ALSO BY SUE FISHKOFF

*The Rebbe's Army: Inside the World of Chabad-Lubavitch*

# KOSHER NATION

# KOSHER NATION

## Sue Fishkoff

Schocken Books · New York

Library of Congress Cataloging-in-Publication Data
Fishkoff, Sue.
Kosher nation / Sue Fishkoff.
p. cm.
Includes bibliographical references and index.
ISBN 978-0-8052-4265-2
1. Jews—Dietary laws.   2. Kosher food.   3. Kosher food industry.   I. Title.
BM710.F56 2010
296.7'3—dc22           2010011326

www.schocken.com

*Book design by Robert C. Olsson*

Printed in the United States of America

First Edition

2   4   6   8   9   7   5   3   1

*For my grandparents*

# CONTENTS

# PROLOGUE

On my bookshelf, tucked away between Mollie Katzen's *Moosewood Cookbook* and Irma Rombauer's *The Joy of Cooking*, is a tattered little yellow book, its worn binding barely held together by a few dusty pieces of Scotch tape.

This is my copy of *Love and Knishes*, Sara Kasdan's 1956 guide to Jewish cooking, passed down to me by my mother, who was presented it by her mother-in-law, my grandma Belle, soon after my parents married in December of that year.

Written in a folksy, Yiddish-inflected narrative tone, *Love and Knishes* offers strictly Old World, Ashkenazic fare: sweet and sour cabbage, stuffed derma, gefilte fish made from live carp, chopped liver with gribenes—all of it swimming in schmaltz, the rendered chicken fat generations of Jewish women used instead of butter for meat meals to avoid transgressing the laws of kashrut (the Hebrew term for keeping kosher).

Grandma Belle wanted to make sure her daughter-in-law knew how to prepare the right kind of food for her new husband, a man who, unbeknownst to my grandmother, wanted nothing to do with boiled brisket or pickled tongue or any other culinary reminder of his parents' roots in the Russian Pale.

My mother tried valiantly for months. I can still make out her scribbled notes on the lokshen (i.e., noodle) kugel page, reminding herself to add chopped apricots and a third egg to the recipe. Finally, my father said, Enough! And out came the Kraft mac and cheese, the spaghetti with meat sauce, and, for a real treat, the Swanson TV dinners.

That cookbook was pretty much all I knew about kosher food growing up in suburban New Jersey in the 1960s and early '70s. Kosher food was something we got once a year at my grandparents' Passover seder, and in my young mind, it became inextricably linked to the history of our people. We would read the Haggadah, the story of the Exodus from Egypt—my only exposure to Jewish text—and then tuck into matzo ball soup, gefilte fish with red horseradish sauce, roasted chicken, carrot tzimmes, boiled potatoes, and noodle kugel.

No green vegetable sullied the table, in accordance with Ashkenazic norms. Kasdan's salad chapter, "Papa Called It Grass," contains just three recipes, only one based on actual greenery. Her explanation—Jews don't do vegetables—is one my dad has always taken to heart.

It was years before I encountered kosher-keeping Jews at close range and began to understand the deep spiritual connection observant Jews have to their food. It certainly wasn't present at the Israeli kibbutzim where I spent much of the 1970s and '80s, the cooperative settlements whose dining halls eschewed the dietary restrictions their founders left behind in Poland and Ukraine.

No, the understanding came later, in 1991, when I spent a year studying Jewish texts at Pardes, an egalitarian yeshiva in Jerusalem. As one of the few students who did not keep kosher, I felt the loneliness on Friday nights when the others refused my dinner invitations.

But I also experienced the rare beauty of a traditional Shabbat meal, where blessings are said over the wine and the bread, where the food has been chosen and prepared according to laws meant to remind us that we are not alone in the world, that we are part of an intricate, carefully balanced network of life and death that existed long before us and extends far into the future.

Jews aren't the only people with a tradition of sacred eating, although our laws are the oldest to have survived into the modern world. How we sow, how we harvest, how we slaughter, how we prepare our food, how and when we eat it—Jews are hardwired to link our food choices to moral and political beliefs, which is probably why so many Jews are active in the organic, locally sourced, and vegetarian movements. What we put in our bodies has a lot to say about who we are and what we value.

Two separate incidents provided the immediate impetus for this book. Some years ago I found myself in Sumy, an industrial city in northeastern Ukraine, researching an article about a young Chabad couple who had moved there from Malibu, California. One afternoon I drove with the rabbi, his wife, and their three children in a rickety Russian-made car two hours out of town to a farm to watch the farmer milk his cow. Many ultraobservant Jews will only drink *cholov Yisroel*, milk that is watched from the time it leaves the cow, and it was so important to these parents that their children enjoy fresh milk that they went to this considerable effort two, sometimes three times a week. I was struck by their determination to keep the laws of kashrut in such a difficult environment.

A year later, while covering a National Havurah Committee retreat in New Hampshire, I sat with a group of young Jews active in the independent minyan movement. The indie minyans, as they are called, are a loosely knit collection of lay-led prayer communities run by and for Jews in their twenties and thirties. In their efforts to be welcoming to all, they explained to me, many of them follow a two-table system of kashrut at their potluck meals. One table is for vegetarian food that carries a *hekhsher*, or kosher certification, and one table is for vegetarian food that does not carry such a label. Thus everyone can bring food and everyone can eat food, no matter his or her observance level— radical inclusiveness tempered by a twenty-first-century sensitivity to religious belief.

Seeing, on one hand, the lengths to which a hassidic family will go to keep kosher in Ukraine, and on the other hand, the determination of young Jewish social-justice activists to honor Jewish tradition while excluding no one, I was struck by how broad the spectrum of Jewish sacred eating has become.

Kashrut is different in America than it was in Europe. For the first time in history, Jews have a choice as to how we express our Judaism— we are neither pushed into it by outside pressure nor compelled by internal religious authorities. And in that choice is contained all the complexity and nuance of modernity.

The kashrut system brings an ancient world of tribal ritual to bear on contemporary sensibilities of inclusivity, pluralism, and the search for meaning. Can the two coexist? Can two-thousand-year-old laws of kosher slaughter bring meaning to the daily life of a twenty-first-century American Jew?

As Jews changed the ways they looked at kashrut, so did America change its relationship to kosher food. The kosher food industry, once the province of this country's small number of observant Jews, has expanded way beyond the population that might be presumed to support it. How did that happen? Why do one-third to one-half of the processed food products in American supermarkets carry kosher certification? Why do Tropicana and Coca-Cola go to the enormous expense of making their products kosher for Passover every spring? Who's buying all this kosher food, and why?

Kosher food and the kosher food system started out as Jewish and, like other immigrant food traditions, have become American. That's what this book is about.

I'd like to acknowledge the many people who have gone out of their way to help me during the eighteen-month endeavor of researching and writing this book. The rabbis and staff at the Orthodox Union, the OK Kosher Certification, and the Star-K Kosher Certification opened their doors to me, answering persistent questions with grace and patience.

I'd particularly like to acknowledge Don Yoel Levy, Chaim Fogelman, and Dovid Steigman at the OK; Menachem Genack, Eliyahu Safran, Seth Mandel, Avraham Stone, Moshe Perlmutter, and Chaim Goldberg at the Orthodox Union; and Avrom Pollak and Tzvi Rosen at the Star-K, along with numerous kosher supervisors in the field who allowed me to tag along as they climbed into flour tanker trucks, hosed down vats of boiling grape juice, and inspected miles of ice-cream bars in factories from rural Pennsylvania to Shanghai. Yakov Yarmove, Yaakov Horowitz, Yitzhok Gallor, Yakov Vann, Reuven Nathanson, Yosef Eisen, Chaim Davids, and Mordechai Grunberg require special mention here.

My heartfelt thanks to Devora Kimelman-Block, Roger Studley, Shalom Kantor, Andy Kastner, Aitan Mizrahi, and the folks at Hazon and the Isabella Freedman Jewish Retreat Center for allowing me to witness a new kind of kosher slaughter, one that hopefully will flourish in the new century. Elie Rosenfeld, Marcia Mogelonsky, and Menachem Lubinsky gave me crucial insight into the world of kosher marketing, and professors Joe Regenstein at Cornell University, David Kraemer at the Jewish Theological Seminary, and Jeffrey Gurock at Yeshiva University helped me navigate the history of kashrut in America. Many other people allowed me into their homes, their kitchens, and their workplaces, and my thanks go out to all of them.

Alisa Kramer was the first to encourage me to write this book, picking it out of a list of topics I presented to her during a morning hike in the redwoods. Kelle Walsh did an initial edit of the entire manuscript, out of the goodness of her very generous heart. My family and friends put up with my crankiness and frequent long absences, and I thank them for sticking by me.

And again, as with *The Rebbe's Army*, I thank my wise and hardworking editor, Altie Karper at Schocken Books, for her careful guidance, devoted friendship, and unwavering belief in my ability to write this book. No writer could wish for more.

# KOSHER NATION

# 1.

# It's a Kosher, Kosher World

## *Kosher Food Conquers the U.S. Market*

IN 1972, Hebrew National launched a television ad campaign that changed the way Americans looked at kosher food.

The commercial, which aired off and on for two decades, shows Uncle Sam about to bite into one of the company's kosher hot dogs. He is stopped midmunch by a sonorous voice listing the additives the U.S. government permits food manufacturers to use in their processed meats. Frozen beef. Artificial colorings. Meat by-products. Non-meat fillers. With each phrase, Uncle Sam's frown deepens.

But don't worry, the voice continues. Hebrew National would never use anything but pure, all-natural beef. "We can't," it declares, as the camera pans upward to a cloud-filled sky. "We're kosher, and have to answer to an even higher authority."

Kosher food manufacturers have been advertising for more than a century. But the early ads for Pillsbury flour and Crisco shortening were aimed at the Jewish consumer, particularly the Orthodox housewife who purchased most of her household's goods.

By the 1960s, companies eager to expand their business began looking beyond their traditional base. Hebrew National was not the first to advertise openly to a non-Jewish audience. In 1960, a popular Levy's ad showed an Irish cop, an African American boy, and a Native American all enjoying the company's Jewish rye bread with the tagline "You don't have to be Jewish to love Levy's." But Hebrew National added a new twist that gripped the imagination of Middle America—the idea that God is involved in the production of kosher food.[1]

"You can't really say that God endorses your food in a commercial, but it's certainly implied," says Mary Warlick, a professor at the School of Visual Arts in New York, who still uses the TV spot with her students.

The commercial was ironic, even comic, but it captured the country's mood. In 1972, the Vietnam War was raging, antiwar protesters had taken to the streets, and America's inner cities were simmering with crime and racial tension. Watergate was on the horizon, and people were losing faith in their government. How could those same leaders protect the country's food supply? Kosher food, on the other hand, "answers to a higher authority," one that is utterly trustworthy. It's better. It's cleaner. It's worth the money. The government may not protect you, the ad suggests, but Jewish law will.

Four decades later that message still resonates, and kosher has become one of the country's hottest food trends.

It happened fast. A generation ago, kosher was a niche industry, the business of the country's small minority of observant Jews. They shopped in small grocery stores in Orthodox neighborhoods, ate in family-owned restaurants serving traditional Ashkenazic fare, and took their own food with them when they traveled.

Today one-third to one-half of the food for sale in the typical American supermarket is kosher. That means more than $200 billion of the country's estimated $500 billion in annual food sales is kosher certified, a remarkable statistic considering that less than 2 percent of the population is Jewish, and only a minority of them keep kosher.

Kosher food is available just about anywhere, and just about everyone buys it, whether they know it or not. Kosher consumers no longer have to seek out kosher grocers or specialty shops; in fact, more than 40 percent of kosher food sales are rung up at Walmart, which has kosher sections in more than five hundred of its stores.[2]

Some of these products are the traditionally Jewish ethnic foods that supermarkets display in their kosher sections, which expand every fall and spring just before major Jewish holidays. These are the jars of gefilte fish, the boxes of matzo meal, the horseradish sauce, and the beet borsch. That "traditional" kosher market hit $12.5 billion in domestic sales by 2008, a 60 percent increase in just five years.[3]

But most kosher-certified products are mainstream foods aimed at the general public, and are made by some of the biggest names in food manufacturing: Pepsi, Coca-Cola, General Mills, Nestlé, Kraft, Nabisco. The Hebrew National and Levy's ads, along with the 1960s "Man, oh, Manischewitz" ad for Manischewitz wine featuring Sammy

Davis Jr., were all part of the same effort to convince the non-Jewish public that kosher is better, and not just for Jews.

"It paralleled what happens with all ethnic food," says Jonathan Sarna, professor of American Jewish history at Brandeis University. "The only way you're going to make money is to make it mainstream."

Kosher food is big and it's increasing at twice the rate of the non-kosher market.[4] In 2007, the "kosher" label was slapped on more new domestic food products than any other label, including "organic," "natural," and "premium." That year 4,784 new kosher products were launched in the United States, versus 2,245 new "all-natural" products and 1,636 new organic products. The United States dominates the global kosher market; it released more than half of the 8,200 new kosher products launched in 2007 worldwide.[5] Nearly one-third of all new food products in this country are kosher certified, including chocolate Easter bunnies and Christmas candies, items clearly not intended for the Jewish consumer.

The biggest surge in kosher certification occurred in the early 1990s, the years when companies including Nabisco, Entenmann's, and Godiva went kosher for the first time. There was a snowball effect: As more mainstream producers went kosher, their competitors followed suit. "If you're Kellogg's or Post, you don't want to eliminate any potential consumer," says Menachem Lubinsky, a longtime consultant to the kosher food industry. "Since you know that a portion of your customer base requires kosher certification, you go ahead and you get that kosher certification."

As kosher food gained ground in the mainstream market, it came out of the closet for observant Jews as well. Kosher meals are offered in hospitals, nursing homes, prisons, and the military, on cruise ships and airplanes. Kosher hot dogs are sold at ballparks, and kosher vending machines serve up knishes and sandwiches in airports and medical schools. Every year more hotels open kosher kitchens, more colleges offer kosher dining plans, more fast-food chains open kosher franchises.

Kosher food travels in the highest circles. In December 2005, the White House kitchen was made kosher for the first time, for the president's annual Chanukah party. In April 2008, a $10,000-per-person kosher fund-raiser was held in Britain's Windsor Castle, home of the royal family, and the Vatican announced that Pope Benedict XVI favored a certain kosher bakery in Rome's historic Jewish ghetto for his biscotti.

Kosher food has gone upscale. Forced to compete in the general marketplace, it must satisfy ever more sophisticated tastes. Kosher restaurants are no longer sequestered in heavily Orthodox neighborhoods in Brooklyn, dishing out cholent and kugel to a captive audience. They have moved to Midtown, and they offer the same organic greens and seared tuna as their non-kosher neighbors. Kosher wines can sell for $200 a bottle, and better kosher butchers are carrying grass-fed elk and bison, along with Kobe beef for $60 a pound. More and more specialty foods now have their kosher equivalents. Chipotle sauce, gourmet gelato, mango salsa, Belgian chocolates, and artisanal cheeses are all being churned out by kosher food manufacturers who vie with one another to anticipate the next culinary trend.

And it's not just Jews buying this food. More than 11.2 million Americans regularly buy kosher food, 13 percent of the adult consumer population.[6] These are people who buy the products *because* they are kosher, not shoppers who pick up Heinz ketchup, Miller beer, or Cheerios because they like the taste or the price. There are about six million Jews in this country. Even if they all bought only kosher food, which is not the case, they would not be enough to sustain such growth.[7]

In fact, just 14 percent of consumers who regularly buy kosher food do so because they follow the rules of kashrut. That means at least 86 percent of the nation's 11.2 million kosher consumers are not religious Jews.[8]

Many are not Jewish at all. They are people turning to kosher food for a wide variety of reasons. They are vegetarians, who trust that a "D" kosher dairy symbol means a product contains no meat. They are lactose-intolerant consumers who know that kosher products without the "D" are dairy-free, or folks with gluten allergies who stock up on kosher-for-Passover items made without wheat. They are people who follow religious or spiritual practices satisfied by kosher food, including Muslims who buy kosher meat when halal is not available, Seventh-day Adventists who eat only biblically permitted animals, and those who look for the *pareve*, or neutral, kosher symbol, indicating food that contains neither dairy nor meat.

All these people buy kosher food for what it guarantees in terms of ingredients. But the growing popularity of kosher certification also has to do with perception, with the belief shared by many people, Jewish or not, that kosher food is cleaner, safer, better. In fact, more Americans buy it for these reasons than any other: 62 percent buy kosher because they believe it is of higher quality than non-kosher food, 51 percent because they believe it is more healthy, and 34 percent because they consider it safer.[9] What with spinach tainted with E. coli, peanut butter laced with salmonella, and beef infected with mad cow disease, Americans uneasy about the country's food supply might well find comfort in knowing that another pair of eyes—a pair of religious eyes at that—is watching over the manufacturing process.

Those extra eyes do not always guarantee quality, but the perception that they do persists and can lead to increased sales. That is why so many food manufacturers and retailers are willing to pay fees ranging from a few hundred dollars to $100,000 or more a year to the rabbis and agencies that provide kosher certification. They are banking on the consumer appeal of that kosher label.

Dr. Avrom Pollak, president of the Star-K Kosher Certification in Baltimore, Maryland, tells of a man who came to his office seeking certification for his bakery. The process would require, among other things, making the kitchen kosher (called kashering), buying new pots and pans, switching suppliers, closing from sundown Friday to sundown Saturday, and hiring a *mashgiach*, or kosher supervisor. There were no Jews in the baker's small town, and Pollak asked him why he would go to such an expense.

"He said, I want kosher certification so when I tell people I use only one hundred percent vegetable shortening, they'll know it's true," Pollak relates.

In certain industries, kosher regulations do act as one more safeguard to good health. For meat to be certified as kosher, the animal must have no diseases or physical flaws. "Downer" cows, animals that are too sick to walk, are not accepted for kosher slaughter, although they do make it into the non-kosher meat supply. In February 2008, the U.S. Department of Agriculture recalled 143 million pounds of non-kosher beef, the largest meat recall in history, after an undercover tape showed plant workers using electric prods to move downer cows through the kill line. Kosher regulations also protect against mad cow disease, which has been linked to animal feed containing infected meat or bonemeal; kosher-certified animals cannot be fed other animals.

As demand for kosher certification continues to grow, so does the need to oversee all those factories, shops, and restaurants to ensure that the food being produced meets Jewish dietary regulations. Thus the upturn in the kosher food market has spurred an increase in the number of kosher certification agencies, from eighteen in 1981 to almost one thousand separate rabbis and agencies offering kosher supervision by early 2009.[10]

In one sense this has produced a very confusing situation, with shoppers forced to distinguish between hundreds of individual rabbis putting their own kosher symbols on food products. In fact, it's not as chaotic as it seems. More than 80 percent of the kosher goods sold in this country are certified by the four largest agencies: the Manhattan-based Orthodox Union (Ⓤ), the Star-K in Baltimore (☆), the OK Kosher Certification in Brooklyn (Ⓚ), and the Kof-K Kosher Supervision in Teaneck, New Jersey (Ⓚ). Between them, these agencies employ thousands of *mashgichim*. These supervisors are the foot soldiers of the kosher food industry, traveling the world to inspect factories, kitchens, tanker trucks, slaughterhouses, bakeries, butchers, and supermarkets. They also oversee meal preparation for hotels, cruise ships, prisons, Jewish schools, synagogues, and summer camps. And they kasher kitchens, clean bugs from vegetables, and watch over the religiously sensitive operations of kosher wine- and cheesemaking.

All in all, kosher certification and supervision is a huge enterprise involving hundreds of millions of dollars, which operates behind the scenes of the food industry, the unseen cost of doing business in today's global market.

This did not happen in a vacuum. A perfect storm of increased religiosity, a strengthening of Jewish ethnic pride, and a growing obsession with healthy eating have all conspired to vault the kosher industry to the top of the country's food chain.

America has always been a religious society, but Jews historically rate lower on the key religious indicators than other faith groups. Fewer American Jews believe in God than Protestants or Catholics, fewer Jews pray privately, and more say religion is not important in their lives.[11] That has been true throughout the twentieth century. But in the past two decades, growing numbers of Jews have been exploring their faith, including its rituals, and more say they are seeking spiritual nourishment. Synagogue membership may be declining, but more American Jews light Sabbath candles, observe the Jewish holidays, and keep at least some of the kosher laws, even if they do not consider themselves "religious."[12]

The 1970s saw an explosion of pride among many ethnic and racial minorities, including Jews. Israel's victory in the 1967 Six-Day War gave an unprecedented boost to American Jewish self-esteem, leading to a growth in Jewish education, support for Israel, and a public flexing of Jewish ethnic muscle. Jews who had previously kept their identity under wraps now proclaimed it in the public arena.

In the waning decades of the twentieth century, dietary practices based on health or ethics, such as eating organic food and vegetarianism, became socially acceptable, even trendy. Announcing that one cannot eat this or that food because of moral or spiritual concerns is no longer seen as rude or unusual; it's more often considered a demonstration of values and self-discipline. Americans are interested in the spiritual and psychological benefits of such diets, and that includes a kosher regimen. Kosher food and the kosher food industry are hot topics of conversation, from front-page articles in the *New York Times* to bestselling kosher cookbooks.

These societal changes accompanied and contributed to a shift in the American Jewish attitude toward kashrut. Many Jews already keeping kosher are keeping it more strictly, and some who don't are more willing to experiment with it.

Orthodox Judaism as a whole has moved to the right, and its attitude toward kashrut is no exception. Practices that would have been acceptable a generation or two ago, such as eating cold foods in a non-kosher restaurant, have fallen out of favor in Orthodox circles. Local *vaads,* or rabbinic committees that oversee kosher restaurants and retail stores, are imposing stricter requirements on what owners of those businesses may and may not do. *Glatt* meat, which requires much more careful inspection of an animal's lungs and was once a stringency observed only by the ultra-Orthodox, is now the industry standard for all kosher meat. More and more kosher dairy restaurants adhere to cholov Yisroel, a stricter standard for milk that requires watching it from the time it leaves the cow; more bakeries proclaim that they are *pas Yisroel*, that is, using "Jewish bread," which means that observant Jews participate in the baking process, at the very least by turning on the oven.

Among liberal Jews, hostility to kosher food has eased up considerably, replaced by curiosity and even pride. Whereas their parents and grandparents viewed keeping kosher as part and parcel of an observant lifestyle that cut Jews off from society at large, increasing numbers of younger Jews, comfortable in their position in America, see it as a mark of Jewish identity, a declaration of membership in the tribe. It's something that can be observed as the occasion demands rather than a permanent restriction on one's dietary choices.

Jewish weddings and bar/bat mitzvahs are more often kosher today than in the past, even if those throwing the events are not observant. Making them kosher is a way to proclaim their Jewish character. Few national Jewish organizations serve non-kosher food at their official gatherings anymore, not because more participants keep kosher than a generation ago, but as a public statement of Jewish inclusiveness. The Reform movement, which declared Jewish dietary laws outdated 150 years ago, has slowly softened that stance. Increasing numbers of Reform synagogues maintain kosher kitchens, and in 2007 the Union for Reform Judaism, the organizational body of Reform congregations in North America, posted a Reform guide to kashrut on its website, something that would have been unthinkable a decade earlier.

A moving illustration of this new attitude occurred in January 2003, when Israeli astronaut Ilan Ramon brought only kosher food with him on the space shuttle *Columbia*. Although Ramon was a secular Jew who did not observe kashrut, he told the media before his ill-fated flight that in space he felt he was representing the entire Jewish world. Keeping kosher symbolized that connection.[13]

KOSHER FOOD is not food that is blessed by a rabbi. It is food that adheres to Jewish law. The vast body of rituals, regulations, and customs surrounding the preparation and consumption of food, collectively known as the practice of kashrut, is based on a handful of verses in the Torah, the five books of Moses that constitute Judaism's central text. Those verses have been argued over by rabbis and scholars for more than two thousand years. Kashrut is a constantly evolving construct; the biblical verses remain unchanged, but the way they are understood and applied has altered over time, from country to country and, more recently, between the different Jewish denominations.

The word *kosher* comes from the Hebrew word *kasher,* meaning "fit" or "proper." Kosher food is food that is appropriate for a Jew to eat. It is not intrinsically holier than other food, and its consumption is incumbent only upon Jews. Interestingly, the word *kosher* does not appear anywhere in the Torah. It is used several times in later biblical texts, but not in reference to food. In the book of Esther it is used to mean "appropriate," similar to its most common usage today in the English-speaking world.

As the Torah tells it, Jews received the commandment to eat differently than other people in about 1200 BCE, after they left bondage in Egypt and became a separate nation with a homeland—Israel—and a constitution—the Ten Commandments.

Before then, according to the biblical story, everyone ate alike. In the Garden of Eden, Adam and Eve enjoyed a purely vegetarian diet, feasting upon the bounty of the earth and the fruit of the trees. They took their diet with them when they were expelled from Eden for eating from the Tree of Knowledge—a dietary transgression that changed the course of human history. It was only after the world was destroyed in a great flood that God permitted Noah and his descendants to eat meat, and then only grudgingly, in recognition of the human lust for flesh. But God specified in Genesis 9:4 that only the flesh of an animal was permitted, not the blood, which contained its soul.

Later in the Torah came the prohibition on eating an animal's sciatic nerve, the part of Jacob's upper thigh touched by the angel during their all-night wrestling match in Genesis 32:25–33. This story has significant financial consequences today for kosher butchers and shoppers, as only the front portion of cattle, sheep, and other mammals are considered kosher.[14]

The rest of the Torah's pronouncements on dietary law date from the Israelites' forty years of post-Exodus wandering in the desert prior to their settlement in Canaan, the Promised Land. The relevant verses are few in number and tersely written, leaving it up to future generations to figure out how to put them into practice.

Several of the verses about dietary law deal with Passover, specifically the prohibition on eating leavened bread and the commandment to eat matzo in remembrance of the miraculous escape from Egyptian slavery.[15] Others command Jews to observe a sabbatical year once they reach Israel, letting the land lie fallow every seventh growing season.[16] One verse exhorts Jews to take challah, that is, set aside for the *kohanim* (priests) in the Temple a small portion of dough before baking bread,[17] and another describes the ritual of the *omer*, the offering of the yearly grain harvest.[18]

But most Torah verses dealing with Jewish dietary practice concern restrictions on food consumption: which animals, birds, fish, and insects may and may not be eaten;[19] how the permissible foods must be slaughtered and prepared;[20] and that meat and milk must not be cooked together.[21] It's these laws that have caused the greatest headaches and generated the most rabbinic ink over the years.

In one sense, the Torah is clear about which creatures Jews may and may not eat, even if no reason is given for those distinctions. Kosher mammals must have split hooves and chew their cud. The camel chews its cud but does not have split hooves, and the pig has the right feet but does not chew its cud; neither is kosher. Kosher fish must have fins and scales, which means shellfish is not kosher. Kosher insects, for those who choose to consume them, must have jointed legs that enable them to hop, such as locusts and grasshoppers.

Birds are more difficult. The Torah does not explain what makes a bird kosher; it simply lists some birds that are kosher and others that are not, leaving it to later authorities to tease out general principles. Eagles, hawks, owls, kites, ravens, and falcons are named as prohibited species, leading many authorities to deduce a blanket prohibition on scavengers and birds of prey. But because the list is incomplete and scholars are not certain of the modern equivalent of some of the biblical names, the custom is to eat only those birds that one's community has a tradition of eating. If your father and grandfather ate pigeon, so can you.

Determining which animals may and may not be eaten is just the first part of a larger, more complicated procedure of figuring out how to put these biblical commandments into everyday practice: How should Jews plant, grow, slaughter, prepare, serve, and eat their food? The Torah states that Jews should not consume the blood of an animal together with its flesh, but how is that to be avoided? What is the correct way to remove the sciatic nerve? Does the prohibition on cooking a kid in its mother's milk apply only to goats or to cows and sheep as well? Should hot food be treated differently from cold food?

As the centuries passed, rabbis considered, refined, and expanded their answers to thousands of such questions. Scholarly opinions piled up, commentaries built on each other, and the regulations and restrictions of kashrut multiplied and became ever more complex.

The first compilation of Jewish laws, including those dealing with kashrut, was the Mishna, a second-century compendium of oral rabbinic discussions that had taken place over the two previous centuries. Three more centuries of rabbinic commentary on the Mishna were summarized and written down as the Gemara. Together the Mishna and Gemara make up the Talmud, the principal guide to Jewish law, or *halacha*.[22] Within its pages, the Talmud contains detailed discussions of Jewish law and practice, much of it conducted in dialectical fashion as a series of questions and answers between leading rabbis. Both majority and minority opinions are set down, and later conclusions can contradict earlier ones.

In the sixteenth century, Rabbi Joseph Caro attempted to reconcile these debates in the Shulchan Aruch, or "Ordered Table." His writings on kosher law are contained in Yoreh Deah, one of the four volumes of the Shulchan Aruch. It is still the main authority for questions of Jewish dietary law and practice, and is what Orthodox rabbinical candidates are quizzed on before receiving ordination. But it is not the only source; the discussion continues.

As the centuries passed, the tendency was for Jewish dietary practice to become stricter as later generations of rabbis built upon the opinions of their predecessors. For example, kosher law today forbids the mixing of meat and dairy. Yet the Torah never explicitly states the two should not mix, only that a baby goat may not be boiled in its mother's milk. Literalists might look at that verse and argue that if an animal is not the offspring of the animal that provided the milk in which it is cooked, the resulting dish is kosher.

That reading was never given serious credence, but a related one was. In the late first or early second century CE, Rabbi Yossi the Galilean held that the prohibition should apply only to creatures that produce milk, that is, mammals. Birds don't nurse their young, so it should be permitted for Jews to cook chicken in milk, as Rabbi Yossi did in his native Galilee. Rabbi Yossi argued the point with Rabbi Akiva in Mishna Chullin 113a, with Rabbi Akiva holding that the cooking of any bird in milk violated a rabbinic prohibition, if not a biblical one. Yossi lost the argument—Rabbi Akiva was a tough opponent—and Jews were forever cut off from chicken Parmesan.[23]

The Talmud noted that the warning against cooking a kid in its mother's milk appears three times in the Torah. Each mention was taken to indicate a different prohibition: one against cooking meat and milk together, one against eating meat and milk that was cooked together, and one against deriving any benefit from their combination, such as selling a cheeseburger. Even these prohibitions require further interpretation. What does "eating them together" mean? Does it mean milk and meat should not be eaten in the same bite? Or can they not even be consumed during the same meal? And how long is a meal? Must one wait a minute, an hour, or longer after eating meat or dairy before consuming the other?

In the absence of a Jewish pope who could decide with global authority, various customs arose in different Jewish communities. Most Orthodox Jews today wait six hours after eating meat before they will consume dairy, but German Jews wait three hours, and Dutch Jews just one hour. Conservative Jews who keep kosher usually wait three hours, but some wait six.

Those are the rules if one eats meat before milk. After a dairy meal, observant Jews have only to rinse out their mouths before consuming meat, on the grounds that milk products do not linger as long in the mouth as meat does. But if the dairy meal includes hard cheese that has been aged for at least six months, it must be treated like meat, and the wait time is six hours—or three, or one, depending on one's country of origin or denominational affiliation.

Once it was decided that meat and dairy products should not be consumed together, the rabbis looked for ways to ensure that they remained as far apart as possible. Perhaps one should keep completely separate sets of pots, pans, dishes, and utensils for meat and dairy. And to avoid inadvertent mistakes, it might be best to keep those items in different parts of the kitchen, even wash them in separate sinks. By the modern era, an observant Jew would never use a dairy plate for a meat meal, or vice versa, even if it had been carefully washed. And dishes used for pareve food, food that is neither meat nor dairy, had to be kept separate from the other two categories. Such added stringencies, called "fences around the Torah," were developed over hundreds of years and eventually assumed the same force of law as the rules they were set up to protect.

Technological advances further complicated the picture, introducing assembly lines and chemical additives into an ancient legal scheme designed for human labor and biologically based foodstuffs. Today it is possible to eat an entirely kosher "cheeseburger," with the burger, the cheese, or both made from soy products. Does that contravene the spirit of milk-dairy separation, or is the dish kosher because no actual dairy is mixing with actual meat? (It's kosher.)

The invention of the airplane made it difficult to count the hours between meat and dairy meals. Should the observant Jew go by what time it is on the ground, or the number of hours passed in flight? (The latter.) Space travel added an entirely new dimension—what time is it when one is orbiting the earth? NASA was forced to call in rabbinic authorities to decide the question for Jewish astronauts.

To outsiders this attention to such minute details of food preparation and consumption might seem obsessive, even silly. But to Torah-observant Jews it can mean the difference between profaning their bodies and making them into holy vessels, the ostensible aim of kashrut. "A person is what he eats," explains Rabbi Chaim Fogelman, communications director for the OK Kosher Certification, giving a mystical, hassidic twist to the biology of digestion. "Once you eat something that is not kosher, it goes into your body and is with you forever. That's why people are very, very particular about kosher. Just like a fat cell, once it appears in the body, it can shrink but it never disappears."

MULTINATIONAL CORPORATIONS don't make kosher food to help Jews turn their bodies into holy vessels. They do it to make money. The Orthodox Union reports that in forty-five years, fewer than a dozen companies dropped their kosher supervision because it didn't help sales.[24] Kosher food shoppers spend an average of $1,000 more every year than ordinary consumers, making them a lucrative market to capture.[25]

That is why Jelly Belly sought national kosher certification in 2008. "It would open new doors to trade we hadn't had, not just from Jewish customers, but vegans and others who look for a kosher symbol," says Bob Simpson, president and COO of the Fairfield, California–based candy manufacturer.[26]

Simpson declines to say how much it cost Jelly Belly to make the switch from a less rigorous kosher agency to the Orthodox Union. Just getting rid of all the non-kosher food starch in its plant and warehouse cost $650,000, and was only a portion of the total expense. But less than a year later, he said the company was seeing a return on its investment. "Now that we can sell to national kosher distributors, they have been inundated with requests from kosher retailers. Our product is flying off the shelf."

Many smaller food manufacturers also ante up for kosher certification, believing it will help their bottom line. Valerie Bono, vice president of sales and marketing for Golden Cannoli, a company in Somerville, Massachusetts, that makes cannoli dough and prepackaged shells, said their products have been kosher since her father and his partner, neither of them Jewish, founded the business in 1978. "At least sixty percent of our business is because we're kosher. It's definitely a selling point," she says. "Whether people are Jewish or not, they think of it as a better product."

Not every company finds going kosher worthwhile. Joseph Farms, a dairy operation in Atwater, California, made kosher cheese for two years before dropping the certification in early 2008. "It was too expensive for us, and we weren't seeing the money from it," says general manager Carl Morris. Kosher cheese production requires a kosher supervisor on the premises the entire time cheese is being made, and the company wasn't making enough profit to warrant that extra salary. But since Joseph Farms dropped its certification, Jewish customers have been writing and calling, asking for it back. One Orthodox congregation in Oakland, California, flooded the company with e-mails, and their rabbi called Morris personally to ask if he would consider doing even one kosher run a week.

Unfortunately, Morris says that's not possible. The plant operates seven days a week and cannot afford to shut down for twenty-four hours to kasher all its equipment, the minimum time required for the process. Plus, he doesn't have the storage space to separate the kosher from the non-kosher cheese. Morris sighs. "I feel for them, and I'd love to help them out, but it's just too expensive."

Changing certification can bring down the wrath of the kosher consumer, and can prove to be just as costly as dropping it altogether. In 2002, rumors began flying that Stella D'Oro, which since 1958 had been kosher and pareve, was about to start using dairy ingredients in its cookies. Kraft Foods, which took over the company in 2000, wanted to use a cheaper chocolate that contained milk.

The outcry was immediate. One of the few widely available brands of kosher cookies made without milk or butter, Stella D'Oro had been a fixture on Orthodox tables for two generations because its cookies could be eaten for dessert after a meat meal. Without pareve status, they were less useful. Boxes of Stella D'Oro cookies, stamped with the new "dairy" labels in anticipation of the proposed changeover, lay unopened for months in kosher grocery stores from Monsey, New York, to Lakewood, New Jersey. In January 2003, Kraft scrapped its plans to change the recipe.[27]

Something similar happened to Duncan Hines when the company switched many of its pareve cake mixes to dairy in 2005. Sales dropped off precipitously, and other manufacturers seized the opportunity to launch their own pareve cake mixes to fill the gap. In September 2006, Duncan Hines reversed its decision after CEO Jeff Ansell said he'd received an earful from customers. Twelve of the eighteen kosher cake mixes that had gone dairy the previous year, representing 80 percent of company sales, returned to pareve status.[28]

Both companies bowed to the power of the Orthodox market, says Elie Rosenfeld, CEO of Joseph Jacobs Advertising, a marketing firm that targets the Jewish consumer. Rosenfeld believes that although kosher-keeping Jews are no longer the majority of people who buy kosher food, they are still the industry's driving force. They shop for Shabbat on Thursday evening and Friday morning, producing a predictable end-of-week sales bump, and they buy high-priced kosher products like meat, wine, and prepared foods. Supermarkets want to keep them coming into the stores, and food manufacturers want them buying new products.

And they are not shy about expressing their opinions. "Jews are vocal," Rosenfeld points out. "When a company like Duncan Hines gets a thousand phone calls, they 'get' it."

There may be just a million or so American Jews who keep kosher,[29] but they are concentrated in five key markets: New York, Los Angeles,

Miami, Chicago, and Philadelphia–New Jersey. That makes it worth-while for supermarkets and discount chains in those regions to carry lots of kosher-certified products. From the food manufacturers' point of view, the tens of thousands of dollars paid out in annual fees for kosher supervision is more than outweighed by the loss of business they would suffer if stores stopped carrying their products. That is particularly true of the larger food companies, for whom kosher certification is an easily absorbed operating expense.

The observant Jewish community—what the industry refers to as the traditional kosher market—is changing, and that, too, affects how and where kosher food is sold. The kosher consumer is growing younger and wealthier; one survey found the largest group of Jews who keep kosher are between the ages of eighteen and thirty-five. They travel more than their parents, and they expect to find kosher food on the planes they take, the stores they shop in, and the hotels where they stay.

The tourist industry has been quick to cash in. The year-round kosher hotels that once dotted the Catskills and held sway along Miami Beach have been replaced by mainstream hotels that "go kosher" for Passover and other Jewish holidays. All-kosher vacation packages are available at the fanciest properties, and they cost a pretty penny. In 2009, the Fairmont Scottsdale Princess in Arizona offered a weeklong Passover stay starting at $3,900 per person. Passover week at the Fairmont Mayakoba on Mexico's Riviera Maya started at $4,000 per person.

Kosher cruises joined the market in the 1990s and can cost twice as much as non-kosher trips. In early 2009, a seven-night Alaska cruise with Kosherica, the country's largest kosher cruise company, started at $1,957, versus $1,025 for a similar non-kosher cruise.

In 2008, nearly a dozen major hotels opened kosher kitchens, including the Radisson at Los Angeles International Airport, a Double-tree in Chicago, a Hyatt in Chicago, and the Tampa Airport Marriott. The Holiday Inn International Drive Resort in Orlando opened a dedicated kosher kitchen that October, in time for Sukkot. Leased to an outside vendor, it has separate areas for preparing meat, dairy, and pareve dishes. Catering director Kathleen Hawthorne said the idea is to allow observant guests to dine in the hotel's restaurant, just like any other traveler, and order a kosher meal off the regular menu. "The meals are frozen and double-wrapped. We just take them out of the freezer, pop them in the microwave, and serve them with kosher silverware that is also wrapped in Saran wrap."

Kosher food at sports events, once a rarity, is growing more common. New York's Shea and Yankee stadiums opened kosher food stands in 1998 after pressure from local officials and the New York Board of Rabbis, and when the Mets and the Yankees debuted new stadiums in 2009, kosher baseball fans were pleased to see not one but four glatt kosher food courts at both Citi Field and Yankee Stadium. Baltimore's Oriole Park at Camden Yards has been serving up kosher fare since 1993. A kosher hot dog cart appeared at Philadelphia's Lincoln Financial Field in summer 2004, and in 2006, kosher hot dogs, Italian sausage, peanuts, pretzels, and soft drinks became available at RFK Stadium in Washington, D.C. Progressive Field, home of the Cleveland Indians, opened a kosher hot dog stand in 2007, and in April 2008, a *Boston Herald* reporter gushed over the new kosher vending machine at Fenway Park.

The minor leagues are also getting into the act. In August 2007, MerchantsAuto.com Stadium in Manchester, New Hampshire, home of the Fisher Cats, served kosher hot dogs, hamburgers, and falafel at its first Jewish Pride Night. The event was put together by Chabad Rabbi Levi Krinsky after he and his family were stopped by security when they tried to bring matzo sandwiches into the ballpark during Passover two years earlier. Stadium policy bans outside food, but the guard allowed the Krinskys through once they explained they would be unable to eat any of the food for sale inside the arena.

During the game, the catering manager approached Krinsky and asked how he might better accommodate the team's Orthodox fans. A night of kosher food and baseball was the happy result.

Observant Jews on the go no longer have to brown-bag their meals. In 2006, Kosher Vending Industries launched its Hot Nosh kosher vending machines that dispense hot dogs, knishes, pizzas, and other snacks from separate meat, dairy, and pareve machines. By 2008, more than one hundred of these machines served airports, hospitals, schools, stadiums, and shopping malls in the Northeast corridor, including JFK's international terminal, NYU Langone Medical Center, the University of Maryland, and the zoos in Brooklyn and Queens.

This growing availability of kosher food is a by-product of American Jews' growing confidence in their position in society. Orthodox Jews had always gone to ball games; they simply accepted that they had to pack their own meals or go hungry. But as the kosher food industry grew and more mainstream food products became kosher certified, Jewish sports fans began clamoring for equal treatment. One New York Jets fan, an observant Jewish accountant who held season tickets to Giants Stadium, told a reporter that he used to eat at home before every game. When the stadium opened its kosher food stand in 2006, it made a big difference to him. "It makes me feel like I'm a real fan," he said. "I can buy a hot dog like everyone else."[30]

American Jews have always tried to balance their desire to be fully American with an equally strong desire to preserve their Jewish identity. That balancing act becomes much more difficult when one is committed to following a kosher diet. Nothing says Fourth of July like a backyard beer-and-wiener roast, yet observant Jews sometimes find themselves on the other side of the fence.

That's why Orthodox families visiting Israel get such a kick out of the kosher McDonald's and KFC outlets in that country. They can order the most normal, all-American food—a hamburger and a (pareve) milk shake, a bucket of the Colonel's Original Recipe or Extra Crispy fried chicken—and still be Jewish. That's why kosher pizza parlors are so popular in America, and why more and more Subway and Dunkin' Donuts franchises are going kosher. "The kosher consumer is no longer Grandma Sadie with her shopping cart; it's a young shopper with a Lexus parked outside," says Menachem Lubinsky. "They want to have every popular food product be kosher."

In the 1930s, Coca-Cola was the most popular soft drink in America. For immigrant Jews eager to fit in to American society, the pull was irresistible. "Coca-Cola was *the* American drink, and American Jews needed to drink it," explains Rabbi Adam Mintz, visiting professor of Jewish history at Queens College in New York.[31]

The problem was no one knew what was in it—the recipe was a closely guarded trade secret. In 1935, Rabbi Tobias Geffen of Congregation Shearith Israel in Atlanta, where Coca-Cola headquarters was located, began receiving letters from Orthodox colleagues around the country, telling him their people were drinking Coke and begging him to find out if the ingredients were kosher. Geffen met with company executives, and they gave him a list of the ingredients in the soft drink—but not their percentages—on condition that he keep the information strictly to himself.

Geffen found two ingredients that were problematic under kosher law: glycerin made from non-kosher beef tallow, and traces of grain alcohol, which cannot be consumed during Passover because grain-based products must be produced in a special way for Passover use. Company executives were so persuaded of the need to satisfy the very small market of kosher-keeping Jews that they agreed to replace those ingredients, an amazing step for a major food manufacturer to take at the time.

Geffen wrote back to his colleagues giving Coca-Cola his stamp of approval. Keeping his promise not to reveal the drink's actual recipe, he referred to its two non-kosher ingredients by the biblical names given to two of the eleven spices used in the daily incense offering in Jerusalem, whose identities were lost when the Temple was destroyed in 70 CE. He knew the rabbis would get his meaning: best to hold off drinking Coke until those ingredients are replaced.[32]

We don't know how much Coca-Cola spent going kosher in 1935, but it was definitely a lot less than Nabisco spent sixty years later making Oreo cookies kosher. And kosher-keeping Jews were just as tickled.

Oreos had always been forbidden in Orthodox homes because they were made with lard. Joe Regenstein, a food science professor and kosher industry expert at Cornell University, says every Jewish child in his hometown of Newark, New Jersey, "knew" the nearby Nabisco plant "was a lard house," that the cookies it made were filled with forbidden pork fat. Kosher substitutes like Hydrox cookies, produced since 1908 by Sunshine Biscuits, didn't have the same taste, crunch, or cachet.

Years later, as a faculty member at Cornell, Regenstein found himself serving on a university advisory council with a vice president from Nabisco. Jokingly, he asked the man what it would cost for the company to go kosher. Six months later, the executive came back with a figure: $8 million, too much to consider.

By the 1990s, however, the project was no longer unthinkable. Saturated fats were on the outs, food manufacturers were replacing them with trans fats (considered healthier at the time), and Nabisco, too, replaced the lard in its food products with vegetable oil. That removed the most difficult obstacle in the way of the company's going kosher, but the complete process took years.

First they had to change suppliers, so that all the ingredients used to make the cookies were kosher. Then they had to kasher the equipment in every Nabisco factory, which meant rabbis crawling inside three-hundred-square-foot baking ovens and burning them out with blow-torches, the standard technique for making ovens kosher. But huge rubber conveyor belts ran through those ovens, and they could not withstand such intense heat. The plants could shut down production while the kashering took place, but that meant significant lost revenue all at one time. Nabisco decided it would be less expensive to work piecemeal, waiting until each belt broke or wore out of its own accord, and sending the rabbis in with their blowtorches when that line had to be taken down anyway to replace the belt.

Nabisco had about ten cookie factories, Regenstein estimates, with about ten belts per plant. Only when all the belts, about one hundred total, had been replaced could the company receive kosher certification. It was, Regenstein believes, "the most complex conversion of a plant that wasn't kosher into a kosher plant that was ever done."

In October 1997, the process was completed, and soon afterward, kosher Oreos hit the shelves. "The news came racing across the Internet with apocalyptic urgency," wrote Rabbi Joshua Hammerman of Temple Beth El in Stamford, Connecticut, in a *New York Times Magazine* article. Better even than a Jewish president was this incontrovertible proof that, as he put it, "Jews have finally made it. After eighty-five years in the Gentile larder, Oreos have gone kosher."[33]

Food writer Jeffrey Yoskowitz was in sixth grade at the Solomon Schechter Jewish day school in West Orange, New Jersey. He recalls his teacher bringing in a box of the newly permissible cookies to celebrate with the class. Regenstein received a complimentary package from Nabisco containing samples of the new products. He passed them out to Orthodox students and faculty in the university's kosher dining hall, "so they should see what a real cookie tastes like."

It wasn't just Oreos. All of Nabisco's products were now kosher, including Fig Newtons, Ritz Bits, Chips Ahoy!, and Honey Maid graham crackers. The excitement was almost too much to bear. "Let's delight in our de-larded Nabisco factories the way the Maccabees reveled after removing swine from the Temple," Hammerman exulted.

The story ended happily for Nabisco. Although the company does not make its finances public, Regenstein says it's clear they are making money, even though it cost them a lot to go kosher. Each of the one hundred belts they replaced cost $150,000 in 1990s dollars, plus they pay yearly certification fees.

The story also ended happily for America's kosher-keeping community, which now had one more popular food product that it was allowed to eat.

But the breakthrough contained a touch of the bittersweet. As Hammerman sat in his kitchen late one night in January 1998, contemplating the kosher Oreo he was about to enjoy, he thought about how kashrut had always set Jews apart from the nations around them. Every time Jews resist the temptation to indulge in a pepperoni pizza or a cheeseburger, they reaffirm their uniqueness. Is eating Oreos a step toward assimilation? What would happen to the Jewish people if they ate like everyone else?

"I shudder," he wrote. "Can we survive this?"[34]

# 2.

# Eating Their Way into Heaven

## The Who, What, and Why of Keeping Kosher

THE WHITE VAN with "888-Go-Kosher" emblazoned on both sides pulls up in front of a newly renovated home on Staten Island, New York. Rabbi Sholtiel Lebovic and his assistant, a young Israeli rabbinical student, leap out and start unloading their supplies: steel wool, paper towels, bricks, aluminum-foil roasting pans, bottles of ammonia, and kitchen cleansers. Finally, a large blowtorch attached to a heavy propane tank emerges, which Lebovic hauls up the front steps, puffing with the effort.

Lebovic is here to kasher the kitchen of Arkady and Marina Sandler, a young couple who have been moving toward greater Jewish observance. As founder and director of Go Kosher, a traveling outfit based in Crown Heights, Brooklyn, Lebovic drives up and down New York, New Jersey, and Connecticut kashering kitchens in private homes, schools, hotels, summer camps, and nursing homes. He is a Lubavitcher, a member of the hassidic movement noted for its outreach to largely nonobservant Jews. Over the past eighteen years, Lebovic has helped make ten thousand kitchens kosher, either doing the job himself or advising people by phone.

Some of his clients are longtime Orthodox Jews who have moved to a new home and want help making their kitchens kosher. These are usually in-and-out jobs, as both parties know what to expect. But 60 to 70 percent of his customers are, like the Sandlers, newly observant Jews who have never kept a kosher home. They are often tentative, afraid of doing the wrong thing or asking the wrong questions. Those are the people Lebovic enjoys helping most. He spends time with them, discussing their motivation, giving them practical tips, and letting them know he'll be there for them.

"That's our mission statement, helping people go kosher from zero," he says. "When you come into someone's house, it's not just the technical aspects of kashering what can be kashered. You have to work with them so they understand what it's all about, what it entails, what it means on a practical as well as spiritual level."

Keeping kosher requires more than knowing which birds, fish, and animals may and may not be eaten. It's a complete lifestyle with precise details of food preparation and consumption. Not only must all food be kosher, so must the dishes on which it is served, the utensils with which it is eaten, the pots and pans in which it is cooked, the knives with which it is chopped, and the kitchen countertops and appliances used in its preparation. Once something has been kashered, it remains kosher unless it comes into contact with any non-kosher food or with mixed meat and dairy products. In such cases, it is usually sufficient to re-kasher the plate, pot, or countertop where the offense occurred.

In the Sandler kitchen, twenty-nine-year-old Marina is kneeling in front of plastic bags filled with her old Tupperware and cooking utensils. Boxes holding small appliances, glasses, and dishes sit off to the side. She looks a bit overwhelmed.

"Can I keep this?" she asks, showing Lebovic a yellow ceramic mixing bowl. Some kitchen items can be made kosher, and some cannot. Glass- and metalware can be dipped in boiling water to make them kosher, but porous materials such as ceramic, rubber, and wood might harbor bits of non-kosher food material in their crevices and so must be discarded. China is problematic: Ideally it should be replaced, but most people are loath to throw away family heirlooms. In such cases, many rabbis counsel not using the pieces for twelve months and then dipping them in boiling water. Knives that have been used to cut non-kosher food need to be scrubbed with an abrasive material and then plunged into a pot of boiling water. Some people bury dishes or utensils in the earth before kashering as a symbolic removal of any lingering food particles, a tradition without basis in Jewish law but one that persists nonetheless.

There will be no burying of dishes in the Sandler home. Is the mixing bowl part of a set? Lebovic asks. It is, Marina replies. Usually he tells people to replace such items, but he doesn't want to cause the couple undue financial hardship, so he takes a fallback position, offering a less strict interpretation of what needs to be done.

"I have to be a psychologist," he explains. "Sometimes people are very attached to certain items, and we have to figure out a way that won't prevent them from kashering their kitchens. I feel it's part of my job to be lenient, so in the big picture they stay on the horse, keep kosher, and are happy with it."

Getting more Jews to keep kosher is his priority. Before he scares off newbies, he tries to figure out their limits. For example, the easy method of making a dishwasher kosher is to run it through three complete wash cycles, but a stricter approach would be to leave the machine unused for a year. Lebovic doubts the Sandlers will go that far, and that's fine. He doesn't expect they will host many ultra-Orthodox friends, the only people who would be concerned about the kosher status of their dishwasher. Playing rabbinic opinions against each other is a useful and accepted way of negotiating such situations. "For people who are just turning kosher, they can run the three cycles," he says. "If they can raise the hot water to a higher temperature, all the better. If some hot bricks can be put inside, to bring the temperature up somewhat, even better."

Kashering a kitchen is a lot of work, so Lebovic brings one, two, even three helpers with him, depending on the job. There's scrubbing, boiling, burning, lifting, and carrying to do. All new dishes and utensils have to be *toyveled*, or dipped in a mikveh, a ritual bath, for spiritual purification. If he's doing that for a client, it means carefully packing up all the plates and glasses, hauling them to the mikveh, dipping them in the water, and getting them back to their owners without breaking anything. The Sandlers have decided to do their own dish dipping, so one assistant was enough for today.

While that assistant fills the aluminum roasting pans with water and sets them to boiling on the stove for dipping the silverware and pouring over the granite counters, Lebovic explains to Marina how to use her microwave for both meat and dairy. According to standard kosher opinion, an oven retains the character of whatever was cooked in it most recently; the steam rising from that dish becomes trapped in the enclosed space and "infects" the next dish cooked. In kosher households with just one microwave oven, it is the usual practice to double-cover all meat or dairy dishes as they are cooking, to prevent this cross-contamination. Like many fervently Orthodox Jews, Lebovic has two microwaves, one for meat and one for dairy. That level of strictness isn't necessary here, so he counsels Marina to heat her meals in tightly covered containers.

The Sandlers have done a lot of prep work in advance of Lebovic's visit. They have marked their utensil drawers and countertops with stickers saying "meat," "dairy," or "pareve" to help them remember to keep everything separate. If, for example, a dairy knife is used to cut meat, it becomes *treyf*, or non-kosher, and has to be kashered—not something one wants to go through on a regular basis.

It's a lot to remember, and Marina, although enthusiastic about the project, is worried. "I'm mostly nervous about the shopping, knowing what to buy," she says. "And when it's Shabbat and my kids want something to eat, how will I manage? It's complicated. You can spend three hours cooking and then make one mistake and have to throw it away."

When nonobservant Jews decide to become "more religious," the defining moment of their new lifestyle often comes when they kasher their kitchen. From that point on, they are reminded of their Judaism at every meal. For many families, like the Sandlers, going kosher is a happy process, the culmination of a spiritual journey. But in some families, one spouse may be more interested in taking on greater ritual observance than the other, leading to all sorts of conflict. It's bad enough when both are Jewish; if one is not, additional factors come into play.

A professional couple in Greenwich, Connecticut, is going through just that turmoil. Speaking anonymously, as they are well known in their community, the wife, who is Jewish, says that she has been moving toward greater observance for a number of years. When the couple moved to a new house two years ago, she wanted to kasher the kitchen but decided not to in the name of *shalom bayit*, the Jewish commandment to keep peace in the home. "My husband isn't Jewish, and he was worried he'd do something wrong in the kitchen or not be able to eat the food he enjoys," she says. To ease him into the process, she started buying only kosher-certified foods, so he would get used to seeing kosher labels in their pantry and would understand that he didn't have to give up tacos or beer. The family is experimenting with kosher substitutes, such as putting avocado on their burgers instead of cheese. "We had a cookout last summer and served a totally kosher meal to our non-Jewish neighbors, and no one noticed," the wife says.

The biggest hurdle to overcome was her husband's insistence that kosher food doesn't taste as good as non-kosher. "We'll be out in a restaurant and he's eating filet mignon, and he asks me if it's kosher," she says. "I say no, it isn't a kosher cut, kind of preparing him." She buys non-kosher beef ribs one week and kosher ribs the next, to show him he can't taste the difference. When he ordered wine one evening in a restaurant, she kept her mouth shut until they got home, then told him it was a kosher brand.

The most important thing to both of them, she says, is keeping conflict out of their marriage. Each has to compromise—he by realizing that she is going to kasher their kitchen sooner or later, and she by accepting that he will continue to eat what he wants. She has made her peace with that. "If he wants Chinese food, he can eat it on paper plates out on the patio," she says. "He can have his filet mignon outside on the grill. We're not going to stress over it." She's incredibly lucky, she acknowledges, that her husband understands how important keeping kosher is for her, and is willing to go along with it.

"Yes, it's easier if two people are Jewish and they agree to keep kosher together," she says. "But that's in an ideal world."

Back in the Sandler home, thirty-two-year-old Arkady has returned from work and is looking over the bowls and utensils that have to be replaced. The juicer can stay, Lebovic rules, as the Sandlers think it's only been used for fresh fruit, but the blades have to be removed, cleaned, and dipped in boiling water, just in case.

Just before dusk, Lebovic steps out on the deck to begin the difficult job of kashering the couple's barbecue grill. They bought it used, and the metal grating is caked with a thick layer of blackened food residue, memories of parties past. The rabbi sprays the grill with oven cleaner, turns the heat to high so the cleaner foams up over the top and drips down the sides to the deck, and then takes his blowtorch to it, moving the torch back and forth across every inside surface. He works slowly and carefully: The flame reaches 1,300 degrees, enough to reduce any food particles, or human flesh, to ash.

Inside, the Sandlers talk about why they decided to make their home kosher. Both were born in the former Soviet Union and immigrated as children to Israel, where they met during their compulsory military service. After they married and moved to New York in 2004, they began seriously exploring Judaism and gradually became more observant. Arkady attends synagogue regularly, and their two daughters are in a Jewish summer camp. When they moved into this new house, they decided to take the opportunity to establish a kosher kitchen as a symbol of their increased Jewish commitment.

"That's why we're doing it, so the kids will know they're Jewish," Marina says. "We want them to feel Jewish, to know Jewish values."

An hour later, Lebovic is still working on the grill, blasting away the last bits of non-kosher encrustation. He's on his third round of oven cleaner, high heat, and blowtorch when the twilight skies suddenly open up and a late-summer storm breaks. Unfazed, he opens an enormous blue-and-white umbrella and stands under it in the pouring rain, a huge flame roaring from the blowtorch he holds firmly anchored at his midsection, intent on the job of making another home safe for kashrut.

FOOD IS CENTRAL to Judaism. Rituals, laws, and blessings are attached to every aspect of its procurement, preparation, and consumption. There is one blessing made over bread but another one for cake and cookies; one over wine but another one for other fruit juices, milk, soda, and water; one for fruit that comes from trees but a different one for produce that grows in the ground. At a meal that includes bread, after the ritual handwashing and recitation of the blessing for bread, no additional blessings need be said for any of the other foods consumed.

Special foods are tied to each Jewish holiday, including Shabbat, the Jewish Sabbath that runs from sundown Friday to sundown Saturday. Jews are commanded to prepare the best meals they can afford to sanctify those days. The overall point of eating is not just to consume nutrients but, in the words of Deuteronomy 8:10, to be "satisfied," both physically and spiritually. Food in Judaism has an inherently sacred quality, which is expressed when the laws of kashrut are obeyed.

Yet despite the intricacies of kosher laws and the attention centuries of rabbis have given to clarifying them, there is nothing in the Torah that specifically states *why* God commands Jews to eat this way.

There are 613 mitzvot, or commandments, in the Torah, which can be divided into three categories. *Mishpatim* are laws that make sense to all people and are needed to keep society functioning, such as the prohibitions against murder and stealing. Most are incumbent upon Jew and non-Jew alike, and form the basis for most societies' civil and criminal laws. *Edot* are laws testifying to the Jewish people's special relationship with God, such as the commandment to circumcise infant boys or to eat matzo, the unleavened bread consumed during Passover in remembrance of the Exodus from Egypt. These laws apply only to Jews. Finally, there are *chukim*, laws that have no rationale discernible to the human intellect but must be obeyed simply because God so commands. These also apply only to Jews. The laws of *shatnes*, which ban garments made of wool and linen woven together, and the laws of mikveh are chukim. So are the laws of kashrut.

Over the centuries, scholars have attempted to tease various principles out of the kosher laws. Many hold that the prohibition against eating meat torn from a living beast teaches humane treatment of animals, as do the rules governing *shechita*, or Jewish ritual slaughter. Others find scientific validation for the ban on pork and shellfish, saying the ancient Israelites must have known mollusks were often tainted and raw pork could carry trichinosis. Still others take an anthropological approach, claiming that the early Hebrews shunned pork to set themselves off from surrounding pagan cultures that worshipped the pig, such as the Canaanite death cult that engaged in ritual pork consumption and the Phoenicians who deified the wild boar.[1]

All of these are projections of the human need to know why onto a text that does not reveal its motivation. The standard Orthodox position is, God said eat this and don't eat that, and that's why we do it. "Kashrut is important because it's biblical, the same reason Shabbat is important and the holidays are important," explains Rabbi Jacob Traub, head of the Orthodox Rabbinical Council, a kosher certification agency in San Francisco.

If the underlying reasons remain shrouded in mystery (or history), the act of keeping kosher can itself teach moral, spiritual, and ethical lessons. One is self-discipline. The twelfth-century sage Maimonides, also known as Rambam, wrote that the kosher laws "train us in the mastery of the appetites," and he didn't mean just those related to food. Traub likes that aspect of kashrut. "Every once in a while there's something you might want that you can't have," he says. "And that's not so terrible. I might want a cheeseburger, but that doesn't mean I have to have a cheeseburger. A person who has disciplined herself not to eat everything she desires is less likely to indulge in acts such as stealing, adultery, or even murder. It's important that people should realize there are limitations," he says.

Although the Torah does not discuss the spiritual benefits of Jewish dietary practice, later rabbis have devoted great attention to the matter. Kashrut, they write, is part of an entire network of laws and rituals that promote the idea of living consciously and thoughtfully in the real world. Judaism neither denigrates nor glorifies the physical world or the physical body; it is neither an ascetic nor a hedonistic religion. The physical and the spiritual are part of a unified whole. Still, although both are essential to the proper functioning of the universe, a thing's true nature lies on the spiritual plane. The job of the observant Jew, according to this understanding, is to elevate the mundane activities of daily life—eating, drinking, sleeping, elimination of body waste—to the level of holiness, where that true nature can be expressed, by following God's laws. Each activity has its own blessing, reminding Jews to stop and think about how its performance connects them to God, the creator of all reality.

"Keeping kosher is a statement of who I am, to myself first, and then to others," says Linda Silvern, who struggles to keep kosher in rural Alabama. "It is a continual reminder of my belief in God. By paying so close attention to something I do at least three times a day, I am reminded of who I am, where I came from, and my many blessings."

Rabbi Eliyahu Safran, vice president of communications and marketing for the Orthodox Union's Kosher Division, points out that hunger is a natural drive, needed to keep any living creature alive. A Jew can enjoy its spiritual benefit only by eating foods permitted by God, in the manner set down in Jewish law, accompanied by the appropriate blessings that connect body to soul. That connection between kashrut and reaching for holiness is made explicit in Leviticus 19:1–20:22, when God prefaces the laws given to the Jewish people by declaring, "You shall be holy, for I, the Lord your God, am holy."[2]

The mystics, rabbis who work in the rarefied field of Kabbalah, delve into the spiritual aspects of kashrut with particular relish. The thirteenth-century Zohar, considered the central text of Kabbalah, describes the heavenly table where the righteous will sit after the coming of the Messiah, dining purely on words of Torah—the ultimate illustration of the physical merging with the spiritual. Yaron Milgrom-Elcott, a doctoral student in Jewish mysticism at New York University, traces the upward spiritual trajectory involved in Jewish consumption back to Genesis 1:29–30, where God gives Adam and Eve the fruit of trees to eat, while animals are given grass and other green plants that grow close to the earth. "So already there's a division," he points out. "People look up to eat, taking fruit from the trees, and animals have to look down."

The Tanya, the central text of the Chabad-Lubavitch hassidic movement, contains a detailed explanation of the kabbalistic way of looking at food. According to Jewish mysticism, at the moment of creation, God's divine Oneness shattered into countless shards of divine light, pure energy, which became enclosed in physical shells. Those shells—rocks, trees, animal or human bodies—conceal the thing's true nature, which is the divine energy within. Every object yearns to have that energy released so that it can be reunited with God, the source of its creation. The job of the Jew is to help release the divine light in things of the physical world by following God's laws.

Rabbi Yosef Jacobson of the Rabbinical College Chovevay Torah in Brooklyn and an expert on the Tanya explains how this applies to eating. Every piece of food contains a divine spark, the purpose for which it was created. In the case of food eaten by people, that purpose is nourishing a human being, which permits that person, in turn, to live and fulfill his or her own God-given purpose. "So when I look at a piece of food, I can't just ask what my interest is in eating it; I must actually ask the food, so to speak, what its interests are," Jacobson explains. "There's something at stake for the food as well. I need the food and the food needs me."

It is a symbiotic relationship: In eating kosher food, the Jew releases the divine energy trapped within it and sends it back up to God, while the food keeps the Jew alive so he or she can pursue goodness in the world—the purpose for which people were created. Jews can work this process only with kosher food. The Tanya says Jews are unable to release the divine energy in non-kosher food, and it in turn cannot sustain them sufficiently to pursue the goodness they are meant to do. Non-Jews, on the other hand, can release the energy in non-kosher food, be sustained by it, and do good in the world. All food and all people have their function.

In this vision of the universe, kosher animals were created for the purpose of being eaten. Their divine sparks are released when the animals are slaughtered, cooked, and consumed according to the laws of kashrut. But every step of the process must be conducted mindfully, or the animal's death and consumption becomes a desecration. For example, no part of the animal may be torn off while the animal is still alive. That is the literal meaning of the word *treyf,* from the Hebrew *toref,* to tear. In casual conversation today, *treyf* refers to any non-kosher food, but its original meaning concerned a specific treatment of animals.

Rabbi Mendel Lifshitz, a Chabad rabbi in Boise, Idaho, teaches a course in Tanya and devotes three sessions to the spirituality of the kosher diet. He tells the story of a hassidic rabbi who had one precious lamb that he slaughtered and served when he ran out of food at a *far-brengen,* a festive gathering of hassidic men. Rather than mourning the loss of his only animal, the rabbi rejoiced; instead of just one lamb saying "*bah,*" a hundred yeshiva students who ate the lamb were walking around praising God, raising the lamb's divine energy to the level of holiness.

This view of the world should inspire respect for all beings, animate or inanimate, as each contains part of the same divine light. "We judge people and things by their cover, their wrapper, their shells," says Rabbi Jacobson. "The Tanya challenges us to look beneath the shell and see things for what they are, their essence. That begins with the food we eat. When I see my body as a conduit for my soul, not just an independent organism of flesh and sinews and blood, then my eating has different significance. It's not just, I'm hungry, so I'll eat; it's that my soul is also hungry to fulfill its mission in the world."

Jewish thinking makes much of the fact that eating involves physically taking something into one's body, a literal interpretation of the adage "You are what you eat." This interpretation teaches that people absorb the personality characteristics of the animals they eat. The cow, deer, and lamb are gentle, communal animals and are permitted under kosher law. But the eagle, shark, and hyena, hunters and scavengers that exhibit bloodthirsty characteristics the observant Jew should abhor, are all forbidden. The Talmud teaches that eating non-kosher food harms the Jewish soul even if the food is consumed unintentionally. It's that dangerous.

Rabbi Yosef Eisen, head of the Vaad HaKashrus of the Five Towns and Far Rockaway, New York, quotes Rambam as saying kosher food has more impact on a Jew than anything else because it becomes part of one's flesh. Kosher food has the power to connect a Jew to the Divine, he says, comparing the process to a television. If a television screen is filled with static, it means the device is unable to connect with its power source. "When a Jew ingests something that is not kosher, he's blurring his screen," Eisen explains. "He can't connect to God anymore. Every Jew is intuitively connected to HaShem,[3] everybody on different levels. The levels depend on how much advice you follow from Torah. With eating non-kosher food, that connection, that wire, that cable is now loosened. With eating kosher food, that opens up the screen. That makes the screen clear."

Doing more mitzvot brings a Jew closer to God, Eisen says, and eating a kosher meal contains a lot of mitzvot. Take a pastrami sandwich: The meat was slaughtered properly, soaked and salted according to the laws of kashrut, seasoned with kosher spices, and made into a sandwich with two slices of bread made from wheat that was planted properly and processed under kosher supervision. "Now it's on your plate, the bread and the pastrami. You make a *bracha* [blessing], and you're now eating something that has more than half a dozen mitzvot attached to it."

Other Jewish thinkers bring up the aesthetic significance of the prohibition on eating meat from diseased or deformed animals or those that have died of natural causes. Before kosher slaughter, animals are inspected to make sure they are free of wounds or disease. Only perfectly healthy animals pass the test. Gnawing on a carcass found in the woods or eating a steak taken from a sick cow is distasteful and shows a lack of self-respect. In this way, kosher laws promote human dignity.

Other moral lessons can be derived from the laws of kosher slaughter. In the twentieth century, as animal welfare became more valued in Western society, Jews increasingly pointed to the Torah's commandments to treat animals with compassion as evidence of the social relevance of their faith. The Torah teaches that domestic animals must not be burdened with loads too heavy for them and must enjoy a day of rest every Saturday along with their masters. When a domestic animal is slaughtered for food, the act must be performed by a quick cut across the neck with a very sharp knife, which is supposed to lessen the animal's pain.[4]

Some Jews understand the Torah's attention to the needs of animals as God's preference for vegetarianism, pointing to the story of Noah as proof. Indeed, there is a Midrash (rabbinic interpretation of Torah) that appears to imply that when the Messiah comes and the world is perfected, humankind will revert to the vegetarian state of Adam and Eve in the Garden of Eden. Jewish vegetarianism became much more popular in the latter part of the twentieth century, particularly among young people, for spiritual as well as practical reasons: It's easier, and cheaper, to keep a kosher dairy kitchen than to worry about having two sets of dishes.

Many rabbis teach that the separation kashrut makes between milk and meat teaches reverence for life. Meat comes from a dead animal, while milk comes from an animal that is not only alive but has recently given birth, the ultimate life-giving act. Keeping them separate reminds one that death and life each has its proper place.

Sometimes Jews who are not religiously observant and do not keep kosher will purposefully buy kosher food. Often they do so for the same reasons as non-Jews: They believe it is healthier, safer, and cleaner. But some also do it for reasons of community, tradition, and Jewish identity. This is particularly true on the Jewish holidays, which have become times for nonobservant Jews to connect with their history by putting Jewish food on the table. Many Jews who don't keep kosher the rest of the year buy kosher wine and matzo for the Passover seder, sometimes out of respect for parents or grandparents, sometimes because it makes them feel more Jewish, and sometimes because of an inchoate feeling that it would be wrong to do otherwise.

Janice Drell of Glenview, Illinois, is not nonobservant; she is simply not fully kosher according to Orthodox standards. She keeps a kosher-style home, meaning she does not bring in pork or shellfish, but she will buy packaged food without kosher symbols. She reads the labels to make sure they contain no lard or other obviously non-kosher ingredients, like most Conservative and some Orthodox Jews. But when her children were growing up, she made the home completely kosher every year for Passover. The kids would draw pictures of skulls and crossbones to put on the pantry where the family sequestered all its bread, pasta, cereals, and other non-Passover foods, to indicate those were off-limits for the week. She would buy kosher-for-Passover food, from matzo to ketchup, even though ketchup without a kosher symbol was good enough the rest of the year.

"Partly it's how I was raised," she explains. "Partly it's a way to identify as Jewish. And partly it's to honor my forefathers and foremothers."

Rabbi Safran of the Orthodox Union believes that even this occasional expression of Jewish dietary practice points to an inner need all Jews have to signal their Jewish connections through food. "One need not be religiously observant to come to the conclusion that life is more than just physical," he says. "And if it's more than just physical, than I need to look for a greater sense of meaning in those physical activities. The act of eating takes on greater meaning when it's infused with something spiritual, and that something spiritual is kashrut. Kashrut says you can't just run wild, eating whatever comes your way. There's a manner, there's a setting, there's cutlery, there's the opportunity to recognize God through the recitation of blessings."

Now that there are so many items carrying kosher certification, it's just as easy to buy kosher as non-kosher food, he says. But there is also something deeper, the *pintele yid*, or Jewish spark, that is supposedly built into every Jewish soul. Once a person feeds that spark with Jewish soul food—a kosher diet—it takes on a force of its own, pushing the practitioner, willing or not, toward greater observance in other areas of life. Eat kosher, the hope is, and more will follow. "That kosher steak can lead from the kitchen door to the living room door and to the bedroom door," Safran suggests.

Jews have suffered and died for kashrut throughout history. The Jewish principle of *pikkuach nefesh*, the preservation of life, takes precedence over almost any other commandment in the Torah. Jews are obligated to give their lives only to avoid perverse sexual relations, idolatry, or murder. But the kosher laws are so deeply ingrained within observant Jews that some will do whatever they can to avoid eating non-kosher food, even in the most dire circumstances. Some observant Jews in Nazi concentration camps and Soviet labor camps fasted on Yom Kippur, and throughout the rest of the year they picked bits of maggoty meat out from their gruel, denying their starved bodies the little bit of nutrition that extra food would have offered.

Kashrut is a force that both unifies and separates. It identifies its practitioners as part of the Jewish community and ties them to thousands of years of Jewish history, while at the same time setting them apart from those who do not keep kosher. Until the nineteenth century, that meant apart from non-Jews. The system works quite well: If you can't sit down to a meal with your Gentile neighbors, you're unlikely to socialize with them or marry into their families. Even today, when observant Jews eat with non-Jewish colleagues in kosher restaurants, mingling (if not marrying) with impunity, everyone at the table is aware that they are there because the Jews will not eat the same food that their colleagues eat. That can be a point of pride, but also discomfort.

Modern Orthodox feminist Blu Greenberg writes about this psychological impact of keeping kosher in *How to Run a Traditional Jewish Household,* her seminal guide to the observant life: "Nowhere do I feel more connected to my community than on those rare occasions when I find myself in a non-kosher restaurant, eating half a cantaloupe while my companions dab at their shrimp cocktails or paté de foie gras."[5]

The Torah does not specifically say Jews should eat differently to separate themselves from other people; it presents this diet as a way for the Israelites to show their closeness to God. But later biblical books do make the point, beginning with Ezekiel's sixth-century BCE warning that the Jews in Babylonian exile should reject the impurity of foreign foods. When Christianity became the state religion of the Roman Empire in the fourth century CE, it became a capital crime for a Christian to eat at a Jewish table.[6]

In the United States, it was precisely the kosher diet's power to separate Jew from non-Jew that brought kashrut into disfavor among some new Jewish immigrants. Looking to get ahead in a secular world that was quietly or openly anti-Semitic, they took steps to disguise or downplay their otherness. That meant changing their names—Greenberg to Green, Hershel to Harry—losing their yarmulkes, and joining their non-Jewish friends and colleagues in non-kosher restaurants.

By the early twentieth century, kosher food had become a battleground. On one hand, many new immigrants considered it old-fashioned. They wanted to be fully American, and that meant discarding the dietary laws that set them apart. Meanwhile, the growth of the processed food industry meant that more kosher food was showing up already bottled, canned, and packaged, and many traditional Jews were reluctant to buy these unfamiliar items, preferring to cook as much as they could from scratch so they would know it was really kosher.

Kosher food manufacturers, store owners, and Orthodox groups locked arms to persuade both kinds of American Jews to buy more kosher food products. They enlisted the media as their ally. Even before the World War I, food manufacturers ran ads in the Yiddish press to introduce the immigrant Jewish population to newfangled products like ketchup, canned soup, crackers, and bottled soda, showing that they were American but kosher, too. In 1913, a Yiddish women's magazine carried a two-page ad for Borden's Eagle Brand condensed milk, pointing out that every U.S. president had immigrant origins and linking that information to the claim that good nutrition leads to success in America. "Unspoken was the promise," writes social historian Hasia Diner, "that with just enough Borden's milk their American-born sons, too, could become president."[7]

To bring lapsed Jews back into the fold, Orthodox groups tried appealing to the same claims of health, hygiene, and aesthetics that had lured many of them away from kashrut in the first place. Kashrut was reinvented for this audience as a symbol of modernity, rather than a biblical commandment. In a society where keeping kosher was a choice, it had to appear as the most attractive one.

They aimed their campaign at nutritionists, many of them Jewish themselves, who had declared the typical Jewish diet fatty, unbalanced, and unhealthy. To counter these arguments, Jewish homemakers were bombarded with advertisements, books, and lectures demonstrating the modernity, cleanliness, and scientific validity of the kosher diet. In 1911, Detroit physician Noah Aronstam defended the kosher diet in these terms at the International Exhibition of Hygiene. In a stunning misappropriation of Darwinian science, he claimed that the fish and mammals permitted by kosher law were more nutritious than non-kosher varieties because they "stand higher on the ladder of evolution." He lauded the ancient dietary laws as ahead of their time, saying they predicted the "doctrines of modern sanitation."[8] Similar articles appeared in medical journals and women's publications, claiming that the milk of kosher animals was easier to digest, or that eating milk and meat together caused stomachaches.

Food manufacturers were happy to lend a hand, emphasizing the sanitary conditions and up-to-date technology in their plants in an era when convenience trumped homemade in the kitchen. A 1920 advertisement by Horowitz Margareten declared, "We have raised the kneading and baking of matzoh from haphazard, careless, hit-or-miss to a science." The company claimed to control its oven temperature to "fractions of an inch" and to bake its matzo according to "carefully computed formulae," rather than relying on those unscientific recipes handed down from Grandma, who clearly could not measure properly.[9]

Manischewitz made similar claims, advertising its matzo as the "purest, cleanest matzo you can get, so clean it is untouched by human hands," says historian Jonathan Sarna, "which is hilarious, because they used to market their matzo as handmade. But now we've decided human hands are full of germs." Later on, matzo was sold as a diet food, and even later, as cholesterol free, in line with America's changing food trends.

In May 1925, the Hebrew Ladies' Aid Society of Fargo, North Dakota, held a picnic for immigrant Jewish women. Representatives from the Mazola company extolled the ease and nutritional benefits of frying Chanukah doughnuts in Mazola corn oil, a product released just a decade earlier. It was kosher, the women were told, but also up-to-date. They could use it without fear of being outed as greenhorns, the pejorative term for newly arrived immigrants.[10]

The Women's Branch of the Orthodox Union mounted a national campaign to show how modern kosher cooking could be. They published cookbooks for the contemporary Jewish housewife and sponsored cooking classes that showed kosher methods for preparing all-American dishes like meat loaf, chocolate-chip cookies, and macaroni and cheese. The kosher laws did not prevent Jews from participating fully in society, they argued. You could serve a completely kosher dinner to non-Jewish friends, including cocktails and dessert, and it would be as delicious and appealing as a non-kosher meal.

A kosher diet led to moral uprightness and self-discipline, the campaigns promised. Kosher meat and shellfish restrictions provided protection from many diseases, promoting good health and longevity. But above all, a kosher diet showed the practitioner's refinement, nobility of character, and impeccable taste. "Kashrut was nothing less than an artistic opportunity, an occasion to demonstrate the aesthetic sensibility of the modern ritually observant Jewish woman," writes Jewish cultural historian and George Washington University professor Jenna Weissman Joselit, explaining this view. "These arguments for keeping kosher sought unmistakably to make the point that observance of the dietary laws was as consonant with middle-class life as handsomely appointed apartments or visits to the opera."[11]

It was, however, a losing battle. The percentage of American Jews who kept kosher declined as the century wore on. Sociologist Marshall Sklare claims that by the 1950s less than 10 percent of third-generation American Jews followed the dietary laws.[12]

America's religious nature also has an impact on Jewish dietary practice. From its founding, this has been a deeply religious society. It is also a religiously fickle culture: 40 percent of Americans practice a different faith than the one in which they were raised.[13] Both factors have contributed to the emergence of many "new Jews." Within a Jewish population of approximately six million[14] are hundreds of thousands of converts to Judaism, as well as an unknown number of *baalei teshuva*, or "returnees to the faith," formerly secular Jews who become religiously observant. These people were not brought up with kosher kitchens. They did not help their mothers bake challah or hear their fathers intone the blessings over the wine at the Sabbath table, which is how Jewish children learned to keep kosher in the old days. These Jews need lessons to learn how to eat according to Jewish law.

An entire educational industry has sprung up to help them. A search for "kosher books" on amazon.com yields more than a thousand titles. Most are cookbooks, but many are guides to keeping a kosher home. When Rabbi Lebovic went to kasher the Sandler home on Staten Island, Marina Sandler was clutching a copy of Rabbi Zalman Goldstein's book *Going Kosher in 30 Days*, a popular guide to taking a family from treyf to kosher in a month.

Jewish institutions are helping their people learn about dietary practice. Increasing numbers of synagogues offer home kashering services for free or at reduced cost to their members, and dozens of rabbis like Lebovic make a living from it. In the past few years, kosher agencies and Orthodox, Conservative, and Reform institutions have begun offering lectures and classes on kashrut, both in the classroom and online, most of them aimed at a lay Jewish audience.

The Orthodox Union is particularly involved in this outreach. Rabbi Safran heads up the OU's public education initiative, which got under way in 2006. His department has produced DVDs for children and adults on topics such as kosher birds, kosher fish, and kosher meat. It has an extensive Web presence, offering archived articles, videos, and live streaming Q&A sessions with rabbinic experts answering callers' questions. It sponsors OU Kosher Coming, a program that sends kosher experts into schools and synagogues, and Kosher Tidbits, an online radio archive offering more than a hundred short seminars on various aspects of kosher observance.

Again, the thinking is that this outreach will encourage more Jews to keep kosher and to observe other Jewish commandments as well. "The less people know, the less observant they are," Safran says.

The Orthodox Union also offers ongoing kosher education for rabbis, yeshiva students, and kosher professionals through its Ask OU program. A five-session how-to series of DVDs issued in early 2009 treated highly specialized subjects such as *nikkur*, the correct way to remove forbidden veins and fats from a kosher animal carcass, and the best methods for checking produce for insect infestation. In summer 2008, the OU partnered with Yeshiva University's rabbinic seminary to offer a three-week program in practical kashrut for rabbinical students, the first time such a course had been offered.

Another kind of kosher outreach that has become popular in recent years takes place in supermarkets, usually before or during major Jewish holidays. Rabbis or synagogue groups set up tables inside the stores; they offer shoppers information about Judaism and kashrut, direct them toward the kosher food section, and give tours through the aisles to show Jews who do not keep kosher how many mainstream products carry kosher certification.

The Chabad movement spearheaded this campaign with Kosher Awareness Week, typically offered in supermarkets before Rosh Hashanah or Passover by Lubavitch emissaries, the men and women who run hundreds of Chabad centers across North America. Often they will move from store to store during the week, to reach as many Jewish shoppers as possible. The program is promotional as well as educational; in spring 2001, Chabad headquarters in Brooklyn tried to get every emissary in the country to run Kosher Awareness Week at the same time, creating a national push to encourage more Jews to keep the dietary laws.

Rabbi Mendel Bendet directs Chabad-Lubavitch of the Poconos in Stroudsburg, Pennsylvania, a farming region with perhaps a few hundred Jewish families. He began running Kosher Awareness Week in spring 2007, to introduce kosher food to this overwhelmingly non-observant Jewish community. "They tend to have stereotypical images of what kosher food might be," he says. "We show them it is not as far out or as hard to find as they think. They are shocked to see the percentage of items on the shelves that have kosher certification."

Miriam Ferris, a longtime Chabad emissary in Berkeley, California, teaches challah baking to Jewish women, another popular Chabad kosher outreach project. Challah is the bread traditionally served at Shabbat meals, so there is a built-in connection between the food and Jewish learning, which Ferris, like other Chabad emissaries, is happy to exploit. "There's a saying, 'ain kemach, ain Torah,' without food you can't study," she says.[15]

On one midwinter Thursday evening, four women gather in her kitchen to help bake what Ferris calls a "kabbalistic challah." She begins by asking each woman to drop a coin in her pushke, or charity box, taking the opportunity to tell them that because baking challah is part of preparing for the holy Sabbath day, it is particularly meritorious to give charity beforehand. Then she passes out her challah recipe. She found it in Ohel Rachel, a book that discusses the three commandments specifically given to Jewish women: lighting Sabbath candles, obeying family purity laws, and taking challah, which, since the destruction of the Second Temple, means removing and burning an egg-size handful of bread dough from each batch made from at least five pounds of flour.

Ferris calls the recipe she is using kabbalistic because it relates each ingredient to a human attribute, the way Kabbalah finds connections between the physical and spiritual worlds. "Salt gets rid of guilt, so who wants to add the salt?" she asks. Next she sifts the flour, "to get rid of the bad while keeping the good," she explains. Sugar is added for emunah, or faith in God. Then she measures out the yeast, which in Hebrew is shmarim, from the same root as shomer, the word for "guard." "That means HaShem guards the Jewish people," she says.

Now water is added to the dry ingredients while Rivka Ferris, one of Miriam's daughters, reads aloud, "The water is the intellect. In Chabad philosophy, it's so your mind should rule over your emotions." Finally, the eggs are mixed in, "so all your endeavors should hatch and come to fruition," Miriam explains. "Okay, now we anoint the challah like a king," she continues, dripping a small amount of olive oil into the bowl while one of the women kneads the dough furiously. Usually Ferris uses vegetable oil, but this challah demands the best.

"Not so hard—you don't want to rip it apart," she cautions the enthusiastic kneader, who by now has both hands buried in the dough past her wrist bones. The woman looks up, expecting a hassidic tie-in to the admonition, but Ferris just laughs. "That's not kabbalistic, just good challah baking."

Only one of the women in the kitchen, Miri Elman, learned Jewish cooking from her mother. The rest, including Ferris, grew up in non-kosher homes. "My mom taught me the throw-anything-in, go wild method of cooking," Ferris says. Elman, on the other hand, has happy memories of helping her mother cook for Shabbat every week. Her job was preparing the cholent, or Sabbath stew. "I'd put it together, and my mother would put it in the oven," she recalls. "She had a special cholent pot she got in 1968 when she got married. I'd put the onion in the bottom, then the chicken or meat, then potatoes, barley, paprika, garlic powder, onion powder, salt, and three bullion cubes."

By now each woman has taken her turn kneading the dough. Ferris tells them that while they're kneading, they should be praying for their friends, family, and the entire Jewish people, and contemplating how they hope to grow spiritually in the coming week. "By kneading in the oil, we are blending in HaShem's presence," she says. With a twinkle in her eye, she adds, "This is the most mystical challah dough I've ever seen."

As more American Jews grow up in nonobservant homes, Jewish religious schools have shouldered the burden of teaching kashrut to children who no longer learn it from their parents. That is true even in Orthodox day schools, which divide the school day between Jewish and secular studies. Not only are some of these pupils' parents newly religious with limited backgrounds in kosher law and practice, even the most Orthodox children are growing up in a world where keeping kosher is a matter of choice, one constantly beset by temptation. Setting a firm foundation early on will, their elders hope, keep them in the fold.

In September 2005, the fifty-thousand-square-foot Jewish Children's Museum opened at the corner of Eastern Parkway and Kingston Avenue in the heart of Crown Heights, Brooklyn. More than a hundred thousand visitors, mostly children, pass through its doors every year. The most popular section by far, says marketing director Chaim Benjaminson, is the kosher supermarket, a kid-friendly mini grocery store and kitchen that gives hands-on experience in making kosher choices.

Kids seem to love it. They rush in, grab pint-size shopping carts, and stuff them full of kosher-certified food products they snatch off the shelves. They ring up their purchases at scanners that give kosher information about the items instead of their price. A colorful video game asks users to answer questions about kashrut. Is this animal kosher? Can you eat this food with that? At a tiny kitchen table, red meat dishes jump away when placed next to green dairy utensils, thanks to hidden magnets. A refrigerator talks each time it is opened, delivering Henny Youngman–style lines like "What kind of fish is a gefilte, anyway?"

"With the Internet and Wii, you have to teach children about Judaism in a fun and interactive way, or you'll never get them out of the house and away from all their technology," says Benjaminson. The exhibit is labor-intensive. Staff have to tape and glue all the product caps on tightly so that the kids don't open them, and they're constantly replacing plastic fruit scarred with child-size bite marks.

Inbal Rejman is visiting from Florida with her sons Aaron, ten, and Harel, seven. It's the fourth time the boys have been to the museum, and they run straight to the kosher supermarket. Aaron grabs a squeeze bottle of Israeli-made honey and scans it. "When can you serve this?" the screen asks. Rejecting wrong answers "only on Wednesdays" and "only with poppy seed," he confidently presses "on bread" and is rewarded with a happy dinging noise.

"The boys love it," Rejman says. "They're the ones who dragged me here. It's important that they know what's kosher, what kind of products to look for."

Jewish schools that do not belong to a particular movement often teach a more nuanced approach to Jewish dietary practice, as their students come from homes with varying levels of observance. The Tehiyah Day School in El Cerrito, California, serves three hundred children from kindergarten through eighth grade. Many of their parents are affiliated with the nearby University of California at Berkeley, a famously left-wing, intellectually rigorous campus. When Rabbi Tsipi Gabai, the school's spiritual leader, teaches her eighth graders about kashrut, she knows they will challenge her at every turn.

One afternoon, the class grapples with the notion of kashrut as a way for Jews to separate themselves from other people. The idea makes many of the students uncomfortable. "It doesn't seem right to be different just for the sake of being different," one girl blurts out. "That's like saying the white race is different so we should have segregation and slavery."

"You have to understand the context," Gabai argues. "Here was a small group of people, the first to believe in one God, and they were surrounded by tribes that worshipped idols and sacrificed their children. So when Moses comes and gives them the mitzvot, the commandments, he says, don't be like these others, don't follow their way of life."

The Torah understood that Jews were going to eat meat, she explains, so it gave them rules to limit that consumption and laws to prevent the kind of brutality they witnessed in surrounding cultures. "So these laws and rules were not about segregation but to protect the community. You think God cares whether you light a fire on Shabbat? The idea is, when you take one day a week to rest, that makes a healthy community. You want to eat meat? Okay, but you can't just chop off a limb and let the animal bleed to death like the Canaanites, or eat a dead animal you found in the road. Don't be like those people. You are *am kadosh*, a holy nation. *Kadosh* doesn't mean 'better,' it means 'different.'"

Another girl raises her hand. "When you are Jewish and you keep kosher, it's kind of a way not to separate yourself in a bad way from the rest of society, but a way of saying, 'Yes, I'm Jewish; yes, I'm proud of it; and yes, I can keep the laws that date all the way back to the Israelites.'"

She pauses for a second, then offers another thought. "I was raised vegetarian, but if my family ate meat, I think we would keep kosher. I know I would."

# 3.

# Big Brother Is Watching

## *The Kosher Certification Agencies*

RABBI MENACHEM GENACK'S office overlooks Ellis Island, the New York Harbor landmark where more than two million Jews entered the United States between 1880 and 1914 as part of the largest mass immigration in American history.

In those years there were no kosher certification agencies, no industrial slaughterhouses, no supermarkets. Jews prepared their own meals from scratch. They bought whole kosher fish from the local fishmonger, freshly butchered meat from the kosher butcher, and bread at the kosher bakery. The most punctilious picked out their own chickens at the chicken market and watched as the shochet, or ritual slaughterer, did his thing. But other than that, they cooked using the same raw materials as everyone else. A person setting up a Jewish household was expected to know what was and wasn't kosher; if you had questions, you turned to your rabbi.

"When I was growing up in the 1950s, my mother kashered her own meat; she soaked and salted it," Genack recalls. "No one does that anymore. It's all done in the slaughterhouse."

Today Genack directs the Orthodox Union's Kosher Division (OU Kosher), the world's largest kosher certification agency. More than four hundred thousand products manufactured in eight thousand plants owned by three thousand companies in eighty different countries carry the OU's well-known kosher symbol, a *U* inside a circle. An estimated one thousand mashgichim supervise the making of those products, their efforts overseen by fifty or so rabbinic coordinators working out of OU headquarters in lower Manhattan. Each rabbinic coordinator has his area of expertise: This one might specialize in oils and baked goods, his neighbor might oversee fish, and the guy down the hall might be in charge of food technology. They collect reports of plant visits made by their mashgichim, help new companies navigate the process of going kosher, keep on top of fraud and delinquency, educate the public about kashrut, and ensure that a steady supply of kosher food keeps rolling off the line. Questions of kosher law go to the agency's *poskim*, Rabbis Yisroel Belsky and Hershel Schachter, who interpret Jewish law to apply to particular kashrut concerns.

Kosher certification is a twentieth-century invention, driven by technology. People don't need a rabbi to tell them a raw apple is kosher. But as soon as that apple is cooked, canned, frozen, freeze-dried, or packaged—as soon as it is changed in any way from its natural state—it becomes subject to rabbinic oversight, to ensure that the laws of kashrut are not being violated in the process. On the simplest level, that might mean a rabbi assuring his flock that a local bakery may be patronized, or that a particular shochet's meat is kosher. That was the extent of kosher supervision until mass production changed the way food got to the table.

In 1925, the average American housewife prepared virtually all the food her family consumed; by 1965, up to 90 percent of the food eaten in American homes was factory processed.[1] No longer was it a question of whether the corner fishmonger used a shrimp knife to cut the piece of halibut Aunt Sadie was buying. Now observant Jews had to be concerned with the kosher implications of canning equipment, assembly-line belts, and spray dryers used in factories half a world away. They had to wonder whether the beef soup mix they bought in the supermarket had been freeze-dried in machines previously used for cream soups, a violation of the prohibition on mixing meat and milk. They had to determine the kosher status of chemicals used to make artificial flavorings and preservatives. The congregational rabbi was no longer enough of a guide; hence, the emergence of the kosher expert.

The Orthodox Union was the first to enter this field. Created in 1889 as the Union of Orthodox Jewish Congregations of America, the umbrella organization for the country's Orthodox synagogues (partly in response to Reform Judaism's Union of American Hebrew Congregations, whose temples were fast gaining ground throughout the United States), the OU soon turned its attention to the need to bring order to the country's kosher food supply. The processed food industry was growing at a tremendous rate, but there were no kashrut standards in factories. That made it difficult for kosher homemakers, who were buying increasing amounts of boxed, packaged, canned, and frozen goods, to ensure the dietary sanctity of their kitchens.

In the early 1920s, the OU came up with a plan to offer food manufacturers a kosher supervision and certification process that would be recognized by Jewish consumers nationwide. Rabbis authorized by the OU would visit plants to ensure that all the ingredients and equipment met kashrut standards, and would give the company permission to put a label on those products attesting to their kosher status.

Individual rabbis had given their approval to factory-produced kosher foods before then, most notably to Passover matzo beginning in the 1880s, but this new collaboration between food manufacturers and national agencies would shift authority from local to national, and eventually global, control.

The first company to take up the offer was the H. J. Heinz Company, which agreed to produce a kosher version of its popular canned pork-and-beans. In 1923, Heinz Vegetarian Beans became the first food item to carry national kosher certification. This also represented the first successful effort to convince a major food manufacturer that the country's growing Jewish population was a lucrative market.

It took years for American companies to buy into that notion in significant numbers. In 1945, more than twenty years later, the OU was certifying just 184 products made by thirty-seven companies. Activists in the Women's Branch of the Orthodox Union, frustrated by the small number of canned and packaged goods they could serve their families, began visiting manufacturing plants to convince owners to seek kosher supervision, in some cases even paying for the laboratory analysis of their products just to get more kosher food on the shelves.[2]

Every time a well-known food product or major manufacturer "went kosher" in those early years, the Orthodox community celebrated and the Jewish press trumpeted the news. When Loft's ice cream and candy received kosher certification in 1935, one Jewish publication called it "an historic event for the Jews of America," and the OU honored the company's non-Jewish president at a kosher banquet at New York's Hotel Biltmore.[3]

By 1961, 1,830 items produced by 359 companies were under OU supervision,[4] still not commensurate with the growth of the processed food industry as a whole. As late as the 1960s and '70s, it was common for Jews who kept kosher to read the ingredients labels on cans and boxes of processed food to determine for themselves whether an item was acceptable or not. By the 1980s, the tipping point had been reached, kosher certification had begun its meteoric rise, and this method of keeping "kosher by ingredient" fell out of favor in Orthodox circles, although many Conservative Jews continued to rely on it. So many products carry kosher certification today that few Orthodox Jews will buy processed food that is not marked with a recognized kosher symbol.

Despite the growth of the kosher food industry, there is no national standard governing what can and cannot be called kosher. About two dozen states have kosher laws, but they are based on consumer protection—as long as you are up front about what you're selling and whose kashrut standards you follow, you are permitted to call it kosher. To a certain extent, the field polices itself through community acceptance. "Anyone can set up a kosher agency," says Rabbi Chaim Fogelman of the OK. "Just get a logo, put out your shingle, and you're in business. The thing is, you have to get people to trust you."

Rabbi Moshe Elefant is one of two executive rabbinic administrators at OU Kosher. As a child in 1950s Brooklyn, he was taught that if a food label did not list lard or tallow, the product was kosher enough to eat. His own children, on the other hand, always look for a recognized kosher symbol. Elefant approves of the increased strictness. "There's greater awareness in the community that you don't self-diagnose," he says. "You're not the doctor. Looking at an ingredient panel, I don't know what those ingredients are or where they were made. The kosher consumers know they need a reputable supervision to make that determination for them."

Today food manufacturers pay for a kosher label because they believe it helps sales. The whole point is to get that kosher symbol on their product. But in the early years of kosher certification, companies were wary of appearing too Jewish. When Heinz first agreed to produce its kosher beans, company executives worked with the Orthodox Union to develop a logo that would not alienate non-Jewish customers. After much negotiation, the OU agreed to drop the word *kosher* from the original design proposal, and came up with the less ethnically specific "circle U" logo still in use.

Well into the 1980s, many American food manufacturers were loath to get kosher certification for the same reason—they felt it would limit them to the niche Jewish market. This is still true in the food industry outside North America. Kosher products in Great Britain, for example, do not carry kosher labels. Products manufactured under kosher supervision in the United States have a hard time finding British distribution because of those labels, and in fact are rarely carried in British supermarkets. The London Beth Din Kashrut Division, the major kosher certifier in Great Britain, publishes an annual *Kosher Nosh Guide* that lists all the kosher products for sale in the country, so observant Jews and others looking for kosher items will know what they can buy.

There's also the generic "K" option, developed in the 1920s by New York marketing expert Joseph Jacobs to give manufacturers of kosher products a symbol that kosher consumers would recognize, but that any rabbi could take as his own mark. It gave companies more choice in determining how much they wanted to pay for kosher supervision, and to whom. The problem was that the "K" symbol was never registered as a trademark, so anyone can use it, one reason why it grows less popular each year. But some companies that pay good money for recognized kosher supervision continue to use the "K" for their own reasons, such as Kellogg's, which is certified by the Vaad Harabonim of New England but chooses not to display the group's kosher symbol on its products.

Other companies understood early on that targeting the Jewish market and being open about their kosher status could be quite profitable. In 1912, Procter & Gamble became one of the first major food manufacturers to ask a rabbi to give his *hekhsher,* or stamp of kashrut, to Crisco, the company's newly developed vegetable-based shortening. Because Crisco was pareve, it could be used instead of butter in the preparation of food served at meat meals in kosher homes. Under the supervision of Rabbi Moshe Zevulun, one of the leading Orthodox rabbis in the country, Crisco was widely advertised as a product "the Hebrew race" had been "breathlessly" anticipating "for 4,000 years."[5]

Until 1935, the Orthodox Union's Kosher Certification Service was the only agency offering nationally recognized supervision and certification. That year Abraham Goldstein, who had headed the OU's kosher effort since its inception, left to form a rival agency, the Organized Kashrut Laboratories. In 2008, the Brooklyn-based OK was the world's second-largest kosher agency, supervising 114,000 products made by more than 1,600 companies. The Kof-K Kosher Supervision of Teaneck, New Jersey, entered the field in 1969, quickly followed by the Baltimore-based Star-K Kosher Certification. Today these four organizations, known as the Big Four, certify most of the kosher food sold in the United States.

By 2009, there were more than a thousand individual rabbis and organizations offering their own hekhshers. Many of them are so-called heimishe hekhshers, kosher approval given by hassidic rabbis whose followers trust only their own leader's rulings. But the Big Four's share of the market continues to expand, both because they work with the largest food manufacturers and because they buy out smaller agencies and take over their accounts. In 2008 alone, the Orthodox Union bought the Half-Moon K, a Los Angeles–based organization that certified such well-known products as Kikkoman soy sauce and Campbell's vegetarian vegetable soup, as well as Western Kosher in Winnipeg, Manitoba, which supervised 120 mostly Canadian companies. These consolidations result in universally higher kashrut standards, as many of the smaller certifications follow less strict guidelines. But it also decreases competition, which some critics fear will lead to higher fees for kosher supervision.

Each of the agencies emerged in a different way that continues to color how it operates.

Rabbi Goldstein founded the OK in order to use his own system of chemical analysis to determine the kosher status of food products. The late Rabbi Bernard (Berel) Levy bought the agency from Goldstein in 1968, adding the thirteen companies Goldstein supervised, including Sealtest, Carvel, Pillsbury, and Kraft Foods, to companies such as Domino and Maxwell House, whose hekhshers Levy had purchased earlier. The OK is led today by Rabbi Don Yoel Levy, who took over as president upon his father's death in 1987. The OK prides itself on its extensive database of ingredients, inert and active, and detailed formulas for every product it supervises; the agency also specializes in supervising and certifying flavorings and other chemicals used in food production.

The Star-K is a lay-led nonprofit agency, created in the 1970s as an outgrowth of the Orthodox Jewish Council, a chartered organization founded in 1947 to oversee religious life for the large Jewish community in Baltimore. The day-to-day work is handled by rabbis working for the agency, but policy is in the hands of a board of directors headed by its president, Avrom Pollak. Rabbi Moshe Heinemann is the agency's *posek,* deciding all questions of kosher law. By the 1980s, the Star-K had moved beyond Baltimore to certify companies around the world. They are best known for supervising food ingredients, kosher meat, and dairy products.

The Kof-K is headed by CEO Rabbi Dr. Harvey Senter, with kashrut standards set by Rabbi Aaron Felder. As at the other major agencies, a staff of kosher food production specialists oversees daily operations, aided by an army of mashgichim and field offices around the world. A committee of rabbis governs kashrut policies, deciding all questions of Jewish law related to food production.

As food technology becomes more advanced, the market share of the Big Four continues to grow. It's difficult for independent rabbis or small, local certification agencies to maintain the technical knowledge to keep up with these advances, the Big Four insist. One example is the steam jacket, an innovation used in many industrial kitchens to heat many huge pots of food at once. If the kitchen is also cooking non-kosher food, even if in another part of the room, the steam from one pot can condense over another pot, mingling non-kosher with kosher food. "A regular rabbi who doesn't know the technology can walk in and say it's kosher," says Fogelman. "Not every rabbi can give certification to every kind of facility."

The same is true of chemical additives and flavorings. The OK has a database of more than half a million kosher-certified chemical compounds. They require a detailed formula for every product they certify, which includes information on every ingredient in that product, where it comes from, and who certifies it. All that is kept in the database, which is constantly being updated and is accessible to the agency's mashgichim. How could one person possibly keep track of so many details?

When a company decides to seek kosher certification from one of the major agencies, it follows a highly detailed application process. While procedures differ slightly between agencies, the fundamentals are the same.

First the company must describe the food product or products it makes, to ensure it is an appropriate candidate for kosher certification. Rabbi Elefant says that when he joined the OU in 1987, food manufacturers outside New York were not particularly knowledgeable about kosher requirements. While he does not recall any requests for kosher certification of ham or bacon, he says there were companies that wanted to certify products that mixed meat and milk, or did not understand the prohibition on animal-based ingredients in pareve foods. "Today that has changed," he notes. "Companies are more sophisticated; they educate themselves before they apply."

Next, an applicant submits a list of every ingredient used in its products, including vitamins, stabilizers, flavorings, and emulsifiers. The company must provide information on where those ingredients are produced and what kind of kosher certification is in force in the factories producing them. All these ingredients and the production processes in their factories of origin have to be vetted by the certification agency. "In this global economy, companies use ingredients from around the world," explains Rabbi Yaakov Luban, a second executive rabbinic coordinator at the OU. "A simple cookie can have ingredients from thirty different countries. A flavor component can have one hundred ingredients."

For example, Health Valley Organic sesame seed multigrain crackers, certified as kosher by the Kof-K, lists fourteen ingredients on the side of its box. They are organic flour, organic expeller pressed oil, organic sesame seeds, organic nonfat dry milk, sea salt, organic toasted sesame oil, organic cane juice, organic black sesame seeds, cream of tartar, organic wheat bran, baking soda, organic wheat gluten, organic rice bran extract, and papain. Along with meeting federal organic standards, each of those ingredients must be investigated from the standpoint of kashrut. Does the oil come from overseas, and if so, how is it shipped to the United States? Is the nonfat dry milk produced under strict kosher supervision, utilizing a properly kashered spray dryer? Papain, a digestive enzyme made from the latex of the papaya fruit, is produced in several stages, including drying the extract, purifying it of contaminants, and then refining it into a powder or liquid form. Is that all done under proper kosher supervision?

Once the paperwork is in order, the certification agency makes an initial plant visit to meet with company representatives and review the factory's equipment to ensure it can be made kosher. If not, new equipment must be purchased. Agency representatives go through a long list of requirements with company officials, such as maintenance of approved procedures, the need to alert the certification agency of any change in suppliers, and the protocol for unannounced inspections by a mashgiach at intervals set by the agency.

Fees for this ongoing supervision are set, ranging from $2,000 to $3,000 a year up to $100,000 or more. In general, the fees depend on how often a mashgiach has to visit. A plant that manufactures packaging material for salt and sugar might need only one visit a year, whereas cheese or wine factories require round-the-clock supervision because of the more complex kosher laws involved in their production. Travel costs for the mashgiach also figure in. A plant that is hard to reach would usually pay higher fees than one located near a major city.

"This is a major financial investment for a company," acknowledges Elefant. "It has to be worthwhile to you. If it isn't, I tell you don't do it, because you're never going to be happy. And if you're not happy you're going to start to cut corners, and when you cut corners I'm going to get angry, and we're going to have a total breakdown of the system."

On the other hand, Elefant says, just about every food ingredient today is available in a kosher version, making it not nearly as cumbersome or expensive to go kosher as it was even a decade ago. As more finished products—the food sold in stores—carry kosher certification, the companies that make those items are requiring that all the ingredients they use also be kosher certified. So down the production chain goes the demand for certification, spreading to the smallest microchemical used in any step of the manufacturing process. Few new food items are launched *without* kosher certification in the United States today, their manufacturers considering it less expensive to pay the supervision fees than risk cutting themselves off from a large part of their potential customers.

"If Nabisco all of a sudden says it will only use one kind of kosher oil for its entire facility, which is huge, there are companies out there that will become kosher just for Nabisco," says Rabbi Yaakov Horowitz, a kosher expert and the longtime senior mashgiach for The Manischewitz Company. "These people may not know anything about kosher or want to know anything about kosher, but they want that Nabisco account."

The next step in the certification process is sending mashgichim into the plant to kasher the equipment. That includes shutting down production for at least twenty-four hours, blowtorching ovens, and running boiling water through all pipes and tanks. Finally, an initial production run is scheduled, which will usually take place under the watchful eye of the mashgiach assigned to the plant or a senior rabbinic coordinator sent by the kosher agency.

Hundreds of companies go through this process every year. The OU alone receives about seventy-five new certification requests a month. Not only does each application require a good deal of legwork, but oftentimes companies are not eager to disclose the intimate details of their manufacturing process, including the complete ingredient list required for certification. Rabbi Don Yoel Levy, head of the OK, once visited a plant that made decorative chocolate shavings. It had special techniques for shaping the chocolate and special knives for cutting it. The knife room was blocked off from the rest of the plant, and Levy was not permitted inside. "The owner said he promised his father he would never show the room to anybody, and Rabbi Levy said he promised God he would not certify anything he didn't check out himself," says Fogelman. The company did not go kosher.

If a factory produces kosher and non-kosher food items, they must do so in carefully separated areas that do not share equipment or ingredients. As an extra safeguard, most agencies do not permit a factory to store kosher and non-kosher versions of the same ingredient, such as a kosher and a non-kosher corn oil, for fear the non-kosher version will end up in the kosher product.

Sometimes that restriction is relaxed, such as when the non-kosher ingredient is much more expensive than the corresponding kosher ingredient, making it unlikely that a company would substitute the former for the latter. That is not a foolproof method, as Rabbi Luban learned when he dealt with a plant that made cookies-and-cream ice cream. The ice cream was kosher, but because Oreo cookies were not yet kosher, the ice cream used a kosher-certified Oreo substitute. A new client wanted the company to make the same ice-cream flavor, but with real Oreos. Obviously that product would not be kosher. The OU did not want the company bringing Oreos into the plant, fearful that the non-kosher cookies would end up in the kosher ice cream by mistake. But company owners convinced the OU that real Oreo cookies were so much more expensive than the kosher substitute that it would never use them in the kosher ice cream.

Six months later, Luban got a call from a consumer who bought some of the company's kosher ice cream and found real, non-kosher

Oreos inside. She recognized them by the logo imprinted in the chocolate cookie wafer. Luban went to the factory and brought half a dozen boxes of the kosher ice cream back to OU headquarters, pulled the lids off every box, put them under hot water to melt them down, and found that every single box contained Oreo cookies. It turned out that the company had purchased $25,000 worth of Oreos to use in its non-kosher ice-cream order and then lost the account. Rather than throwing out all those cookies, they used them in the kosher ice cream, thinking no one would notice.

Luban notified the company that the OU would no longer certify it. The owner called back in a panic, saying he had just purchased the company for $20 million, and the distributors were specifically interested in OU supervision so they could place the ice cream in major supermarkets. If he lost those accounts, it would destroy his business. A compromise was reached, but the penalty for continued kosher supervision was steep. The company had to fire its entire management team, which could no longer be trusted to uphold kashrut standards, and was forced to hire a full-time mashgiach for $20,000 a year, a significant sum at the time.

That was just one instance where the carefully controlled kosher supervisory system broke down. Because it is financially prohibitive to place full-time mashgichim in every factory, the certification agencies have to depend on spot checks, regular lab reports, and human honesty. That requires a delicate balancing act between keeping up good relations with the company, making sure that what the kashrut agency asks of the company is not so onerous that it can't be maintained, and ensuring all the while that the rules are observed.

"Companies are not hostile to us, but we're still a pain in the neck for them," Luban admits. "Some rabbi with a beard in New York is deciding which ingredients they can buy? It's an interference."

WHEN THE KOSHER certification agencies first emerged in the early twentieth century, they limited their supervision to processed food items. That skirted the main problem: kosher meat, a field that has long been plagued by charlatans and cheats out to make a buck by substituting less expensive non-kosher meat and poultry for the real stuff.

As far back as the eighteenth century, Jews complained to religious and secular authorities about kosher meat fraud. The first recorded complaint was lodged against a New York shochet named Moshe in 1771. The first court-ordered revocation of a kosher butcher's license came in 1774, when the widow Hetty Hays charged that her shochet was selling non-kosher meat.[6] Various attempts by New York rabbis throughout the nineteenth century to impose standards on kosher meat and poultry production failed. In 1925, New York City's Commissioner of Markets claimed that 40 percent of the meat sold as kosher in the city was actually non-kosher, despite a kosher law that had been enacted in 1915.[7]

Part of the problem had to do with the voluntaristic nature of American society. When Jews came to this country, they left behind the Jewish communal structures of Europe and the Russian Empire, most notably the *kehilla*, a local body that controlled religious life and provided the necessities for Jewish observance, including shochtim. In the absence of these central authorities in each Jewish community, the kosher food system in America became a free-for-all.

Jeffrey Gurock, professor of American Jewish history at Yeshiva University, tells of a woman named Rachel Samuels who wrote home to Germany in 1790 to complain about the sorry state of Jewish observance in Virginia. "She wrote, 'I'm stuck here in Charlottesville, and there's no *Yiddishkeit* [Jewish life]. The shochet doesn't know what he's doing and often substitutes treyf meat for kosher. I have to get out of here.'"

In the 1700s, synagogues in the larger Jewish communities along the East Coast assumed responsibility for providing their congregants with kosher meat and poultry. The synagogues hired and fired shochtim and monitored local kosher butchers to the extent they could, but the system was unreliable. "Sometimes these guys were skilled, sometimes they didn't know what they were doing, and sometimes they were corrupt," Gurock says. "They were constantly being investigated."

Congregation Shearith Israel in New York hired a shochet even before its doors opened in 1730. The man was constantly being accused of fraud, as were the local butchers who sold his meat back to the congregation. Synagogue trustees tried to clamp down on kosher practice, inspecting congregants' kitchens for kashrut violations and quizzing Jews who traveled outside the city as to what they consumed on the road. They imposed fines on women who didn't clean their utensils properly,[8] a holdover from the European system of Jewish communal authority that would hardly be tolerated today. But they couldn't control the meat situation.

Shearith Israel was the only source for kosher meat in New York until 1825, when newly founded Congregation Bnai Jeshurun hired its own shochet. As each new synagogue in the city was established, it hired a shochet and made arrangements to sell the meat to its congregation through local butchers. But by 1850 there were so many Jews in New York that ritual slaughterers and butchers began to set up shop on their own, outside the system of synagogue or communal oversight.[9] In 1813, Avraham Jacobs became the first independent shochet in the United States. He was followed by many more shochtim who were not affiliated with any synagogue or rabbinic board and were often badly trained. This led to a rapid decline in the standard of kashrut for meat in the second half of the nineteenth century. Several times during the century—in 1845, 1854, and 1863—groups of Orthodox synagogues in the city tried to get together to regulate kosher slaughter and butcher shops, but their efforts never lasted more than a few years. The field was growing too fast; the opportunities to cheat were too many.

In 1887, Hungarian immigrant Moses Weinberger painted a damning portrait of kosher poultry slaughter in New York City. He described the scene at one slaughtering place outside the city limits, anticipating Upton Sinclair's exposé *The Jungle* by two decades:

It is very narrow and forever filled with rivers of mud, mire and blood. Throngs of frightened, impetuous people stand crowded together, pushing each other. The shochatim lack room to turn, hardly able to even move their hands. Since most of the poultry is slaughtered on Sabbath eve or on Thursday, every slaughterhouse boss wants to get a head start to get to market as early as possible. The shochet therefore must sometimes slay as many as 200 birds "in one breath." Woe to the pious and God-fearing. . . . The shochet knows that he did not properly sharpen the knife, inspect it more than once, and even then in a great hurry. But what can the wretchedly poor shochet do? He has to maintain his wife and children.[10]

Ten years later, a union was formed by shochtim to improve the level of kashrut and to protect their wages.

By 1902, there were 1,500 butcher shops claiming to sell kosher meat in New York City. In 1909, ten thousand head of cattle a week were slaughtered in New York for the kosher market;[11] the following year, the president of the Kosher Butchers Retail Association in New York claimed that 65 percent of the meat sold through kosher butchers was not kosher.[12] The price difference between kosher and non-kosher meat provided constant temptation: In 1935, non-kosher beef liver wholesaled for 15 cents a pound, while kosher liver went for 40 cents a pound.[13]

Rabbis provided little protection from this abuse. America did not have any formally ordained rabbis at all until 1840, the year Rabbi Abraham Rice arrived from Germany and took a job at Congregation Nidchei Israel in Baltimore. He was followed by a trickle of other German-educated Orthodox rabbis, but the system of lay control was already established in American synagogues. Rather than rabbis enforcing kashrut standards in their congregations, the congregations set their own rules, which might be more lax or stricter than what the rabbis called for.

"If the rabbis were too outspoken one way or the other, they got bounced," Gurock says. "One of the early Orthodox rabbis had seven pulpits in seven years. Every time he tried to put the hammer down, the congregation turned on him and he was out the door." Rice himself resigned barely eight years after assuming his pulpit in Baltimore, following his unsuccessful efforts to enforce Orthodox standards within his congregation.[14]

Back in Europe, the leading Orthodox rabbis of the nineteenth century urged their followers not to immigrate to America, a heathen land where their religious life would suffer. These warnings had little effect on the 1.3 million Jewish immigrants who set sail for the New World over the next fifteen years. And while many Jews' observance levels dropped off the longer they lived in America and the farther they moved from New York, this growing Jewish population still provided a market for kosher food. In 1917, when the Orthodox population reached its height, a million consumers bought 156 million pounds of kosher meat.[15] More than half the poultry sold in New York City between 1920 and 1930 was kosher slaughtered.[16]

Money was at the root of corruption and fraud in the kosher food industry, whether it was butchers substituting less expensive non-kosher meat for kosher, or unscrupulous rabbis charging fees for kosher supervision they did not really provide.

In 1895, Rabbi Moshe Wechsler of New York was charged with running a fake kosher certification operation. He promised non-Jewish food manufacturers that he would drum up Jewish business for them, then took large fees for his supposed supervision that often amounted to little more than providing the companies with "kosher" labels to put on their products. He charged $100 for ads in a newspaper he published, then printed only enough copies to distribute among those who placed the ads. He solicited ads for silverware and baking utensils by telling Gentile-owned companies that Jews threw out all their kitchen supplies every Passover and had to buy new dishes and utensils after the holiday. He told a chocolate company that local Jews would accept their chocolate as kosher because it contained no fat, a complete falsehood.[17]

The Wechsler case was the most well publicized, but many other rabbis and alleged rabbis were running around supervising kosher slaughterers, butchers, and food establishments with no central control. It was largely to enforce kashrut standards that eighteen Orthodox congregations in New York, Philadelphia, and Baltimore got together in 1888 to bring Rabbi Jacob Joseph from Vilnius, Lithuania, to New York as America's first and only chief rabbi, a sort of Jewish pope for the New World.

Rabbi Joseph's tenure was short-lived. He created a system in New York whereby mashgichim appointed by him would supervise poultry slaughter and would affix a *plumba*, or lead seal, to every chicken, indicating that a kosher supervisor had approved it. A tax of one penny was added to the retail price of every chicken to cover this added supervision, and Joseph declared chickens without plumbas to be non-kosher. The money collected went to an association set up by the eighteen congregations, and they paid Joseph from their coffers.

Opposition to the plan was immediate. Consumers complained

about the price increase on kosher poultry, the Jewish press made allusions to the system's similarity to the hated kosher meat taxes levied on Jewish communities in Europe, and butchers and shochtim complained about supervisors looking over their shoulders. A group of New York rabbis, incensed that the job of chief rabbi went to a foreigner instead of one of them, set up a rival *bet din*, or rabbinic court, and declared that any meat carrying Rabbi Joseph's plumba was non-kosher.

The rabbis' dissatisfaction had a financial component: Rabbi Joseph's arrival threatened the fees they collected for their own supervision of kosher slaughter and butcher shops in the city. At a time when rabbis' salaries were minimal, the extra money a rabbi earned for kosher supervision was a jealously guarded privilege. As this rival group hammered away at the chief rabbi's authority, Rabbi Joseph extended his supervisory efforts from poultry to meat, and then to Passover wine and matzo. The battle over kosher supervision went back and forth, as various shochtim, butchers, and meatpackers in the city aligned themselves with one or the other faction.

By 1889, so few kosher establishments were paying into the association's central system that Rabbi Joseph's salary of $2,500 a year could no longer be covered. In desperation, the association decided that the city's wholesale butchers would pay his salary directly, in return for receiving kosher supervision. Rabbi Joseph argued vigorously against this, realizing that if he were paid by the same businesses he purported to oversee, he would not be seen as impartial.

Indeed, that is what transpired. Rabbi Joseph's reputation plummeted, and in 1895 he fell ill and took to his bed, where he remained until his death in 1902. Even his demise did not bring unity to the city's kosher industry; for months after his death, thousands of stores continued to advertise that he still supervised them.[18] Never again did American Jewry attempt to hire a chief rabbi.

Kashrut, a dietary system used throughout the centuries to keep Jews together, was tearing the American Jewish community apart. Kosher slaughterers, butchers, and supervisors regularly tried to undermine their rivals by declaring them non-kosher, engaging in tit-for-tat exchanges of insults that confused and angered the kosher-keeping public.

There were battles for control of kosher meat in towns across America. In 1894, during kosher meat wars in Brooklyn's Brownsville neighborhood, street fights broke out and an angry mob upended the buggy of one Rabbi Wisinetzky and beat him up because he supported a rival group of butchers and shochtim. In Rochester, New York, the Hebrew Children's Home and the Hebrew Sheltering and Guardian Society maintained two separate Jewish orphanages, not because there were so many abandoned Jewish children, but because the sponsoring organizations could not agree on kashrut standards.[19]

In 1906, the Jewish community of Paterson, New Jersey, hauled to court the rabbi they hired to supervise kashrut, claiming he was so incompetent the local shochtim refused to allow him to inspect their knives, which a kosher supervisor must do to ensure the blades are sharp and free of nicks. The rabbi admitted that the shochtim and kosher butchers did not respect him—one had even locked him inside a meat freezer, he told the judge—but he insisted he was doing the best he could, considering his miserable salary of $5 a week. Another rabbi was brought down from New York to replace him, and the sordid affair came to a head when the two rabbis got into a public fight in the synagogue, an incident that did nothing to enhance the reputation of kosher supervision in that town.[20]

When Jewish communities suspected kosher butchers of price-fixing, they erupted in fury. In May 1902, kosher butchers on the Lower East Side of New York raised their meat prices from 12 cents to 18 cents a pound, and the next day Jewish women declared a boycott. On May 15, twenty thousand Jewish women took to the streets, breaking into kosher butcher shops, dousing the meat with gasoline, and setting it afire. Angry crowds ripped kosher meat out of the hands of shoppers, flinging it to the ground. After weeks of violence, during which several shops were burned and dozens of women arrested, New York's kosher butchers agreed to restore the old prices.

Kosher meat riots prompted by price-fixing broke out again in 1917 in New York and Chicago, and in 1916, Jewish women in Pittsburgh angrily protested price increases by the city's kosher bakers. In these cases, too, the consumers prevailed and the old prices were restored. In May 1935, the largest boycott of all by women in New York City shut down two-thirds of the city's kosher meat shops. By mid-June of that year, one thousand shops had given in and reduced their prices.[21]

The kosher poultry business was rife with racketeering and violence. In 1914, Barnett Baff, owner of several wholesale and retail poultry markets in New York, was suspected of price-fixing and of underselling his rivals. He was shot and killed on the street, as were two eyewitnesses to his murder who had offered to testify in court. One of Baff's shooters later confessed that one hundred kosher poultry retailers in the city had raised $4,200 to pay for the murders.[22]

Strong-arm tactics prevailed for decades and turned particularly ugly after the New York Live Poultry Chamber of Commerce gained control of the city's poultry slaughterers and retailers in 1927 and forced retail merchants to buy only from selected wholesale slaughterhouses. At state hearings in September of that year, a poultry wholesaler testified that his right hand had been broken after he sold to a retailer the chamber had not assigned to him.[23] In August 1928, the home of a noncompliant poultry dealer was bombed; the case was dropped when the witnesses, including the victim, refused to testify.[24] In 1929, the *Forward* reported that sixty-six people, all of them Jewish, were found guilty of conspiring to fix the prices of kosher poultry in New York in collusion with the chamber of commerce, Teamsters Local 167, and the Kosher Slaughterers Union. The newspaper reported that the city's Kosher Chicken Trust was "terrorizing butchers and kosher slaughterers and ripping off customers," and concluded that the kosher chicken industry "was rife with corruption and filled with gangsters."[25]

There was even more money to be made in the kosher beef business, and by midcentury organized crime was rumored to have penetrated the industry. "The Italian Mafia was heavily involved with kosher meat; that was the buzz on the street," says Rabbi Yitzchok Adlerstein, professor of Jewish law and ethics at Loyola Law School in Los Angeles. "When I was growing up, the story was that [one hassidic sect] in particular had been involved with the Mafia, and they weren't the first. It wasn't for any outlandish reason. They needed a bridge loan for their meat business and they got that bridge loan, but they didn't step out of the business after the loan was paid back."

Corruption and scandal also plagued the processed food industry. In the early twentieth century, the fastest-growing part of that industry was kosher-for-Passover food. As is true today, Jews who were lax about kosher observance the rest of the year found their faith, and their wallets, at Passover. Before the national certification agencies emerged, companies that produced Passover food items would hire individual rabbis to inspect their plants. Some of those rabbis did little more than walk through the factories and leave "kosher for Passover" labels behind for workers to affix to the products on their own, without supervision.[26]

Ostensibly to correct such abuses, leading matzo producers including The Manischewitz Company and Horowitz Brothers & Margareten formed the National Matzoh Bakers Association in 1918. But an antitrust suit brought against the association in 1930 suggests that its real goal might have been controlling, not regulating, the industry.[27]

A kosher law went into effect in New York in 1915, largely to control the kosher meat industry. In 1926, the New York State Department of Foods and Markets created a "kosher squad" to inspect kosher retailers in accordance with the new law, but the squad itself was not free of corruption. In 1930, a Brooklyn butcher, brought to court for the fourth time for selling non-kosher meat, told the judge his only offense was refusing to bribe the state inspectors. Other butchers confirmed that this extortion system flourished in the department.[28]

The national kosher supervision agencies attempted to stop the most egregious cases of fraud in the kosher food system. But incidents continued to pop up, and if they lacked their earlier frequency, they made up for it in audacity and scale.

The processed meat business was particularly problematic, as meat came into the processing plants from various sources and was difficult to monitor. One common ploy used by plants caught with treyf meat was to claim they were holding it for Christian friends. In the late 1960s, Rabbi Sheppard Baum, head of the Kosher Law Enforcement Bureau of the State of New York, found treyf salamis on the shelves of a large packing plant that serviced a number of Jewish institutions, including summer camps and rabbinic seminaries. The plant owner insisted he was holding the meat for a non-kosher company whose truck had broken down, a claim that was later found to be completely fictitious.[29]

In 1961, Rabbi Morris Casriel Katz of the Sons of Jacob Synagogue in St. Paul was sent to investigate a large Midwest kosher sausage plant. Seven years later he chronicled what he found in a scathing indictment of the industry. "Big racketeering" was making "millions of dollars," he wrote, by sneaking non-kosher meat into factories that made kosher delicatessen meat products, to the point where "up to 80 percent" of the processed meat sold as kosher nationwide was treyf.[30] In one year, he claimed, more kosher-labeled pastrami and corned beef was sold in the United States than the total weight of all the animals slaughtered in the country's kosher packing plants.[31]

Everyone was at fault, Katz charged: plant managers who paid tens of thousands of dollars; "kosher-front" rabbis willing to look away as cheap non-kosher meat was brought into the factories they supervised; rabbinic organizations that refused to crack down on their dishonest members; and the bookkeepers, distributors, and retailers who went along with it all.

One Friday night, acting on an employee's tip, Katz staked out the plant he had been sent to investigate. Around midnight he watched as a truck pulled into the factory's back entrance and unloaded barrels of treyf briskets, beef tongues, and meat trimmings from the non-kosher plant the same company operated twenty miles away. This went on every Shabbat, he discovered, a time when the kosher plant was supposed to be closed and no supervisors were on duty. Again, money was to blame: Kosher brisket sold for $1.40 a pound, versus $1 a pound for non-kosher brisket.

When he relayed his findings to the local kashrut board, the rabbis were angry—at him, for breaking up what was a lucrative operation for them as well as the factory manager.

Independently owned butcher shops also fell prey to financial temptation. Rabbi Jacob Traub of San Francisco remembers a congregant coming to him in the early 1970s to complain about a butcher he suspected of selling non-kosher livers. Traub and a fellow rabbi drove over to the shop at 3:00 a.m.—the usual time meat was delivered to the place—parked outside, turned off their lights, and waited. At 4:00 a.m. a van pulled up and two men began unloading boxes.

"We walked over, wished them good morning, and asked to see what was in the boxes," Traub relates. One of the men started to shake. "He got totally white; I thought he was going to have a heart attack. He says, 'As of this moment I am no longer in the butchery business; I quit.'" The livers were indeed non-kosher, and the offending butcher was fined $1,800 and forced to hire a full-time mashgiach for his store.

Orthodox-owned kosher businesses have been among the worst

offenders, able to get away with such practices because their customers trust them. Kosher eating establishments from Catskills hotels to Brooklyn restaurants were routinely busted from the 1940s on for serving cheaper non-kosher meat and poultry to their Orthodox guests, particularly during the lucrative holiday seasons when kosher food prices increase. In September 1983, Tessler's Resort Hotel, a kosher establishment in the Catskills, was charged with fraud for serving non-kosher meat to observant diners at Rosh Hashanah. Agents from the state's kosher law enforcement division seized twenty-five non-kosher chickens, twenty-five veal breasts, and eleven packages of pork loin from the hotel kitchen. The owners were fined $1,000.[32]

Sometimes kosher caterers finger their own suppliers. In December 1987, Rabbi Victor Segal, who ran a kosher catering firm in Chicago, sued three Chicago poultry suppliers for selling him thousands of pounds of non-kosher chickens. The fraud affected customers in twenty-two states and was the largest case of fraudulent mislabeling of kosher food in the country. In February 1988, the three companies settled out of court, agreeing to leave the kosher business.[33]

One of the most notorious cases was the chicken scandal that rocked Monsey, New York, in September 2006. Shevach Meats, a kosher butcher shop that rented space in the Hatzlocha Grocery, was discovered selling non-kosher chicken that it bought and repackaged using fake kosher labels. Local rabbis uncovered the deception by making a surprise visit to the store and inspecting the poultry, finding the color of the skin and lack of salt residue proof that the birds had not been kashered. The scam had been going on for at least eight years.

Orthodox Jews in the Monsey area, many of them hassidim, spent weeks furiously kashering their kitchens, scrubbing down countertops, boiling pots and silverware, and cursing the name of Moshe Finkel, the shop's owner and butcher who had been known in the community as a pious Jew. Hundreds prayed for repentance or gave money to charity, traditional ways to atone for sin. Some Orthodox men fasted for a day. "It was devastating for the people who live there," said Rabbi Genack of the OU. "The sense of betrayal. The person was somebody from the community itself."[34]

Kashrut agencies throughout the United States met for months afterward to discuss how to tighten their controls. Some suggested that

observant Jews should stop buying kosher meat in supermarkets altogether. The group agreed that butchers should not repackage kosher
meat and poultry unless the butcher's kosher supervisor put his name
on each new package. Some of the national agencies decided to mark
their products with holograms, which are difficult to fake, and there
was discussion of how better to monitor kosher meat all along the distribution network.

But most kosher scandals are the result of unintentional error, often
made by workers who do not fully understand the observant Jew's commitment to kosher food.

In March 2009, a riot erupted at Cheskel's Shawarma King in
Borough Park, a heavily Orthodox Brooklyn neighborhood, when a
patron discovered the hot dog he had just purchased looked unusual.
He asked to see where it came from, and a naïve staffer showed him a
package of decidedly non-kosher Bar-S jumbo chicken franks. It turned
out that the shop had run out of its regular brand of kosher hot dogs,
and the non-Jewish worker sent to buy more decided to save time by
heading to the grocery store across the street, where he picked up what
looked to him like mighty fine wieners.

More than one hundred angry hassidim mobbed the Shawarma
King, spitting at workers and banging on the counters. One man
punched manager Yosef Baron in the face, prompting Baron to fend off
his attackers by brandishing an electric knife. The police arrived, no
one was arrested, but the restaurant was shut for two days while rabbis
threw out the offending hot dogs and kashered the entire kitchen and
all its utensils.

It was, said the shop's kosher supervisor, Rabbi Naftali Meir Babad,
a "terrible accident."[35]

The case of the non-kosher hot dogs pales beside the Great Girl
Scout Cookie Mishap. Girl Scout cookies are certified kosher by the
Orthodox Union. In November 2008, during the height of cookie-
selling season, a customer noticed that his Thin Mint cookies were
missing their usual kosher label. It turned out that it was inadvertently
left off 14 million boxes of Thin Mints, which account for about
25 percent of annual cookie sales.

Chastened, ABC Bakers of Richmond, Virginia, the company that
manufactured the offending cookies, sent out letters of apology to

Scout councils nationwide, along with proof of kosher certification from the OU.

No one messes with the Girl Scouts.[36]


THE BIG FOUR kosher certification agencies rarely have to deal with such scandals, but they do devote great time and effort to protecting the integrity of the kosher food supply and their own good names. Their staffs answer consumer inquiries, alert the public when non-kosher food is being sold as kosher, and monitor the unauthorized use of their trademarked symbols.

Much of that work is educational, answering people's questions about kashrut in general as well as the kosher status of particular products. The first such service was the OU's *Kashruth Column*, a printed newsletter launched in 1933 that fielded questions sent in by consumers such as: Is Aunt Jemima pancake mix kosher? Can we eat Hershey's chocolate bars? Today all the major agencies, as well as private kosher organizations and individuals, run websites that provide such information to the public.

But the public has to care enough to pay attention. Avrom Pollak of the Star-K says his agency used to supervise a kosher pizza parlor on Long Island. When the agency decided to withdraw its certification and sent a letter stating that to the restaurant's owner, the owner posted it in his front window. Apparently he figured that because it was printed on Star-K letterhead, customers looking for a *teudah*, or kosher certificate, would glance at the letter quickly and assume the restaurant was supervised, instead of reading the document and realizing it said the exact opposite. "You'd be amazed at how easy it is for people to allow themselves to be fooled," Pollak says.

Trademark infringement is something the Big Four take very seriously. According to the kosher agencies themselves, the unauthorized use of kosher symbols increased by nearly 30 percent between 2007 and 2009.[37] That does not always mean the mislabeled food is non-kosher. Sometimes the company has simply stopped paying for kosher supervision but continues to use the kosher symbol of the agency that used to supervise it; the food is still produced in exactly the same way and is technically kosher, but the use of the kosher symbol is fraudulent. In such cases the damage goes beyond money, the agencies insist.

It involves a violation of the trust on which the entire system depends. If a company is willing to use a symbol it has not paid for, it's reasonable to assume it will try to cheat in other ways that would affect the actual kosher status of the food.

In some cases, serious fraud is involved. The Orthodox Union is particularly diligent about protecting its trademark, devoting an entire department to chasing down wrongdoers. In September 2008, the Wilder Spice Company in Reisterstown, Maryland, was ordered to pay the Orthodox Union $300,000 for willfully using its kosher label without permission. The company went so far as to forge a letter of certification from the OU, which it displayed in its offices. "It was pretty serious activity, and the court took it pretty seriously," said attorney David Butler, who represented the OU in that case.[38]

In court, the agencies use language appropriate to the legal system. "You can't go to a judge and say, 'Your Honor, this man has eaten treyf.' It's not a big issue to him," says Rabbi Baruch Cywiak, a former member of the OU's department of trademark infringement. "But you can say, 'Your Honor, I own this mark, it's a trademark I have registered federally and internationally, and this company is willfully and knowingly infringing upon it.'"

The OU's trademark infringement team investigates several hundred cases a year, but few end up in court, says Howard Katzenstein, the agency's director of business management.

Some cases involve little more than a printing error. A major New York supermarket chain produced a new line of canned vegetables, and its graphics department used the label on an existing line that was under OU supervision for its design mock-up. They copied the OU symbol onto the new label without understanding what it meant.

Sometimes a company puts an "OU" on its product in the mistaken belief that it is a universal kosher symbol. That happened with a jelly producer in Turkey, which was certified by local rabbis but put the "OU" on its label when it sent the product to the United States. They did it, they explained, so American shoppers would recognize it was kosher.

Rabbi Mayer Kurcfeld of the Star-K says that in the 1980s his agency saw an OU label on Fuji film. There is no reason why film would need kosher certification, so the Star-K alerted the OU, which contacted Fuji headquarters in Japan. The company apologized and said they had been told that products with this symbol "sell better in the United States," Kurcfeld says.

Such offenses are usually rectified with a visit or phone call. Intentional fraud is much less frequent, and more difficult to correct. The OU handles thirty to forty such cases a year.

A company that does not have kosher supervision might label its product as kosher just to increase sales. Maybe it even applies for supervision, has product labels printed with the agency's kosher symbol, and then decides the supervision is too expensive, but it uses the labels anyway. Some manufacturers make up entirely fraudulent kosher symbols, hoping to deceive shoppers into thinking the product is certified. In 2007, some Russian-made products were spotted bearing the letter *K* inside a white *Q*, a poor imitation of the legitimate symbol used by Rabbi Aryeh Spero's Quality Kosher certification. With more than one thousand listed kosher certification symbols in existence, it's hard enough for experienced kosher shoppers to know which are valid and which are not. How are retailers supposed to keep track?

Hauling businesses to court is a sideline for the national agencies. They spend much more time putting out consumer alerts to keep people from inadvertently buying non-kosher products. The OU, OK, Star-K, and Kof-K all have "kosher alert" sections on their websites, where they post cases of fraud, mislabeling, and unauthorized trademark use, including the names of manufacturers and retail establishments that are no longer under kosher supervision. If a violation involves actual non-kosher food being sold as kosher, a special alert may be sent out, posters put up in neighborhoods where the product is sold, and consumers who spot the offending items urged to contact agency headquarters.

If they call the OK, they'll reach Miriam Wudowsky. As head of the OK's department of unauthorized products, Wudowsky spends her days fielding consumer inquiries, tracking down suspicious products, and reporting kashrut violations on the agency's website.

One Monday morning, she sits at her desk in Crown Heights, Brooklyn, peering at a picture of a vitamin bottle on her computer screen. A woman had called to say that her nutritionist advised her to take vitamins that were allegedly kosher certified. She bought a bottle, it had an OK label, but when she looked on the OK website, the brand was not listed as being certified by the agency. Wudowsky asked the woman to take a digital photo of the label and e-mail it to her.

"She's right," Wudowsky says, pointing to the slightly blurry image on the screen in front of her. "It's not listed in our database, and it's not a new product that hasn't been listed yet, either."

Wudowsky gets about twenty calls and fifty to sixty e-mails a day from people trying to figure out whether they've bought a non-kosher item. Investigating these complaints takes a lot of detective work. Sometimes it's hard to identify which company makes a given product. It might operate under a different name than the one listed on the label, or the address might be wrong or missing. Once she locates the manufacturer, she has to determine who, if anyone, is giving the product kosher certification. If it's one of the Big Four, that's fine; she'll call that agency to verify. But the hekhsher could be from an individual rabbi or from an organization not known to her, and that is more difficult to check.

Most complaints come in by phone or e-mail. But sometimes—not as often as in the past—the suspicious item shows up physically in her office. Wudowsky has received candies, cookies, butter, and cheese in the mail from anxious kosher consumers. Once an elderly gentleman sent her a crushed juice box that he had not fully emptied. Wudowsky opened the package, and grape juice spilled all over her desk. "I'd asked him to send me the label, and he didn't quite understand," she recalls.

But that wasn't as bad as the fish. "They mailed it in some kind of Styrofoam box," Rabbi Fogelman recalls. By the time it arrived at OK headquarters, it had defrosted and was in terrible shape. "You have no idea what it smelled like. Took three days to get the smell out of the office."

# 4.

# On Fire for Kashrus

## The Life and Times of a Mashgiach

IT'S 1:30 A.M. on a Saturday night in October, and fifty-five-year-old Rabbi Yitzhok Gallor is behind the wheel of his van, on his way to kasher the apple juice tanks at the Tree Top plant in Prosser, Washington.

His eyes are red-rimmed and his voice is rough, and that's not from the cigarettes he sneaks every chance he can get. He has just driven four hours across the Cascade Mountains from his home in Seattle, where he spent a rare Shabbat with his wife and children, leaving after sundown for the trip back to the central part of the state. He's exhausted but has to head straight out to the plant. They're starting a kosher run in the morning, and workers used the equipment earlier that day for a test run on non-kosher grape juice—all Tree Top products are kosher except the grape juice—so they can't use it for tomorrow's apple juice until Gallor works his mashgiach magic.

All the really cool work of kosher supervision takes place in the middle of the night. That's when factories are able to shut down production long enough to allow mashgichim in to kasher their equipment, sending up a blazing show of fire and water.

"There is no time here; there are no days or nights," Gallor says, as he drives through the darkness. "It's after midnight. Am I beginning my day or ending my day?"

Gallor knows he has two to three hours of hot, dangerous work ahead of him. Running boiling water through miles of pipes and in and out of enormous holding tanks requires that he keep his wits about him. But he's invigorated by the cool night air and the quiet of this lazy agricultural valley where the only light marring the perfect black sky is the twinkling of faraway stars.

Washington's Yakima Valley is the nation's grape juice capital, with twenty-four thousand acres of Concord and Niagara grapes, the most popular varieties for making grape juice, jam, jelly, fruit snacks, and flavorings. Overall, Washington State grows nearly half the country's Concords and 40 percent of its Niagara grapes. All four of its grape-processing facilities—Welch's, Milne Fruit Products, Smucker's, and Valley Processing—are located between the sleepy towns of Sunnyside and Prosser. In 2008, those plants turned 180,000 tons of grapes into millions of gallons of juice concentrate, shipping it all over the world.

When the grape harvest begins in early to mid-September, the entire valley shifts into overdrive to make sure the fruit is picked and processed before it rots or freezes on the vine. Work continues around the clock, the processing plants keeping up a steady hum as trucks pull into the loading docks overflowing with ripe purple globes. A faint aroma of grape bubble gum wafts gently over the fields. That's when Gallor leaves home and heads for the motel that will be his headquarters for the season.

Gallor is in charge of kosher supervision at Milne, Smucker's, and Valley Processing on behalf of the Orthodox Union. (Welch's is under different supervision.) A full-time mashgiach, he has dozens of other accounts during the year, but the Yakima Valley grape harvest, which he's worked since 1994, is his most labor-intensive assignment. He and his six assistants, most of them yeshiva students looking to supplement their income, spend the entire harvest every year here in central Washington, from the time the first grapes reach the processing plants until the last fruit is picked. This year unexpectedly cool weather means the season will be short, maybe five weeks. Last year it lasted for ten weeks, until after Thanksgiving.

Grape processing requires full-time kosher supervision, like meat and cheese. The plants run seven days a week, twenty-four hours a day, so these young men work twelve-hour shifts, two guys per factory, as well as every other Shabbat. When a Jewish holiday abuts Shabbat, their shifts can last forty-eight hours or longer. As observant Jews can't technically work on these days, the mashgichim walk around with non-Jewish plant workers, checking things visually and watching the workers turn knobs on and off under their supervision.

The mashgichim sleep at the plant when they're on duty, in small rooms or trailers provided by the company. Every two to three hours, day or night, they do an inspection tour to make sure kashrut standards are being observed. They must check that the grapes arrive uncrushed at the receiving docks, and once the juice is extracted, it cannot be touched by anyone other than an observant Jew until it is flash pasteurized. They monitor the temperature inside the pasteurizing tanks to make sure it remains at the boiling point. They check all incoming materials to guard against non-kosher intrusion. If systems break down, they supervise repairs. And a few hours later they do it all again.

Thirty-one-year-old Aron Weitz flies in from Israel every year to work the harvest with Gallor. A full-time Torah scholar, he studies in a *kollel*, a yeshiva for married men, in Jerusalem. His part-time work with troubled teens doesn't bring in enough to support his wife and four children. He earns a third of his yearly income every fall in the Yakima Valley.

"I love it here," he says. "I love nature; I like to get away. There's a Gemara that says if you want to hear the world turning, you have to leave the city. I do my best learning out here, my best being a Jew out here."

Weitz grew up in southern Florida, where his father runs a kosher certification agency in Broward County. He started helping out at fifteen, supervising Passover programs at hotels and nursing homes. When he flies to Washington, he usually stops off in Florida to see his parents, and his mother loads him down with kosher food to take to the wilds of the West Coast. This year she packed twenty individual Shabbat meals, homemade dinners that she froze for him to carry on the plane. "She thinks I'm still seven years old," he says, grinning.

The grape harvest extends through the Jewish High Holiday season, meaning Gallor and his helpers spend every Rosh Hashanah, Yom Kippur, and Sukkot away from their families. That's particularly hard on the married men. Weitz wishes his wife would come one year with the children to be with him, but they can't afford the plane fare. So he makes the best of things.

"If you don't have a positive mind-set, it can be very depressing," he says. "But if you take it in the right way, it can be very, very special, very nice."

Some years Gallor says it's hard to find mashgichim willing to work the Yom Kippur shift in particular. Praying the daylong service alone in a windowless room deep inside a factory while fasting for twenty-four hours can be tough. This year, however, he was lucky: Three of his helpers volunteered. "That rarely happens," he says. "Nobody wants to do it. It takes a strength of character most people don't have, to sit by yourself like that."

On the other hand, there's something to be said for enforced solitude during a holy day focused on introspection. Gallor pulled Yom Kippur duty one harvest season and found it a deeply spiritual experience, perhaps the most meaningful Yom Kippur of his life. "A lot of times at Yom Kippur when you're in shul [synagogue], you let the chazzan [cantor] do your work for you. When you're in the factory by yourself, it's only you and God. It forces you to have a reckoning with your maker and talk to him in a real way."

All mashgiach work demands integrity, flexibility, and great attention to detail. Working the grape harvest requires that and more. These men are alone most of the time, in charge of supervising very complex operations where the potential for accidents and mistakes is great. Most of them are in their twenties, more at ease studying Torah than driving combines, and they have to assert their authority with big, burly factory workers who aren't used to dealing with religious Jews.

"It takes a certain personality to be able to do this," Gallor notes. "You have to be able to be in a factory by yourself sometimes for forty-eight or seventy-two hours. You have to be honest. You have to be excited that you're here and also scared to be here—scared you'll do something wrong. You have to be on fire for kashrus."

Kosher certification is managed on the macro level by agencies, but the actual day-to-day work is in the hands of the mashgichim. More than one thousand work for the OU, another three hundred for the OK, and hundreds more for Star-K, Kof-K, the Chicago Rabbinical Council, and a host of other, smaller kosher certification agencies. At any given time, hundreds of these supervisors are crisscrossing the country on their way to factories, restaurants, nursing homes, schools, bakeries, and slaughterhouses, peering into cooking pots, checking ingredients, washing down production lines, climbing into tanker trucks, and bustling around bagels.

Perhaps the misconception that kosher food is blessed by a rabbi persists because so many mashgichim are indeed rabbis or rabbinical students. But those men in yarmulkes are not blessing the food; they are watching it to make sure no non-kosher contamination takes place. They function more like security guards than priests.

Until a decade or so ago, the only way to learn how to be a mash-giach was by word of mouth, from other mashgichim. Today mashgi-chim hoping to work for one of the Big Four agencies must pass a test, and throughout their career they can participate in conferences and courses offered by their agency. The job has become professionalized.

Even so, mashgichim are not highly paid—Rabbi Levy of the OK says $15 to $17 an hour is typical—and the job does not carry much prestige. Few little boys want to grow up to be a mashgiach, particu-larly one who works in factories. It's lonely, you're always spying on people, and you spend a lot of time on the road. As Gallor puts it, it takes a certain personality.

Gallor has that personality. He's gregarious, able to talk to anyone about anything, but he's also a loner, a man who sets his own agenda and isn't afraid to ruffle feathers. He smokes (a lot), he drinks (just a l'chaim), and he plays a mean guitar. Every year he gathers a new team of mashgichim to join him for the grape harvest. About half are from Israel, and most are returnees. They, and the workers in the grape-processing plants he supervises, call him Father Harvest, a moniker that fits his gray beard, rustic dress, and love of the outdoors.

Driving to the Tree Top plant that October night, he breathes deeply of the autumnal air and talks about the connection between Judaism and nature, a connection that helps him feel at home in this farming valley where Jews are a rarity and Jesus saves. Both he and the valley residents share a deep faith in God, which helps them get past their cultural differences.

"People who live here live nature; they live the harvest. It's all based on faith," he muses. "It's based on God bringing the rain at the right time." If the wind kicks up after the grape plants have flowered, it can blow away the pollen, and that year's harvest suffers. If it rains too early, the pollen becomes sticky and can't travel easily from plant to plant, leading yet again to a bad harvest. "So everything is based on faith and God and connection to the land, to the times of the moon, the harvest festival, the planting festival. I feel more connected here than in the city, where people are far from nature. I feel a connection to the people who live here, because we all have faith."

Inside the plant, the night foreman rushes Gallor over to the equip-ment that needs to be kashered: two twenty-five-foot-tall stainless-steel holding tanks; a couple of decanters, or centrifuges, that spin the juice away from the fruit; and a complicated series of pipes that carry the juice from process to process. Boiling water has to be passed through every pipe, tank, and decanter, and it must overflow the open tanks to ensure the outsides are kashered as well.

It's Gallor's job to monitor the temperature of the water, to make sure it's at least 185 degrees by the time it hits the farthest piece of equipment. That's the temperature the Orthodox Union requires for kashering vessels. He stands carefully to the sides of the tanks, gingerly holding the end of a too-short thermometer that he plunges into the bubbling cauldrons below, dodging as best he can the boiling liquid that drips intermittently from pipes passing overhead. Hoses are shooting out steaming water on one side of the tank, pipes are dripping on the other, and the entire operation looks mighty dicey.

Sure, mashgichim get hurt on the job, Gallor says. One rabbi he knows fell into a tank as it was being filled with boiling water and was badly scalded. Hand, face, and arm burns are hazards of the trade, compounded if a mashgiach is tired and not paying proper attention.

The last-minute job at Tree Top was unexpected; Gallor has to be up at six the next morning to say his prayers and finish the previous week's paperwork before making sure the noon shift gets to work on time, their stomachs nourished with a hot breakfast. Gallor's motel room is Kosher Central for the team, the refrigerator and pantry stocked with whatever kosher food they can find at the local grocery store. Supermarket runs are the highlight of the week. They comb the shelves to find a new product, and no matter the cost, they bring it home: a package of smoked cheese, a new brand of frozen fish, a fresh pineapple.

Gallor has a father-son relationship with his team. He cooks for them, listens to their troubles, and sorts out roommate conflicts. He throws parties, makes them pizza and popcorn, and brings his wife's cakes and cookies back with him after home visits in a constant battle to keep the team's excitement level high, their inner fires burning. Boredom is the enemy of vigilance, he says. If the guys get lazy and rely on the factories' automated systems to monitor kashrut instead of expecting the unexpected, the *yetzer hara*, or evil impulse, will take over, and kashrut standards will suffer.

One of Gallor's assistants, thirty-one-year-old Yisrael Sackon, made wine in his motel room this year. His father is a winemaker in Israel, and he knows the basic process. He collected a few bags of Concord grapes from the vineyard behind the motel, which the public is permitted to do after the harvest. He crushed the grapes by hand, added sugar, and put the mixture in a one-gallon glass container, which he kept in his closet for three weeks to ferment. "It tasted great," he exults. "I was surprised at how good it was. I tried to make wine last year when I was here, but it spoiled—I didn't have the right equipment."

Gallor looks askance when he learns of the project, but keeps his mouth shut, as it is a done deal. If it helps keep the yetzer hara at bay, so be it.

Early Sunday afternoon, Gallor pays a visit to the Milne plant, where Dov Soltz is about to set off on the first inspection tour of his shift. Milne is a huge operation, with the capacity to make 80,000 gallons of juice a day and storage space for 2.8 million gallons. The company pays $80,000 a year to the Orthodox Union for kosher supervision. President Randy Hageman says the fee is "a good ten to twenty percent more" than other agencies would charge, but he believes it's worth it. "Kosher has a reputation for purity," he says. "We have many customers who insist upon a kosher label, and the OU symbol carries a lot of weight in the juice industry."

Soltz and the other young mashgiach assigned to Milne share a cramped trailer in the plant's parking lot; it's equipped with a sofa bed, a toilet, and a dining nook that doubles as a workstation. Laundry hangs on a line strung hastily across the unmade bed. Jewish books are lined up beside the microwave: *Sifrei Maharal*, the writings of Rabbi Yehudah Loew of Prague, and Brachot, a tractate of the Talmud. When the guys aren't sleeping or making plant inspections, they're studying.

Next to the trailer is a small wooden hut called a sukkah. The week-long Sukkot holiday,[1] also known as the Festival of Booths, begins five days after Yom Kippur and commemorates the period following the Exodus from Egypt, when the Israelites lived for forty years in temporary dwellings as they wandered in the desert. To observe the holiday, Jews build small wooden or canvas structures near their homes where they sleep, eat, and spend time with their families. Gallor and his mashgichim might miss out on the holiday feasting and family time, but they cannot abandon the religious obligation outlined in Leviticus 23:42–43: "You shall dwell in booths seven days . . . that your generations may know that I made the children of Yisra'el to dwell in booths when I brought them out of the land of Mitzrayim."[2]

To accommodate this religious requirement, the three plants they supervise set up sukkahs in their parking lots, which the men decorate with handmade cutouts and photos of their children. When they're on duty, the mashgichim take their meals in these sukkahs and, despite the near-freezing night temperatures, try to sleep there at least once or twice.

Weitz got hit with a double whammy this year, pulling Shabbat duty during Sukkot. Because of the Sabbath prohibition on carrying items from one place to another, he cooked a cholent ahead of time and brought it into the sukkah at Valley Processing before sundown Friday. Then, in accordance with the prohibition on turning electricity on and off during a holiday, he unplugged the outdoor generator. That turned off the automatic heating element he needed to keep the cholent warm. So it wouldn't spoil, he stuck the pot in a garbage bag filled with ice. Nothing like ice-cold bean-and-potato stew for three straight meals.

"I had a beautiful Shabbos," he insists. "I had candles, because there were no lights. I was by myself; I sang a little. It was pitch-black, very cold, but it was very sweet. It was"—he searches for the right word— "a growthful experience."

The sukkah at Milne is more makeshift, about eight feet square, built of plywood with bamboo fronds thrown across the top so the stars can be seen, in accordance with Jewish law. Inside are a table and folding chair, a few empty seltzer bottles, a blanket, and a battered pot sitting on a hot plate. Soltz lifts the lid, winces, and quickly replaces it. Domestic skills are not a high priority with these guys.

Soltz loves the technical aspects of his work. He is a part-time yeshiva student in Israel but is also studying graphic design, and he has drawn a detailed flowchart of the plant's processing procedure, numbering every tank and showing correct temperatures, sequence, and directional flow of the juice, to assist him on his tours. He's not the only one who uses his chart; the plant manager posted copies on bulletin boards for the rest of the workers. A mashgiach needs to be thoroughly versed in all the equipment and procedures used in the plant he supervises. He needs to know what should be passing through every pipe and every holding tank at what time, so he can catch mistakes. The more he can stay actively interested in the factory's work, the better his supervision will be.

First Soltz goes over to the receiving dock, where a truck has just pulled in and is starting to dump a full load of grapes into the hopper. There's not much to see at this stage, he explains, but it's important that the workers know he's liable to show up anywhere. "If they think you don't know what's going on, they can send things through the pipes that don't belong," he says.

Soltz grew up in an Orthodox neighborhood in Baltimore and now lives in Israel, so he's never spent much time around non-Jews, particularly the Evangelical Christians who populate this valley. He's been pleasantly surprised by the respect the workers have for him and his fellow mashgichim, all of whom they call "rabbi," although none has yet been ordained. Because the workers are deeply religious, he says, they understand the Orthodox commitment to kashrut and are unlikely to take shortcuts or try to cheat the system. "It makes us more comfortable to know we can talk religion with them and they can relate," he says. "Their eyes will light up. I've talked with some workers who have read the Bible five or six times."

Gallor encourages his mashgichim to build relationships with the workers in their plants. On one hand, they are here representing the Jewish people. But, even more important, workers often tip off a mashgiach when kashrut is violated. That has happened many times to Gallor, he says, especially if the worker is a religious Christian who feels a kinship with the rabbi as a man of God. "They feel it's the right thing to do," he says.

Back at Milne, Soltz continues his inspection tour. From the hopper, an auger pushes the grapes onto a conveyer belt that drops them into the de-stemmer, where stems, leaves, and other debris are removed. The resultant grape mash moves through pipes into the factory and enters the heat exchanger, a double-tube pipe system where it is heated to 181 degrees for flash pasteurization. This is the most important part of the kosher production process, for if the grapes are not heated high enough, they will not become *mevushal*, or ritually cooked. The Orthodox Union considers grape juice kosher at 175 degrees but requires plants to maintain a slightly higher temperature as a buffer. Computers monitor and record the heat inside this mechanism, and a mashgiach checks and signs the printout every twenty-four hours. He also visually checks temperatures during each walk-through, and if it's too low he uses a "rabbi divert," pushing a handle that closes off the main pipe and sends the grape mash back to the hopper to repeat the entire process.

Once the juice is correctly pasteurized, it is kosher, and supervision is easier from that point on. Milne instituted this system in the early 1990s, and the other plants adopted it. Before then the juice was not pasteurized until the end of the process, and two mashgichim had to work each shift. Now just one is needed.

From the heat exchanger the juice is cooled down and moved into two-thousand-gallon treatment tanks, where enzymes are added. Then it moves through a series of re-pulpers, filters, and decanters for further refinement and is sent through concentrators that extract the liquid essence used to give grape aroma to other products. Finally, the now-pure grape juice concentrate ends up in 180,000-gallon stainless-steel storage tanks. From there it might be blended with other ingredients, which the mashgiach must constantly monitor for kosher status, or it might be sent directly to Snapple, Ocean Spray, Minute Maid, Tropicana, or one of Milne's many other clients for final blending and packaging.

Soltz is proud of his job and eager to show visitors the inner workings of this enormous plant. He scrambles up a ladder to the top of one of the storage tanks to demonstrate how he looks inside to make sure that the right hoses are pumping out juice, that nothing noncertified is being added to the mixture. He points out the sugar shack where incoming grapes are put in blenders and tested for sugar levels, and explains that he must constantly check to make sure that this mash, which has become juice under non-kosher conditions, is not mistakenly dumped back into the processing system.

"That's our job," he says, "to make sure."

RABBI FOGELMAN of the OK is fond of telling people that a kosher restaurant or factory with no problems is probably hiding something. No one is perfect, he says. What counts is how a place handles its mistakes, how transparent its business practices are, and how quickly it corrects errors, recalls products, or fires workers responsible for fraud.

The mashgiach is the front line in this defense. Yet there's a built-in conflict of interest: If a mashgiach reports such flagrant abuse that a kosher agency withdraws its certification from the restaurant or factory he supervises, that could mean he's out of a job. Some agencies pay a severance fee in such cases—the OK gives two weeks' pay—but it's still a financial hardship. That's why integrity is so crucial in a kosher supervisor, as is personal commitment to kashrut itself. If the mashgiach believes it's a sin for a Jew to eat non-kosher food, he won't tolerate any violations in the places he supervises.

Rabbi Yaakov Luban of the OU also sits on the kosher vaad of Raritan Valley, New Jersey, which certifies kosher restaurants and retail food establishments in three central New Jersey towns. In the mid-1980s, he oversaw a kosher pizza parlor in Highland Park that used cheese made from cholov Yisroel. Because such cheese requires greater supervision when it's made, it's more expensive than ordinary kosher cheese. The shop kept a freezer stocked to the hilt with packages of this ultra-kosher cheese and had a full-time mashgiach on the premises, but Luban would drop by for spot checks.

On one visit he saw a can with no label in the shop's pantry, an immediate red flag. He asked the owner what it was, and the man said it was peas. Luban asked for the can to be opened, and it turned out to be plums. The product was kosher, but the fact that the owner lied put Luban on alert. What else might be wrong?

"I knew he had an office across the street, and I thought maybe he's storing material there, so I asked to see it," Luban recalls. The two men walked to the other building and started downstairs to the office, which was in the basement. As they were descending, Luban noticed a number of black garbage bags under the stairwell.

"You can find out a lot of information from the garbage," Luban says. "So I started snooping around while he was fidgeting with the key to open the office. He saw me looking through the garbage bags, so he grabbed one and started dashing up the stairs with it. I took after him in hot pursuit."

Luban chased the man down the street, his tzitzit, or ritual fringes, flying. The man wove in and out of buildings and finally stashed the bag under a truck. Luban crawled under the truck, retrieved the bag, and looked inside. It was filled with empty packages of non-kosher cheese. The owner told Luban it was very old garbage, but the expiration dates were new and the truth soon emerged. Pizza shops routinely grate cheese ahead of time to keep in buckets for quick use during the busy workday. This man would sneak into his own restaurant in the middle of the night with boxes of cheap non-kosher cheese, grind it up, and put it in buckets for the next day.

"Whenever the rabbis came to inspect, we saw the freezer full of kosher cheese, but that's not what he was using," Luban relates. "Those packages were years old. He was saving a thousand dollars a month by using non-kosher cheese." The shop's kosher supervision was immediately terminated, and Luban decided never again to supervise a place where the owner was not religiously observant.

The point is not just to be observant, but to care deeply about preserving the food's kosher integrity. That's what Mordechai Feinberg of Santa Cruz, California, believes. Feinberg is a freelance mashgiach, working jobs across the country. One of his recurring gigs is at a cheese plant in Rupert, Idaho, that produces the cheese used in Cheez-It crackers, a Kellogg's product.

Making hard cheese requires full-time kosher supervision. The process utilizes rennet, an enzyme that comes from the stomach lining of calves. Although most kosher agencies hold that rennet is so far removed from the actual cow that it is not in itself considered food, and virtually all rennet used in the United States is now vegetable based, the process is still carefully monitored. Only an observant Jew is permitted to add the rennet during the cheesemaking operation. In old-fashioned factories, this is done by hand—the mashgiach pours in the bucket of rennet whenever the coagulation stage is reached. In most modern plants the process is automated, but kosher certification agencies still require that a mashgiach press the activation button that sends the rennet through the system.

Feinberg works Jewish holidays at the Rupert plant, filling in for the regular mashgichim so they can be home with their families. It's good money, he says—$2,000 a week plus a food allowance. And he doesn't mind spending the holidays alone. He brings his books and gets a lot of studying done.

The work itself is not difficult. The factory operates on an eighteen-hour schedule, from 6:00 p.m. to noon. During that time there are twenty-seven production runs, which means that every forty minutes the mashgiach has to push the rennet button for a new batch of cheese. The button used to be on the plant floor, Feinberg says, which meant the mashgiach had to get up and go to it, but now it's in the rabbis' sleeping room, which makes things a lot easier in the middle of the night. "A little bell sounds; you wake up and push the button. If you don't wake up, the phone rings. They can't work if you don't push the button."

It's not easy to get to Rupert, a three-and-a-half-hour drive from the nearest airport through mountainous passes that are often covered in snow. And life in Rupert is lonely for a religious Jew. Temptation to cut corners is high: No one watches what a mashgiach does in a factory like this, except the heavenly judges. "You really have to care about kashrut," Feinberg says.

Very few women work as kosher supervisors. This is not due to any prohibition in Jewish law. Although Orthodox authorities say that rabbis and cantors must be male, Jewish tradition holds that women may decide Jewish law in the kitchen. In most Orthodox homes, it is the woman who keeps the dishes correctly separated, who knows whether a piece of meat has fallen into the cream soup and whether it is large enough to make the entire pot non-kosher.[3] Kashrut supervision is one of the few areas of Orthodox Jewish life where women have the same legal status as men. But professional kashrut supervision involves a lot of physical work—hauling, climbing, and crawling—and factory supervision requires constant travel, which is difficult for women with small children. Most women who work in kashrut supervision oversee restaurants, schools, and catering halls rather than factories or slaughterhouses. And they are more often found outside major cities, where there are fewer Orthodox men.

But as the kashrut industry grows, there is an increasing need for supervision, and the number of *mashgichot* (female kosher supervisors) is on the rise. In fall 2009, the Star-K held the first national training program for mashgichot. Like similar programs held for male kashrut supervisors, the weeklong seminar included proper procedures, a review of kosher laws and policies, and field trips to kosher facilities.

Rabbi Kurcfeld of the Star-K, who organized the course, says women often make better supervisors than men because they are particularly careful about details. "They're very meticulous," he says. "They don't deviate—either something is right, or it's not."

Evelyn Prizont has worked as a kashrut supervisor for three years in Seattle. Her job is full-time, but most of the mashgichot she knows choose part-time work because of their family obligations. She went into the field when her children reached school age. "I do it for the glamour," she deadpans. "And the tremendous respect."

Prizont has quite a few establishments under her purview: a retirement home, a Chinese restaurant, a bagel shop, the deli section of a grocery store, some health-food shops, and the Hillel kitchen at the University of Washington. She's a real hands-on supervisor, washing vegetables herself and poking through the bulk-food bins in the health-food stores to make sure the dried beans, rice, and granola mixes are kosher certified. And while this slender, softspoken woman may not inspire immediate fear in the people she supervises, she has other ways of getting what she needs.

"Never underestimate the power of lipstick," she offers. "I do a lot of information gathering. I'm there as the narc, right? I'm in and out of these places, so I have to rely very heavily on my relationships, on getting people to speak to me openly and honestly." It also helps that she speaks Spanish, the first language of many kitchen workers. One restaurant employee kept her abreast of kashrut violations, fingering a coworker who routinely mixed dairy with meat equipment and used produce that had not been checked for infestation. "He begged me not to tell anyone it was him," she says. "I have nice relationships with the people I work with—when I'm not pulling their certification!"

That she did only once, at a different Chinese restaurant in the city, and only after months of trying to help them stick to the rules. "I could tell they were having a tough time, so I'd go in and work with them," she says. Noticing that the restaurant's produce was often spoiled, she bought the owner a lettuce spinner, which the woman had never seen before. One elderly cook used to bring his own non-kosher lunch into the kitchen, which kashrut agencies forbid. "I felt bad for him—he's an old man—so I brought in kosher food for him, to help him out," Prizont relates.

When she finally had to come in and take their kosher certificate off the wall, she says the owner understood, but it was still hard. "We were thirty percent of their business," she notes. "My husband counted the yarmulkes one night and figured it out."

Prizont believes she is seen as less threatening than a man, something that helps her gain people's trust, but she's not afraid to come down hard on violators. "I work with some high-powered chefs, huge guys with sharp knives. They're very powerful, but they start to sweat when I come around. They see me shaking my head at something across the room, and they get nervous. I wield power, and they know it."

SOME PEOPLE would kill for Rabbi Binyamin Kaplan's job at the Häagen-Dazs plant in Bakersfield, California. As the OU mashgiach, he sniffs sorbet, pokes at pistachios, monitors the mango, and charts the chocolate. Everyone who works in the factory seems to be smiling—either they get paid a lot, or they are filled to the gills with Häagen-Dazs frozen dessert.

Kaplan, on the other hand, has never tasted the stuff. "It's not cholov Yisroel," he explains. He keeps to that higher standard of kashrut, and so he must decline even a bite of the coffee almond crunch ice-cream bars smothered in chocolate coating that whiz by him on the assembly line.

Ice-cream production is not as delicate an operation as cheesemaking from the standpoint of kashrut, so Kaplan visits the Häagen-Dazs factory only periodically. He won't say how often, to keep the company on its toes. This plant produces 15 million pounds of ice cream, sorbet, and frozen yogurt products every year, so there's a lot for him to track.

Most of his responsibility is paperwork. On the laptop he carries through the plant he has a copy of the factory's Schedule A, a list of every ingredient that it uses in every product. Those ingredients have all been approved by the OU experts. During his inspection, he walks around looking at boxes and bags to make sure no unauthorized materials are present. He checks product codes and country of origin information, all of which must match his list exactly. He also has a copy of the plant's Schedule B, a list of all the final products it manufactures, and matches that list to what's written on the labels and packages.

In the chocolate warehouse, he finds a discrepancy. Stacked ceiling-high are plastic vats of dark chocolate, from 850 to 1,800 pounds each. He checks the product code on the outside of one vat against his Schedule A list and notices that the numbers don't match. Quality engineer Michael Carter, who is accompanying Kaplan on his inspection, calls over the warehouse manager, who explains that the chocolate arrives in raw form, is sent out to another OU-certified plant for processing into a fudgelike material, is then sealed in vats, and is sent back in different packaging.

The procedure sounds all right, but Kaplan makes a note to check with headquarters. "I'm sure it's just a paperwork problem," he says.

There are storage rooms kept at 40 degrees, for perishable flavorings and fruits. Another room kept at a brisk minus 10 degrees houses chocolate chips, toffee crunch mix, and more delicate varieties of nuts. Chocolate coating is kept toasty in the hot room at 95 degrees, so that it stays liquid for easy pouring over ice-cream bars.

Kaplan passes by one-ton storage tanks holding Baileys Irish cream flavoring used for the company's ice cream. The liqueur carried in liquor stores is not kosher certified, but Baileys makes a kosher flavoring that it ships in special numbered containers to the Häagen-Dazs factory. The containers are sealed at the Baileys plant with red and yellow tags that can be unsealed only by another kosher supervisor. Today's containers do not appear on Kaplan's Schedule A, so he writes down all the numbers on the tags for double-checking with New York.

At the end of the tour, Kaplan has five discrepancies noted in his report. He's certain they are all items that were not properly recorded at one end or the other. None, he's confident, involves kashrut violations. But no matter how well a mashgiach gets along with a company—and Kaplan's relationship with the Häagen-Dazs team is as friendly as can be—he can't forget he's there to police them.

"It's like Ronald Reagan said: 'Trust, but verify,'" quips Rabbi Reuven Nathanson, who is accompanying Kaplan on today's inspection. Nathanson is the West Coast coordinator for OU Kosher, overseeing the agency's accounts west of the Rockies, from the Canadian to the Mexican border. He is one of three national rabbinic field representatives who between them carve up the agency's kashrut supervision work coast to coast. In addition to collating the reports of the ten or eleven mashgichim in his territory, including Kaplan's, he also serves as the mashgiach for eighty to one hundred of his own plants. Altogether, he is responsible for ensuring kashrut standards are met in hundreds of factories.

"California is a huge territory," he says. "The usual OU schedule is four plants a day, four days a week, but in California you can spend an entire day driving to one plant."

Nathanson has been working for OU Kosher since 1991, after a career in hospital administration in New Orleans. His first job was freelance. The OU called the Chabad rabbi in New Orleans to ask if the man would supervise the agency's lone factory in Louisiana, to replace the rabbi they were currently flying in from Chicago. The Chabad emissary didn't want the job but suggested Nathanson.

"They called me, and I was so annoyed that someone was actually flying from Chicago to New Orleans every month to look at frozen yogurt that I said yes," Nathanson recalls.

That first job paid $40 per visit, plus $10 for gas. But as the Medicare system went into slow decline and kosher food production soared, more and more OU jobs came his way until he and his wife picked up and moved to Los Angeles, where in 1992 he went to work full-time as a kosher supervisor.

Like every other industrial mashgiach, Nathanson is on the road more often than he is home. His typical workweek has him driving up and down the West Coast, covering hundreds of miles at a stretch. On the rare weekday he sleeps at home, he might be up at 4:00 a.m. to catch a 6:00 a.m. flight, arriving home at midnight or later and hitting the road again the next morning. But he likes the adrenaline rush, the variety of traveling from place to place, meeting different people, and learning how food production works.

The relationship with companies under supervision is not purely adversarial. Often a mashgiach will help a company find a kosher ingredient it needs or suggest workable alternatives. Nathanson says he helped a snack-food manufacturer save $50,000 by suggesting they start making a product they had been buying, at a stiff price, from another company. And no, he didn't take a cut on the savings. That's not how kosher agencies operate—not the legitimate ones.

All kinds of backgrounds come in handy. After the visit to Häagen-Dazs, Kaplan and Nathanson dropped by to inspect a plant that packages dry foods such as sugar and salt for chain restaurants and discount stores. The ingredients come in from other manufacturers, and this plant pours them into single-serving-size packets.

The company wanted to begin packaging Buffalo hot sauce, a spicy dipping sauce. As the plant manager was showing Kaplan the new machine the company had purchased to keep the hot sauce separate from the dry goods—a kashrut requirement—Nathanson noticed two rolls of labeling tape lying on a countertop. He picked them up and saw that the partially used roll read "OU," while the newer, still-wrapped roll read "OU-D," indicating a product that contains dairy ingredients.

"What's this?" he asked the manager. The man beamed. "We had some of your old labels left, so we thought we'd save money by using them up before opening the OU-Ds," he said.

If Nathanson hadn't lived so long in Louisiana, or if he were not a *baal teshuva*, or newly observant Jew, meaning he grew up eating non-kosher food, he would not have known that Buffalo hot sauce contains butter. Any packages that went out without dairy designation might not only compromise a Jewish customer's kashrut, but could prove deadly to someone with dairy allergies. He got rid of the old labels and explained why to the manager.

That's job satisfaction, he says.

Back in the Yakima Valley grape fields, it's Sunday night and Rabbi Gallor and his team are getting ready for their annual Sukkot party. To cheer up the guys and relieve the tedium, Gallor always plans at least one homespun holiday celebration. Tonight's party will be held in the sukkah in the Smucker's parking lot. Gallor did a supermarket run earlier in the day and is back in his motel room heating up frozen French fries and making popcorn. He has brownies from his wife; cookies from the store; bottles of Pepsi, Sprite, and seltzer; pretzels; fruit; some cheese and crackers—whatever he can dig out of the pantry that looks festive.

Logistics are tricky. The party has to be timed between inspection tours at all three plants. Precisely at 10:00 p.m. he sends his son Shaul, who works as one of his mashgichim, to pick up the two supervisors at Milne and Valley Processing. Gallor drives over to Smucker's with the three young men who are not on duty, and they meet up in the sukkah with the Smucker's mashgiach, who has just finished the last inspection on his noon-to-midnight shift.

During the ride, Gallor reflects on the larger purpose of his work. "I'm a rabbi," he says. "Kosher is just part of my job. God puts me in these places for a reason." A few days earlier, Gallor was buying a light-bulb in a hardware store, and the cashier turned out to be an Israeli woman who was eager for Jewish connections. Gallor invited her for Sukkot, her first in a long time. He gets letters and gifts from people he's met, thanking him for his advice or comfort. Once he received a laminated print with a thank-you note saying Gallor had changed the sender's life. The note was unsigned and Gallor has no idea who sent it, but he relishes opportunities to pay it forward.

"God is an intricate part of the ecosystem," he says. "When you're a mashgiach you have a different life than most people. I'm always traveling; I'm on a plane, looking down. I think, Look at all those cars, all those houses; God is in all those places. And that's only what I can see from the plane. He is in everybody's head, in everybody's life, intimately. When you multiply that by the entire world, the cosmos, the workings of the universe, it's mind-boggling."

By eleven, the party is in full swing. The guys have crowded eight plastic chairs into the sukkah, squeezing them in next to the folding table filled with party food. Gallor plugs in a space heater, takes out his battered guitar, and launches into a series of Hebrew songs while the others bang out the rhythm on congas, plastic buckets, and cooking pots. His repertoire includes *"Ivdu et Hashem B'simcha," "Al Ha'neesim,"* and other favorites from religious summer camp, along with hassidic *niggunim*—wordless melodies that Gallor composed himself. Their voices ring out with feeling, the sound cutting through the dark night. Workers arriving early for the midnight shift must wonder what is going on in that brightly lit wooden hut on the edge of the parking lot, the little shack rocking with joy and song.

"The main thing is to be together and enjoy the gifts that God gives us, even in a parking lot," Gallor says. "We talk Torah, to remind us of the reasons why we are at the grape harvest in the first place."

As the midnight whistle blows, the three mashgichim starting the next twelve-hour shift rise from their seats and head for their factories. The juice doesn't wait.

# 5.

# Pastrami on Rye

## The Jewish Deli

THE SECOND AVENUE DELI is no longer on Second Avenue.

Two generations of New Yorkers swore by the kreplach, chicken soup, and mile-high pastrami sandwiches served up at this renowned East Village kosher eatery by famously grumpy waiters who barked out orders and yelled at customers who didn't finish their food. The boisterous show at the corner of Tenth Street and Second Avenue in the heart of what was then a heavily Jewish neighborhood was orchestrated by Abe Lebewohl, the restaurant's larger-than-life owner who stood at the helm from the time the doors opened in 1954.

Lebewohl was a character only New York could produce, a guy who once made a statue of Paul Bocuse out of chopped liver to celebrate the French restaurateur's visit to the city. He built a Walk of Fame to honor his favorite performers from the nearby Yiddish theater, carving their names in the sidewalk outside his front door. The restaurant was filled with celebrities and politicians; long lines snaked out the door for Sunday brunch.

Regular customers had their favorite servers. For Berkeley, California, writer Sharon Rudnick it was the waitress with the white makeup, red lipstick, and black bouffant wig who would quip, "You're the richer, I'm the pourer," as she poured matzo ball soup into customers' bowls. "It was a mixed blessing to get her because she was incredibly slow," Rudnick says. "But she was so entertaining it made up for the service."

It all came to a screeching halt the morning of March 4, 1996, when Lebewohl was shot and killed on his way to making the deli's daily bank deposit. His brother Jack took over the business but shut it down in January 2006 over a rent dispute with the landlord. Jewish New York mourned until the restaurant reopened two years later a mile uptown, on East Thirty-third Street.

Much remains unchanged in the new place. There is the same dish of pickles plunked down along with the menu, the same matzo ball soup with one enormous, fluffy softball floating in broth flecked with golden globules of chicken fat, the same chopped liver sandwich, a little dry and with just the right amount of pepper.

But a lot is different. The decor is more uptown, as are the prices— $22 for a sandwich, unheard of in the old neighborhood. There is a full bar, also new, and an appetizing case near the front door filled with expensive cuts of nova and sable along with pickled herring and whitefish salad. Most noticeably, the surly Jewish waiters have been replaced by polite youngsters who smile and nod as they write down orders. "I'll yell at you if you'd like," offered one African American waitress, eager to please a table of longtime customers.

The original Second Avenue Deli was the last of Manhattan's historic kosher delis, one of thousands of kosher restaurants that dotted Brooklyn, the Bronx, and lower Manhattan at the turn of the last century. In Europe, the laws of kashrut pushed Jews into the food trades because certain items, such as wine, bread, and meat, could be eaten only if produced by fellow Jews. They brought their skills with them to America, opening restaurants, grocery stores, bakeries, and butcher shops. There were pre–World War I dairy restaurants like Ratner's on the Lower East Side and the Famous Dairy in Brooklyn, serving cheese blintzes, potato pancakes, and beet borsch. In 1908, Barney Greengrass, known as the Sturgeon King, opened his famous fish store on Fifth Avenue. There were steak houses run by Romanian Jews, loud, smoky joints that masked the toughness of their kosher cuts with heavy sauces and free-flowing liquor. There was the appetizing store, an American innovation that displayed every kind of smoked and dried fish alongside cheeses, nuts, and candy.

Chief among these Jewish culinary marvels was the meat delicatessen. First brought to New York by German immigrants in the 1820s, the Jewish version, which emerged in the 1870s and '80s, modified the original treyf recipes to create kosher substitutes. They used schmaltz, or rendered chicken fat, instead of lard, and prepared ptcha, or jellied calf's foot, instead of pig trotters. Strictly kosher were Lou G. Siegel's and Ben's Best. The Stage and the Carnegie in Midtown opened as "kosher-style" delis, as did Katz's, founded in 1888 and today the last remaining original Jewish deli on the Lower East Side.

Above all, Jewish delis were famous for their meat: pickled tongue, roast brisket, spicy corned beef, and tender steamed pastrami. These delicacies were born of necessity. Not only did pickling, smoking, and salting serve to preserve meat in the days before refrigeration, but kosher meat must be soaked and salted within seventy-two hours of slaughter, depriving it of enough time to hang and tenderize. Slow braising, curing and pickling, salting, stewing, and steaming, all characteristic of Ashkenazic cooking, counteract the toughness.

Pastrami was brought to America by Romanian Jews. The word refers to a cooking technique in which meat is rubbed with a spice mixture, left to cure, and then smoked and steamed. In Romania, Jews made it from goose or duck; in New York, they adapted the technique to this country's plentiful supply of beef. Deli aficionado David Sax, a Toronto-based food writer, says no one knows who sold the first pastrami sandwich in America, but he quotes writer Patricia Volk's claim that it was her Lithuanian great-grandfather, who ran a kosher butcher shop on Delancey Street in the late 1880s. Putting it between two slices of rye bread, which Volk says he did on a customer's suggestion, was the happy accident that led to that pinnacle of deli cuisine, the hot pastrami sandwich.[1]

The first Jewish delis in New York were mostly on the Lower East Side and virtually all kosher. There was no reason for them not to be; their customers were kashrut-observant Jews. Originally they were freestanding butcher shops, replacements for the earlier pushcarts that sold knishes, bialys, and herring snacks to Jewish immigrants pouring in from Eastern Europe and the Russian Pale of Settlement. Patrons would order their meat along with a small quantity of spicy brown mustard and take it home to eat. By the turn of the century, some of these delis offered sit-down service. They were patronized mainly by men, bachelors or married men working to bring their families over from Europe, and they served the same simple food customers were used to at home.

In the early 1920s, Jews began moving away from the Lower East Side, first northward to the Bronx and eastward to Brooklyn, then eventually out into the suburbs. Most of the kosher restaurants followed, but the delis stayed. They had become firmly identified with New York as a whole, not just with its Jews; by the mid-1930s, there were about five thousand delis in the city, both kosher and non-kosher.[2]

Within that world, the Second Avenue Deli did not have a monopoly on mean waiters. They were standard issue, as beloved as they were maligned. "People walk into a Jewish restaurant, they expect to be insulted," says Jack Lebewohl. Catskills comedians milked the genre. One favorite joke had a customer ask his waiter what a fly is doing in his soup, to which the waiter retorts, "The backstroke." In another, a customer complains about his soup, saying he's had much better, and the waiter shoots back, "Not here, you haven't."

Food critic Arthur Schwartz's grandfather waited tables in two of Brooklyn's legendary kosher eateries, both now closed. "He was a mean Jewish waiter," Schwartz says. "In the late fifties, he went to work at the Famous Dairy, in the side room where all the politicians sat. He was mean because he hated the customers. He didn't like us too much, either."

Jack Lebewohl's son Jeremy sees no reason to take pride in bad service. Just twenty-five years old when he took over the new Second Avenue Deli in December 2007, Jeremy is an energetic young man eager to preserve the New York institution his uncle Abe created, but just as eager to bring it into line with modern aesthetics. The napkins are white linen. The display cases shine. The waiters beam. The toilets are spotless. Jeremy happily steers visitors into the women's restroom to admire the rotating plastic seat covers and the wall mosaic that lovingly re-creates a 1970s street scene outside the original restaurant.

He's also proud of his food. Most of the old menu has been preserved, and new items have been added. "Try the egg salad," he urges, pushing an overflowing serving bowl across the table. It's warm, salty, full of onions, mushrooms, and schmaltz—absolutely delicious, and obviously sinful. Nonsense, Jeremy retorts. "My grandparents, your grandparents, this is how they ate, and they lived to a ripe old age. They weren't obese." Chicken fat? Look at the ingredients in canned soups or TV dinners. "It's garbage, stuff you don't want to put into your body," he says. "This is pure, natural schmaltz—simple, delicious."

Schmaltz is a staple in Eastern European Jewish cooking, used instead of butter in dishes served at meat meals. The Second Avenue Deli is a meat restaurant, so schmaltz is in heavy use. They make it from the drippings left over from gribenes, the fried chicken skin snacks set out in small bowls on every table.

One evening a few months after the restaurant's grand reopening,

Rabbi Josh Plaut, his wife Lori, and their eight-year-old son, Jonas, are happily munching on their gribenes, waiting for their food to arrive. "Jonas loves gribenes, and I grew up on it," says Josh. "My Russian-born grandmother used to make it for me." Lori waxes nostalgic about her grandmother's schmaltz, which was kept hardened in a jar in the refrigerator. "My grandfather used to spread it on radishes," she recalls.

The Plauts are longtime Second Avenue Deli fans. When Josh was a pulpit rabbi at a Reform synagogue in Connecticut, he would bring his congregation to the original eatery on their way to tours of Ellis Island and the Jewish Museum. "This new place is more cheerful, and the bathroom is a lot cleaner," he says. And Jonas? "He likes it because it's old-style. When he had a cavity filled, he wanted to come here afterward."

Comfort food. That's the real draw with Jewish delis. Chicken soup, boiled brisket, stuffed cabbage, homemade coleslaw, crunchy dill pickles. Sharon Rudnick's grandfather, Irving Blumer, operated Hobby's, a kosher-style deli in Newark, New Jersey, from the 1940s until the early 1960s. As a young girl, Rudnick would follow the waitresses around and was allowed to mix cherry syrup with seltzer to make cherry sodas in the back room. To her, a deli is all about the smells. "That greasy pastrami smell, the pungent corned beef smell. It's a visceral sense memory that makes me feel calm and good. And the sawdust—I loved to kick it with my Mary Janes. It had a real evocative smell."

The Second Avenue Deli is filled with the smells of cooking meat and boiling soup. Jeremy shows off his downstairs prep kitchen, where he pickles his own corned beef and steams his own pastrami. You can't buy a good steam box commercially, he says, and making pastrami is a delicate operation. "If you don't steam it enough, it has a rubbery texture and is tough, but if you steam it too long, it falls apart and crumbles when you pick up the sandwich," he advises.

Jeremy loves the deli business. He grew up in his uncle's restaurant and did not want to see the tradition end with Abe's death. On the other hand, he knows he has a tough act to follow. "My grandfather came in when we reopened. He wanted steak—rare—with potato soup, a side of coleslaw, and a little tongue. Later he called me up and said the soup's no good. My customers like it, but it wasn't good enough for my grandfather."

It took a lot of money, and guts, to reopen the Second Avenue Deli.

Most restaurants of any kind fail within the first three years, according to the National Restaurant Association. And delis, with their heavy stews, fatty meats, and liberal use of schmaltz, are not on the cutting edge of food fashion. There were five thousand Jewish delis in New York City sixty years ago. Today Sax counts about twenty-five: fifteen in Manhattan, five or six in Brooklyn, two in the Bronx, and another two in Queens. Elsewhere in the country the situation is even more dire, as city after city sounds the death knell for its last traditional delicatessen.

"The Jewish deli is dying," says Sax, who in 2009 parlayed his love for this quintessential slice of American Jewish history into *Save the Deli*, a wistful paean to a disappearing world. The thirty-year-old spent three years visiting more than 150 Jewish delis to research his book, part of his mission to rally support for the few remaining stalwarts while mourning the passing of others. "Each time I hear a deli has closed, something inside me dies," he says.

If the Jewish deli survives, it will be because a new generation has fallen in love with the food and the world it represents. In a handful of cities, new Jewish delis are opening. Their young owners and chefs aren't looking to innovate so much as to return to tradition, reviving the original hands-on way of doing things. They are brining their own pickles, salting their own beef, and stuffing their own sausages, just like their forebears a century ago.

There is one big change from the old days: Few of these new delis are kosher. Sax lists his favorite newcomers in Boulder, Philadelphia, Toronto, and Portland, Oregon, all run by younger Jews. None is kosher. But all are heimishe, focused clearly on traditional Ashkenazic foods. It's all style and atmosphere, Jewish diet without Jewish law. Detractors call it "kitchen Judaism," an easy way for nonobservant Jews to express their communal attachment and cultural identity—by eating Jewish food.

"Many Jews still cling to food traditions," writes food critic Leah Koenig, who says she, too, is a culinary Jew. "They are the Jews derided as 'bagel and lox Jews' by their religious contemporaries. They are the ones for whom chicken soup is as much a marker of their identity as the shofar. And they are growing in number."[3]

The phenomenon first emerged in nineteenth-century Europe, where it was known as *fressfroemigkeit*, German for "eating religion." It referred to assimilated Jews who symbolically rejoined the community on Jewish holidays by eating traditional ethnic meals. But kitchen Judaism really flourished in the New World, where Jewish immigrants, in their quest to be accepted as real Americans, were eager to cast off the ghetto trappings of kashrut, religious garb, and Yiddish but did not want to give up their favorite foods.

Kashrut standards themselves were more relaxed in early America than they are today. Esther Levy's 1871 *Jewish Cookery Book*, the first Jewish cookbook published in this country, counsels rubbing a scarlet fever patient's entire body with "fat bacon," which would be anathema today, but she did not suggest eating it. (The same book included a recipe for mutton leg, a part of the animal not considered kosher today, and made Sunday rather than Friday dinner the most festive of the week, in consideration of American customs.)[4]

Levy's cookbook was kosher, but other Jewish cookbooks of the same era boasted openly treyf recipes, indicating the changing standards in many Jewish American households. *Aunt Babette's Cook Book*, a Jewish cookbook published in 1889, included recipes for dishes containing shrimp, oysters, and ham. The author excused those ingredients on the grounds that "nothing is '*trayfa*' that is healthy and clean."[5]

The conflict many Jews felt between preserving their Jewish identity and fitting into American society increased as Jews moved out of predominantly Jewish neighborhoods and found themselves next to non-Jews at work, school, and play. In 1922, Rabbi Mordecai Kaplan, the founder of Reconstructionist Judaism, feared that imposing strict kashrut observance on American Jews would lead them to abandon the faith altogether, and he predicted that the dietary laws would have to change if Judaism was to survive.[6]

Some Jews developed a practice known as "eating out," keeping kosher at home but not outside. Jenna Weissman Joselit writes that kashrut "was not only redefined but repositioned as a growing number of American Jews restricted its observance to the home."[7] There were variations in this practice, from the more observant, who ate salads or kosher varieties of fish in non-kosher restaurants, to Jews who did not follow any kosher restrictions when outside their home.

Brooklyn homemaker Joy Devor grew up in Los Angeles in a Sephardic family that kept strictly kosher but would eat selectively in non-kosher restaurants because there were hardly any kosher ones. "There was the deli, and that's it," Devor recalls. "We got a pizza shop when I was in eighth grade, and that was so exciting." One day when the family was dining in a non-kosher restaurant, Devor's sister said her tuna fish salad "tasted wrong." It turned out the waiter had brought chicken salad by mistake. "My father said, That's it, we are never eating out anymore," Devor says.

Today "eating out" is more common among Conservative Jews, although some Orthodox Jews will do it. According to a 2006 Conservative movement survey, while 75 percent of Conservative professionals and 65 percent of lay leaders keep kosher homes, 94 percent of the professionals and 98 percent of the lay leaders eat in non-kosher restaurants. One-third of the professionals and more than half of the lay leaders will eat meat in those restaurants. The same survey showed that 87 percent of Conservative rabbis and cantors eat in non-kosher restaurants, although just 9 percent will order meat.[8]

Even though Conservative Jews may observe kashrut differently than Orthodox Jews in certain ways, the movement itself accepts kashrut as a commandment. Once kashrut is no longer considered a divine commandment but more a marker of Jewish identity, the entire conversation shifts. As the twentieth century continued, increasing numbers of nonobservant Jews ate Jewish to feel Jewish, and that's not something they needed to do all the time. In many homes, Jewish ethnic foods became limited to Shabbat and holiday meals, the times when less observant or secular Jews wanted to underscore their membership in the tribe. At these meals, observance of the laws of kashrut was symbolic. The matzo balls and gefilte fish might be kosher, but the roast chicken might not be, although it would most likely not be slathered in cream sauce or sprinkled with bacon bits. Butter, however, might be placed on the table next to the kosher challah.

This new way of eating became known as kosher-style. It involved a reimagining of Jewish dietary practice, a tweaking of the laws without their wholesale abandonment. The motivation was to bring Jewish eating in line with contemporary American values, such as proper hygiene and good nutrition, while preserving at least the semblance of kosher practice. Milk was considered healthy for children, so Jewish mothers newly arrived in America began serving it at every meal, even meat meals. The meat, however, was usually still kosher.

There was little logic to these choices. A lot of the decisions were made on gut feelings, which varied between households: Did a certain leniency still feel Jewish, or did it go too far? Arthur Schwartz remembers his mother feeding him a ham-and-cheese sandwich with a glass of milk one afternoon in the late 1950s, and his grandfather exploding in anger when he came upon the scene—not because of the treyf sandwich, but a glass of *milk*, too?

Jewish delis quickly took to kosher-style. In the early twentieth century, kosher-style delis differed from their kosher counterparts mainly in their hours of operation—kosher restaurants closed every Shabbat, whereas most kosher-style eateries closed just for the major Jewish holidays. The food itself was still kosher. No pork or shellfish was served, and meat and milk were kept separate. But as the decades passed and kosher-style delis followed the Jewish population out into the suburbs, standards grew more lenient in accordance with changing tastes. By the time the kosher-style deli reached its height in the 1950s and '60s, whipped cream had appeared on the Jell-O served after a meat meal, and bacon was close behind.

Certainly these transgressions of the laws of kashrut illustrated American Jewry's growing assimilation into Gentile society. But the persistence of the Jewish deli itself, with its focus on traditional Ashkenazic food, indicated something else: that even the nonobservant Jews who owned and frequented these places had certain red lines they were loath to cross.

"Kosher-style delis had canonical foods that were eaten in canonical ways," says David Kraemer, Talmud professor at the Jewish Theological Seminary and author of *Jewish Eating and Identity Through the Ages*.[9] "They were highly restricted, not by kashrut rules, but by what were perceived to be Jewish rules. So by and large, even if they had both dairy and meat, they separated them."

Meat dishes and dairy dishes might be served to the same person, but they were kept in separate parts of the deli case and listed on separate sections of the menu. This symbolic distinction, a nod to kashrut, came to characterize the Jewish deli. And it proved popular with generations of American Jews. Immigrant parents and grandparents who had fallen away from strict Jewish practice felt at home with the familiar menu, and their American-born children were drawn in by the nostalgic appeal. Either way, it was a completely Jewish, if not strictly halachic, atmosphere.

"You didn't go to a kosher-style deli to assimilate; you went there to eat Jewish," Kraemer points out. "The people who went didn't care about kashrut anymore, but they did care about being with *landsmen* [Jews with similar geographic origins]. And where would you find landsmen? In the kosher-style deli."

L. John Harris, writer and codirector of the documentary *Divine Food: One Hundred Years in the Kosher Delicatessen Trade,* says the Jewish deli contributed to social integration, bringing non-Jewish Americans in to experience Jewish cooking and allowing Jews to try new American foods in a safe, comfortable setting. "It's where both groups could come together," he says.

By the end of the twentieth century, Jewish delis came in three varieties: glatt kosher, which served only glatt kosher meat; ordinary kosher, which might serve non-glatt meat such as Hebrew National and often did not have a full-time mashgiach on-site; and kosher-style. As time went on, the ordinary kosher variety was slowly squeezed out.

The new Second Avenue Deli is one of those restaurants. It displays a teudah signed by an Orthodox rabbi in its front window. All the ingredients used are kosher certified, the meat is kosher, the kitchen has been properly kashered, and the rules of kosher cooking are strictly observed. But although it is down the block from the Midtown branch of Yeshiva University, the flagship Modern Orthodox institution of higher learning, few Orthodox Jews will eat there. That's because the restaurant is open on Shabbat. It always has been. The Lebewohls make use of a loophole in Jewish law that forbids only a *Jewish*-owned business from operating on Shabbat. They do this by employing a *shtar mechira,* a contract by which they sell the restaurant to a non-Jew every Friday evening and buy it back every Saturday night. So, technically, it is not Jewish owned during that period.

There was a time in New York's Jewish history when this sort of arrangement was accepted, the years when synagogues held early services on Saturday morning to accommodate worshippers who had to work later in the day. Not anymore. Today's Orthodox Jews are much stricter than their parents; most consider the rabbi who certifies the Second Avenue Deli a maverick and will not accept his supervision.

This generation gap is evident in the Lebewohl family. Jack doesn't think twice about being open on Shabbat, while his son Jeremy, who keeps kosher at home, would prefer to be closed. But he's not prepared to make that change yet. The business climate is cutthroat, and many of his customers are non-Jewish. He doesn't have a captive audience like glatt kosher restaurants do. If his customers find the deli closed when they want to eat, they will go elsewhere.

There's another argument for staying open on Shabbat, one Jeremy offers to his own rabbi: If he closes, where will his nonobservant Jewish customers eat a proper Shabbat meal? At the Second Avenue Deli, he points out, they can say *kiddush,* the blessing over kosher wine, and *motzi,* the blessing for bread, over kosher challah. They can enjoy a cholent on Saturday afternoon or roast chicken on Friday night. "For a lot of people, this is their only Jewish connection," he insists. "There's a certain aroma here; it's how your grandmother used to cook. We're providing almost a religious experience for someone who doesn't keep Shabbat at home."

The Second Avenue Deli manages to survive because it's in Manhattan, which has a large enough Jewish population to sustain a wide range of kashrut standards. It is also, like all New York delis, heavily dependent on the tourist market—eating at a Jewish deli is a required part of many visitors' trips to the city. But in most parts of North America, the old-fashioned, non-glatt kosher deli has fallen into disfavor as those Jews who care about kashrut demand the stricter glatt standard.

"Either people want a Jewish deli that also serves other food, or they want glatt kosher," says thirty-nine-year-old Ziggy Gruber, a third-generation deli man and co-owner of Kenny and Ziggy's New York Delicatessen Restaurant in Houston, Texas. "The kosher delis in the middle are dying out. They're going to have to make a choice—go glatt or just be kosher-style and serve everything."

Glatt kosher meat first became popular in this country after World War II, brought in by fervently Orthodox Hungarian hassidim. When their shochtim would find adhesions on the lungs of slaughtered cows, which supposedly indicated a diseased animal and would require additional rabbinic inspection before the animal was declared either kosher or treyf, they would simply discard the entire carcass. *Glatt* is Yiddish for "smooth," and the lungs of a glatt animal can have absolutely no adhesions. As the Orthodox world began moving to the right in the 1980s, fewer rabbis would certify restaurants, butchers, or caterers that used non-glatt meat. Today none of the major kosher agencies will do so, and few kosher meat suppliers even carry non-glatt meat.

Glatt meat is more expensive than regular kosher meat because fewer animals pass the smooth-lung test. And it's more expensive to run a glatt kosher restaurant, as the kosher certifiers require a full-time mashgiach on the premises before they will give their certification. The restaurant must pay his salary, which runs about $40,000 a year—not much for the mashgiach, but more than some small restaurants can afford.

"It backs owners into a corner," charges Sax. "People won't eat there if they don't have a hekhsher, but the cost of the hekhsher could put them out of business."

The kosher agencies don't buy that argument. If a restaurant complains about the cost of a mashgiach, it demonstrates a lack of commitment to kashrut that should put up red flags in other areas. "If an owner says he can't afford fourteen dollars an hour for the mashgiach, maybe he's cutting corners elsewhere. Maybe he's not buying the seven-dollar kosher oil, either," says Rabbi Fogelman of the OK.

Gruber's deli in Houston is kosher-style. His family ran a string of strictly kosher delis in New York for many decades, starting with the Rialto, which his grandfather Max opened on Broadway in 1927. The Rialto was the first Jewish deli on Broadway, and it drew celebrities like the Marx Brothers, Milton Berle, and Ethel Merman. The family went on to open other popular kosher delis, including Berger's on 47th, Wally's Downtown, and the Griddle on 16th.

When Gruber was eight, he started working at his father's kosher deli in Spring Valley, New York. Grandpa Max taught him how to pickle, cure, and smoke meat, and how to cook all the Eastern European specialties. He adored the business, continuing on to the Cordon Bleu culinary school in London and apprenticing at three-star Michelin restaurants, but he finally returned to the family deli. He loved the place.

"You'd have the Mr. Goldbergs coming in, first-generation Americans who ate this food five, six times a week. This was the food they knew. Today Jews think sushi is Jewish food. If you had given my grandmother chicken tikka masala, she'd go, *Vos is dus?*" he says.

For years the family delis didn't need a mashgiach. Inspection by state kosher authorities was sufficient. But by 1989 Orthodox Jews were becoming stricter, and customers started demanding glatt kosher and asking who the restaurant's mashgiach was. Gruber had never heard of glatt, so he asked one of the state inspectors what it meant.

"He said, it's *bubbe meises*, old wives' tales," Gruber recalls. "Either meat is kosher or it's not. He said this is something they cooked up to make money."

Nevertheless, customers were demanding the new standards, so Gruber asked a local cantor if he would supervise the restaurant. "He said he wanted ten thousand dollars. I thought, that's a lot of money, but if he gives it to the synagogue, no problem. But he said no, I want it in cash and I want it in my pocket. That blew my whole vision of kosher."

Soon afterward Gruber moved to Los Angeles, where he opened Ziggy G's on Sunset Boulevard, his first kosher-style establishment. "I found it less of a headache," he reports. "Also, it was becoming the trend. There is no middle today, it's either glatt or not kosher."

In 1999, he moved to Houston, and with partner Kenny Friedman, a Bronx restaurateur, he opened Kenny and Ziggy's, also kosher-style. The restaurant has a huge menu with more than two hundred selections. Gruber serves all the old Ashkenazic favorites, from chopped liver and gefilte fish to kasha varnishkes and sweet-and-sour tongue. But he also offers ham-and-cheese omelets and BLTs with real bacon, items one would never find in the old kosher-style delis. Those earlier places would serve a slice of cheese on a separate plate if customers asked for it with their salami; now the two come together in a sandwich.

Sitting in his office at the Jewish Theological Seminary, David Kraemer digs around in a desk drawer and pulls out a menu from Artie's Delicatessen, a kosher-style Jewish deli that opened in 1999 at Broadway and Eighty-third Street. It reads pretty much like the menu at Kenny and Ziggy's: heavy on the farfel, whitefish salad, and triple-decker sandwiches, and lots of weak Jewish jokes and folksy Yiddishisms. Also like Kenny and Ziggy's, Artie's does not try to conceal its non-kosher status. The menu lists several varieties of Reuben sandwiches—a deli staple that combines meat, cheese, sauerkraut, and Russian dressing—as well as a turkey-and-bacon club.

But, Kraemer points out, none of those treyf items is pictured on the menu he has. Kosher-style delis try to maintain some Old World aesthetic. Artie's serves bacon, but the salami is Hebrew National, kosher by Conservative standards. The restaurant also offers "shiva platters" for sending to families who are mourning deceased relatives. Artie's may not be kosher, but it's "100 percent Jewish," Kraemer says. "Image-wise, it's absolutely clear what they're doing here," he explains, moving his finger from item to item on the menu. "Look, they have Jewish penicillin, emergency chicken soup. Here's the Moshe Dayan sandwich, on challah. And the desserts—rugelach, cheesecake, Jell-O—all the mid-twentieth-century suburban Jewish food. The only beer they serve is Maccabee, Israeli beer. I mean, it's pure fetish."

Is that what the deli has become—museum fodder? Not at all, says L. John Harris. "The Jewish deli is *not* dying," he insists. "The history of the deli in America is a series of changes." People have been killing off the Jewish deli for years, he says. "But it's always being reborn, like the Jew himself."

Harris is sitting in Saul's Restaurant and Delicatessen, a kosher-style deli in Berkeley, California. It's the monthly meeting of the Deli Mavens, a group of deli lovers that has been getting together for nine years at Saul's to eat, kvetch, and share deli memories. Harris organized the group when Saul's reopened in 2000 and he noticed the new waitstaff was not familiar with Jewish food. He and a few friends would spend a couple of hours a week serving as restaurant hosts, walking the floor and kibitzing with customers. They were paid in pastrami.

The core membership of the Deli Mavens is about twelve people. Most have lived in Los Angeles, a great deli town, they agree. One woman talks about frequenting the little Jewish delis up and down LA's Fairfax Avenue when she was a child. They're all gone now, she says, except for Canter's, a venerable kosher-style institution that has been around since 1931.

Nah, counters seventy-year-old Brad Bunnin; Los Angeles doesn't do deli right. And New York is overrated. Chicago is the place for authentic Jewish deli. "That's where I was born and bred," he says with pride. "When I was a kid, there was a deli in every Jewish neighborhood, if not two or three. We'd go two or three times a month. I don't think there were any 'famous' delis because there were so many of them."

But San Francisco? The group sighs. There's nothing sadder than a Jew looking for deli in Northern California. Saul's serves great pastrami, made from Niman Ranch beef, antibiotic- and hormone-free, humanely raised, and organically fed. But it is the only Jewish deli in the East Bay and, according to Harris, the only Jewish deli worth the name in the entire Bay Area, a region with four hundred thousand Jews, the fourth-largest Jewish community in the country.

The Bay Area is a foodie's paradise. It's where California cuisine was invented, where California wine made its name, where world-class chefs create marvels from organic produce, locally sourced meat, and artisanal cheese. It is also a melting pot of various ethnic cuisines, from Vietnamese to Ethiopian. But somehow Eastern European Jewish cooking never caught on. Jewish delis have come and gone, none of them lasting very long. The most recent failures were the SF New York Deli, a kosher deli run by four yeshiva graduates, and the kosher-style California Street Delicatessen in the San Francisco Jewish Community Center, its menu designed by celebrity chef Joyce Goldstein. Both opened in 2006; the JCC deli closed in mid-2007, and the SF New York Deli folded a year later.

It takes a Jewish neighborhood to sustain a Jewish deli, and San Francisco does not have Jewish neighborhoods. The city's Jewish community was founded in the mid-nineteenth century by German Reform Jews. Not only did they not particularly like Eastern European food, which they considered low class, but because they did not observe Shabbat traditionally they did not need to live within walking distance of a synagogue, so they spread out throughout the city. The only long-time Jewish deli to survive is David's Deli near Union Square. Opened half a century ago by Holocaust survivor David Apfelbaum, it became the flagship of sixteen David's Delis that once blanketed the city. The other branches have all closed, and the lone holdout tries mightily but is no longer a go-to destination.

Sax remains hopeful that the region's talent, money, and natural resources will spur a renaissance for the Jewish deli. Harris shares that hope. Saul's Deli is trying; co-owner Peter Levitt used to cook at Alice Water's Chez Panisse, the legendary restaurant two blocks away that launched the sustainable food revolution. But it's a lot to pin on one deli, and a non-kosher one at that. A future for *kosher* delis in San Francisco? *Fuhgeddaboudit.*

The trick, some experts suggest, is to serve kosher food with a wink and a nod. Restaurants don't have to put Hebrew lettering or "kosher" on their sign; an unobtrusive kosher certificate in the window will clue in the Orthodox diner without alienating those who don't know what it means. "What the restaurants always tell me is, they don't want to be known as a great kosher restaurant, they want to be a great restaurant that happens to be kosher," says Elan Kornblum, publisher of *Great Kosher Restaurants* magazine.

Great restaurants that happen to be kosher can thrive in New York or Montreal, both cities with large observant Jewish populations. Even there, however, the profit margins are so slim and popular tastes so fickle that a bad month or two can push a place over the edge. In other cities, upscale kosher restaurants are even more vulnerable. Chicago has only about five, according to Kornblum, and Las Vegas, widely touted as the city with the fastest-growing Jewish population, has three. Los Angeles has more, but closings are frequent. In December 2006, Manhattan's popular Prime Grill opened a branch in Beverly Hills. It lasted just over a year, closing in February 2008. A month later Mamash, an Asian fusion restaurant in the heavily Jewish Pico-Robertson neighborhood, closed three months after its opening, quickly followed by The Magic Carpet, a popular Yemenite restaurant that had hung in for fifteen years.

The Prime Grill's failure was the biggest surprise, considering its splashy, well-publicized opening and the money behind it. Amy Klein, writing about the closure in the *Jewish Journal of Greater Los Angeles*, reported that some experts blamed the restaurant's high prices, others blamed its location, while still others said it was seen as an "outsider" in a city that protects its own. All agreed, however, that the kosher restaurant business is twice as tough as the ordinary restaurant business.[10]

In 2009, there were just two kosher restaurants in San Francisco: the Sabra Grill, serving Israeli food, and Shangri-La, a Chinese vegetarian restaurant. The East Bay also had two: the Holy Land and Amba, both Israeli restaurants in Oakland. South of San Francisco, a region with a large Jewish and Israeli presence, there was just Izzy's Brooklyn Bagels in Palo Alto.

The last gourmet kosher restaurant in the San Francisco Bay area, Bar Ristorante Raphael in Berkeley, closed in 2007 after a fretful four years. Founder and co-owner Noah Alper, who developed Raphael's after selling off Noah's Bagels, his chain of kosher bagel shops, spent almost a million dollars getting his white-tablecloth kosher dining establishment off the ground. Raphael's was an Italian dairy and fish restaurant, serving pizza and pasta along with Italian Jewish specialties. Despite good reviews, the customers never materialized. Alper says the restaurant "almost broke even" for four years before he decided to close.

"There weren't as many strictly kosher Jews as I'd thought, and most of them eat dairy out at non-kosher restaurants, so they had other options," he says. "Maybe if it had been a meat restaurant, we would have locked them in. But someone will pick up the gauntlet."

That someone is twenty-five-year-old Chaim Davids, chef and mashgiach at The Kitchen Table, a California-Mediterranean restaurant that opened in May 2009 an hour south of San Francisco in Mountain View. Davids graduated from culinary school in Baltimore, trained as a kosher butcher, and worked in the wine cellar at the Herzog Winery before being invited to develop the menu for what is currently the only high-end kosher restaurant in Northern California. When he got the call in mid-2008 that the restaurant was ready to roll, he quit his job in Baltimore, packed everything he owned into his car, and headed west. He stopped off in Wyoming for the Rainbow Gathering, an annual campout of ex-hippies and artsy types, and pitched in with the cooking at the Jerusalem encampment, preparing kosher vegan meals in an oven built of cans and bricks.

One morning, Davids breezes into the prep kitchen in the home of Silicon Valley venture capitalist Bobby Lent, the principal investor in the new kosher eatery. He will spend the day testing recipes he will later teach to the restaurant's Italian chef, who is unfamiliar with kosher cooking.

Davids empties two bags of groceries onto the kitchen counter: a dozen Thai eggplants, half a dozen eggs from cage-free vegetarian-fed hens, a selection of forest mushrooms, a package of sprouted soybean tofu, two onions, a red pepper, a couple of carrots, baby potatoes, and organic mixed herbs. The first two dishes he will try are a curried, brined eggplant appetizer and a vegan burger made of fresh vegetables and organic tofu.

He slices the eggplant and sets it to roast in the oven, then rummages through the Lents' spice pantry for the right combination to throw into his brine. "Maybe I'll use garam masala, make it kind of an Indian eggplant," he muses. While the brine bubbles away on the stovetop, Davids talks about his culinary philosophy. He's a purist in the kitchen, he says, and the new restaurant's menu will focus on sustainably grown food, organic ingredients, and home-cured meats.

Davids will make his own kosher pastrami, the old-fashioned way. "I don't want to ship in produce," he says. "I won't use dextrose, sucrose, xanthan gum. No chemicals."

At one point Lent wanders into the kitchen to see what Davids is up to. Lent's primary reason for backing this venture is to provide a place where observant and nonobservant Jews can eat together, but he also knows the menu has to be enticing enough to draw the general public. He expects more than 80 percent of the customers will not be Jewish— there aren't enough kosher-keeping Jews in Silicon Valley to sustain a restaurant. And Northern California diners have high standards, he says. They're not going to patronize a place just because it's kosher. The food has to be terrific.

By opening day, the vegan burger has been scrapped. Davids couldn't get the patties to hold together properly. The brined eggplant appetizer, on the other hand, is a hit. Davids is hard at work in the kitchen, prepping a large bowl of lamb chunks for his masala-spiced lamb kebabs, which are served with wild arugula, couscous, and a homemade kosher nondairy yogurt sauce. "You can't buy pareve yogurt commercially; we had to make it ourselves," he says.

The restaurant is on a busy shopping street and curious passersby stop by all afternoon that first day to check out the menu. None seem to realize the place is kosher. It is not stated on the menu. All the wines are kosher, but the wine list doesn't say so. The only indications of the restaurant's Jewish identity are a few items like the matzo ball soup and pastrami. That's the point, Davids says: not to hide the Jewish connection, but to add it as another layer. The food has to say, We're artisanal, we're sustainable, and we're hip, but we're also Jewish.

"I was on the front page of the *Palo Alto Daily News,* wearing a big red yarmulke—on purpose," Davids says with a grin. "I wanted everyone to know here's a *frum* [religiously observant] Jewish kid making his own kosher corned beef in downtown Mountain View. That's what it's about, right?"

# 6.

# Beyond Manischewitz

## *Kosher Wine Aims High*

LUNCH AT Jeff and Jodie Morgan's home in Napa, California, reflects the rarefied sensibilities of the Bay Area foodie.

A salad of organic greens, lightly drizzled with olive oil and balsamic vinegar, is followed by wild rice with sautéed mushrooms and pasture-raised baby lamb chops—grilled rare—part of an entire lamb the couple bought from a local farmer.

A soft October breeze plays across the deck of their yellow farmhouse, circa 1889, located on a quiet street in the heart of California's greatest winegrowing region. In the yard are fruit trees—peach, orange, plum, fig, olive, pomegranate—and a small enclosure where Jodie is raising half a dozen chickens that have just begun laying eggs. A more bucolic Napa Valley scene could hardly be imagined.

On the table is a bottle of red wine: a 2006 cabernet sauvignon Morgan made himself under his Covenant label. No Napa Valley meal is complete without a glass of wine, preferably made by one's host. The wine is delicious, fragrant and full-bodied, garnering an enviable score of 90–92 points from noted wine critic Robert Parker of *The Wine Advocate*. It's expensive, $90 a bottle. And it's kosher.

"Kosher wine is at the precipice of a renaissance in quality," insists Morgan, former West Coast editor of *Wine Spectator* who, like Napa transplants before him, succumbed to the lure of the vine, quit his day job, and started making his own wine.

He did it almost on a dare. In summer 2002, when he was working as wine director for the Dean & DeLuca gourmet food chain, he found himself pouring rosé at a synagogue fund-raiser next to company owner Leslie Rudd. Rudd, who was pouring a red from his own winery, turned to Morgan and asked, "Why does kosher wine suck?"

Not all of it does, Morgan started to explain, noting that he'd tasted a few delicious non-mevushal wines made by the Herzogs, a longtime kosher winemaking family that started making quality dry kosher wines in the mid-1980s. But it's true, he continued, most kosher wine is mevushal, or cooked, which means it is heated almost to boiling during the winemaking process. That is done to circumvent the prohibition on Gentiles touching the stuff and rendering it non-kosher. Boiling wine, while presumably protecting against desecration by the uncircumcised, rarely does anything to improve taste. Even though the mevushal wines of today are not technically boiled, just flash pasteurized for about ninety seconds, he said, it's still a shame to put a good wine through the process.

But why did it have to be that way? Why couldn't he and Rudd, who is also Jewish, combine their expertise and make great, non-mevushal kosher wine? Morgan didn't want to make kosher wine because he was observant, but because he was Jewish. He wanted to be proud of the wine his people made. "I wanted to take the paradigm and turn it on its head," he explains. "From the folks that brought you psychotherapy and the atom bomb, we can also bring you really good wine."

At first Rudd was leery, agreeing to come on as financial backer but not to give Morgan grapes from his vineyard. If the wine turned out badly, he didn't want his name attached to it. So Morgan found his own grapes; flew off to New York; met with Nathan Herzog, chief of sales for the Herzog wine company; and got permission to share their kosher staff and winemaking facilities in Southern California. That's where Morgan made his first four vintages of Covenant Cabernet Sauvignon, starting in 2003.

That first release drew rave reviews. Parker gave it 93 points in *The Wine Advocate*, gushing, "Covenant may be the finest kosher wine made in the United States." *Wine Spectator* gave it 92 points. With each vintage since then, the kudos continued.

It's wine that brought Morgan back to his Judaism, he says. He grew up in a nonobservant home and, after a brief flirtation with Judaism in college, spent the next fifteen years as a professional saxophonist. In 1988, he turned his attention to wine, first working at a winery on Long Island, then writing a wine column for a local paper that turned into a gig with the *New York Times*. In 1992, he was recruited by *Wine Spectator* to write their annual Passover issue on kosher wine.

Morgan admitted to the editors that he didn't know anything about kosher wine. "They said, You're Jewish, aren't you?" he recalls. For that first article, he embarked on a crash course to learn everything he could about kosher wine, tasting the best and the worst. He organized a blind tasting for winemaking friends on Long Island, secretly serving only mevushal wines, including some top brands from Israel. One man turned to him in the middle of the event and remarked, "These are the weirdest wines I've ever tasted."

For seven years he wrote about wine, deepening his knowledge of kosher wines in the process. The problem, he came to believe, is that American Jews don't care enough about the quality of what they put in their mouth. "We take food and wine very seriously in terms of their spiritual essence, but the sensual essence has taken a backseat. If you look at Jewish literature and religion, it's filled with sensual imagery. Look at the Song of Songs. So why are we so divorced from the sensual aspect of eating and drinking as compared to other cultures?"

Morgan wants to raise the bar for kosher wine, which won't happen, he says, until Jews demand a better product from kosher winemakers. "It's ninety-nine percent attitude and just one percent delivery," he insists.

He's got a job ahead of him. Bad kosher wine is almost a point of pride with American Jews, the butt of many a Jewish joke. It exists because it can. Unlike Borscht Belt comedians, kosher winemakers have a truly captive audience. Observant Jews need kosher wine, no matter what it tastes like, for the kiddush blessing before the Friday night and Saturday afternoon Sabbath meals, for the post-Sabbath havdalah service, for Jewish holidays, and for religious services such as weddings and circumcisions.

But that's poor excuse for the sticky-sweet bottle of Concord Grape Uncle Morrie has stashed away in the corner cupboard, the one he drags out each spring for the Passover seder. "We are known as the worst winemakers in the world, and we are the people with the oldest codified relationship to wine," Morgan says.

Wine has had a place in Jewish practice since the days of the ancient Israelites. Israel itself was described in Deuteronomy 8:8 as a land of grapevines, and several varieties are mentioned in the Bible, including spiced wine in Song of Songs 8:2 and "strong" wine in Psalms 75:9.

Wine was an integral part of Temple rituals in Jerusalem more than two thousand years ago. Specified amounts were offered along with the daily burnt sacrifice: a quarter of a *hin* of wine, about one and a half quarts, if a sheep was being sacrificed; a third of a hin with a ram. Wine was poured on the top of the altar as a signal that the choir of Levites should begin their daily chanting of the Psalms.

Wine was so prized during the First and Second Temple periods, according to Israeli wine critic Daniel Rogov, that men who planted vineyards were exempt from military service.

After the destruction of the Second Temple in 70 CE, Jews carried their winemaking skills with them into the Diaspora. Jewish life could go on without priests or Jerusalem, but not without wine to fill the kiddush cup, a ritual dating back at least to the first century BCE. Jewish winemakers plied their trade throughout the Roman Empire and into the Middle Ages. Rashi, the great eleventh-century Torah commentator, was reputed to have made wine from his own vineyard in Troyes, France, helped by his three daughters who labored beside him in the fields.

Jews have lived and made wine in some of the best winemaking regions of the world. But when they came to North America, it's as if they forgot everything they'd learned. In fact, what happened was that the few French and Italian Jews to hit these shores were overwhelmed in the late nineteenth century by the masses of Jewish immigrants from Eastern Europe and the Russian Pale of Settlement. And these newcomers landed in New York, home of the lowly Concord, rather than California, where they might have happened upon the more versatile zinfandel or cabernet.

"When my father came to this country, the only grapes he could get were New York State grapes, Concord grapes," relates sixty-two-year-old David Herzog.

David Herzog, uncle to Nathan Herzog, is a seventh-generation winemaker. He and his brothers Philip and Herman run the Royal Wine Corporation, which makes kosher wine under the Herzog, Baron Herzog, Weinstock, and Kedem labels. More than a century ago their great-grandfather Philip Herzog was the exclusive wine supplier for Austro-Hungarian emperor Franz Josef, who rewarded him with the title of baron, a rare privilege for a Jew. Their father, Eugene Herzog, carried on the family tradition, making wine in his native Czechoslovakia before fleeing the postwar communist government for New York in 1948. There he started making wine on New York's Lower East Side, but he was unable to find the grapes he wanted. He made do with the native Concord, which produces a bitter juice winemakers describe as "foxy."

"You can't make a very good wine out of Concord grapes," explains David, who gave up a career in investment banking to join the family business in 1971. "You have to add a lot of sugar to it."

Nevertheless, Concord grape became the industry standard for kosher wine in America, supplemented by blackberry, cherry, and other sugary, fruit-flavored fortified wines, all made for sacramental purposes. The country's first commercial kosher wine, developed in 1899 by the Schapiro Kosher Wine Company on New York's Lower East Side, carried the dubious slogan "Wine so thick you could cut it with a knife." If not particularly elegant, these syrupy libations are blessed with longevity. Some can be capped and stored for years, even decades. In a Jewish culture that frowns upon heavy drinking, this is a big selling point.

Interestingly, these sweet kosher sacramentals are enjoying a kind of cultural revival, celebrated with ironic fascination by young hipsters similarly entranced with their grandparents' brisket and klezmer music. At launch parties for her 2008 book *Cool Jew*, author Lisa Alcalay Klug of Berkeley, California, served a drink she named the Manitini, a retro cocktail made with Rose's lime juice, vodka, seltzer, and Manischewitz Blackberry—the coolest drink in the reimagined shtetl.

Alcalay Klug didn't choose Manischewitz wine by accident. It's been around for a century and, with annual production of more than 975,000 cases, still controls close to 65 percent of the country's kosher wine market. Manischewitz wine was created almost as an afterthought by The Manischewitz Company, founded in 1888 in Cincinnati, Ohio, as the country's first commercial matzo bakery. According to a history compiled by Rabbi Yaakov Horowitz, the company's longtime mashgiach, Manischewitz wine was created in 1901 to deal with a surplus of grape juice, used to make egg matzo. The wine soon became a bigger seller than the matzo that spawned it.

Manischewitz wine is what most people think of when they think of kosher wine, particularly the flagship Concord grape, with its distinctive taste reminiscent of grape bubble gum. It has been poured into so many tiny plastic cups in so many synagogues that even Jews who purport not to like it can't imagine a Shabbat or Passover without it.

The same holds true for Mogen David Concord, a sweet wine that controls a third of kosher wine sales in North America. Both wines sell for about $5 a bottle.

Manischewitz wine is no longer made by Manischewitz but by the Centerra Wine Company in Canandaigua, New York, which leases the Manischewitz name. Mogen David wine is produced by The Wine Group, a San Francisco–based corporation. And Jews are not the only target audience for these wines. Both Manischewitz and Mogen David sell well abroad, particularly in Asia, which is emerging as the next big wine export market. Korea's annual import of wine jumped from $30 million in 2002 to $100 million in 2004. According to the USDA Foreign Agricultural Service, kosher American wines—especially Mogen David Concord—control a "significant share" of the American wine market in that country.

The American South is another hot market for sweet kosher wine, where it is purchased largely by African Americans. Laurie Schaefer, a spokeswoman for Manischewitz wine, acknowledged they are the company's second-largest group of buyers after Jews.[1] A study by Joseph Jacobs Advertising, a marketing firm focusing on the Jewish market, compared Jewish and African American wine consumption. Almost none of the Jewish respondents had tasted Manischewitz in the two months since Passover, whereas 50 percent of the African Americans had drunk some in the previous two weeks.

But nostalgia is a powerful force. Many Orthodox Jews who may be familiar only with wine used for kiddush feel that all kosher wine should be sweet. They wrinkle their noses at dry wine, calling it "sour." Some say it burns their throats. Chani Gold, owner of Food Affair, a kosher catering business in Brooklyn, says the very religious crowd doesn't go through much wine at her affairs. When they do drink, "they like the five percent [alcohol] moscato," a wine she describes as "soda pop."

That is what the Herzogs were up against in 1985 when they decided to make nonsweet kosher wines. That first year, working out of a rented facility in California, the company made white zinfandel, chenin blanc, cabernet sauvignon, and chardonnay. The publicity effort for their new line, a full-page ad in the February 24, 1983, *New York Times*, proclaimed, "Kosher wine needn't be sweet, just special."

It took years to get that message across, says David Herzog. What turned the tide, he believes, was the influx of baalei teshuva, or newly observant Jews, into the ranks of the Orthodox in the last decades of the twentieth century. Used to drinking good wine in secular America but now constrained by the laws of kashrut, these new kosher consumers were no longer content with inferior hooch. They wanted good wine, and they were willing to pay for it. "They helped us a lot," he admits.

Over the past two decades, baalei teshuva helped drive up the quality and price of all kosher wine in both Israel and North America. Good reviews followed, capped in early 2008 by cover stories on Israeli wines in *The Wine Advocate* and *Wine Spectator,* and a series of sterling reviews of Israeli wines that judged kosher next to non-kosher wines and found both surprisingly good. At a wine tasting for two hundred industry leaders in January 2008 sponsored by the *Wall Street Journal,* a kosher Goose Bay Pinot Noir proved more popular than a non-kosher French burgundy and a non-kosher Oregon pinot noir. The tasters were not told that the Goose Bay was kosher, the paper later reported, because "it wasn't relevant." The wine was chosen for the tasting "simply because it was good."

In 2003, Herzog Wine Cellars moved out of its rented space to open its own $15 million, 77,000-square-foot facility in Oxnard, California, with the capacity to make two hundred thousand cases of wine a year. The Royal Wine Corporation's Kedem Winery in Marlboro, New York, is larger, but in addition to wine it produces a million cases of kosher grape juice annually. Herzog Wine Cellars is located four hundred miles south of Napa Valley, far from the grapes used for its wine but close to Los Angeles's large Orthodox population, which supplies the company with the observant workforce it needs.

In spring 2009, Herzog Wine Cellars released its most expensive wine yet, three hundred cases of cabernet sauvignon made exclusively out of grapes from the prestigious To Kalon vineyard in Napa Valley. The wine is not mevushal, is kosher for Passover, and retails for $200 a bottle. Gary Wartels, owner of Skyview Wine and Spirits in Riverdale, New York, took sixty bottles for his store and sold out almost immediately. "Even at that price, it's been very popular," he says. "It's perfect for Passover. You're supposed to use high-quality wine for the seder, and this certainly qualifies."

Royal Wines still makes sweet wine but only under the Kedem

label, to keep it separate in consumers' minds from the more upscale California lines. According to the company, both Kedem and Herzog Cellars wines enjoy annual growth figures in the low double digits.

David's brother Philip Herzog says even hassidic Jews are developing a taste for drier wines. The Herzogs often hold tastings of the kosher wines they make or import at their Bayonne headquarters. One such tasting in July 2008 drew more than three dozen hassidic leaders. "We didn't taste any sweet wines," Philip says. "These people are spending eighty or ninety dollars a bottle for wine for Shabbat. They learn it from the non-Jews."

Philip says his wife used to drink only sweet wine, particularly Tokay, but now prefers chenin or sauvignon blanc. Cabernet, he says, is "a little strong for her."

"It was a risky decision we made twenty-five years ago, that Jewish people are trendy," David interjects. "Americans were drinking more wine, so Jews began drinking more wine. We Jews are behind the curve, but we get there eventually."

WINE HOLDS a special place in Jewish tradition, as it does in many other cultures. It is one of the few consumables, along with bread, to merit its own blessing: *Baruch ata HaShem elokeinu melech ha'alom borei pri hagafen*, "Blessed are you Lord our God, King of the Universe, who has created the fruit of the vine." Both bread and wine are required at the Sabbath and holiday tables (with matzo standing in for bread at Passover, of course).

Because of its ritual importance, wine used by Jews is subject to a bevy of restrictions regarding who may drink or benefit from it. Grapes are kosher in and of themselves. There is no special kosher procedure for growing or harvesting them. It is when the grape juice separates from the pulp during the crush and begins to flow that restrictions set in. From that point on, the liquid must not be touched by a non-Jew, or even by a non–*shomer Shabbos* Jew, one who does not observe the Sabbath. In order to be considered kosher, wine must be handled only by observant Jews from the time the juice appears until the finished wine is corked and sealed in a bottle. When the wine is uncorked it must again be poured by an observant Jew or it becomes non-kosher.

In a modern winery, where much of the process is mechanized, "handling" the wine includes pushing any buttons or otherwise starting and stopping machinery, all of which must be done by a mashgiach, or at least a Sabbath-observant Jew. Even if a non-Jewish worker is operating the forklift used to dump half-crushed grapes into a receiving bin, the mashgiach must push the buttons controlling the process. These restrictions apply not only to wine but to any kosher product made from grapes, including jams, jellies, and juice.

The prohibition against drinking non-Jewish wine dates back to biblical days. Deuteronomy 32:38 is interpreted to prohibit a Jew from partaking of *yayin nesekh*, wine that may have been used in idol worship. This law emerged at a time when Jews lived in a majority pagan society.

When Christianity replaced paganism as the dominant religious culture, the prohibition against non-Jewish wine focused on the need to prevent intermarriage. The rabbis of the Talmud warned against *stam yaynam*, or "ordinary wine," wine made by a non-Jew for everyday use, on the grounds that wine drinking was a social activity that would bring Jews into contact with non-Jews in an atmosphere where inhibitions became lowered. That could lead to sexual intercourse, which could lead to intermarriage. Keep Jews away from stam yaynam, the argument went, and they'll keep away from Gentile women.

Ensuring that only Sabbath-observant Jews come into contact with wine at any step in its life cycle is a cumbersome regulation. That's where mevushal wine comes in, the presumption being that pagans would not offer boiled wine to their idols. By boiling wine, Jews believed they were protecting it against secret offerings by a non-Jewish servant who, while bringing wine to his Jewish master's table, might stop off to pour some in front of his gods.

Although precious little idol worship went on in Christian Europe, the custom of heating kosher wine to near boiling point persists to this day. Once wine is cooked, it may be handled by anyone and still remain kosher. That is why virtually all kosher restaurants in this country permit only mevushal wine, so that any waiter or customer may pour it without compromising its kosher status.

There are two major opinions concerning how high a temperature wine must reach for it to be considered mevushal. Some rabbis and kosher certifying agencies follow the opinion of Rabbi Moshe Feinstein, who held wine is mevushal at 165–175 degrees Fahrenheit. Others follow Rabbi Levi Yitzchok Greenwald, the late Tzelemer Rav, who held that 190 degrees was the halachic minimum. Some Jews won't drink wine certified by agencies following the competing rabbi's opinion.

Not only that, some strictly Orthodox Jews won't use mevushal wine of any kind for kiddush or other ritual purposes. They will use only wine made start to finish by Sabbath-observant Jews, as if heating the wine to circumvent that restriction constitutes a kind of cheating. Some hassidic Jews go further, prohibiting *rayis akum*, the glance of a non-Jew, meaning no Gentiles may even gaze upon the wine while it is being made, but none of the major certifying agencies follows this practice.

Like many other kosher laws, those regulating wine were understood differently at different times. In 1608, Leon of Modena (a Venetian rabbi and teacher who was himself the subject of some controversy) wrote that his fellow Italian Jews commonly drank their Gentile neighbors' wine, and had done so "from time immemorial."[2] The sixteenth-century Polish rabbi Moses Isserles, known for his commentary on the Shulchan Aruch, suggested that Christians in his day were not idolators, so their touch did not make turn kosher wine into wine from which a Jew could not derive benefit. But these leniencies were not widely accepted. The majority opinion, and practice, has always been to avoid wine made or touched by Gentiles, a position that does not sit well with liberal Jews in today's multicultural America.

First to abandon the notion of kosher wine was the Reform movement, which in its Pittsburgh Platform of 1885 discarded the laws of kashrut as outmoded and ill suited to life in modern society.

The Conservative movement, which accepts kashrut as binding, decided two decades ago that the laws of kosher wine needed to be reevaluated. In 1985, Rabbi Elliot Dorff wrote a responsum for the movement's law and standards committee proposing lifting the restriction on wine made by non-Jews. "We can presume that Gentiles who produce and serve wine in the Western world are not 'idolators' in the halachic sense of that term," he wrote. Moreover, he continued, it does not appear that avoiding Gentile wine has helped stem the rising tide of intermarriage among American Jewry. Since that was the main goal of the prohibition, he recommended that the Conservative movement follow the lead of its membership, many of whom were already drinking non-kosher wine, and "let the prohibition fall into disuse without protest."[3]

Even among liberal Jews who drink non-kosher wine on an every-day basis, it is nevertheless customary to use kosher wine for kiddush and special occasions such as bar mitzvahs and weddings. "It certainly should be a standard for our movement that only certified wines be used for sacramental purposes at home as well as in the synagogue," Dorff wrote. Using Israeli wine for Shabbat and holidays is also applauded by many Jews, observant and nonobservant, as a mark of identifying with the Jewish State.

Jeff Morgan of Covenant Wines experienced this recently when he was asked to show up at a Napa wedding to make sure there was a prayer quorum of ten Jewish adults. "What did they have at the chuppa?" he says, referring to the Jewish wedding canopy under which a toast is made and the groom then steps on and shatters the wineglass. "A cheap, white mevushal wine. Because (a) the bride was afraid she might get red wine on her dress and (b) nobody cared. They just knew they needed kosher wine. And then they drank non-kosher wine for the rest of the meal and served oysters."

Some younger Jews don't buy into this sentimental use of kosher wine for sacred purposes. In fact, members of Tikkun Leil Shabbat, an independent minyan, or prayer community, in Washington, D.C., found the idea of kosher wine so repugnant they sought to ban it.

Tikkun Leil Shabbat is a group of Jews mostly in their twenties and thirties who get together every third Friday for Shabbat services. The minyan encourages social activism, sponsoring a lecture by a local social service group during the prayer service, as well as gender equal-ity and religious pluralism. They put out a basket of yarmulkes for wor-shippers to wear if they choose, but only after long argument about where to place the basket so it would be available but not coercive.

The minyan draws an eclectic crowd, including a fair number of converts and intermarried couples. In early 2007, some members of the coordinating team, which functions like a board of directors, announced they were offended by wine carrying a kosher hekhsher. How can we use wine for a sacred purpose if the non-Jewish parents or spouses of those who take part in our community are not allowed to touch it, they asked? How can we, as a community committed to social justice, ignore the ethnocentric overtones of this practice?

The coordinating team decided that from then on kiddush would be made over wine without a hekhsher at all communal functions.

That created problems, recalls Joelle Novey, the minyan's twenty-nine-year-old administrator. "A lot of people were upset by our decision," she says. "They didn't feel it accommodated their needs." It in effect excluded more-observant Jews from saying kiddush for the group, since they were no longer allowed to use kosher wine, the only kind of wine they could drink.

Throughout the spring of 2007, meetings were held between the minyan's leadership and disgruntled members to heal the rift. Various solutions were put forward. Some people suggested making kiddush over two cups of wine, kosher and non-kosher. Others proposed that the weekly prayer leader, who already had the authority to pick and choose from the worship service, also choose which wine to use.

None of those ideas was acceptable to those opposed to kosher-certified wine. "They *never* wanted to see someone hold up wine and say, This is kosher because no non-Jew has touched it," Novey explains. "One person said, If you walked in the door and saw a sign, 'No black people were involved in making this food,' would you eat it?"

On the other hand, the observant Jews in the minyan were just as committed to using kosher wine, for spiritual as well as halachic reasons. "They said, I find it meaningful to sanctify Shabbat over wine made by folks who also sanctify Shabbat," Novey relates. "It's not about xenophobia or racism, they said; it's about wanting to use food prepared by others who share this Shabbat thing with me."

The minyan came to a compromise: Instead of the traditional communal kiddush after Friday night services, empty cups would be set out for worshippers to make their own blessings, and both kosher-certified and noncertified wines would be available. The blessing would still be said in unison, but over many cups instead of one. The new policy, called Many Hands, Many Voices, remains in effect. It's not perfect, Novey admits, but it's a policy they can all live with.

There are more than two dozen independent minyanim in the country, but as far as Novey knows, Tikkun Leil Shabbat is the only one to have seriously considered banning kosher-certified wine. The conflict so intrigued organizers of the 2008 National Havurah Committee, an annual gathering of North American prayer communities, that they took it to the Sanhedrin, a role-playing session based on the supreme religious council of ancient Israel that each summer tackles a different issue of Jewish law. Participants in the session argued the pros and cons of using kosher-certified wine according to positions assigned them on pieces of paper.

Looking back at the controversy, Novey says it opened her eyes to the delicacy of ritual language. "It was an exploration of something I'd never questioned. For me, it was just part of the wallpaper of what Jews do."

IT'S A CRISP, sunny September day at Hagafen Cellars in Napa Valley, and the first cabernet sauvignon grapes of the season are being brought in for the crush.

The winery's mashgiach sits in a chair by the de-stemming machine, deeply engrossed in a ragged paperback biography of Moshe Dayan. He hardly looks up as a cherry picker lifts half-ton crates of dark purple grapes high in the air, pouring them through a triangular stainless-steel funnel into a series of whirring augers that separate the grapes from the stems and leaves, the first step in the winemaking process.

But Chaim Davids, hired as a second mashgiach for the busy harvest season while he awaits the opening of the new Silicon Valley kosher restaurant he moved here to work for, is bursting with excitement. Wearing cargo pants, tzitzit, and a purple T-shirt reading "Nikayon Zion," the slogan of the Israeli environmental program he attended the previous summer, he stands on a ladder and leans over the de-stemmer as the piles of grapes tumble in.

"It's awesome," he exults, a huge grin on his face. "Every year I think, what a privilege it is to do this."

Hagafen, whose name is Hebrew for "grapevine," is California's first kosher winery, one of just five kosher wineries in the state. It is small, producing ten thousand cases of wine per year. Jews are well represented in California's wine industry as growers, vintners, managers, and wine writers, but very few make kosher wine. Some attempts failed, including Gan Eden, a short-lived kosher winery in Sonoma County, just west of Napa, which folded in 2005, and St. Supery Winery in Rutherford, which made a kosher wine called Mt. Madrona in the 1990s.

Yet Jews have been making wine in the Napa Valley as far back as the 1860s. Some founded commercial wineries, none of them kosher. The 1920 passage of Prohibition caused the bottom to drop out of the California wine business, and many secular wineries turned to making sacramental wine, the only kind of liquor exempt from the nearly fourteen-year-long federal ban on alcohol production. Because rabbis and synagogues were allowed to buy wine for ritual purposes, some congregations saw their numbers swell during Prohibition. Rabbi Horowitz says membership in Los Angeles's historic Breed Street Shul jumped from 100 to 1,500 people during that period, a statistic not unrelated, he believes, to the fact that members could legally buy wine.

Bootleggers were quick to exploit this loophole, paying off rabbis to run liquor through their synagogues. Over a twelve-month period in 1926 and 1927, the *New York Times* carried a series of stories about rabbis arrested for illegal distribution of wine. Shamed, the Reform movement began using grape juice instead of wine in its rituals; Conservative rabbis quickly followed suit.[4]

When Prohibition was repealed in 1933, three Jewish entrepreneurs in Napa founded the Metropolitan Fruit Distillery, where they proposed to make brandy. As Lin Weber tells it in *Under the Vine and the Fig Tree*, her history of Napa Valley Jews, one of the men was Abraham Schorr, an Orthodox rabbi from Czechoslovakia whose family made liquor for years in Europe. Schorr wanted the distillery to operate under kosher laws, a position his partners opposed as too difficult and expensive. He was adamant, and the argument turned ugly. At one point, the wife and niece of one of his partners confronted Schorr about his excessive spending, and he struck them. The women retaliated by taking out scissors and snipping off the rabbi's beard, then charging him with assault. The distillery folded soon afterward.[5]

That was Napa's only kosher offering until 1979, when Ernie Weir, a winemaker at Domaine Chandon, bought twelve acres of vineyard land along the Silverado Trail and started making his own kosher wine in his free time, calling it Hagafen. He'd spent a year on an Israeli kibbutz after graduating from the University of California at Los Angeles in 1971, and although a self-described secular Jew, he had a strong sense of his Jewish roots. "I'm Jewish, I'm cultural, I'm proud of it," he says.

In 1997, Weir quit his job at Domaine Chandon to devote himself full-time to Hagafen Cellars, opening the winery's current facility and tasting room in 2000. His wife is Israeli, and the family spends significant time in Israel. In 2001, he worked as a consultant to several top Israeli wineries, including Carmel, Yarden, and Margalit, and he lectures to Israeli winemakers on what he's learned making wine in California.

Despite his years of expertise, as a nonobservant Jew, Weir can't touch his wine during much of the winemaking process. He tells the mashgiach which buttons to press, but from the time the grapes are separated from their skins in the de-stemmer until the unfermented juice passes through the pasteurization tank, neither he nor his staff can have direct contact with it. Blue OU kosher seals on every barrel in the cellar proclaim their hands-off status. It's a restriction that comes with the territory, he says with a shrug.

Hospitality director Yair Caduri is showing visitors around the winery as the grapes are being pressed. He points to cellar master Emilio Felix, who is hooking up a tube between one of the holding tanks and the pasteurization tank. The mashgiach waits for Felix to finish the connection, then flips a switch to start the juice pumping from one tank to the other.

"The mashgiach doesn't know anything about winemaking. Emilio has to tell him what to do," Caduri tells his visitors.

Like Morgan, Weir says his goal is to show people that kosher wine can be excellent. Unlike Morgan, Weir produces only mevushal wines. He used to make non-mevushal wines as well but switched to all-mevushal in 1993 to get OU certification. The OU, like the rest of the national kosher agencies, will certify only mevushal wines. "I'm not one who believes flash pasteurization changes the taste at all," he says. Hagafen wines have won numerous awards, dating back to the first 1980 vintage. Many of those awards are displayed in the winery's small tasting room, along with menus from White House dinners honoring visiting Israeli dignitaries where Weir's wines were served. One is from a September 1981 dinner at which President Ronald Reagan and Israeli prime minister Menachem Begin shared a 1980 Hagafen Riesling.

Weir goes to great efforts to present his wines as gold-medal winners that just happen to be kosher. Most visitors to the Napa winery are not Jewish, he says, and have no idea the wines are kosher. That's not something pointed out during the tasting room spiel. The Hebrew name might be a tip-off, but only for the Hagafen wines, not those produced under the European-sounding Don Ernesto and Prix labels. And you have to look closely to see the tiny OU symbols.

"I'm not hiding anything," Weir insists. He just doesn't want customers to be scared off by kosher wine's lackluster reputation, a reputation he has worked three decades to change. "I don't think HaShem had it in mind that we'd make kiddush on wine we didn't like," he declares.

The difficulties involved in making kosher wine go beyond hiring a mashgiach and keeping non-Jews and nonobservant Jews away from the wine as it is processing. Various measures taken by contemporary winemakers to improve their product pose problems for observant Jews. One is adding tartaric acid to increase a wine's acidity, common in warmer climates like California when the grapes are harvested late or exposed to too much heat on the vine. Tartaric acid is collected from grape crust left in wine barrels after the wine is removed. Because of the danger of a winery taking crust from barrels used to make non-kosher wine, the OK Kosher Certification agency asked its mashgichim working in Israeli wineries to collect the crust from their company's barrels. That material, collected over a two-year period, was processed in Israel, refined abroad, and sent to kosher wineries around the world.

Another winemaking practice that poses a challenge for kashrut is maloactic fermentation, a second fermentation process that many better wineries use to help stabilize the wine and add character and flavor. The process involves lactic acid, derived from milk, which, among other things, cannot be used to produce wine that may be drunk as part of a meat meal. The OK found a company willing to produce nondairy maloactic culture, which it now uses.

Wine barrels themselves are problematic. The staves that hold them together are sometimes bound by a gluey substance made of dough, which makes the wine forbidden for Passover use. Cork, used as stoppers in most wine bottles, is becoming scarce, so many companies now build stoppers by gluing together pieces of used corks, using glue made from glycerin and fats from mostly non-kosher animals. These are just some potential pitfalls that have to be addressed by kosher wineries and the agencies that certify them.

The agricultural cycle and Jewish law itself pose built-in challenges to kosher winemaking. The grape harvest takes place in September and October, a heavy Jewish holiday period. Work cannot be performed on

Rosh Hashanah or Yom Kippur, during much of Sukkot, or on any Shabbat, and the workday before each of those holidays is also truncated. The typical fall calendar at a kosher winery could have half the days crossed off. Furthermore, during fermentation a good winemaker checks the wine every day to make sure the temperatures are correct, the sugars are right, and the mixture isn't fermenting too quickly or slowly. Larger facilities can put some controls on automatic, but that doesn't help the smaller operations. Jeff Morgan notes that he and his partner sweat through every Shabbat and holiday, and then rush to their tanks after sundown, often working until dawn to make up for lost time.

Throughout history, when kosher wine was not readily available, Jews made their own. That was true in America at least through the middle of the last century. Thelma Levy, a woman in her mideighties, has worked at the OK's Brooklyn office since her late husband, Rabbi Bernard Levy, bought the certification agency in 1968. She describes how, when she was growing up in the Bronx, her mother used to make homemade wine. "She and my father would buy the grapes, and they'd make it," she relates. "It was delicious! Of course, we only used it for kiddush and Passover. In those days you couldn't just go to a liquor store and buy kosher wine."

In the twenty-first century, homemade wine again came into vogue, along with homemade bread, cheese, and other foodstuffs, not out of necessity but due to the growing organic movement and the increased popularity of locally grown food. This is particularly true in California, where boutique wineries are springing up in urban centers as well as rural farmhouses.

Few one-man wine operations are as romantically remote as Four Gates Winery, a kosher winery run by sixty-year-old Benyamin Cantz on top of a mountain in Santa Cruz, a sleepy coastal town seventy-five miles south of San Francisco.

It's not easy to get to Four Gates. The mile-long drive up a potholed dirt road includes hairpin turns that veer dangerously close to sheer drops into redwood canyons, making it clear why Cantz does not encourage visitors.

Another reason is that he's just too busy. While he usually calls in friends to help harvest his three-and-a-half-acre vineyard in the fall, he does everything else himself, from pruning the vines to hauling the grapes in by tractor, from crushing and fermentation to bottling and labeling, even packing up the orders and driving them down the mountain in his pickup truck to mail off to customers. Cantz's methods are strictly old-school. The only way to order his wine is by fax or phone: He has a computer, but it's not hooked up to the Internet. "I'm so backward I write out the invoices by hand," he admits.

Cantz has been living here since 1971, when he graduated from the University of California at Santa Cruz and moved up the mountain to work as a handyman for his art teacher, who owned the property. The land includes a sunny, sloping plateau that had been used as a vineyard in the late 1800s. Some of the old vines had never been removed.

In 1979, another mountaintop resident planted about a hundred chardonnay vines but soon abandoned the site. Cantz took it over and began making his own kosher wine in 1985. In 1991, he finished planting his vineyard; the first year of commercial operation was 1997. Four Gates produces about four hundred cases a year of chardonnay, merlot, cabernet franc, and pinot noir. The grapes are certified organic, but Cantz adds small amounts of sulfur dioxide during bottling to prevent oxidation, so he cannot call the finished product an organic wine.

Although raised nonobservant in Los Angeles, Cantz rediscovered his Judaism in the 1980s and is now Orthodox. That permits him to make non-mevushal wine himself. All Four Gates wines are non-mevushal, so nonobservant visitors are not permitted to set foot in the rickety barn Cantz uses as a winery, an inconvenience he explains with profuse apologies and some embarrassment. It's hard to explain to inspectors from the federal Bureau of Alcohol, Tobacco, Firearms and Explosives and California Certified Organic Farmers that they have to conduct their business from outside the front door.

Cantz lives alone now on the property, with a couple of cats, some horses, and a few goats he keeps for their manure, which provides excellent free fertilizer. Five years ago he added a living room to the main house, but not much else has changed in three decades. His is a rustic lifestyle, filled with cooking and reading and chores. There is no television, just Jewish books piled up in every corner. On a small table near an overstuffed armchair lie *The Essential Tanya* and a selection of writings by Rabbi Moshe ben Nachman, the thirteenth-century Bible commentator known as Ramban. Cantz tries to study a little every day, mostly Torah and Shulchan Aruch, but says he doesn't have time to learn as much as he should.

Cantz is a gentle, soft-spoken man, with piercing blue eyes and white curls that stick out from the bottom of his baseball cap. He likes to sit on a plastic chair set up at the edge of his property, from which he can look out over the vineyard, the surrounding mountaintops, and, on a clear day, as far as the Pacific. If only he'd planted the rows farther apart, he muses, he'd be able to get a tractor through them and his work would be a lot easier. Instead he has to walk the vineyard by foot, clambering up and down the hillside, whether he's pruning or spraying or carrying bags of goat manure. But that's just the way it is.

For Cantz, kosher winemaking is a calling. He didn't study agriculture in college but was exposed to the New Age fascination with growing things, and started a vegetable garden when he first moved up the mountain. As he became more religious, the idea of making his own wine for kiddush grabbed hold. "It says in the Gemara that something you make yourself, you like nine times more than something you get someplace else," he says.

Winemaking has deep spiritual significance for him, an idea he explains slowly, as if he's just now putting it into words. The process of turning seeds into grapes and grapes into wine parallels, in material form, the spiritual elevation that hassidim believe takes place every Shabbat. "It's a going up, from the manure to the vine to the fruit to the winemaking process to kiddush on Friday night, which sanctifies the whole Creation," he describes. "That's the Jewish image that motivated me to get into this. That is what our relation to God is in the world— using the physical world for a holy purpose."

He is amazed that more people have not gone into kosher winemaking. The market is growing, and wine is easy to make, he insists. Just the other day he taught a friend how to do it. "Piece of cake," he shrugs. When he first started making wine in the 1980s, he assumed California was on the cusp of a kosher wine boom that never happened. "I guess American Jews aren't so much into the agricultural part," he says. "They tend to go to graduate school."

The world of kosher winemaking is small and tight-knit. Those involved all know each other. Many have worked together. Jeff Morgan started making his wine five years ago at Herzog Wine Cellars, where he met Jonathan Hajdu, who is now his partner and mashgiach at Covenant. Chaim Davids, hired as a second mashgiach by Morgan and Ernie Weir, also did a stint at Herzog and showed up this year at Four Gates to help Cantz harvest his pinot noir.

And now Morgan and Hajdu are helping the newest addition to their posse, Rabbi Eli Tenenbaum. A Lubavitcher hassid from Brooklyn, Tenenbaum and his young wife moved to Napa in 2007 to open a Chabad center. He was given Morgan's name as a local Jewish contact, and somehow the pair started talking about wine. Tenenbaum didn't really care for wine and knew little about gardening or planting or anything outside a yeshiva, but that fall he ended up going through Morgan's grapes after harvest, gathering about fifty pounds, and making wine in his home.

The Tenenbaums rented equipment and spent an evening de-stemming the grapes, crushing them by hand, and pouring the must, or grape pulp, into a container to ferment. The container sat in the couple's garage until the weather turned cold and Tenenbaum moved it into their bedroom. He was in New York for a week during fermentation, so his wife had to take the wine's temperature and punch it down every day, with Tenenbaum talking her through it on the phone. He ended up with twelve bottles, one magnum, and an infatuation he couldn't shake.

In December 2007, Morgan suggested Tenenbaum take over a tiny vineyard that belonged to the widow of a man who used to make wine for his friends and family. The vines had been untended for six or seven years, and the woman hated to see them go to waste. It didn't take much to persuade Tenenbaum, and in February 2008 he found himself in charge of four hundred vines of zinfandel, syrah, and carignan grapes in a 110-year-old vineyard.

Now the real work began. In February he pruned. Then he weeded, sprayed on sulfur to protect the vines from mold, fertilized, and weeded again. The work seemed never-ending. After his first shift he couldn't move for the rest of the day. The second, third, and fourth times he worked in his vineyard, he couldn't move for three days. Hajdu worked alongside him, advising him all the way and pitching in to help harvest the grapes in mid-September.

Tenenbaum tries to make wine the way it was made in biblical times, with just a few modern improvements. He does all the work by hand and lets the grapes ferment naturally in open barrels. As he and Hajdu harvest, they leave some grapes on the vine in accordance with the exhortation in Leviticus to leave a corner of one's vineyard untouched for the poor and the stranger. The widow's husband, the former owner of the vineyard, had this quote inscribed over the doorway of his barn, and Tenenbaum refers to it often as a constant reminder of the ethical imperatives of his work.

One hot, dusty summer afternoon, Tenenbaum drives out to his vineyard to examine the vines. He stands at one edge of the property, looking down the rows, fingering some of the grapes gently to test their ripeness, popping a few in his mouth. "You have to chew the seed to get an idea of the acidity or something like that," he mumbles uncertainly. "I can't really tell what's going on." He wants to leave the grapes on the vine as long as he can, so the sugars will rise, but if he waits too long they will turn to raisins, "which is only good if you want to make jam," he notes.

This is all very new to him, and he worries about doing it right. He's still not sure how he, a Brooklyn boy, ended up in California running a vineyard. "I've been out here working in the heat and the cold, all the elements, and I'm thinking to myself, What on earth am I doing?" he muses. He believes that a power beyond himself pulled him to this project, as a way of connecting to the Divine and to his biblical ancestors. "I'm following the direction I was given, and it's phenomenal, truly phenomenal."

Bordering the tiny vineyard are fruit trees, tomato plants, and a chicken coop. It's a gorgeous setting, pristine and pastoral. Tenenbaum wanders through the garden, picking a few tomatoes, gathering a pocketful of eggs to take home, shaking his head now and then as if he can't believe his good fortune. He begins talking about why wine is holy, even magical. There are mystical connections among God, nature, wine, and the soul's secrets, he points out. In the kabbalistic system known as gematria, *yayin,* the Hebrew word for "wine," and *sod,* the word for "secret," both have the numerical value of seventy. "The Talmud says, 'When wine goes in, secrets come out.' You really see the essence of a person when he drinks, both the depths and the shallow waters."

The numerical value of Elokim, one of the names of God, is the same as that for *teva,* the Hebrew word for "nature," suggesting a holistic way of understanding reality. "Nature is a level of godliness; godliness is the energy that makes all this happen," he says, waving his arms to indicate the grass, the trees, the vines. "Scientists are figuring out what energy is, and Abraham figured out how to connect to that energy. That's what Judaism is about, connecting. It's not something I read. It's not academic. It's something I experience."

The previous week's Torah portion included the phrase "man is a tree of the field." Tenenbaum repeats it. *"Man is a tree of the field.* Isn't that powerful?" As trees have to be thinned out in order to grow stronger, so people need to thin out their negative attributes. The same with a vineyard; it must be pruned to stay healthy.

Suddenly Tenenbaum pulls out a shofar and begins to blow the short, long, and truncated blasts of the High Holiday call to worship: *tekiah . . . shevarim-teruah . . . tekiah.* It is three weeks before Rosh Hashanah, the period when observant Jews blow the shofar every morning to prepare for the impending High Holy Days. Tenenbaum says he likes to bring his shofar to the vineyard and let the mournful sound of the ram's horn ring out down the rows, connecting him through the vines to his Judaism and his history.

"We have an incredible four-thousand-year heritage that is vibrant and growing and meaningful, and it's only getting better," he says. "And all of these insights come from this one little acre. Imagine that."

# 7.

# Good-bye, Moisha's

## Supermarkets Replace the Corner Store

YAKOV YARMOVE STANDS in front of the kosher deli counter at the Jewel-Osco store in Highland Park, Illinois. Inside the display case rests a wide assortment of ready-to-slice meats (turkey, roast beef, corned beef, salami) alongside stainless-steel bins brimming with fancy prepared foods (herbed roast chicken, potato pancakes, noodle kugel). Overhead stretches a large blue-and-white banner reading "Kosher Marketplace."

Catty-corner is the supermarket's regular deli department. It looks exactly like the kosher section: The counter is just as long; the food signs use the same lettering; the workers are similarly dressed. There is, however, ham next to the turkey, along with sliced cheeses, a detail lost on all but the observant Jewish shopper. To most customers, the two are indistinguishable.

"That's my goal," Yarmove says. "I want to mimic this," he says, sweeping his arm toward the non-kosher deli section, "over here," indicating the kosher deli counter, "but with kosher rules. I want to give our customers a world-class shopping experience."

Yarmove is the main kosher buyer for Supervalu, the parent company of 2,500 retail grocery stores nationwide, including the Acme, Albertsons, Shaw's/Star Market, and Jewel-Osco chains. He decides which products go into the 1,500 stores that have dedicated kosher sections. He also decides which of them, like the Jewel-Osco in Highland Park, will get kosher "stores within a store," a decision determined by the Jewish demographics of the area. Supermarkets in neighborhoods with a large, tightly concentrated observant community get a level-one kosher store, with a meat department, fish department, bakery, kosher dairy case, and a greatly expanded selection of kosher packaged and frozen foods. A smaller but still significant observant population might merit a level-two store, with a kosher meat department or bakery but rarely both, while a level-three store would usually have just the expanded kosher grocery section. Nationwide, Supervalu operates ten level-one, ten level-two, and close to a hundred level-three kosher stores.

Yarmove has no hard numbers to help him determine where to place those stores. The U.S. Census does not track people's religion, and local Jewish leaders are, Yarmove says, prone to exaggerate the size of their communities. He visits towns, walks around, stops in at synagogues, and does a lot of shmoozing before giving his superiors his best guess.

The kosher store in the Highland Park Jewel-Osco opened in 2001, the first level-one kosher store in the Jewel-Osco chain, which with 186 stores controls 40 percent of the grocery business in greater Chicago. Completely remodeled in late 2008, the store is spanking new with soft, modern lighting, wide aisles, and parquet floors. Right inside the front door is a large Purim display, with Kedem wine and grape juice, *hamantaschen,* or special Purim cookies, and a selection of Purim toys for the kids.

"That's important to the kosher customer," Yarmove says. "A display like this says, We understand your holiday. It's not just about borsch and matzo." Immediately to the right is the kosher deli section. In front is the prepared-foods display, which offers precut fruit salads and fresh sushi from the in-house kosher sushi department. Next to this is the kosher bread display—all pas Yisroel, some baked in the store's in-house kosher bakery and some purchased from local bakeries. "That's part of our philosophy, to support local businesses," Yarmove says.

Yarmove trains the workers in his kosher departments to smile and greet people with a lively hello, mimicking the local butcher or fishmonger who knows his customers and their families. "Listen, we were forty years in the desert. We drove Moses crazy," he points out. "We wanted meat, he gave us quails; then we wanted manna, so he gave us manna. We cried. We wanted to go back to Egypt all the time. We can be very demanding. So we train our people to look past what they see and try to make the customer's day cheery."

When a supermarket like Jewel-Osco announces it is opening a big kosher section, independent butchers, bakers, and corner grocers often feel threatened. Their fear is well founded: Independent food concerns, kosher as well as non-kosher, are imperiled nationwide as big-box stores continue to muscle in. Why would anyone choose to buy groceries in several different stores when they can pick up everything they need in one location? Even shoppers who insist they prefer the personal service of an independent find themselves lured in by the convenience, variety, and competitive pricing a chain is able to offer.

Avrom Pollak of the Star-K remembers how his grandmother would take a full day to do her shopping in the Brooklyn neighborhood where he grew up. "She went to the kosher butcher, she went to the fish store, she went to the produce store, and then she went to the place that sold milk, butter, and cheese." As a boy, he loved watching the fish swim around in the big tank in the front window of the fish store. Customers would point to the one they wanted, and the counterman would scoop it up in a big net and bang it over the head with a wooden rolling pin. Then he'd skin it and clean it, a process that could take forty-five minutes or more. Nobody minded, Pollak says. "They'd catch up on everybody's news. They had patience. Today people don't have time for that. They want one-stop shopping, a supermarket that has the bakery, the meat department, the groceries, and the take-out food."

There wasn't much outcry from the Highland Park Jewish community when the level-one kosher store opened in their Jewel-Osco in 2001. It was a different story when a billboard went up in August 2004 on Devon Avenue, the heart of Chicago's historic Jewish neighborhood, announcing a brand-new kosher store inside the North Side branch. The community protested immediately. Signs appeared in kosher restaurants asking people to "please patronize the real jewels of the community, the *heimische*-owned groceries and restaurants." A group of leading rabbis mailed an appeal to thousands of Jewish homes, asking residents to continue patronizing the independents and warning against the strong-arm tactics employed by big-box supermarket chains.[1]

Yarmove himself was pilloried in the press. A front-page story in the *Chicago Tribune* portrayed him as Goliath to the local Davids.[2] The incident still rankles. "There were all kinds of comments about me on blogs, in articles," he recalls. "People were screaming at me in shul. My boss said, 'Yakov, you can't let it get to you. You gotta take it on the chin.'" Yarmove insists he is not out to ruin the independents. But his priority is making life easier for kosher-keeping Jews, and if super-markets do it better, that's just progress. "No disrespect meant, but the independent kosher stores were run like most local stores—limited hours, limited promotions, customer service at a minimum," he says.

Yarmove has been in the business for eighteen years, almost half his life. He is forty now, and when he was a boy in Cincinnati, the only kosher options in his city were two butchers, neither of them glatt. His family drove to Cleveland once a month, a six-hour trip, to buy all their meat and cholov Yisroel dairy products. They would bring the food home packed in ice. "I grew up thinking all kosher milk was frozen," he says. "When I went away to yeshiva at the age of twelve and they served me fresh milk, I was sure it wasn't kosher."

When he and his wife got married in the early 1990s, they would do their grocery shopping at night after work and get excited at each new kosher-certified product they found. "We'd say, look, that salsa has an OU! I don't like salsa, but it has an OU so I'm going to buy it because at least it gives me more variety than what I had before."

Yarmove recalls the kosher stores of his youth as unpleasant places. "They were dirty; they had an odor. Yes, the butcher was nice, he knew everybody's name. But they weren't up to standard. The kosher section in the supermarket was never more than four feet long. It would have Manischewitz matzo, borsch, and gefilte fish. You'd walk past the meat aisle, you'd walk past the bakery, you knew you couldn't buy any of that.

"Now, fast-forward, the kosher consumer can walk in and get the same level of service, the same departments their Gentile counterparts have had their whole lives. Mind-boggling."

At the Highland Park store, he hurries through the aisles like an excited schoolboy, grabbing items off the shelves. Look, kosher organic cereal! Look, Belgian chocolates! He fingers the kosher cheeses lovingly, noting the triple crèmes and the mushroom brie. "When I was growing up, you had shredded mozzarella, cheddar, and processed American cheese," he remarks. "That's about it. Fresh baked bread, I'm telling you, when I was a kid we'd walk past that department saying, I wish, I wish. Now just look at this—French bread, kosher, pareve, pas Yisroel, right here in the supermarket. Look at our pas Yisroel birthday cakes. You can put your kid's picture on this cake and it's still afford-able. It's a whole new world."

Kosher food has been available in mainstream stores for a century, but only in certain cities and at certain times of the year. As early as the 1910s, grocery stores in the Northeast set up small kosher sections to sell Jewish ethnic foods at Passover and the High Holidays. In the 1920s and '30s, the Macy's flagship store in Manhattan operated a Passover section in its food department every spring, walled off from the rest of the store, where it sold Manischewitz matzo, honey, dried fruits, and kosher Carmel wine "imported from Palestine."[3] By the late 1960s, frozen kosher poultry and meat began showing up in super-markets in neighborhoods with significant Orthodox populations, chipping away at the fresh butcher and fishmonger business.

But it was only when mainstream supermarkets began opening full-service kosher departments complete with in-store butcher counters and bakeries that the real change got under way. The first supermarket to offer such a wide kosher selection was the ShopRite in Lakewood, New Jersey, which opened its Kosher Experience in 1979. Kroger in Atlanta was next, opening a year later, then an Albertsons in Dallas and a Price Chopper in Colonie, New York, just outside Albany.

In the 1990s, the phenomenon mushroomed, moving beyond tradi-tional Jewish population centers into the Midwest and West Coast. Today there are several thousand supermarkets with year-round ko-sher sections, several hundred of them offering in-store bakeries, delis, butchers, or fish departments. National chains such as ShopRite, Path-mark, and Albertsons have invested heavily in upgrading their kosher offerings. So have Walmart, Costco, and other big-box retailers. By 2003, Albertsons had kosher sections in every one of its 1,750 stores. For the kosher-keeping customer, it is indeed a whole new world.

ShopRite does the most kosher business of the major chains. Its two hundred stores in New York, New Jersey, Connecticut, Pennsylvania, and Delaware serve an area that is home to more than half of America's six million Jews, including most of those who keep kosher. In addition to the wide variety of mainstream kosher-certified products carried in those stores, the company offers its own private-label ShopRite Kosher brand, launched in 2005. The first item produced under that label was a challah for Rosh Hashanah. Three years later ShopRite Kosher was producing 1,100 items under its in-house label, from canned soups and spaghetti sauce to household cleansers. More than a dozen ShopRite supermarkets have full-service kosher meat, fish, and deli departments, along the lines of Supervalu's level-one kosher stores.

Marketing for these kosher sections is more sophisticated today. Industry consultant Menachem Lubinsky says that twenty years ago, supermarkets would advertise their kosher offerings once a year, at Passover. Today not only do they runs ads before other holidays like Purim, Rosh Hashanah, and Sukkot, they offer special promotions, hold cooking demonstrations, and bring in Israeli holiday items.

If food manufacturers are persuaded to pay thousands of dollars a year for kosher certification because consumer interest in kosher food is continuing to rise, they are also pushed to do so by the supermarkets and discount chains that stock their products. These stores are after the observant Jewish shoppers, who are known to spend more money than other consumers. Kosher marketer Elie Rosenfeld says one of his largest clients, a major national chain, claims Jewish customers spend close to a billion dollars in its stores, between 200 and 300 percent more every week than non-Jewish customers. A lot of those sales are residual: Lured in by the kosher offerings, kosher-keeping Jews may end up doing the rest of their shopping in the same supermarket, picking up toilet paper, paper towels, salt, sugar, and other staples along with their meat and sushi.

Yarmove is a professional, out to make money for his bosses. But there is a religious component to his career choice, as there is for many people who work in kosher certification. It feels good, he says, to provide kosher food to Jewish people. When he was put in charge of opening the first kosher store inside a supermarket in his hometown of Cincinnati, he fairly burst with pride. "It was amazing to bring kosher to my city," he says. "To me, this is more than a job—it's a mission. I'm not just selling diapers; I'm bringing kosher to places where hopefully it is needed."

These dedicated kosher sections in supermarkets are built primarily to serve kosher-keeping Jews, but the kosher agencies hope it will also promote kashrut among nonobservant Jews. Aaron Leff is a mashgiach in Livingston, New Jersey, where he oversees the kosher departments at the local ShopRite. He says even Jews who don't keep kosher stock up on the products, particularly the delicatessen and fresh meat.

"How many times do I look in people's shopping carts, and it's full of non-kosher stuff, but they're also buying kosher," he says. "There's a Talmudic concept that says there are two kinds of Jews. There's the Jew who eats non-kosher because he doesn't like God and he's doing it deliberately, and there's the Jew who just says kosher is inconvenient. It's hard. It costs more money. He doesn't hate Judaism; it's just too difficult to find the kosher. But if you put it in front of him, and it's just as easy to get both, he'll choose the kosher, no question."

Leff drops by ShopRite to inspect the kosher deli three to six times a week. During one visit, a customer told him he was buying kosher meat for the first time in twenty years. Leff didn't know whether to laugh or cry. "Before we opened, there used to be a kosher butcher a tenth of a mile away. Or you could drive to Elizabeth, the next town. There's been kosher meat in New Jersey for the last eighty years. But when you put it in ShopRite, right in front of them, they buy it."

In 2008, almost two dozen new kosher stores opened nationwide. Some were full-service kosher departments inside mainstream supermarkets. But others were all-kosher supermarkets, a more recent innovation that marries the kosher corner store to the modern shopping experience. In August of that year, Pomegranate, a twenty-thousand-square-foot kosher supermarket, opened in the Flatbush section of Brooklyn. Two years in the planning, the store stretches along an entire block of Coney Island Avenue, home to numerous kosher eateries, Judaica shops, and other retail stores catering to the neighborhood's very observant community.

With wood-paneled floors, soft mood lighting, and aisles wide enough for three shopping carts plus a stroller or two, Pomegranate is much more upscale than anything else on the street, including the run-down kosher grocery store it replaced. It is consciously based on the Whole Foods model, boasting a wide range of organic products, ethnic specialties, and fresh produce along with an in-store butcher, bakery, and sushi department. The fresh meat section with butchers at the ready is a thing of beauty, offering aged prime rib at $34.99 a pound and stuffed ready-to-cook lamb chops. The store bakes its own bread, mixes and blends its own cheeses, grinds its own peanut butter, packages its own salads, and slices its own smoked fish in three separate kitchens: meat, dairy, and pareve. Fresh kumquats and kosher-certified panko breading are aimed at well-heeled upscale shoppers, while the homemade knishes and frozen-food cases filled with Syrian specialties and a dozen brands of gefilte fish serve consumers with more traditional tastes.

A month after opening day, store manager Mayer Gold was still beaming. "We expected to be extremely successful, but it's gone beyond our dreams," he says. In the produce section, Nancy Kaminash is fingering the apples. "They're beautiful," she murmurs. Kaminash lives in Park Slope, a trendy Brooklyn neighborhood with a largely nonobservant Jewish population. She does not keep kosher, but her friends said she had to check out the new store. "They're all raving about it," she says. "Look at all the organic! It's so fresh." Clair Pellach comes in from Staten Island to do her shopping. "The selection is so much more varied, and it's clean and the aisles are wide," she says. "And the meat is so beautiful! Red and not too fatty. And they have the filet mignon with the pepper; you don't see that anywhere else."

This is a level of service and choice most urban shoppers have come to expect, but it is very new to the kosher world. Customers at Pomegranate don't have to look at any labels to make sure they're buying kosher; they can just breeze through the aisles and choose at will. They can do that in the small kosher grocery stores as well, but there they don't get the organic produce, the imported chocolates, and the $30 bottles of wine. They don't get the same aesthetic experience, either. "This proves what we've known all along, that the kosher consumer is ready for the next step," Gold says.

It's not just about the luxury items. Pomegranate looks fancy, but most of what it sells is also available in the independent stores—Pomegranate just charges less. Big supermarkets can buy in bulk, which the smaller stores cannot do. One woman Gold passes in the cheese section picks up a package of kosher-certified cheddar. Turning it over skeptically, she squints to see the price, then purses her lips in surprise. "Fifty cents cheaper than down the street," she pronounces, waving it in front of her girlfriend's face. "Ha!"

For months before Pomegranate opened, business owners up and down Coney Island Avenue watched the building go up with a mixture of pride and trepidation. One popular Orthodox blog surmised that the owners of Moisha's Discount Supermarket and Glatt Mart, two popular kosher grocers on the streets, were "quaking in their boots."[4]

But change had already come to the street; Pomegranate's arrival was more confirmation than impetus.

Baruch Pinson has operated Happy Home, a housewares and Jewish gift shop, on Coney Island Avenue since 1993. When he opened, the neighborhood was filled with small, casual kosher restaurants serving deli, pizza, and Israeli specialties. Almost all are now closed. Two doors down from him stood Shop Smart, a longtime kosher grocery store that went out of business when a discount store opened nearby. "The guy who owned it, he cried," Pinson says. "It was a horrible day for him."

New restaurants have opened, most trying to capitalize on current food trends. Japanese is big—the street's third kosher sushi restaurant opened in January 2009. Café Venezia, a fish restaurant, opened in summer 2008, as did Barbounia, a Turkish-Mediterranean place. Kosher Tex-Mex made its debut in the spring of '09 with Carlos & Gabby's. Some of the new restaurants do well, Pinson says, but most come and go fairly quickly, often changing hands among the same group of local owners and then reappearing under a new name. The feel of the old street is fast disappearing. It's not gone, but it's definitely endangered. One milestone was the closing of the neighborhood's last kosher butcher shop, which shut down in 2006 when owner Shimon Goldman retired. A girls' dress shop took its place.

Goldman doesn't like to talk about the butcher shop. He is sitting in his modest kitchen in Crown Heights with several of his children and their spouses, and his wife, Esther, who does most of his talking for him. He sips a cup of tea, sighing now and then, as his family members interrupt each other to tell his tale.

Born in 1925 in Poland, Goldman escaped the Holocaust when his yeshiva was evacuated to Shanghai in advance of the German invasion. He arrived in New York as a war refugee, married in 1949, and in 1951 opened his first butcher shop in East New York after two years as a kosher slaughterer. In the early 1960s, he relocated the business to Flatbush, following the Jewish migration.

Goldman was a neighborhood institution. Customers would stop by just to hear him tell stories—Yiddish folktales, stories from the Bible, hassidic words of wisdom. His career spanned the changes in the world of retail meat, from the early days, when he would go to the market every morning, pick out his chickens, slaughter, pluck, and kasher them himself, to the final years, when the meat and poultry arrived clean and already kosher. Even then he continued to kasher livers for his customers, a process that requires broiling under high heat to draw out all the blood. "So they wouldn't have to dirty their ovens," Esther explains.

When supermarkets came into Brooklyn, it definitely hurt his business. "Women in those days wanted their chickens warm," Esther states. "Today, are you kidding? They want them frozen."

Goldman did not move with the times. He refused to stock frozen meat or poultry. No prepared foods, either. Just old-fashioned fresh beef, veal, and chicken, cut to order. But it got harder and harder to make a living, as younger Jews patronized the newer stores and the price of kosher meat continued to climb. By the time he closed, he was more than ready to get out of the business.

And he made sure none of his four children would go into it. His oldest son, Yosef, a Chabad rabbi in South Africa, says that was never an option. "He wouldn't even let me do his deliveries," Yosef says. "He told me to sit and learn Torah, and if I needed pocket money he'd give it to me. I don't even know what a shoulder steak looks like."

Goldman nods in approval. "I wouldn't want my children to be in this business. There are much easier jobs that make more money. This is not a good profession."

Rabbi Genack of the OU told a *New York Times* reporter that the same scenario is repeating across the country. "The little stores are hurting as more and more people opt for the convenience of one-stop shopping and better prices that they can get in large-scale stores, and it's only going to get worse," he said.[5]

The Northeast and Midwest were hit first, as shrinking cities lost their older Orthodox populations, but the trail of failed independents stretches across the nation. Charlotte, North Carolina, lost its last kosher butcher in 1989. The last one in St. Paul, Minnesota, closed in the early 1990s. In 2006, Irv's Kosher Market went under in Cincinnati, and in January 2007 Bilkers Fine Foods closed after ninety-nine years, leaving that city without a family-owned kosher butcher or grocery store. Beacon Kosher, the only glatt kosher market in Brookline, Massachusetts, closed in June 2007, followed in September by Bob's

Butcher Block & Deli, the last independent in Sacramento, California. Owner Bob Gittleman told reporters he couldn't compete with Trader Joe's prices.[6]

Buffalo, New York; Orlando, Florida; Kansas City, Missouri. The dominoes continued to fall. In December 2008, the *New Jersey Jewish News* mourned the passing of Goldberg Kosher Meats in Old Bridge, the last traditional kosher butcher shop in that area of central New Jersey. Owner Dave Goldberg said he was doing one quarter of the business he did twenty-five years earlier. Younger customers preferred the ease of prepackaged meat and poultry from the supermarket, he said. "In the 1950s we had all the refugees who came over and wanted kosher meat," he told the *Jewish News*. "In the 1970s we were dealing with their children. Now we're dealing with their grandchildren, who could not care less."[7]

All these closings are economically related. But there's an additional factor: Children are no longer taking over the family business. No one else is, either. Dave Goldberg offered his business for free to anyone who wanted it, but there were no takers. When the owners of Bilkers Fine Foods retired, they, too, were unable to find a successor.

The same thing happened in kosher food manufacturing and distribution, fields that used to be made up of family-owned businesses that were handed down from father to son. That automatic succession began to disappear midcentury when the American-born second generation became doctors and lawyers. As the original founders died, their businesses closed or were sold to the fast-rising kosher food corporations.

"It's all consolidation now," says Marty Stein, an account manager in the Albany, New York, branch of Tree of Life, a mammoth specialty food distributor founded in the Netherlands. In 1932, Stein's father established Stein Food Products, a kosher food distributor that carried Goodman's noodles, Manischewitz matzo, and all the other traditional kosher products, selling them to kosher and mainstream grocery stores. In those years, kosher food distribution was handled by regional family-owned all-kosher businesses like Stein Food Products, which sold to stores in the Northeast. "He was a pioneer, getting supermarkets like Grand Union and Price Chopper to have kosher food sections in the 1950s," Stein says of his father. But as the industry grew, national distributors emerged to service national chains, carrying a wide variety of ethnic foods, not just kosher. Stein closed his father's business in 1982 and two years later joined Tree of Life.

Small, independently owned kosher stores have trouble keeping pace with rising customer expectations. Aesthetics are important to a younger generation not willing to step over piles of boxes or rummage through cramped shelves.

When Bexley Kosher of Columbus, Ohio, closed in March 2008 following the owner's stroke, several longtime customers said they felt sorry for him, but they weren't unhappy to see Kroger move in with a newly expanded kosher section. One regular shopper said she no longer found what she needed at Bexley's and would often stop off at the supermarket anyway. Even Philip Froehlich, who worked at the store for years, admitted that it needed new equipment and a coat of paint.[8]

Those independents that manage to stay afloat often find new angles to outflank the better-funded competition. Some specialize in gourmet kosher food, situating themselves in upscale Jewish neighborhoods like Manhattan's Upper West Side or Boca Raton, Florida, where a critical mass of moneyed kosher-keeping customers are willing to pay top dollar for personal service and quality product. Some give up trying to persuade their own children to take over the business, and focus on other people's kids. At Robert's Fish Market, one of the few surviving kosher fish markets in Chicago, ninety-year-old founder Robert Schuffler, a Latvian immigrant, handed the keys to his protégé and friend, thirty-nine-year-old Mexican American Arturo Venegas. Venegas is now the only Latino owner of a kosher fish market in the city.[9]

Others get really creative. Springfield Smoked Fish, a family-owned kosher fish processor founded in 1934 in Springfield, Massachusetts, "wasn't doing very well" by 2007, admits forty-nine-year-old owner Alan Axler, who had taken over recently from his father. The clientele for his three dozen varieties of smoked fish had aged and moved to Florida, and their children and grandchildren were not as fond of herring and mackerel. Casting about for a way to jump-start his business, Axler turned to the lure of treyf, investing thousands of dollars to develop Brekfish, a bacon substitute made from smoked salmon. He got the idea from the twelve-year-old son of one of his best friends, whose family keeps kosher at home. The boy loved bacon, but his mother would not allow him to eat it, so he asked Axler if there was such a thing as kosher fish bacon.

Axler was intrigued and experimented with recipes until he found something he liked. He test-marketed it locally. People loved the taste but had trouble with the logistics. It came in strips, like regular bacon, and needed to be separated and fried in a skillet. Axler got so many inquiries from kosher-keeping customers unfamiliar with bacon, asking how to cook it, that he decided to sell the product precooked.

His unusual project caught the attention of *Fortune Small Business*, which in 2008 sent three experts to help him market the titillating yet entirely kosher product. A year later, after a website makeover and some fancy new packaging, Axler was ready to make his pitch to Whole Foods, the world's largest retailer of natural, organic, and regional foods. If he can sell nationwide, his fish-processing operation has a chance at a second life, he says hopefully.

Still other independents manage to survive in the neighborhoods where they've always been, although few are sanguine about their prospects. Shlomo Moinzadeh has owned Shlomo's Kosher Meat in Baltimore for twenty-two years. The shop itself is more than one hundred years old and is one of just two kosher butcher shops left in Baltimore, a city that once had more than 120 kosher butchers. Moinzadeh was an engineer in his native Iran but fell into the butcher trade after he fled to the United States following the Islamic revolution in 1978. He doesn't care for the work much, but he had to make a living in his adopted country, and this was available. "It's hard work, very physically difficult," he says. "And the customers—they want this, they don't want it that way—very demanding."

None of his children wants to take over the business. And neither do any of his customers, although he offers it to them regularly. "There's very little money in this," Moinzadeh says.

Baruch Weiss is the owner of East Side Glatt, a kosher butcher shop on Grand Street in Manhattan, the main shopping street of what survives of the Jewish Lower East Side. Founded in the 1930s as I. Goldberg and Sons, it is probably the oldest kosher butcher shop in continuous operation in the United States. Weiss bought it fifteen years ago from its third owner.

"People go to supermarkets. There are not too many of us left," he laments. It's a Thursday afternoon in September, and Weiss is standing behind the counter, bracing himself for the after-work, pre-Sabbath rush. He is an amiable, red-haired Vishnitzer hassid. His father-in-law, a ritual slaughterer, got him into the meat business. His first job was the predawn shift on the receiving dock of a meat warehouse in Midtown.

At East Side Glatt, Weiss buys all the meat personally, grinding, cutting, and trimming it himself. "The older people want to see how I cut the meat," he says. Scrunching up his face in imitation, he cackles, "Trim this, clean that." Six years ago, he bowed to the competition and opened a take-out department, a refrigerated case offering stuffed cabbage, kasha varnishkes, roast chicken, kugel, and other Eastern European dishes.

"The takeout, even the non-Orthodox Jewish people buy," he says. "Most are not frum, but they like to eat kosher food for Shabbos. And now, before the holidays, you see them a lot. They want gefilte fish—we make it here. And they want brisket. Even on Thanksgiving, people who don't eat kosher, they want a kosher turkey." Weiss smiles and shrugs. Whatever the customer wants, it's not for him to argue.

DESPITE THE INCREASE in kosher-certified food products, supermarkets in areas without significant Jewish populations rarely stock food specifically aimed at kosher-keeping customers, except for Jewish holidays. So while observant Jews in Idaho or North Dakota can find plenty of breakfast cereals and canned items that just happen to have kosher certification in their supermarkets, very few of those stores would bother to carry the always more expensive kosher meat and poultry.

Linda Silvern lives in Auburn, Alabama, two hours from the nearest kosher butcher in Atlanta. She and her husband are part of a community of twenty-five Jewish families, just two of whom keep kosher. When her husband began studying for Jewish Renewal rabbinic ordination in 1992, the couple started to keep a kosher-style home, avoiding forbidden meat and shellfish and keeping meat and dairy separate. After his 2002 ordination, they made their kitchen completely kosher. "I said, You can't be a rabbi and not keep kosher," she says. "Anybody you invite has to feel comfortable eating in our home."

For most of their food, Silvern just checks ingredients labels carefully. Because she didn't grow up kosher but consciously chose the practice as an adult after years of watching her husband lead their local congregation, she says she had the opportunity to think the decision through carefully. She decided that she didn't need her food to be certified; she was as good a judge as anyone else of what was acceptable and forbidden. "I understand the desire for those who keep strictly kosher to have everything certified as such, but emotionally and practically, I find it unnecessary," she says. "If foods are certified as vegetarian, why pay extra to have a rabbi periodically show up and say yes, it is also kosher. I believe that each new generation of rabbis has had a need to make the walls higher and higher, whether for their own political reasons or to try to stem assimilation."

But kosher meat, she says, "is in a special category." That's straight from Torah. So the Silverns make the trek to Atlanta every three months to stock up on their meat and poultry.

America's westward migration created the kosher meat supply difficulty. When the West opened up for settlement in the early nineteenth century, Jewish peddlers followed the pioneers, filling their backpacks with tools, sundries, and clothing to sell from homestead to homestead. Keeping kosher on the road was hard for these traveling salesmen. They ate what they could find, supplemented by carefully hoarded stocks of kosher salami and canned fish. Eventually some settled down, married, and had children, building the first small Jewish communities along the mercantile trail, from Missouri to Texas and on to California.

It was difficult for these frontier families to keep kosher if they wanted to keep eating meat. Some gave up and stuck to vegetarian diets. Traveling rabbi-shochtim became a familiar sight. They would go from town to town, leading worship services, conducting weddings, and slaughtering enough chickens, lambs, and cattle to see people through the winter. Jews in out-of-the-way places also depended on the railways for their kosher meat, along with other supplies. When the transcontinental railroad was completed in 1869, kosher meat could be shipped for the first time from the slaughterhouses of the East to the Great Plains and points west. Often it arrived spoiled.

Refrigerated train cars solved that problem, but the logistics remained unwieldy, even after the big slaughterhouses moved to the Midwest to be closer to their source of beef. Seventy-four-year-old

Marvin Strait brought up his children in Lamar, Colorado, a city with no real Jewish population. In the 1950s and '60s, he and his wife would order kosher meat from Adler's, a kosher meat market in Kansas City. The store would put the meat on a train—the main line of the Santa Fe Railroad went through Lamar—and the Straits would pick it up at the local depot. "We had a big freezer, and we'd order every month or two," he recalls.

Everyone who kept kosher in those days had big freezers, says Gary Altman, who is sitting with Strait at a Jewish federation luncheon in Colorado Springs. When Altman and his wife, Jill, moved to the sprawling air force town in 1981, they helped organize a kosher meat co-op with nine or ten other Jewish families. The group ordered meat four times a year from Sinai Foods in Chicago, and Altman remembers that he'd get a call in the morning telling him that the delivery truck was on its way. "It would drop the food at the temple, with everybody's name on their order, and we'd go pick up the boxes before they defrosted," he says.

Today about twenty families in town keep kosher. None of the local supermarkets carries kosher meat. One gets in frozen Empire chicken for Jewish holidays. The co-op disbanded recently, but the Altmans and some of their friends still bulk order from a supermarket in Denver that carries frozen kosher beef. Next week, says Jill, a rabbi who used to serve their congregation is visiting from Denver and has promised to bring them a kosher turkey. "I asked my supermarket to get in kosher meat," she says. "They told me it's too much trouble."

It's not surprising that kosher food is in short supply in rural Alabama or small-town Colorado. But Florida? The 650,000 Jews of South Florida constitute the nation's third-largest Jewish community; the 58,000 Jews in Boynton Beach alone make that city the most densely populated Jewish area outside Israel.[10] But another 80,000 to 100,000 Florida Jews live outside Miami-Dade, Broward, and Palm Beach counties, the epicenter of the state's Jewish population explosion. Many are older, on fixed incomes; for the observant among them, obtaining kosher food is just as difficult as for the Altmans and Silverns.

Those are the people Shalom Dadon of Daytona Beach set out to serve in March 2008, when he launched Kosher on Wheels, his traveling Jewish grocery store. Five or six days a week, the thirty-five-year-old father of four hooks up his truck to a trailer filled with fresh, frozen, and packaged Israeli and Jewish ethnic foods, and sets out for isolated Jewish communities along Florida's northern and western coasts, bringing them goods they cannot find in their local supermarkets. It's a business, but it's also a mitzvah, or good deed, he says. "It was pretty difficult for my wife and me to get kosher food. Imagine what it's like for the elderly people who can't drive to Miami."

By late 2008, Kosher on Wheels was serving two dozen locations. Dadon might find himself driving hundreds of miles a day, depending on the route. Every other Sunday, he crosses the state for a west coast run, hitting Palm Harbor at nine, then heading down to Tampa University, Bradenton, Sarasota, and finishing up in Venice at seven. By the time he gets home, he's been on the road for sixteen hours. He spends an hour or two in each location, parking at a Jewish community center, school, synagogue, or Chabad center. Every three weeks he heads north into Alabama and the Florida Panhandle, making stops at Conservative synagogues in Mobile and Pensacola, and outside a gift shop in Destin, a Panhandle town with too few Jews to support a synagogue.

Today is Thursday, so he sets out from home at 4:00 a.m. for the 265-mile drive to Miami, where he picks up most of his food supplies. Then he heads back north 105 miles to a Chabad center in Palm City, his first stop of the day, arriving at noon. Sharon Kapner is already waiting for him outside her car.

"It's my first visit," she says, as she steps inside the cramped trailer. "I don't keep kosher, but it's for the holidays. My husband just loves stuffed derma and kishka." She picks out frozen packages of those two ethnic delicacies, along with some fresh challah and frozen chicken. "I figure for Shabbos tomorrow, I'll make a nice meal."

Chanukah begins in a week, so Dadon has stocked up on kosher candies and other sweets, including packages of frozen dough for *soufganiot*, Israeli-style Chanukah doughnuts. Dadon grew up in Israel and has modeled his operation after a typical Israeli corner grocery store. Shelves of grocery items line the walls of his trailer: Osem soup mixes, Telma couscous, cans of Beit HaShita pickles, Bissli and Bamba snack packs. Refrigerators and freezer cases are crammed with meat, poultry, and prepared foods. Freshly baked challah and cakes are stacked up in front of open bins of sunflower seeds, which Israelis love to crack between their teeth, spitting out the shells. A pot of thick Turkish coffee is brewing near the door for customers, next to a jar of sugar and a common spoon. Ground beef is his biggest seller, Dadon says, along with cholov Yisroel dairy products for his most observant customers. He has a loyal Israeli clientele, and nonobservant American Jews show up in force before Jewish holidays.

Today is Carol Shapiro's first visit to the traveling store. She and her husband grew up in kosher homes in the Northeast but stopped observing long ago, although they retain a fondness for the Jewish dishes of their youth. They retired five years ago and moved to Palm City from Connecticut. Shapiro's eyes light up when she steps inside the trailer. She walks around slowly, picking up various items, asking what they are, comparing ingredients, reluctant to tear herself away from food that conjures up so many memories.

"This is the food I grew up with," she says quietly. "I miss it." There used to be two kosher butchers in West Palm Beach, a half-hour drive to the south, she says. But that was twenty-five years ago; they're gone now. Her mother buys meat at a kosher butcher in Boynton Beach, but that's too far for her to drive, particularly as she doesn't keep kosher. She just likes the idea of "Jewish" meat on Friday nights. Finally, after nearly an hour in the trailer, she buys derma, frozen potato pancakes, two dozen falafel balls, and dough to prepare soufganiot.

While Shapiro is making her selection, she is watched by Daniella Uminer, who with her husband, Rabbi Shlomo Uminer, runs the Chabad center where the Kosher on Wheels trailer is parked. There are about four thousand Jews in the two nearby counties, but fewer than ten are concerned about kashrut, and only one woman besides the Uminers keeps a kosher home. "I'm worried; I don't know how long he'll keep coming to us," Daniella says. "We're trying to encourage people to buy from him, but for people who don't really keep kosher, it's hard. They want fresh."

Before Dadon started his business, the Uminers would drive an hour and a half to the nearest kosher grocery store in Boca Raton every Friday, taking orders for challah and kosher chicken or meat from other Jewish families in town. "*We* were the Kosher on Wheels," says Rabbi Uminer. "People knew that every Friday I'd drive down and pick it up. I was glad to help them out, especially the older people, who are more into kosher and don't drive so much anymore."

For selfish reasons, the Uminers are happy to see Dadon. They no longer have to truck fresh cholov Yisroel milk and yogurt up from

Miami every week; he brings it right to their door. So it's in their interest, as well as part of their religious mission, to ensure that he has enough business to keep afloat.

"I tell people, the truck is not just if you keep kosher," Daniella says. "One time, instead of shrimp, why don't you try cooking a meal with kosher meat?"

# 8.

# Killing It Softly

*Kosher Meat—Who Makes It, Who Eats It*

THE RAPID EXPANSION of the kosher food market is well documented, but exactly how much kosher food is sold in this country, and who is really buying it?

The most-quoted numbers come from the Mintel International Group, a consumer, media, and market research firm that released its first report on the kosher market in 2003.[1] Its January 2009 report put the country's dedicated kosher market, meaning food purchased because of its kosher symbol, at $12.5 billion, versus $195 billion in annual sales for all products with kosher certification, most of which is purchased by people who don't know or don't care whether a product is kosher.

But Mintel's figures are little more than estimates. Lead researcher Marcia Mogelonsky says it is impossible to get hard data on kosher food sales. Scanner data, which is what such reports usually look at, does not track for kosher versus non-kosher, and no one has the time to go through sales slips from every store in the country. Companies themselves rarely release sales figures, she adds.

For its first kosher report in 2003, Mintel focused on just five food categories—chocolate, candy, crackers, salty snacks, and cookies—and did the painstaking work of comparing sales figures from supermarkets, chains, and drugstores for kosher versus non-kosher products in each category. The result was a clear picture of kosher sales in those five food groups but "useless," Mogelonsky says, in helping to determine the size of the kosher market as a whole. It did not include kosher meat and poultry, a huge part of the market, or kosher wine. Nor did it include sales figures from small kosher stores, convenience stores, kiosks, or vending machines.

Beginning in 2007, Mintel shifted the focus of its research away from how much kosher food is being sold to who is buying it and why. For its January 2009 report, the firm surveyed 2,500 adults in October 2008 about their food-buying habits. Thirteen percent, or 335 respondents, said they regularly buy kosher food. Of those, at least 86 percent are not observant Jews, but that does not mean they are not Jewish. Twenty-five percent said they buy kosher food out of respect for their own or their partner's family traditions, which probably means they *are* Jewish, simply not kosher observant. And more than half said they buy kosher products "occasionally," which Mogelonsky says the researchers chalked up to Passover, Rosh Hashanah, "and when the mother-in-law comes to visit." Holiday shoppers are a big part of the kosher market. Manufacturers of so-called traditional kosher foods, such as matzo and gefilte fish, typically do 40 percent of their business at Passover alone.

But the majority of those who consciously buy kosher food are buying it for other reasons, mainly having to do with health and food safety concerns. This is not new, says Jonathan Sarna of Brandeis University. Non-Jews have been buying kosher meat since late colonial times, believing it to be healthier than non-kosher, he says. Americans in the late nineteenth century who were influenced by the health and wellness diets promoted by Kellogg's, Post, and other emerging food giants also sought out kosher meat and poultry.

Seventeen percent of the 2009 Mintel survey respondents said they buy kosher food because of allergies or food sensitivities, usually to milk. According to a 2002 study at UCLA, between 30 million and 50 million Americans are lactose intolerant, meaning dairy products give them nausea, cramps, bloating, gas, and diarrhea. The condition affects 75 percent of African Americans and 90 percent of Asian Americans. While an ordinary food label might not list minuscule amounts of dairy-based additives, a kosher nondairy label guarantees that the food was not even made on equipment used for dairy.

Thirty percent of the Mintel respondents buy kosher food for religious reasons: 14 percent because they keep kosher, 10 percent because they follow a religion with food laws similar to kashrut, and 6 percent because they observe halal. The largest two groups in that category are Muslims and Seventh-day Adventists. But neither faith group looks for all food to be kosher certified; they just want to make sure they're not eating "unclean" animals.

North America's one million Adventists do not follow the later rabbinic laws of kashrut, explains DeWitt Williams, director of Health Ministries for the Seventh-day Adventist Church North American Division. But they do avoid what he calls "unclean meat," the animals, birds, and fish forbidden in the Torah. "We go by Leviticus eleven and Deuteronomy fourteen," he says. "I'm sixty-nine, and I've never had a ham sandwich or oysters or any of those unclean animals. We're very particular about fins and scales. I've never had catfish."

This restriction is a preference, not a church law. Ultimately, the church wants its members to abstain from meat altogether, as Williams has done since 1983. But for those who can't resist, kosher meat is the recommended option. Processed, precooked meats are the biggest concern, and that's why Adventists patronize kosher delis. "We instruct our members, if you eat a hot dog, eat a kosher hot dog," he says. "We know it won't have bacon, pork, or any other unclean meat mixed in it. Especially with hot dogs, salami, bologna, you don't know what's in them."

Williams believes that most Adventists follow this practice. Even in prison, church members will request a kosher diet to avoid ingesting unclean meat. But now that all-beef hot dogs are more prevalent and ingredients lists are more carefully regulated, he suspects younger church members don't seek out kosher meat as often as their elders did.

The Adventist interest in biblical practice also extends to observing the Sabbath on Saturday rather than Sunday. In February 2009, Edith Martinez opened Abraham's Kosher and Pareve Bakery near Chattanooga after years running a kosher bakery in Miami. Martinez learned the Adventist approach to kosher practice from her husband's family, including abstaining from work on the Sabbath. Her bakery closes before sundown Friday, and not just to please the rabbi who certifies them. "We're not Jewish, but the bakery is shomer Shabbat," Martinez says, using the Hebrew for "Sabbath observant."

Observant Muslims follow halal, a stricter dietary practice than that followed by Seventh-day Adventists, one whose details are outlined in the Koran. *Halal* is Arabic for "fit" or "proper," the same meaning as the Hebrew word *kosher*, but the halal diet is much less complex than kashrut. Except for the absolute ban on alcohol, the laws of halal apply only to meat.

First, halal meat must come from a "clean" animal. The Koran's list of permitted animals is based on the Torah, with some differences. Birds of prey, carnivorous animals, and pigs are banned, as are land animals without external ears, such as reptiles, but all fish, including shellfish, are permitted, and permitted mammals don't have to have split hooves and chew their cud. Gelatin, enzymes, emulsifiers, and other chemically altered food ingredients are *mashboob*, meaning "questionable," and observant Muslims generally avoid them.

A second requirement for halal meat is that it be slaughtered in a specific fashion, again similar to but slightly different from shechita. As with kosher meat, the animals themselves come from the same farms and feedlots as those slaughtered by non-kosher factories—the only thing that makes the meat kosher, or halal, is how the animals are killed.

Kosher slaughter is a highly technical procedure. The shochet must be an observant Jew. He must use a very sharp knife without any nicks, to cause the least pain to the animal. With mammals, the trachea and esophagus must be severed in one continuous motion; with poultry, cutting through one of those two pipes is sufficient. The shochet says the appropriate blessing before slaughtering his first animal or bird, and that blessing suffices for the entire run unless he takes a break, in which case he must repeat the blessing before resuming work. An experienced shochet can slaughter a chicken in a matter of seconds, meaning hundreds of birds can be shechted on the strength of one blessing.

There are many further requirements; for example, the shochet must not hesitate during the cut or apply too much pressure on the knife, and the blade must be exposed during the entire procedure. If any part of the shechita is carried out incorrectly, the carcass is not kosher. Traditionally, a shochet studies and trains at length, and is only permitted to slaughter animals after receiving *kabbalah*, a document from recognized authorities testifying to his skill and piety. In fact, Jewish housewives into the twentieth century would kill their own chickens when a shochet was not available, and in Italy women worked as shochtim until World War II.

Like kosher meat, halal meat comes from a permitted animal whose throat is slit with a sharp knife, allowing the blood to drain out. While it is preferable for the act to be performed by a Muslim, meat slaughtered by any "people of the Book," which includes Jews and Christians, is acceptable to less strict Muslims. That is why many Muslims will eat kosher meat when halal is not available: They know the slaughter is performed by a religious Jew, whereas in non-kosher slaughterhouses people of many faiths, or none, are doing the kills. Shawkat Toorawa, a professor of Arabic literature at Cornell University in Ithaca, New York, says his wife keeps halal, but when they can't get to the nearest halal butcher, who is an hour away, she will buy kosher meat. "She doesn't want to handle non-kosher meat," he says.

The Koran requires that the name of God be pronounced before each slaughter. Many strict Muslims will therefore not eat kosher slaughtered meat or fowl, because only one blessing is said by the shochet at the beginning of a slaughtering session.

Pig is banned in the Torah but is just one of many prohibited species. The Koran, however, singles it out for particular disdain as the most filthy and abhorrent of creatures. The Muslim disgust for pork is visceral, even among the nominally observant. Nouf Al-Qasimi, a twenty-eight-year-old food writer, grew up in her father's native United Arab Emirates but spent summers on Cape Cod with her mother's Lebanese American family. Her memories of those visits "revolve around a trusty backbone of kosher products we were never without in our Muslim household: kosher hot dogs and Hydrox cookies instead of Ball Park franks and Oreos." Her parents do not keep strict halal, but when the family went to Denny's for a meal, they studiously avoided pork. That's why the hot dogs her mother threw in the shopping cart were always kosher—she knew they were all-beef. "My parents would *never* eat pork," Al-Qasimi says. "It's the one thing they're strict on."

Baruch Weiss, owner of East Side Glatt in New York, says 10 percent of the customers at his kosher butcher shop are not Jewish. Some are Muslim. One of his steady customers, an Egyptian Muslim, told Weiss one day that kosher meat was getting so expensive, he was becoming a vegetarian.

In summer 2008, two Middle Eastern men came in and asked if Weiss chopped his own meat. He said he did, and they said they wanted to buy it from him unchopped and vacuum-packed, so they could chop it themselves. They were quite insistent, and eventually told Weiss that they worked for the Secret Service of Dubai and were assigned to a high-ranking sheikh staying at the Waldorf. They told

Weiss they were buying kosher because they couldn't find any halal meat.

Islamic religious authorities grant their followers permission to eat kosher meat grudgingly, and only in places where halal is not available. The world's 1.6 billion Muslims support a global halal market estimated at $632 billion annually, according to *The Halal Journal*. But very little of that is sold in the United States, home to between two million and eight million Muslims.[2]

In 2007, 4,477 new kosher-certified products were launched in this country, compared with just 15 new halal products.[3] There are fewer than sixty halal certifiers in North America, compared with hundreds of kosher certifiers, and most of them certify food for export to Arab countries. And while frozen kosher meat and poultry have been available in American supermarkets for decades, the first halal meat showed up only in 2004, and in very few stores. Retail establishments that offer halal food are limited to cities with large Muslim populations like Dearborn, Michigan, where a McDonald's franchise began selling halal Chicken McNuggets in September 2000. Within a year sales had doubled, an increase fueled almost entirely by the halal meals.

Slowly, the domestic halal industry is growing. Muhammad Munir Chaudry, head of the Islamic Food and Nutrition Council of America, says the Muslim community in the United States is sixty years behind the Jewish community in terms of having its dietary needs recognized, but he promises it won't take them sixty years to catch up. He insists there is no longer a need for any Muslim in the United States to seek out kosher meat, since halal is so much more available. In the early 1970s, there was just one halal store in Chicago; today, he says, there are nearly one hundred. In 2006, the World Ethnic Market show in Anaheim, California, featured both halal and kosher-certified food products in what organizers claimed was the nation's first trade show to pair the two. About three dozen Albertsons in Southern California now carry frozen halal chicken and beef, and several sell chicken nuggets certified as halal and kosher.[4]

Chaudry disputes the results of the Mintel reports, saying they inflate the number of non-Jews who buy kosher food. The people who pay for these surveys want to persuade more food manufacturers to seek kosher certification and more stores to carry their products, he charges. "The kosher organizations have to promote their business. The number of Jewish consumers is not growing, so they try to say that Muslims buy it, Hindus buy it, vegetarians buy it, people who have allergies buy it. I don't give too much credence to surveys like that."

One area where halal is making inroads is on the college campus. More than one hundred North American campuses offer full or partial kosher dining plans. Not only do many Muslim students eat these meals, but a handful of schools have created joint halal-kosher dining programs, usually adding halal to a preexisting kosher plan.

The California Institute of Technology in Pasadena created its kosher meal plan in 1998 to keep a promising Orthodox graduate student from defecting to the Massachusetts Institute of Technology, which had a large kosher dining program. Three years later the school got Sunni certification for its kosher kitchen from the Islamic Center of Southern California; the Sunni students agreed to eat kosher meat. In 2003, however, Caltech added a separate halal kitchen that served halal-slaughtered meat to the school's more observant Shiite Muslims. Joel Weinberger, executive kosher chef and director of the school's kosher and halal dining programs, says only a handful of students patronize either option. In 2009, two people signed up for the kosher meals and six for the halal.

The main problem kosher kitchens face when they try to serve Muslim students is avoiding any ingredients with even a trace of alcohol, a list that includes vanilla extract, balsamic vinegar, and a host of other flavorings and condiments. "We have wine available for Shabbat, but it makes the Muslim students uncomfortable, so we keep it in storage and bring it out on demand," Weinberger says.

The perception that a halal option is simply an add-on to a kosher meal plan can keep Muslims away. At Cornell University, school officials took over a preexisting kosher dining program in 2001 and tried to re-create it as a multicultural option. They went through hoops to appeal to Muslim students, avoiding all alcohol and ingredients containing alcohol and changing the meal plan's name from the Kosher Dining Program to the more generic 104-West, after the building in which it was located. But Professor Toorawa, who doubles as advisor for the school's Muslim students, says he doesn't know any Muslims who eat there.

"It's perceived as a Jewish space," he says. "It started out as a kosher dining hall, they have Sabbath dinners on Friday evening, and it's closed on Jewish holidays." There are very few practicing Muslims at Cornell versus the school's 3,500 Jewish students, he adds. Those who do care about halal tend to eat from a kosher dining station elsewhere on campus that is part of a food court that focuses on many ethnic cuisines and has no particularly Jewish atmosphere. And because so few of the Muslims at Cornell are observant, he says, most are happy eating in any dining hall and sticking to fish or vegetarian meals.

At some schools, a kosher-halal dining plan can foment interfaith dialogue. In 2007, a Caltech transfer student from the American University in Beirut came to Weinberger's office to inquire about halal options on campus. "She took one look at me and walked out," says Weinberger, who wears a yarmulke. "I heard her in the hall saying, 'He doesn't look like the right person,' and someone said, 'No, he's the guy you need to talk to.'" The student came back in, introduced herself, and the two had what Weinberger describes as a friendly discussion of her dietary needs. "I told her we'd take care of it," he says. "She said she'd never met a Jew before, and it was a very good experience how I treated her."

At some campuses, a kosher-halal dining program is created when smaller, separate dining plans are combined. That happened at Mount Holyoke College in 2000. According to Howard Blas, who wrote about the project for *The Jerusalem Report*, the Jewish students at this small Massachusetts school agreed to forgo dishes prepared with wine, which would violate the Islamic prohibition on alcohol, and the Muslim students agreed to eat kosher meat rather than demanding halal slaughter.[5]

Some schools with neither dining option decide to create a joint program from the start. At Dartmouth College in Hanover, New Hampshire, where all students must sign up for a meal program, college officials realized in 2000 that theirs was the only Ivy League school without a kosher dining option. Wanting to attract more Jewish students, they announced that one would be established. A group of Muslim students requested a halal program be set up as well. In 2001 the college built three kosher kitchens—for meat, dairy, and pareve— and a separate halal kitchen in the middle of the busiest food court on campus. Manager Robert Lester says that by 2009 the two programs were serving eight hundred meals a day on a campus with four thousand undergraduates.

His biggest challenge is ensuring a steady supply of meat. "The students begged us not to limit them to a vegetarian option, but it's very hard to find kosher and halal meat in Hanover," he says.

HANOVER'S supermarkets, like those in Boise and Colorado Springs, may not be well stocked with kosher meat, but they are increasingly in the minority as the kosher industry continues to swell. And as more kosher-friendly supermarkets, served by the growing kosher industrial slaughterhouse system, changed the shopping habits of kosher consumers and forced independent butchers and grocery stores to shut down, they also changed the lives of rabbis and shochtim.

Through much of the past century, local shechita was the norm. It was actually protected in many cities to help local vendors. In the nineteenth and early twentieth centuries, kosher meat coming into New York City from outside slaughterhouses was sometimes declared non-kosher by city rabbis, although those bans never lasted long. The advent of refrigerated train cars and the growing power of the national certification agencies, which observant Jews began to trust more often than their local rabbis, signaled the demise of local shechita, beginning midcentury on the East Coast and moving slowly westward.

"There used to be shechita in every neighborhood," says Moshe Yurman, a former New York shochet. "It all stopped. Now it's outsourcing, going to South America, to Uruguay; there are even shochtim going to Manchuria to shecht for Israel. It's easier to fly out a crew of people than to do it locally."

When Rabbi Jacob Traub arrived in San Francisco in 1966, all the kosher meat and poultry for sale in the city was slaughtered locally. He and his fellow pulpit rabbis either did or supervised the work. On Mondays they would slaughter beef and lamb at Allen's, a large slaughterhouse on the waterfront where AT&T Park, home of the San Francisco Giants, stands today. The meat was sold through three kosher butcher shops.

For poultry, Jewish shoppers would go to Israel's Kosher Meat Market in downtown San Francisco, a mall with half a dozen kosher purveyors. They would choose their live chicken, and the butcher would shecht it on the spot. Traub remembers women bringing their slaughtered chickens to him for examination. "They'd bring them right here to the synagogue, upstairs to my office," he says. "They'd lay them out on my desk, entrails and all, and say, this doesn't look good; the gallbladder is more greenish than it should be. And I would have to decide if the chicken was kosher or not. To me this was a little bit alien, but I knew the rules and regulations, at least from books. So here I got the hands-on."

Local slaughter of both meat and poultry in San Francisco stopped around 1976, Traub remembers, when supermarkets began carrying frozen Empire chicken and, later, frozen kosher beef. No one brings chickens to his office anymore. He doubts that any rabbis younger than himself would know how to handle such a situation.

Retired Brooklyn shochet Laibl Posner remembers back further than Traub. He learned to shecht as a yeshiva student in Crown Heights in the 1940s. Many young Lubavitchers did the same, he says, to equip themselves with a wide range of Jewish skills as part of their mission to spread Judaism. Until the late 1940s, a large slaughterhouse called New York Butchers stood in Midtown Manhattan on the East River, on the present site of the United Nations building. On days when it was taken over for kosher slaughter, up to twenty shochtim would work there at once. Posner and his yeshiva buddies would sometimes be permitted to watch them work, the closest they got to hands-on experience until their teachers felt they were ready.

Posner shechted his first cow in 1949, at the age of nineteen. That was the year he received his kabbalah. He spent all summer practicing in his hometown of Pittsburgh, helped by his father, who was also a shochet. "He taught me at home," Posner recalls. "There was a chicken market in Pittsburgh. He used to go, buy some chickens, and shecht them for us for dinner." Posner would hang around the kosher butchers at the market, and when a non-Jew bought a chicken, the shochet would let him kill it, knowing that if the young man made a kashrut mistake, it wouldn't matter. Posner still teaches yeshiva students how to shecht if they call and ask. He takes them to a non-kosher chicken slaughterhouse in Brooklyn, buys a bird, takes it out back, and goes through the procedure until they can do it themselves.

"The hardest thing to learn is the grip," he says, demonstrating in pantomime in his Brooklyn dining room. Pretending to have a chicken wedged under his left armpit, he grabs its imaginary neck with his left hand, pulling the head back so the trachea and esophagus are fully extended. That frees the right hand, which holds the *halaf*, or shechting knife. The halaf should be twice as long as the width of the animal's neck, to ensure that one quick back-and-forth motion is enough to sever the required pipes. "If you shecht properly, there's a minimum of pain," he insists.

In 1951, Posner accepted a position as rabbi and shochet for the tiny Jewish community of Marinette, Wisconsin. He stayed for three years, filling the Jewish needs of even smaller populations in the surrounding region. A couple of times a month he would drive north to Iron Mountain, Michigan, to teach Torah to the adults and Hebrew to the children, and to shecht whatever animals they needed.

This was how Jewish communities existed outside the major cities. But by the time Posner took that job, the landscape was already changing. "Before the war, just about every town had a shochet," he says. "Maybe not a rabbi, but definitely a shochet, who was usually the cantor, too. Then Empire came in, they sold it all prepared, and people bought it. Young people moved out of the small towns, and the Jewish communities couldn't support a shochet any longer." Even the large slaughterhouses worked differently. Outside New York, a slaughterhouse would receive an order from a kosher butcher for a certain number of animals, and the shochet would show up and shecht them. It was all done to order. Today slaughterhouses produce as much as they think they can sell.

Rabbi Dovid Steigman, one of ten rabbinic coordinators at the OK kosher agency in Brooklyn, worked as a shochet from the early 1970s until the mid-1980s. Starting at a slaughterhouse in York, Nebraska, he moved to one in Rochester, New York, and finally spent ten years at Falls Poultry, also in upstate New York. All three places have since closed.

There was a lot more kosher beef slaughtered in those years, Steigman says. In the early 1970s, at the peak of the market, there were four or five kosher slaughterhouses in Sioux City, Iowa, another two or three in Omaha, and at least one in Missouri. They were enormous operations. One facility in Spencer, Iowa, used to slaughter 1,000 to

1,500 head of beef a day, more than all the kosher slaughterhouses in the country today combined.

Unlike Posner, Steigman didn't choose to become a shochet. In 1971, after graduation from yeshiva, he went to Mexico City to work as a teacher and Torah scribe. He learned to shecht in order to make a living. He finished his training in Nebraska and settled into the life of what was then a well-paid profession with job security. The shochtim's union was very active; as late as 1970, it supported eighty retired slaughterers on pension.[6] "Nowadays, shochtim don't make the kind of money we used to make," Steigman says. "We were part of the Teamsters. If someone misbehaved, his trucks disappeared. If you really misbehaved, you were locked in a cooler."

A shochet's work is not pleasant. The Talmud teaches that a person chooses the career that suits his or her innermost nature, so a shochet must be sublimating some sort of bloodlust. Killing chickens is one thing—they go by so fast, hundreds an hour, that it quickly becomes a blur. But slaughtering a full-grown steer requires looking it in the eye and running a knife across its neck with tremendous speed and accuracy. There is a lot of blood, a lot of noise, and a lot of physical exertion.

Steigman is a kindly, soft-spoken man, not the sort you'd imagine enjoys killing animals. That's not why he did it. He did it for the money, first of all—with a wife and children to support, the paycheck was hard to beat. But he also found great personal satisfaction in bringing Torah down to earth, fulfilling what he learned in such a practical way. "Providing kosher meat for people is a tremendous thing," he says. "If people eat kosher, it affects their davening, the way they make a living, everything. It's a very satisfying thing to give people authentic kosher food."

Rabbi Seth Mandel oversees all the OU-certified kosher slaughterhouses in North and South America. About 90 percent of the glatt kosher beef produced in the United States is under the OU. He is also in charge of approving and firing those slaughterhouses' shochtim, whose work he checks during surprise visits. "Shochtim don't get any respect," he notes. "People look at them like, How can you go into this dirty line of business? But it's not only a necessary business, because Jews want to eat meat, it's a holy business. A shochet should do it saying, God commanded us concerning the proper way to slaughter animals, and I want to do God's will. He should be conscious of the fact that he answers to a higher authority. It's not me he should be worried about; he should be worried about the Guy Upstairs who's looking over his shoulder."

That's how Moshe Yurman feels about his *halafim*. Yurman is one of just three men in North America who make the ritual knives used in kosher slaughter, and he treats his work as a holy art. Each halaf is made by hand, usually from stainless steel. While Yurman won't say how many he produces a year in his Brooklyn basement or how long it takes to make one, he does say that the best halafim can cost $1,800 or more, and their working life rarely extends beyond five years.

Halafim used to be made of high-carbon steel, which is easy to sharpen to a very fine edge but rusts easily and is more fragile than stainless. Stainless steel was a 1950s innovation. Until a century ago, most halafim were converted from ordinary commercial knives, refashioned to a shochet's specifications. All knives were handmade in those days, he notes, so shochtim just had to find a good blacksmith to work with. Barbers' straight-edge razors were good for making into halafim for chickens, as they are about the same five inches in length.

As the machine-made knife industry developed, these sources for halafim disappeared. When Yurman went into the field in the 1980s, he started out reshaping kitchen knives into halafim. As he grew more experienced, he began working from scratch. As good as the best commercial knives are, he says, the companies make them to wear out, so they have to be replaced more often than a shochet would like.

A shochet grows very attached to his halafim, because they're expensive and because they have to fit the hand so precisely. Most shochtim are so used to their own that they will never borrow a colleague's. "A shochet is married to his halaf," says Mandel. "You get used to its feel; you get used to how it sharpens; you get used to how you work the blade. You want a halaf that is like an extension of your hand, so you are thinking about the chicken and not the halaf. You don't want the shochet thinking about anything except killing the animal quickly, according to Jewish law."

Shochtim will usually keep two, three, or four halafim in working condition and tend to hold on to them after they wear out, often bequeathing them to their sons and grandsons. Many shochtim collect antique halafim; it's a point of pride to compare collections, to see which have the most elegantly carved handles or most unusual shapes.

Yurman has an extensive collection of vintage halafim and is happy to show off a selected few to visitors, laying them out on his dining room table. "This is an old European knife used for lamb or goat, or maybe a very small calf," he says, running his finger along the shank of a twelve-inch knife, a length rarely seen today. It has a beautifully carved bone handle that has been eaten by worms over the years. A halaf blade cannot have any mark or nick on it, so halaf makers use the handle to express their artistry, often putting their mark on a brass bolster attached to the handle to indicate who made it.

"And here's an even nicer one," he continues, taking a small hinged knife with a bone handle out of a dark wood box. "It's German made, at least one hundred years old, high carbon, well polished when it was made, and well taken care of so it didn't discolor. It was very rarely used; you can see that." He turns to a third halaf, much longer than the first two, a full two feet in length and very heavy, more than two and a half pounds. It has a black handle made of ebony, hand-worked with a crosshatch pattern to give it a better grip. "This was definitely made for beef," he says. "You can see the patina on it, from the rust." A long halaf was more useful in past decades, when cattle were slaughtered by the shackle-and-hoist method, a technique now forbidden in the United States whereby the live animal was hoisted by its hind legs and the shochet had to jump in and out quickly when he was slaughtering to avoid injury. Every extra inch of blade gave him more time to get out of the way.

The men who make halafim jealously guard the sources of their steel, as the number of foundries doing custom work declines every year. Yurman does not travel to factories to choose his product; instead, he researches high-grade stainless steel available to the custom knife market online and in trade publications. Currently he prefers European steel, especially Swedish. But the ordering is hit or miss. "You buy some, try it, and sometimes you fall on your face," he says. "There's constant ongoing development of steel in the trade—Is it too brittle? How long can it hold an edge? Is it resistant to corrosion?—all the things a knife needs."

Once he settles on a particular steel, he buys five hundred to one thousand pounds at a time in raw sheets that are at least ten feet long and about a foot wide. For a halaf destined to be used on cattle, he cuts out a piece twenty-four inches long and twenty-seven inches wide. The shank, or blade, of the finished halaf would usually be eighteen to twenty inches long, not including the handle.

First he drills a hanging hole in the steel and heat-treats it in a furnace. The next step is grinding the shank to create a bevel from the spine to the edge of the blade. That's done by machine, and he usually sends the job out to plants that have paper-knife machines, used in the book industry to trim the edges of pages. The raw piece of steel is placed on a magnetic bed and held in place by the magnetic pull while stones move back and forth across it to create the bevel. The steel rests in a water-and-oil emulsion to remain cool. It's a delicate procedure: If the machine works too quickly, the steel can heat up enough to bend or buckle, and the blade is ruined.

From grinding, the halaf goes to polishing. Yurman uses a belt grinder for his polishing, to bring the steel to a mirror finish. He sells his halafim fully sharpened but not nick-free. A shochet will resharpen his halaf to his own preference; some prefer a sharper edge, while others feel that makes the blade harder to check and more subject to nicks. A shochet checks his knife for nicks between every large animal, and every fifteen to twenty minutes when slaughtering poultry. There is no law prescribing this; it's purely a financial consideration. If a nick is discovered in the blade, every animal slaughtered since the previous check is no longer kosher. Fifteen or twenty minutes' worth of chickens is a lot less expensive than losing even two head of cattle.

Like everything else in the kosher food industry, the history of the halaf is not free of politics. At one time it was at the center of a bitter struggle pitting hassidim against their rabbinic opponents, the *misnagdim*. In the late eighteenth century, a new technology for making the blade of a halaf emerged in Germany. The way Seth Mandel tells it, the news spread to Eastern Europe, where Rabbi Dov Ber of Mezeritch, who in 1760 succeeded the Baal Shem Tov as leader of the fledgling hassidic movement, seized upon the new halaf as a way to separate his hassidim from other Jews and unite them as a group. Mandel says Dov Ber directed hassidic shochtim to adopt this new technology, and led them to believe that shechita performed with the old halaf was invalid. "The reason for a lot of the rancor between the hassidim and misnagdim was conflict over this new knife technology," Mandel maintains. "It was done purely for political reasons. It became a huge brouhaha and led to civil war inside the community."

All shochtim use the same kind of halafim today; it is no longer a political issue. Other conflicts have taken its place. When Yurman, Posner, and Steigman were working as shochtim, there were many kosher slaughterhouses and most shochtim had full-time jobs. Today most depend on contract work, and because of industry consolidation and better shipping methods, fewer shochtim are needed. As more and more Orthodox American men opt for "white collar" professions, the field is increasingly left to hassidim.

That doesn't mean non-hassidic Orthodox don't want to become shochtim, Yurman says. But the rightward shift of the Orthodox community as a whole, and its growing preference for *hassidishe shechita*, or slaughter performed by hassidic Jews, makes it increasingly difficult for non-hassidic shochtim to find work. There is no difference in technique, he points out. It's all about image, the notion that a more observant-looking shochet will be less likely to cut religious corners. Companies use that belief to advertise their meat as "more kosher" than the competition's—reasoning that makes less sense as almost every kosher slaughterer now uses hassidishe shechita. But not having that stamp on one's meat can hurt a company's bottom line.

"When a company can advertise 'hassidishe shechita,' it's sellable in the Five Towns as well as Williamsburg, but if you can't advertise that, you can sell in the Five Towns but not Williamsburg," Yurman explains, using the heavily hassidic Brooklyn neighborhood of Williamsburg to epitomize the captive market represented by all hassidim, the fastest-growing segment of the Jewish population. Why should a kosher meat operation limit its sales by hiring a non-hassidic shochet, when for the same money it can hire a hassidic shochet, whose meat is acceptable to all Orthodox Jews?

"It's the companies that invented the term 'hassidishe shechita,'" Yurman charges. "They invented the premium price for it; they invented the need for it. You can't do a Passover program today without cholov Yisroel, without a *daf yomi* [daily page of Talmud study], without hassidishe shechita. The whole community is on the march to the right, and it affects every part of the industry, not just the beef."

# 9.

# Please Don't Eat the Broccoli

## Bug Infestation Takes Salad Off the Table

AT 8:30 A.M., Rabbi Meir Waks pulls up outside Dougie's, a kosher barbecue restaurant on the outskirts of Brooklyn's Borough Park neighborhood. He sits inside his three-wheeled cart to finish a cigarette—it's been a long night, much of it spent patrolling the streets with a Neighborhood Watch group. After a final drag, Waks steps out of the vehicle, flips through a heavy key ring hanging from his belt loop, unlocks and lifts the metal grill protecting the storefront, and opens the door.

As Dougie's main mashgiach, thirty-year-old Waks is the first person inside every morning. At night, either he or the afternoon mashgiach is the last to leave, turning off all the pilot lights and making sure everything is locked up. They are the only people who have keys to the place, a requirement of kosher supervision. Not even the owners can get in without them.

Dougie's doesn't open until lunch, so Waks has about an hour before the rest of the staff arrives. He takes that time to call in to his rabbinic supervisor at the OU, turn on the convection ovens and the pilot lights, and walk through his stockroom, freezer, and refrigerators, taking note of what needs to be reordered. Canned tomatoes, check. Beef ribs, check. Seasoned salt, check.

He readies the eggs for the day, breaking six dozen into a large bowl and inspecting them for blood spots that would render them nonkosher. If it's a busy morning and he doesn't have time, he'll let one of the non-Jewish staff break the eggs, but then he has to trust that worker to call him over each time he sees a suspicious red dot. That's asking a lot of cooks who are always under pressure, so to encourage them to stop and alert him, he pays a dollar for each blood spot they find. One guy made $50 a week that way.

The money comes out of his salary, but Waks takes the religious ramifications of his job very seriously. He has a friendly, easy way with the staff, but he—and they—never forget that he's there to watch them. The restaurant's meat is kept in a locked freezer, and all the liquor is shut up in Waks's office overnight. A security camera records everything that goes on in the kitchen, and Waks does spot checks on the tapes. Twice they helped him catch workers sneaking in their own beer, which the kashrut agencies do not allow. The men were fired.

At 9:30 a.m., he heads downstairs to the prep kitchen, heaves a large plastic tub of celery onto one of the stainless-steel counters, and starts looking for bugs.

Checking fresh vegetables for bug infestation is the most time-consuming part of a restaurant mashgiach's job. First, Waks sets up his light table, covering it with plastic wrap so water from the wet produce doesn't get inside. Then he takes a stalk of celery, cuts off the leafy top, and throws it away. It's too hard to clean the tops, he explains. Bugs hide in the soft leafy folds and have to be lured out by soaking in a mixture of water and vinegar—not too much vinegar, he cautions, or the vegetable will become marinated. The procedure is not worth the time in the fast-paced world of an urban restaurant.

He holds the stalk in his left hand under a stream of water, slowly running his right forefinger down the entire length, front and back. Then he places it on the light box, and looking through a jeweler's loupe, inspects it with the utmost care. The bugs most often found in celery are brown aphids that bore their way into the vegetable's flesh and follow the lines of the stalk, leaving pencil-thin light brown trails. To the untrained eye, the trails look just like the celery's natural ridges, or perhaps some slight discoloration. It takes long practice and hawk-like vision to pick out the slight wavering that indicates the lines were made by a crawling insect.

Waks inspects a dozen stalks before settling on one that has a shaky, barely visible beige trail about an inch long down one side. He runs his finger along the marking and carefully inserts the tip of a small sharp knife at one end to see whether the bug is still there. It's not, so he cuts away that part of the stalk and throws the rest into the soup pot. The next two stalks have tiny live bugs, barely discernible, but enough for him to reject the entire vegetable.

At the end of an hour, Waks has cleaned enough celery for the day's soup, throwing away close to one-third of what he started with. "That's pretty clean," he says. Sometimes he has to discard half or more of the raw produce he cleans. "That's how they tell us to do it," he says with a shrug. "You just follow the rules, even if you don't always know why."

Waks is lucky he works in a restaurant that specializes in barbecue. In restaurants that serve a lot of salads, the mashgiach can spend hours every morning poring over frisée, parsley, chives, and mushrooms, washing, checking, rewashing, rechecking, cutting away, and throwing out. The average head of lettuce contains as many as thirty thrips and aphids, according to one kosher expert. Not only is this mind-numbing work, it can add plenty of zeros to the cost of a kosher event.

Separating milk and meat and avoiding prohibited foods such as pork and shellfish are the most well-known and widely observed kosher laws. Few nonobservant Jews, and virtually no non-Jews, know that Jewish law also forbids ingesting the insects that lurk in fruits and vegetables. What could be problematic about strawberries? Or broccoli? They seem the most innocuous of foods.

They are not, at least not to an observant Jew. While all vegetables and fruits are inherently kosher, the bugs they attract are not. The Torah warns against consuming insects no less than fifteen times. Jews may not eat an insect that crawls. They may not eat an insect that flies. They may not eat an insect that floats on the water. Chomping down on a piece of curly lettuce that has a bug hiding in its folds could put a Jew in violation of four, five, or more Torah prohibitions, depending on the species and on whether the bug is dead or alive.[1]

"Actually, insects are more unkosher than pork," says Rabbi Yochanan Friedman, who works as a mashgiach for several food-manufacturing plants and prisons near his home in Santa Cruz, California. "The Torah emphasizes the prohibition against eating creepy-crawly things much more often than pork. If you eat a ham sandwich, it's one violation. If you eat a bag of lettuce without washing it, you could be eating many, many bugs."

The prohibition derives from the Torah, but the strictness with which the law is observed is relatively recent, dating back just a few decades to America's ban on DDT use in agriculture. DDT may present serious health hazards to humans, but it does a bang-up job of killing bugs. The increased popularity of organic produce, which is grown entirely without pesticides, adds further to the infestation problem, rabbis say, making today's fruits and vegetables more bug-ridden, and potentially more unkosher, than ever. The problem doesn't affect kosher homemakers overmuch; they can serve whatever they want, so long as they wash and examine all produce carefully. But it has made kosher supervision of prepared foods, manufacturing and packing plants, catered events, restaurants, and other retail food establishments much more complicated and has added greatly to the mashgiach's workload.

"It is taking the mashgiach away from his primary responsibilities and turning him into a lettuce washer," says Rabbi Yakov Vann of the Los Angeles–based Rabbinical Council of California.

Rabbi Yosef Eisen, head of the Vaad HaKashrus of the Five Towns and Far Rockaway in New York, is a national expert on the kosher problems of bug infestation. He was part of the original team that the OU asked in the 1980s to collect data about just how infested America's produce had become. The team's research found that certain fruits and vegetables, because of their shape and attractiveness to bugs, tended to become so infested that they required special attention or should not be eaten at all. Oranges, winter squash, and other fruits and vegetables that are peeled before eating were fine to eat, as were hard, smooth vegetables such as carrots and green beans that only require a thorough washing. But romaine lettuce, with its sweet taste and tightly folded leaves, must be washed by hand with soap, leaf by leaf, and held up to the light for careful examination. Asparagus, cauliflower, and broccoli must be washed under a strong stream of water and vigorously swished in a bowl of water. Brussels sprouts, dill, curly parsley, watercress, strawberries, raspberries, blackberries, and wild blueberries can require more work than they're worth, so they have become cuisine non grata in kosher kitchens, particularly at the commercial level.

Kosher authorities announced these new restrictions, which upset many Orthodox Jews. "There was a tremendous amount of resistance in the beginning," Eisen recalls. "People said, 'How can you say there are insects in the lettuce? My grandmother wore a *sheitel* [wig] down to her nose, and she ate parsley and dill and broccoli. She never saw any problems. This must be something contrived by the ultra-Orthodox rabbis just to scam us.'"

The agencies realized it would take hard numbers and an outreach campaign to win over the kosher public. In 1992, the OU gave Eisen a $20,000 grant to hire mashgichim in New York, New Jersey, Florida, and California to collect data on a wide variety of the most problematic fruits and vegetables over a two-year period. They kept track of which kinds of insects they found, how many, where they tended to be lodged, how deeply they bored, and how best they could be removed.

One mashgiach examined cabbage in a New Jersey coleslaw plant every week for two years, checking one hundred heads per visit. Eventually he recognized a pattern: Infestation was greater in certain months than in others, cabbage attracted thrips rather than aphids or mites, and the thrips generally were found in the first seven leaves. From this information, the OU developed a policy of checking the first three or four leaves of a cabbage head. If those are completely bug-free, there is a 90 percent chance that the rest of the head is clean, and the entire cabbage may be used.

The 90 percent figure is a halachic leniency. It is impossible to guarantee that no insects have infested a given amount of produce, and Jewish law prohibits a Jew only from knowingly ingesting an insect. To that end, the major kosher certification agencies developed rules stating that only those fruits and vegetables with a significant probability of infestation needed to be checked.

Persuading the kosher public came next. The OU, OK, Star-K, Kof-K, and other kashrut authorities put out consumer guides to checking and cleaning the most common fruits and vegetables. The information is posted online and continually updated, as standards change and different years produce more or less infestation of particular crops.

Not only do standards change, different rabbis have different standards for the same product. Strawberries were declared particularly problematic in 2007, when that year's crop was found to be unusually infested. The announcement produced something of a panic. Kosher caterers quickly removed the offending fruit from their menus, and kashrut agencies upgraded their policies for checking and cleaning strawberries. Some rabbinic authorities advised soaking them in warm, soapy water for three minutes before rinsing and cutting off the leafy tops. Others said soaking was not necessary and that the berries should be washed and then rinsed three times under steadily flowing water. Some agencies advised peeling each berry and then washing, as the tiny white bugs that attack strawberries are particularly difficult to see.

And still others, including the kosher committees in Lakewood and Brooklyn, banned the use of fresh strawberries entirely.

Ultimately, it's up to the individual to decide how strict he or she wants to be. Rabbi Friedman says he eats strawberries in his own home, but washes and checks each one before putting it in his mouth. "Cutting off the tops only helps a little," he says. "It's not really where the bugs hang out. All the bugs I have found on strawberries have been around the seeds." Once, Friedman relates, he was visiting a mashgiach friend who checks strawberries commercially. The friend was about to dive into a plate of fresh strawberries for lunch when Friedman suggested they try an experiment. Friedman picked three berries at random and found live bugs crawling around on two of them.

Still, he says, these things need to be taken in stride. "The truth is, people eat bugs all the time without realizing it. If that really grosses you out, better sleep with a mask. You can get neurotic about it, but there's no point. The question is, how far should you go to make sure you're not eating something non-kosher?"

Pretty far, says Freyde Ilowitz, a hassidic mother of eight who lives in the Williamsburg section of Brooklyn. She has made it her mission to warn observant Jews about the spiritual dangers they face every time they sit down to a salad. She began her work in the early 2000s, lecturing in Yiddish and English to Jewish day schools and adult groups in the Greater New York area.

As a hassid, Ilowitz holds a kabbalistic view that suggests that people appropriate the behaviors and personality traits of the animals they eat. "At each presentation I talk about what happens to a person's *neshama* [soul] when the bugs go in," she says. "When it goes into a person, it becomes part of the person. All of the bad character traits of that insect, like the ones that go into a field and eat up all the crops, also go into the person, and you can't get rid of it. It enters the bloodstream and your blood becomes poisoned. It's the only transgression in the Torah that takes over your heart; the heart becomes clogged and you can't learn Torah."

Ilowitz is deeply alarmed by this scenario. She has put together a video that she takes with her to lectures, a forty-five-minute examination of fruits, vegetables, and grains, and the bugs that love them. It opens with a baby boy sitting in a high chair and Ilowitz's voice-over asking whether the parents in her audience want to "poison this precious soul" by feeding him non-kosher food.

From there commences a parade of horrors sure to delight any seven-year-old boy. Onions are infested with thrips. Rice hides weevils and beetles. Cherries are filled with worms. Broccoli and cauliflower are so ridden with aphids, thrips, spider mites, and other insects that washing, soaking, even burning over an open flame aren't enough—the florets have to be cut off and only the stalks can be used. Scallions, leeks, raspberries, and blackberries shouldn't be eaten at all. There are close-ups of spider mites oozing out of dried apricots, beetles burrowing into dates, and maggots crawling in people's dinner plates.

Here's what the video says about figs:

> Figs are very problematic. They are extremely infested with wasps and other insects. You need to be a real expert to know how to inspect them. Figs from California are usually cleaner. Figs from Turkey should not be used at all. With dried figs, the way to inspect them is, cut them in two and then turn every piece inside out. With fresh figs you need to check carefully because the white insects are very similar to the fibers of the fig. If you see one bug, do not use that fig. If you don't see anything you should put the fig into a glass bowl with water and check to see that no white insects float to the top. Then wait a few minutes and put the glass bowl on a black object. If you see white insects, don't use it.
>
> On figs you'll find a round hole on the other side from the stem. There you might find a black wasp that is very small, approximately one millimeter. You should cut out that piece from the top because it's very hard for the human eye to see if the wasp is there. For those who are not experts and want to eat figs, there's an easy way out—just scrape out with a spoon all the seeds from the inside and discard, then wash the peel with warm water, rubbing it with your hands. When you examine a fig you should do it with the attitude, "The fig I am about to inspect has bugs; I just have to find them."

It's not easy to eat in Ilowitz's world, something she freely acknowledges. But the zeal and passion with which she approaches her work come from a deep, heartfelt belief that this is what God demands of the observant Jew. She is a gentle woman with a ready smile who welcomes a stranger into her home with cookies and tea even as toddlers are grabbing her ankles and she's trying to cook her Friday night meal while advising a teenage son what to pack for a Shabbat trip.

In 2004, Ilowitz wrote a book based on her video, in Yiddish with full-color illustrations. She hopes to begin lecturing at non-hassidic Jewish schools and perhaps release her book in English. The standards will be more lenient in that version, she says. Few non-hassidic Jews will go to the trouble of cutting nuts in half to look for insects, a difference she accepts. The main point is to keep as many Jews as she can from eating insects.

"I'm happy if I can help another Jew stop eating broccoli and cauliflower," she says, nodding her head with conviction.


A *humra* is a stringency, a practice of observing Jewish law according to a strict understanding of that law. As the rabbinic discussions in the Talmud illustrate, the Torah's commandments and prohibitions have to be interpreted in order to come up with standards of observance. And no two rabbis interpret alike. Those who approach the Torah more broadly dictate observance practices that are more lenient, more forgiving of human weakness. Rabbis who take a more narrow view of the Torah, and who demand more of themselves and their followers, come up with standards and practices that are rife with humras.

In early-twentieth-century America, Jewish observance was much less strict than it is today. The Jewish immigrants who left their homes in Europe and the Russian Pale were rarely the most religious of their compatriots. They were the wanderers and the seekers, pioneers ready to tackle an unknown world and make their living in a foreign, non-Jewish society. If that meant cutting off their side curls, ditching the sheitel, and giving up or seriously modifying their kashrut, that was part of the price of the adventure. This changed after World War II. Survivors of the Holocaust poured into North America, including the remnants of a yeshiva world that felt it could no longer survive in a Europe that had betrayed it so horrifically. These deeply observant Jews moved into Jewish neighborhoods in urban centers like Brooklyn, Chicago, and Montreal, bringing their ultra-Orthodox beliefs and behaviors with them. They set up day schools and yeshivas; they opened butcher shops and bakeries; they wore yarmulkes and beards in public. Slowly they influenced practices in the larger American Jewish community, particularly its Orthodox contingent. Synagogues that permitted mixed seating in the 1930s now set up *mechitzot* separating men and women during worship. Orthodox women in heavily Jewish neighborhoods began covering their hair and lowering their hemlines.

The post-Holocaust immigration also had a big impact on Jewish food and dietary observance. The new arrivals were not the adventure seekers of their parents' or grandparents' generation. Ripped by force from their prewar all-Jewish world, they were not eager to leave their way of life, or their way of eating, behind; instead, they brought it with them. The hassidim introduced cholov Yisroel, relatively unknown in America until then. The Hungarian arrivals of the 1950s upped the ante for kosher meat, encouraging wider reliance on their own stricter standard of glatt, which slowly became the accepted standard for all kosher meat in America. As the century wore on, Orthodox Jews stopped eating in non-kosher restaurants where their parents and grandparents had been willing to order salads and other cold, non-cooked food.

David Kraemer of the Jewish Theological Seminary calls this the humratization of American Jewry. In *Jewish Eating and Identity Through the Ages*, Kraemer chronicles the history of Jewish dietary practice from biblical to modern times largely as one of increasing strictness. The pace increased in the last decades of the twentieth century. Observant Jews have always been careful to wash their vegetables and fruits before eating to remove visible insects. But practices such as buying light tables for their kitchens, peeling the skins off strawberries, and avoiding bagged salad mixes are very recent humras.

In his book, Kraemer surveyed articles in the Jewish press from the 1980s and '90s. He found one of the first references to insect infestation in a 1984 issue of *Kashrus Magazine*, a newsletter put out by Rabbi Yosef Wikler of Brooklyn. In that article, Rabbi Moshe Heinemann, rabbinical authority of the Star-K, opines that if one cannot see the insects in broccoli, spinach, and other leafy vegetables with the naked eye, the rule of one-in-sixty nullification pertains and the vegetable may be eaten.[2]

Twenty years later the Star-K, along with the other major kosher certifying agencies, demands careful inspection and cleaning of all green leafy and floreted vegetables and advises against the consumption of artichoke hearts and Brussels sprouts.

By the early twenty-first century, other food items that were eaten without a second thought by Orthodox Jews just a decade or two earlier were being carefully scrutinized. By 2008, fresh broccoli, cauliflower, asparagus, artichokes, blackberries, raspberries, and strawberries had disappeared from kosher restaurants and catered events. Processed foods also were revisited. With canned artichokes, the OU now will give kosher certification only to the bottom of the vegetable; the complete heart is off-limits.

In February 2009, the annual convention of local kashrut committees in West Palm Beach, Florida, turned its attention to raisins. The previous year, kosher consumers had raised the alarm of increased infestation in various brands of packaged raisins, especially imported varieties, and the certification agencies were pressed to look into it. The Association of Kashrus Organizations, the umbrella group of the world's major kosher certifiers, held several emergency meetings in 2008 and determined that Jews could eat raisins without further inspection, but experts continued to explore the matter, and each local committee had to come to its own conclusion.

At least one certification agency, K'hal Adath Jeshurun (KAJ), reported that its own inspection of several brands of raisins revealed that many were infested. Raisins were immediately banned from KAJ establishments and kosher events until further notice, and the agency predicted that raisins would soon join strawberries and leafy greens as food items requiring careful cleaning and checking.

Humratization affects more than fruits and vegetables; even New York City water came under attack. In June 2004, the *New York Times* reported that kashrut authorities had found tiny crustaceans called copepods in samples of the city's tap water. They were alerted to the problem by kosher consumers who complained of finding the insects in lettuce they were buying from Alei Katif, an Israeli company. The bugs were present in the lettuce even after careful washing and rinsing, said the complainants. Rabbis in Brooklyn checked into it and discovered the insects weren't in the lettuce; they were coming out of the faucets.[3]

New York City tap water is among the nation's cleanest, the *Times* reported, which is why federal authorities don't require it to be filtered before it's pumped into residents' homes. And environmental authorities insisted the copepods presented no health risk. But from a religious viewpoint, the water was non-kosher. Until Jews knew copepods were in the water they could drink it, but Jewish law forbids *knowingly* ingesting insects. As Rabbi Chaim Fogelman of the OK explains while holding a glass of Brooklyn tap water up to a window and pointing to several ghostly white comma-shaped creatures flailing around in it, "Once you know they're there, you start seeing thousands."

That summer, Orthodox institutions around the city installed expensive filtering systems for their water supplies, and observant residents bought rabbinically approved home filtration devices. Tap water was banned from kosher restaurants in all five boroughs; even today only bottled springwater may be served.

Kraemer is not alone in thinking the bug business has gone too far. In *Jewish Eating and Identity*, not only does he mention with pride that the Conservative seminary's cafeteria continues to serve fresh broccoli, he points to rabbis throughout the ages who have ruled that the Torah prohibits only bugs that can be seen with the naked eye. More recently, Rabbi Ovadia Yosef, former Sephardic chief rabbi of Israel, agreed with that position, as did Rabbi Moshe Feinstein, one of the major halachic deciders of the twentieth century. Feinstein went further, saying that Jews who demand such stringencies cast aspersions on the piety of past generations, which is not to be tolerated.[4]

Other experts have a different take. They say the increased stringency in contemporary Jewish dietary practice is the happy result of technological advances and a more Jewishly educated populace, both of which allow Jews to observe the Torah's commandments more fully. Leniencies are developed to deal with hardships; they are never preferable, simply necessary. For example, when Jews moved out of the major population centers and kosher meat had to be shipped over long distances, the regulations on how often the meat had to be washed during transit were relaxed. With today's improved transportation methods, they say, those leniencies should no longer be employed.

"When a Jewish community is growing and you're trying to provide them with kosher food, you sometimes look for leniency as the best modus vivendi between adherence to kosher laws at the highest standard and keeping up with the demand for kosher food," says Rabbi Yitzchok Adlerstein of Loyola Law School in Los Angeles. "People say it's a push to humratization—there's some of that also; I don't mean to deny it—but that would be a simplistic way of looking at all of the changes in America. Methods that are tolerable under emergency circumstances pass when the emergency is over. Additionally, Orthodoxy has matured in America. With each successive generation, more people benefit from longer and more sophisticated Torah study. More people are aware of different standards within the law and insist on stricter ones."

That may be true, says Aaron Leff, the mashgiach in Livingston, New Jersey, but as far as he's concerned, the increased strictness regarding bug infestation is because with fewer pesticides, there are simply more bugs in produce. And the federal standards determining what level of infestation is permitted do not measure up to what kashrut demands.

"Organic vegetables are popular, but organic just means there's no pesticides and there's a higher percentage of bugs," he says. "It would nauseate ninety-nine percent of the people if they actually read what is considered to be free of bugs. I mean, it may be healthy because there's more protein sitting on the lettuce leaves, but it's not necessarily kosher."


"YOU ASK IF WE'RE CRAZY?" says Rabbi Yochanan Friedman with a wry smile. "If you think the reason we don't eat pork is because we don't want trichinosis, you're right: We are crazy. We're absolutely out of our minds. But if we're doing it because HaShem said, 'Don't eat things I don't like,' what are we going to do? Call us crazy; we're not eating bugs."

Friedman is leaning up against his car outside the Dole Fresh Vegetables packing plant in Soledad, California. It is seven on a chilly, foggy Monday morning, and he has just driven two hours from his Santa Cruz home for his daily inspection of the romaine lettuce picked by Dole workers the previous day. Friedman is a mashgiach for the Star-K, and the lettuce he approves will be packaged and sold as precut salad mix in the kosher sections of major supermarkets.

There is no kosher problem with selling whole heads of lettuce, or indeed of any other vegetable. Fresh, whole produce does not need certification; it's up to the person who prepares it to ensure that proper kashrut procedures are followed. But packaged, canned, frozen, or otherwise processed food items need hekhshers before kosher consumers will buy them. Packaged fresh vegetables are subjected to the strictest inspection. There are more lenient standards for frozen vegetables, having to do with the insects' bodies disintegrating during processing until they are no longer considered "bugs" according to Jewish law.

Soledad is in the heart of Monterey County's Salinas Valley, the nation's top lettuce-growing region. Its rich, dark soil produces 63 percent of the lettuce grown in California, which itself produces 86 percent of all the lettuce grown in the United States.

One of the fastest-growing and most lucrative parts of the lettuce industry is value-added products, chief among them bagged salad mixes. Precut salads have been on the market since 1984, the year Earthbound Farms in Carmel Valley, just west of Salinas, packaged its first hand-washed organic lettuces.

From the beginning, kosher certification agencies looked askance at these precut fresh products because of the difficulty involved in guaranteeing they were bug-free. A few, including the OK, did give hekhshers to certain bagged lettuce mixes for a time. Those certifications did not last long; the infestation problem was simply too great, and the agencies did not want to risk their reputations by putting their names on products that had a great likelihood of being infested. Salad-packing plants tried to come up with more sophisticated washing and rinsing systems to rid the leaves of enough insects to satisfy kashrut authorities, but none proved successful.

By 2007, kosher certification had been withdrawn from virtually all bagged salad in the United States. Rabbi Eisen of the Five Towns notes that Dole, Ready Pac, and Fresh Express, the three leaders in the field, approached the OU for kosher certification of their precut salads; all were turned down.

The only major kosher certification agency that continued to certify precut bagged lettuce was the Star-K. As of 2009 they certify the Dole plant in Soledad and two plants operated by Fresh Express. It was a long haul getting to the point where the Star-K felt it could give its hekhsher, especially to romaine lettuce.

"Romaine was our nemesis," says Rabbi Tzvi Rosen, who works at Star-K headquarters in Baltimore. Iceberg lettuce, with its firm, tight leaves, is easier to clean to kashrut standards. But romaine, which has soft, curly leaves where insects can burrow, is a more popular salad green in America and is a staple on the seder plate.

Rosen explains that precut-vegetable-packing plants have cleaning systems designed to prevent E. coli and other bacterial infections. But kashrut standards are more rigorous than those of the United States Department of Agriculture, which considers mushrooms infested only if there are twenty or more maggots per hundred grams. Up to sixty insects per hundred grams of frozen broccoli are permitted, as are fifty insects per one hundred grams of frozen spinach. According to Jewish law, the presence of even one insect makes the fruit or vegetable unfit for human consumption.

In the late 1990s, working with company quality assurance teams at Dole, River Ranch, Earthbound Farms, and Fresh Express, the Star-K began doing random samplings of green, leafy vegetables after they had been washed. For a while some of the products passed muster.

"It was going along pretty smoothly, and the product was being distributed in Pathmark, Waldbaum's, and other major chains," says Rosen. "Then rabbis found there was more infestation than met the eye. The companies' quality assurance teams were not sophisticated enough to find the small aphids and thrips we were spotting with our light boxes."

Friedman has been working as the mashgiach at Dole's Soledad plant since 2006. Founded in Hawaii in 1851, Dole Food Company, Inc., is the world's largest producer of fresh fruits and vegetables, with 2007 revenues of $6.9 billion. The Soledad facility was built in 1994 as the world's largest precut-vegetable plant. It grows and packages forty-eight varieties of salad mixes featuring lettuce, cabbage, spinach, and other greens. According to the company, more people around the world eat Dole prepackaged salads than those of any other company. In North America, more than two million bags are sold every day.

Five mornings a week Friedman leaves his home at five for the drive to Soledad. He checks in at the front desk, dons his white lab coat, covers his beard with a hairnet, and walks down a long corridor to the plant's lab room, where five pounds of romaine are waiting for him in a wire basket. He examines the lettuce after it's been through the company's intensive washing and rinsing system; what he okays goes directly into bags that are shipped out for sale.

He fills up a white plastic bucket with hot but not boiling water, to which he adds a squirt or two of liquid dish soap. This lettuce will be discarded after testing, so he doesn't have to use the more expensive but edible vegetable wash most kosher consumers use at home. As the bucket is filling up, Friedman explains his inspection system. He relies on a *hazaka*, a legal assumption, established by the Star-K for this product. Obviously a mashgiach cannot check every single leaf of lettuce before it is bagged; today's harvest at Dole came to 8,600 pounds. Instead, Friedman selects five pounds of lettuce at random and checks it minutely. If he does not find a single insect, the halachic assumption is that the rest of the lettuce is also clean and may be bagged under the Star-K label. But if he finds one bug in those five pounds, the entire day's haul has to be sold as non-kosher.

"My inspection is very thorough," he says. "Very often I give it a no. Depending on the season, I can go three or four weeks with just one yes. And they have to pay the Star-K for me to be here whether it's approved or not."

When his bucket is full, Friedman puts in the lettuce and swishes it around in the warm, soapy water for several minutes. Then he removes the lettuce with a colander, leaving behind a bucket of slightly green water. It is the water he checks, not the lettuce leaves. Across the lab's stainless-steel double sink he stretches a sheet of vinyl "thrip cloth" that has mesh fine enough to trap any debris, and pours the green water through it. Then he spreads out the cloth on a two-by-four-foot industrial light box and starts poking around, using the magnifying glass on a jeweler's loupe to help him distinguish the tiny bugs from specks of dirt.

If it was hard to spot the brown aphids in Rabbi Waks's celery stalks, at least they left a trail. The bugs in this romaine are much more difficult to pick out. Friedman refers to a wall poster in the lab that illustrates the insects most often found in leafy greens. "The most common are the red aphid and the white potato aphid," he says. "The red aphids are the easiest to find. The green, you have to look for legs, which is hard when they're not moving. Thrips also come in different colors and are two-toned. The brown lettuce aphid I don't think I've ever seen, but even after doing this for a couple years, my eye keeps going to the brown things on the cloth. And they're not bugs; they're pieces of dirt."

Friedman continues his careful poking for a full five minutes and raises his eyebrows. No bugs. None at all. Amazing. The day's harvest is declared kosher and will go out under the Star-K label. Friedman wants to underline how extraordinary an accomplishment that is— not for him but for Dole. The company developed such a high-tech washing system, he says, that it cleans even romaine lettuce more thoroughly than an individual could do at home, with or without a light box.

"There's no way the average person in their kitchen is ever going to find all the bugs in their lettuce," he says. "It's nice that more people feel that enthusiastic about making sure what they eat is kosher, but they shouldn't kid themselves." It's possible, he admits, that a person could open a package of precut lettuce with a hekhsher on it and still find insects—that's the downside of the hazaka system, which relies on percentages. But Friedman insists the industrial wash in place at this plant is significantly better than what the average person could do on his or her own. Of course, very observant Jews might still want to rinse the lettuce after they take it out of the package; for his part, he doesn't feel that's necessary. River Ranch and Fresh Express, both of which have packing plants nearby, use similar wash systems that are just as thorough, he says. But neither of them has tackled romaine. Both produce kosher-certified precut iceberg lettuce, cabbage, and other less tricky vegetables.

Certifying precut romaine as kosher is expensive, but it's worth it to the company, says Donna Skidmore, Dole's director of consumer services. "We wouldn't be able to get into certain markets without it," she says. "This is the price of doing business."

Before Friedman came to Dole two years ago, he worked as a mashgiach at another company that tried and failed to produce precut romaine that would satisfy kosher authorities. The problem was, he explains, the company wanted to certify all its romaine, not the small percentage he certifies for Dole. And that, he says, is impossible. Lettuce grows in the ground, and that's where the bugs are. You can't get rid of them all.

Yet that is exactly what Rabbi Yakov Vann is trying to do three hundred miles south of Soledad. Vann heads the Los Angeles–based Rabbinical Council of California, which provides kosher supervision for local restaurants, caterers, butchers, and other retail food establishments. He is obsessed with the idea of growing bug-free vegetables. Sophisticated cleaning systems may be useful in industrial food production, he says, but in small-scale settings the best wash-and-rinse system is only as good as the person doing the work. Especially in restaurants, where mashgiach salaries are low and turnover high, it's easier for a kosher agency to ban hard-to-clean fruits and vegetables than stake its reputation on the skill and patience of someone who may not be up to the task.

There is a better way, Vann believes: Figure out how to grow the stuff without bugs in the first place.

On a hot summer day in late August, Vann is down on his hands and knees in the dirt inside a greenhouse near Oxnard, California, carefully examining the leaves on a head of romaine lettuce. He is wearing a pair of telescopic goggles that make his eyes look so enormous they fairly start out of his head.

The greenhouse belongs to Bender Farms, one of two Jewish-owned farms in this dusty valley where Vann experiments with various growing methods designed to minimize, if not eliminate, bug infestation. The techniques he uses were developed by farmers in Gush Katif, the Jewish zone in the Gaza Strip that produced halachically bug-free produce for the Israeli and North American kosher markets. When Gush Katif was leveled in 2005 as part of the Israeli pullout from Gaza, the kosher-certified vegetable industry suffered. Orthodox Jews around the world saw their supply of fresh and frozen produce diminish and become more expensive. Since then, entrepreneurs in North and South America have been trying to replicate the success of those Israeli farmers, using what is now simply called the "Gush Katif" method, but none of their efforts proved commercially viable. As of 2009, Vann seemed closest to succeeding.

Sitting back on his heels at Bender Farms, Vann pushes the bug-eyed spectacles back on his head and frowns. He's found a red spider mite in the lettuce he was examining, which means the entire greenhouse, one of six owned by the farm, has to be sprayed and the lettuce reexamined the following week. "It's a curse," he sighs. "If we find a new bug, we have to send it to UC Davis so they can tell us what chemical to put on it." Like Rabbi Friedman in the Dole plant, Vann doesn't inspect each plant; he selects a certain number of plants from the perimeter of each greenhouse and tests them as proxies for the whole. Insects that attack these vegetables creep in from outside the greenhouse, and would thus appear in plants along the perimeter before making their way to the center.

Vann has been at this since 2006. Because the Rabbinical Council of California supervises small-scale kitchens in restaurants, hotels, and retail shops rather than large manufacturing plants, his interest focused on providing fresh produce that local mashgichim could clean easily and effectively.

In early 2006, Vann heard about a company growing lettuce in Mexico aimed at the kosher market. He contracted with it to ship produce to kosher retail establishments in Southern California, but after millions of dollars and eight months spent setting up the distribution system, the company failed. It was not able to grow the lettuce clean enough to meet kashrut standards.

Meanwhile, an Israeli company invited Vann to Las Vegas, where it was launching another attempt to import the Gush Katif method of lettuce growing. Vann was impressed with the company's high-tech methods—"it looked like something out of *Star Trek*," he says—but it, too, failed.

In early 2008, Vann decided to go it alone, working with Bender Farms and another nearby farm owned by Yossi Asyag of AOF Agricultural Export, Ltd. Both farms covered their greenhouses with OptiNet, special fine-mesh netting imported from Israel designed to keep out thrips. Apparently it blinds them as they try to fly toward the plants. It's not foolproof, so the farms use the netting in combination with pesticides. It's impossible to grow pesticide-free leafy greens to kashrut standards, Vann says. "We tested chemicals without the netting and netting without the chemicals, and both methods failed. The only way that we can be successful is to have a greenhouse together with chemicals."

The two farms focus on specialty lettuces but also grow parsley, dill, cilantro, spinach, and mint, and are trying to grow broccoli and cauliflower. They employ different growing methods. Bender Farms grows its vegetables directly in the ground, relying on the right combination of netting and pesticides to keep away insects. Asyag raises his beds of organic soil three feet off the ground in aluminum containers, making it more difficult for crawling bugs to reach them, and tries to use as little spray as possible. It's a technique he learned in Israel, where he worked with hydroponic agriculture.

For months, crop after crop failed to meet kashrut standards, but Vann persisted. "This is a work in progress," he says. "We learn. We implement. We've had human error along the way. Nature is unforgiving; if you don't have your system down and you don't follow it to a T, if you forget one spray, the bugs are there instantly. You have to know exactly how often to spray, and you learn by hit or miss."

The first successful crop was harvested in March 2008, just before the busy Passover season. One thousand heads were sent to restaurants, caterers, and a handful of kosher markets in heavily Jewish areas of Los Angeles. The next few crops were not up to Vann's standards. "I want zero dead bugs, only the best of the best," he says. Lettuce has a six-week growing cycle, so there's plenty of nail biting and breath holding as a new group of green heads emerges from the soil and pushes its way skyward. When it's ready to pick, the farms send samples from each greenhouse to Vann at home, and he spends all night inspecting them for infestation. If it's good, the lettuce goes to market. If not, the greenhouse is resprayed and everything that was harvested goes into the Dumpster. Growing this produce is so expensive, it's not worth the farmers' time or money to sell it in the non-kosher marketplace. The netting is expensive. The labor costs of growing in a greenhouse, where every plant has to be tended by hand, instead of in an open field that can be worked by tractor, are enormous. The pesticides are pricey: One ten-gallon can costs $1,000, and once a chemical cocktail is mixed, it has to be used right away and the leftover discarded.

By late 2008, both farms had had several successful lettuce harvests, which were sold as whole heads to markets and restaurants in the Los Angeles area. In addition, Asyag was shipping his romaine to a kosher market in Denver and had joined forces with an Israeli company growing cauliflower and broccoli in Mexico. He moved his lettuce operation to Santa Barbara and hoped to begin shipping a truckload a week to the New York area under his new Alei Katif USA label.

You have to be obsessed to bother with this kind of thing. But kashrut is an obsession. There are easier ways to make money. This level of patience and effort is driven by religious imperative.

"I can't tell you how many times we had failure here," Vann sighs.

"You have to be on top of it all the time, like a mother hen checking her flock. And everyone's a critic. Some people tell me I'm too strict in my standards. Some tell me I'm too lenient. I say, get out here and get down in the dirt with me, then tell me what I'm doing wrong."

If any of his crops pass his brutal inspection standards, Vann says, it's only because God has blessed the project. He doesn't know why; he's just grateful for every clean head of lettuce his farms can send out. "Ultimately, you have to pray," he says. "Before I sit down to check, I always say a prayer: 'God let there be no bugs, but if there are bugs, let me find them.'"

# 10.

# Made in China

*Kosher Food Production Goes Global*

IT'S 6:30 A.M. in Shanghai, and the streets are clogged with cars, taxis, buses, trucks, motorbikes, bicycles, and pushcarts as China's largest city of 20 million jostles its way to work. Rabbi Mordechai Grunberg is in the backseat of a Chinese-made Buick minivan, punching out e-mail messages on his BlackBerry to OU headquarters in New York as his driver heads out of the city and he settles in for the three-hour drive to Jiangsu province.

Grunberg is on his way to inspect two kosher food plants. A full-time kosher supervisor for the Orthodox Union, he spends about two-thirds of every year in China. Once a month he leaves his home in Jerusalem and flies to Beijing or Shanghai, where he spends two or three weeks inspecting factories that produce kosher-certified foods and food ingredients for export. A typical day will have him up at five for morning prayers, then on the road by seven, driving for hours to visit far-flung factories in the Chinese countryside. If he's headed to the airport to fly to another city, he leaves his hotel by six or earlier. He's back home by seven or eight at night, and after dinner and evening prayers he dozes off for a few hours, rising at two to respond to e-mails from New York before the head office closes twelve time zones away. Then it's back to sleep for an hour or two until five, when the cycle starts up again.

Today Grunberg is visiting the Jiangsu Xinwei Food Industrial Company, which produces kosher-certified rice crackers, and Shanghai Kerry Oils and Grains, which refines crude oil and sells it to Chinese companies that export finished products to the United States. It's just a day trip, so he's traveling light, he says, patting the badly worn, soft-sided black leather duffel bag on the seat beside him. The bag is his filing cabinet. It's stuffed with the inspection forms he fills out for each plant visit, as well as background material on the companies, his laptop, and an emergency change of clothes. "It's been through the mill; it's ripped on the bottom," he says. "But I can't find another bag to replace it. I've had it ten years already."

Grunberg is in China for twenty days on this visit and will be taking fourteen separate flights. The oversize suitcase he brought with him from Israel is filled almost entirely with kosher food, which is ironic since he spends his time in factories that produce the only food in the country he could actually eat, if only it were sold there. For this trip he packed a dozen long-life meals, radiated dinner trays from Meal Mart in Maspeth, New York. "They're called Amazing Meals; they can last up to two years without refrigeration," he says, which he guesses is pretty amazing. He eats one of those meals every evening, heating it up on top of the water kettle in his room. Sometimes during the day he'll pull out a package of smoked salmon or dig into a can of tuna. And if factory managers insist on serving him something during a visit, he will ask for a piece of fruit or a cup of hot tea, making sure the drink comes in a disposable cup and the fruit is whole, so he can cut it himself with a plastic knife. But the long-life meal at night is what keeps him going. "It's a nice portion. You get salmon or chicken or lasagna or steak, with a side dish like kugel or farfel or tzimmes," he shrugs. "It's very filling."

Globalization has had a profound impact on kosher food production, as indeed it has had on the food industry in general. Even in the early 1980s, says Rabbi Genack of the OU, U.S.-based food manufacturers supervised by his agency relied upon domestic supply sources. Today a package of frozen vegetables or a can of soup can contain ingredients from a dozen different countries. Each of those ingredients, and the plants where they are produced, must be kosher certified in order for the final product to maintain its own certification. Economics drives the industry, creating bizarre scenarios like the Michigan dairy producer that in April 2008 began exporting kosher milk to Israel, a Jewish variant on bringing coals to Newcastle.[1]

As food companies hunt for ever cheaper sources of food ingredients, they are turning increasingly to China. The People's Republic is the fastest-growing producer of kosher food and kosher food ingredients in the world, with nearly two thousand factories under kosher supervision, all by foreign agencies. All the major American agencies are working there—the OU, OK, Star-K, and Kof-K—as well as smaller ones such as the kosher vaads of St. Louis and Vancouver, the big Israeli and European kosher agencies, and dozens of ultra-Orthodox heimishe certifiers representing their own hassidic communities. Most of the fifty or sixty mashgichim who supervise those plants fly in from Israel, Australia, or the United States, although the agencies also hire Chabad rabbis resident in China, who are happy to do a little moonlighting.

Grunberg has been traveling to China for the OU since 2001, six years after the agency first started certifying factories in that country. The field grew fast. From seventy Chinese factories in 2002, the OU found itself certifying three hundred in 2008 and four hundred in 2009. The agency employs eight mashgichim for those factories: Grunberg and a second rabbi who fly in from Israel, and six Chabad rabbis living in Shanghai, Beijing, and Hong Kong. Each plant needs two or three visits a year, so that means eight rabbis sharing 1,200 inspections a year among them.

China is a big country, but Grunberg is always running into his fellow supervisors. Five years ago he was usually the only foreigner on flights to provincial cities. Today those flights are filled with foreigners. There are, he says, "a lot of rabbis running around China."

China's economic muscle is staggering, even in a time of global financial slowdown. The country has taken advantage of a trade surplus that reached $290 billion in 2008, an elevenfold increase in five years, to overtake the United States as the world's largest exporter of manufactured goods.[2] Many of the country's export-oriented companies are homegrown, but a sizable number are Chinese branches of multinational corporations based abroad, looking to take advantage of China's inexpensive labor pool and favorable business climate. More than fifteen thousand foreign companies establish a presence in China every year.[3]

China is also the fastest-growing supplier of food ingredients to transnational food corporations. In 2007, its food export sales totaled $2.5 billion, an estimated half of which is kosher certified. None of this kosher food is destined for the domestic market—it's going overseas, primarily to the United States and Israel. China's five thousand Jewish residents could hardly eat it all themselves.

Most of the kosher goods made in China are food ingredients that will be sold to U.S.-based manufacturers: flavorings, additives, vitamins, oils, enzymes, coloring agents, texturing agents, salt, and spices. But finished products are catching up, especially snacks, cookies, candies, and dehydrated fruits and vegetables. Some regions have particular specialties, Grunberg says, ticking them off on his fingers: pharmaceuticals from Zhejiang, fish from Ningbo and Dalian, dried vegetables from Shandong province, candy from Guangdong. One large candy company under OU supervision finds it worthwhile to make its candy in the United States, ship it to packing plants in China, where it is sealed in individual packets, and then send it back to America for distribution.

As fast as China's manufacturing star is rising, so is the country's reputation for producing tainted food, the unhappy result of loose state control over a money-hungry business class and lax or nonexistent environmental regulations. Agricultural pesticides and chemical fertilizers are used with abandon to boost crop yields, livestock and farmed fish receive heavy doses of antibiotics, and industrial pollution contaminates soil and water supplies. In 2007, the U.S. Food and Drug Administration turned back about two hundred food shipments from China every month, ten times the number refused from competing countries.[4]

The government-controlled Chinese media is filled with stories of farmers and business owners working in collusion with plant managers to produce substandard goods for profit, and those are just the examples the state allows into print. Two very well publicized cases brought things to a head. In April 2007, thousands of North American cats and dogs died from Chinese-made pet food containing wheat gluten contaminated with the toxic chemical melamine, which artificially boosts a product's protein content. Then, in fall 2008, six Chinese babies died and more than three hundred thousand were sickened by tainted infant formula. A Chinese middleman company was discovered buying milk from farmers, watering it down to save money, spiking it with melamine to fool quality-control agents, and selling it to manufacturers of infant formula. The incident, which the World Health Organization called one of the worst food scandals in history, forced a worldwide recall of infant formula and other products containing Chinese powdered milk, including Cadbury chocolates and Nabisco Ritz cheese crackers.

Reporters investigating the milk scandal in late 2008 found that such adulteration had been going on for years. Farmers in Hebei province, home of the offending middleman, told the *Wall Street Journal* it was common practice to add so-called protein powder to the milk of undernourished cows so it would pass quality-control checks. Salesmen would go from farm to farm peddling the stuff in brown paper bags, and farmers desperate to sell their milk would buy it, not knowing it contained melamine, which can cause severe kidney damage in young children.[5]

Melamine was also showing up in other food products. After Hong Kong authorities discovered in October 2008 that eggs imported from mainland China were contaminated with melamine, the state media admitted that the toxic chemical was "probably being added to animal feed on Chinese farms on a regular basis."[6] The animals eat it and pass on the toxins to their eggs, milk, or offspring.

The punishment for offenders is swift and brutal. In July 2007 the head of China's food and drug safety agency was executed for taking bribes to authorize new drugs, and in January 2009 two key figures in the spiked milk case were sentenced to hang, while others received life sentences. That is little comfort, however, for the Detroit shopper anxiously scanning ingredients lists in the supermarket for anything that smacks of Chinese origin. A Reuters/Zogby poll in September 2007 showed that 78 percent of Americans were concerned about the safety of food imported from China, and 25 percent had stopped buying it altogether.

Worried about losing access to the U.S. market, the Chinese government in late 2007 began requiring all domestically produced food destined for export to carry a state-generated China Inspection and Quarantine, or CIQ, number on the package label. Each CIQ number is entered into a database that allows authorities to trace any food product, and all its ingredients, back to their point of origin in case of a recall. Apparently Chinese food manufacturers don't trust the system completely, or don't believe the foreign companies they deal with will trust it, because Grunberg says applications for kosher supervision in China doubled in the first six months after the milk scare as the Chinese sought to reassure American consumers that their food was safe.

Kosher certification seemed just the ticket. The major kosher agencies working in China have had their own CIQ-like tracking system in place for years, enabling supervisors to see with one glance at a box's label which factory a particular food ingredient has come from. The OU created the system in 2001, and the other agencies adopted it well before the Chinese government instituted its own control procedures.

It's nearly 10:00 a.m., and Grunberg is gazing out the car window at the passing scenery. He's been on the road for three hours, and it's been one enormous factory after another the entire way, smoke-belching testimony to China's commitment to industrial expansion. It's like that all over the country, he says. At least highway construction has kept pace: A trip that used to take him six or seven hours by car now takes just two or three.

Grunberg grew up in Far Rockaway, Queens. He received a BA in accounting from Queens College and an MBA from Adelphi University before continuing on for rabbinic ordination, working his way through seminary kashering hotel kitchens for weddings and bar mitzvahs. He began with the Orthodox Union's kosher department in 1981, taking a job at the New York headquarters. Just three men worked in the department then, supervising four hundred companies around the world, about the same number the OU now has in China alone. One of his first assignments was to travel to Shanghai on behalf of a large kosher-certified beverage company that wanted to source citric acid from China. The country was virgin territory for Western business in 1981, and Grunberg had no idea what to expect.

"I landed in the old airport, showed a taxi driver a piece of paper with the name of my hotel written in Chinese, and off we went," he recalls. "I got to this dilapidated hotel, totally run-down, and the people at the front desk had no idea what I was doing there." In those years Westerners had to have a formal, state-approved invitation and a Chinese citizen escorting them at all times. They couldn't just show up at a hotel and check in. Grunberg's contact was nowhere to be found; no one at the hotel could read his letter of invitation, which was in English; and his request for a telephone met with blank stares.

"I figured the guy was just late, so I sat down in this rickety chair in the lobby to wait," Grunberg continues. "It's ten o'clock, eleven o'clock at night, and I feel something tugging on my right leg. I look down and there's a rat looking up at me, waiting to be fed. He's about a foot long. I said, I'm outta here. I jumped back in the taxi, showed the guy my plane ticket, and he took me right back to the airport. I sat up all night and took the first flight out the next morning." He didn't return to China for twenty years.

By 1995, the Orthodox Union and Star-K were supervising kosher food production in the People's Republic, and other agencies quickly followed. In the early years, Chinese food manufacturers had little understanding of what kosher meant. What they did know was that the U.S.-based corporations they were trying to sell to were demanding that Chinese imports carry a kosher symbol. Paying a few thousand dollars a year for that access seemed a small price.

They soon discovered that not everything could be made kosher. Companies that made products containing shrimp paste or pork, or that mixed dairy and meat, would clamor for certification and become angry when they were turned away. Some offered the agencies more money as if it were simply a matter of bargaining. One mashgiach working for the Star-K says a manufacturer of pork sausage begged him for certification, claiming an American distributor had ordered sixty-five container loads of his product. The man became distraught when the mashgiach refused. Rabbi Shimon Freundlich, who works for the OU from his home in Beijing, once fielded a call from the owner of a Chinese furniture company trying to get kosher certification for his tables and chairs, certain it would lead to greater sales in the United States.

Translation errors led to humorous situations. On Avrom Pollak's first trip to China for the Star-K in the mid-1990s, he visited a plant that produced caffeine for export. At the end of his tour, he found himself in the front lobby surrounded by employees and company officials, all staring at him. "I got a sense that they were waiting for something to happen," Pollak recalls. "They finally asked the interpreter, Where's the rabbit? They had received a letter from their exporter that a rabbit was coming from America to determine if they're kosher." Apparently plant officials with limited English had looked up *rabbi* in their Chinese-English dictionary, and the closest word they could find was *rabbit*.[7]

Such naïveté is rare today. Chinese food manufacturers quickly grasped the concept of kosher supervision, and when a mashgiach arrives for an initial plant visit now, he finds company representatives well versed in what he wants and needs to see.

Grunberg enjoys the adventure of his work. He likes being on the road, meeting new people every day, figuring out the culture. It's a constant rush you don't get at a desk job, he says. In 1994, he moved his wife and seven children from New York to Israel so he could travel to the Far East more easily, and started supervising kosher food production in India, Thailand, and Indonesia, as well as Eastern Europe. He wears a cap or beret rather than a yarmulke in China, and his full white beard is the only sign that he's not a typical Western businessman. His calm, quiet demeanor fits in well with the Chinese way of doing business. He's not a slap-on-the-back kind of guy, but neither is he stiff or officious. When a plant manager says something that alerts him to a possible kashrut problem, he doesn't scowl or yell. He watches, waits, and smiles politely before pouncing.

Of all the countries he's worked in, Grunberg says China has the best security. That's important to a foreign kosher supervisor, who is constantly traveling, sometimes in unsafe areas. India was hardest for him. The roads were awful, and terrorism was a constant danger. Like all mashgichim working in Asia, Grunberg was deeply shaken by the November 2008 terrorist attacks in Mumbai in which Israelis were singled out for particularly gruesome deaths and six people were murdered in the city's Chabad House, including three rabbis who worked as kosher supervisors. That would never have happened in China, he maintains. "Everywhere you go there are barracks of soldiers hidden, on alert. You don't see them, but they're there."

China's vigilant security forces pose a different problem. Right before the 2008 Beijing Olympics, China clamped down on foreign travel to and from Tibet, nervous that Tibetan nationalists would use the press attention on China to stage street protests. Grunberg was arrested at a roadblock that summer on his way from the Tibetan capital of Lanzhou to a village in the southwest, where he planned to inspect yak milk production. He was kept in his car all day in the hot sun while phone calls went back and forth between the plant management and local government officials. Travel in Tibet eased up after the Olympics, but he doesn't need to go there as often now.

Grunberg first went to Tibet looking for a cheaper source of casein, a milk protein by-product that is used in food and pharmaceuticals. He found it among village yak farmers and set up a network to collect the casein produced from dried yak milk. It was hard to travel to Tibet, but Grunberg was fascinated by life in the villages, which hadn't changed in hundreds of years. The farmers had no electricity, no running water, and no gas heat, and they used the sun to dry their milk. Because there was no refrigeration, they had to dry the milk the same day it came from the animal to avoid spoilage. Eventually the OU decided the system was too difficult to monitor, as each villager was boiling down and drying yak milk in his own home without supervision. The project has since ended.

It's almost 11:00 a.m. before Grunberg's car navigates through the dusty streets of Xie Jia Tang village and pulls up at the entrance to the Jiangsu Xinwei Food Industrial Company, a long, low building in the town's industrial zone. Grunberg is quickly ushered into the conference room to wait for Chloe Hsu, the company's sales director. She breezes in, a cheerful, perfectly groomed young woman of thirty-three who, like increasing numbers of her generation, earned her higher degree abroad—in her case, an MS from the University of Glasgow.

Before the gritty business of going over company records begins, there is small talk and an offer of tea or Pepsi. The company has been kosher certified for three years, and they know to hand the rabbi his drink in a paper cup and not to bother putting out cake or cookies. Hsu's grandfather founded the company forty years ago in Taiwan. Her father moved the production plant to China in 1995, although headquarters remain in Taiwan, where he lives. Joint ventures between the two countries are growing, Hsu says. With $1.25 billion in capital, the company is the largest producer of rice crackers in China.

Hsu's father sought kosher certification in order to expand his export business into new markets. "Especially in America, there are so many Jewish people," Hsu says. "We found customers were asking us whether we had kosher certification." The plant makes kosher rice crackers for the United States and non-kosher crackers for Japan. The only difference between the products, she says, is the nori, or dried seaweed, used to wrap some of the crackers destined for Japan. Ninety percent of their production is for export, and only about 10 percent is kosher certified, all of it sent to two California-based companies that use it in a packaged snack mix.

Hsu says the company has not seen sales increase much in the three years they've been kosher certified. Other Chinese manufacturers do report sales bumps. The Nanjing BioTogether Company, which sells fructose, salts, and amino acids to U.S.-based companies that make sports drinks, pharmaceuticals, and flavorings, reported an elevenfold increase in export sales to $62 million in its first year of kosher certification.[8] But Hsu says it's still worth it for her company to pay the OU $7,000 for two or three visits a year by Grunberg, because the company is trying to increase its penetration of the North American market and customers there demand the kosher symbol on all imports.

Hsu's familiarity with the U.S. market is typical of China's new business elite. In the early years of kosher supervision in China, most of the requests for certification of Chinese factories came from foreign distributors who were looking to source products in China. Today the vast majority of the applications come directly from the local factories, from people like Hsu's father. But the Chinese look at the process differently than their colleagues in the United States, where food manufacturers tend to view kosher certification as an aspect of product quality. Companies in China get kosher certification because they have to. It's strictly a business decision, driven by customer demand.

"If they want to sell their product in the United States and they are not kosher, no one will buy it," points out Menachem Lubinsky. "Coca-Cola won't buy it; Kellogg's won't buy it. They'll be cut out of the market. If you're in China or Thailand and you want to export, you have absolutely no choice but to seek out kosher certification." Some companies get certification to fill one order from a U.S.-based manufacturer and then drop it when the order is complete, only to reapply when the next order comes in.

American food manufacturers had been buying ingredients from the Far East for decades before the kosher agencies thought to examine in person how those ingredients were produced. Rabbi Don Yoel Levy, head of the OK, says that as late as the 1960s, kosher authorities did not question the kosher status of flavorings, enzymes, or other chemical compounds on food labels because few people understood what they really were. In the early 1970s, his father, Rabbi Berel Levy, former head of the OK, became the first Western kosher supervisor to visit Malaysia, Singapore, and Indonesia to inspect factories producing oils and oil derivatives such as fatty acids and glycerin used as food ingredients. He returned home with astounding news: Vegetable shortening could have nonvegetable ingredients blended into it, and palm oil could be transported in the holds of huge tanker ships that previously carried non-kosher hot liquids, rendering the oil non-kosher.

Once those kosher problems became known they couldn't be ignored, and the kosher agencies were forced to take their complex systems of supervision and certifications overseas, following the trail of American kosher food manufacturers.

Rabbi Donneal Epstein is one of the OU's two rabbinic administrators in charge of overseas supervision, and he has mixed emotions about the very globalization he oversees. "As an American, I'm a little bit troubled that everything is moving overseas," he says. "There's no manufacturing done in this country anymore. What are people going to do for a living?"

From the viewpoint of kashrut, he's even more ambivalent. When it's the middle of the night in New York and a mashgiach in Asia has a pressing question, where should he call? "We have to have personnel available throughout the world, in different time zones and different cultures, with different languages," he says. "That's something I never dreamed of when I first started working here." Understanding foreign laws and foreign ways of doing business, finding supervisors willing to live on the road, trying to explain to bosses who have never heard of Judaism why they should care if a worker brings her non-kosher lunch onto the factory floor—it's a constant headache. And as companies cast farther afield in their search for ingredient sources, the logistics become more difficult. Sending a rabbi once a month to India is one thing, he says, but try finding one willing to fly to tuna-processing plants in the Marshall Islands, a tiny collection of atolls in the middle of the Pacific Ocean just west of the International Date Line. They come back cursing, telling him it's not worth it to go to the ends of the earth for tuna.

Most kosher food products coming into the United States arrive from Asia and South America. China is by far the biggest source in Asia, followed by India, Japan, and then Thailand. The sixty-five OU-certified plants in India manufacture dairy products, along with chemicals, vitamins, and botanicals used mainly for flavoring. Japan specializes in chemicals and enzymes, while Thailand and the surrounding smaller countries deal with a lot of fish processing.

Each kosher agency has slightly different rules on how often a plant needs to be visited. The Orthodox Union requires just an annual visit for plants that make simple ingredients like cornstarch or rice powder, so-called Group 1 products manufactured through straight chemical synthesis. If that is all a given plant manufactures, the visits can be scheduled in advance and mainly involve document verification. Group 2 and Group 3 products, which involve more complex manufacturing processes, such as fermentation, or the addition of meat or dairy require more visits as well as surprise spot checks. Fees for OU supervision in China begin at $4,500 a year and go up to about $10,000 for two or three visits a year. The other major kosher agencies charge a little less.

Each year the number of Group 2 and Group 3 plants under kosher certification in China increases, which industry experts fear leaves the field open to abuse. An October 2007 article in *Kashrus Magazine* noted that Chinese factories producing food items that would require twelve or more kosher inspections a year in America were getting only two or three visits, because there are too few mashgichim in China.[9] In 2008, Rabbi Sholem Fishbane, kosher administrator for the Chicago Rabbinical Council and head of the Association of Kashrus Organizations, the umbrella for the world's leading kosher agencies, visited kosher-certified factories in China. He reported back that not only do most mashgichim working there not know Chinese, they often schedule plant visits in advance, eliminating the element of surprise.

Chinese companies have been discovered forging letters of kosher certification. A week before his current visit to China, Grunberg says a salesman for an OU-certified company producing frozen fruits and vegetables was caught in such a scheme. He wanted to sell the company's broccoli overseas, but the OU, like most major kosher agencies, does not give kosher certification to vegetables such as broccoli and cauliflower that are prone to high levels of bug infestation. So the salesman took letterhead from OU certification of other company products and forged his own certificate, using his home computer. The OU terminated the company's kosher supervision, and Grunberg says once that happens, none of the other kosher agencies will pick up the account.

This doesn't occur often. The kosher system is built on trust, yes, and in China factories can go months between inspections, giving them ample time to sneak in nonapproved ingredients. But they rarely do it, because if they're caught, they lose their kosher status and, along with it, their foreign accounts, which in China means financial ruin. To add another layer of surety, mashgichim look at every suspicious box and label during their plant visits, taking photos and sending documentation to their head offices for verification. They periodically take random samplings of products, which are tested for animal by-products and other unauthorized ingredients at an independent lab in Beijing.

But concerns remain. "China is the most daunting place for kosher supervision," says kashrut authority Rabbi Eliezer Eidlitz, rabbinic administrator of the Los Angeles–based Kosher Information Bureau. "First of all they eat a lot of dogs and cats. Even today the government admits to at least fifty thousand dogs canned a day in China. So you have to come in and, in a delicate but forceful manner, see every bit of the operation, twenty-four hours a day, to make sure they are not canning animals, not using shellfish, not doing other types of things."

Mr. Li, the quality assurance manager at the Wuxi Genencor Bio-Products Company, would be appalled to hear this assessment. For this sixty-year-old gentleman, neatly dressed in a tie and jacket, trust is everything. "Loyalty is most important in an employee," he states in his clipped, careful English, the product of a dual major in chemistry and English at Suzhou University and a one-year United Nations development course in Vacaville, California. "We keep our word. It's a must."

Mr. Li greets Grunberg at the front door of the towering Genencor plant in Wuxi, an industrial city two hours from Shanghai. He walks Grunberg through the cavernous Scandinavian-designed lobby with its floor-to-ceiling glass walls into the Forbidden City Conference Room, where plates of bananas and oranges, bottles of water and Coca-Cola, and a pot of hot tea await. Li sits on one side of the conference table with his deputy, a young woman who speaks even better English than he does, while Grunberg sits across from them.

A division of Danish food chemical giant Danisco, Genencor opened in China in 1997 and moved into this gleaming new building in 2007. The plant manufactures glucoamylase, an enzyme used in high-fructose corn syrup, the ubiquitous sweetening agent demonized in *The Omnivore's Dilemma*, Michael Pollan's critique of the global food industry. The factory has been kosher since its inception, because it produces only for export. It requires six visits a year from the OU, as it uses a host of Group 3 ingredients, which require the most intensive supervision.

Grunberg pulls out his laptop, brings up his copy of the factory's Schedule A, which lists all the ingredients it uses, and takes care of basic paperwork. Is the plant making any new products since his last visit? Li says no. That's a standard first question; any new products have to be approved by OU headquarters, or they can compromise the entire kosher status of a plant. Grunberg circles the Group 2 and Group 3 ingredients on his list—those are the items he must physically inspect—and heads off for the plant's two warehouses with Li in tow.

The first warehouse is a cold-storage area, kept at a brisk 45 degrees Fahrenheit. Grunberg walks slowly down each aisle, looking up at enormous bags of ingredients stacked to the top of fifteen-foot shelves and writing down their identification numbers to make sure they tally with those on his list. "Where is your glycerin coming from?" he asks, pointing to a dozen large drums. "Do you have the paperwork for this shipment?" Glycerin is a sensitive ingredient because it can be made from animal products. Li pulls out a document showing this glycerin comes from another Chinese factory certified by the OK, so that's fine with Grunberg. The major kosher agencies accept each other's certifications for most, but not all, ingredients.

Grunberg is careful to examine anything the plant uses for fermentation, including peptones, which are protein derivatives that could involve animal products. He checks the origin and identification numbers on every chemical ingredient to ensure none are made on equipment that might have been used to make dairy products. Lactose is a concern here, and when Grunberg sees it on the company's Schedule A, it raises a red flag. Not to worry, Li assures him; the company considered using lactose for fermentation years ago, but it proved too expensive and was never purchased.

"At the beginning, we didn't know what the OU was," Li says. "But after training, we learned the importance of everything, everything being kosher. And we keep our word. I know the significance of kosher for the factory's success, and I take it seriously."

Li is immensely proud of his plant, which is so immaculate it's hard to believe any food passes through its doors, much less cats or dogs. Grunberg doesn't need to see the entire place, but he indulges Li's need to show it off and follows him through the bowels of the stainless-steel behemoth. The floors and walls sparkle. There is no smell anywhere.

The employees are dressed in crisp uniforms and are all wearing safety masks and shoe coverings. Grunberg is seemingly the only man in Chinese factories who needs a beard net, so he's brought his own.

"We have the cleanest plant in Genencor," Li states emphatically. "I am very proud to work here." One half expects him to launch into song, and a line of pigtailed girls waving red flags to leap out from behind the back wall.

He frowns and smiles at the same time. "China is so often misunderstood by Americans."

KOSHER AGENCIES are always happier certifying simple Group 1 products rather than finished foods in China because of all the difficulties involved. Most won't certify dairy or meat from China at all. The Orthodox Union will, but very gingerly.

Rabbi Grunberg talks about doing kosher beef slaughter in China in the near future, and in February 2009 the OU certified its first Chinese-made milk chocolate candies, from the Tastychoco Foodstuff Company. Zhen Jun Ying, the company's vice president, says it took four years to make the changes needed for kosher certification, including making sure all their raw materials were kosher certified, cleaning or buying all new factory equipment, and setting up approved shipping methods. Tastychoco pays $10,000 a year in fees to the OU. The company originally sought kosher certification because their importers in Israel and the United States requested it, but with the collapse of the global economy, now the company itself believes kosher certification will make their chocolate stand out in the international luxury food market. "It's a big investment, but it will help to make our product more attractive," Ying says.

Kosher fish production is very global. In the 1990s, most kosher fish came from North America or Europe. Now sardines come from Morocco, salmon is farmed in Chile and China, anchovies are brined in Peru, and tuna arrives from the Far East. Some fish is processed where it is caught, but a lot is caught or farmed in one country; shipped to another for cutting, steaming, and canning; and sent to a third for labeling and distribution. These piscine world travelers have to be supervised for adherence to kosher regulations all along the way.

The first step in kosher supervision of fish is determining whether the species itself is kosher. The Torah says a kosher fish must have both fins and scales, but the Talmud later noted that every fish with fins also has scales, so it is only necessary to check for scales. Shellfish are non-kosher, having neither fins nor scales, but in order to decide which other varieties were kosher, the rabbis had to figure out what kind of scales the Torah was talking about. By Talmudic times, they decided a kosher fish had to have scales that could be removed without tearing the skin. Sharks, for example, are not kosher; removing their scales causes the skin to rip. Some fish lose their scales when they are removed from the water, such as tuna, herring, and mackerel. They are still considered kosher, as are fish of a known kosher species caught very young before their scales have developed.

The debate over kosher species of fish continues today. The Conservative movement considers swordfish kosher, but Orthodox authorities have forbidden it since 1951, when Rabbi Moshe Tendler of Yeshiva University examined a swordfish under a microscope and ruled it had no scales. His opinion has come under increasing fire from other Orthodox rabbis and scholars, but the major kosher agencies continue to honor it.

Buying fresh kosher fish from a non-kosher fish store requires more consumer knowledge than picking up a can of tuna and looking for the kosher symbol. If the fish has been filleted and no longer has its skin, kosher authorities rule there is no reliable way of determining what species it is. It's the same with fish sent to packing plants after filleting, so kosher agencies require that a patch of skin remain attached to filleted fish to prove its provenance. Even that method is not foolproof. Fishermen have been caught gluing skin patches from less expensive non-kosher fish onto kosher fish and shipping it to fish stores, restaurants, or canning plants. Kosher supervisors can catch this by looking for cut marks around the skin patch, which would be absent if the patch was glued on. They can also soak the fish in hot water to see if it falls off.

Some kosher agencies, notably the OU and OK, rule that filleted salmon does not need a patch of skin to be left on, because the flesh's distinctive reddish color is enough identification. Other authorities, such as the Star-K, feel non-kosher fish can be made to look like salmon through artificial coloring.

Lists of kosher fish species are not useful, because fish are known by

many different, sometimes overlapping names. There is no federal protection for the names of fish—anything can be called "whitefish," and
cod, escolar, and snapper are names used for a wide variety of fish.
Asian catfish is sold in the United States under more than a dozen
names, including basa, tra, Pegasus, and China sole. That is confusing
for kosher consumers, as sole is kosher but catfish is not.

This lack of regulation leaves the door open to fraud, a concern for
those who keep kashrut, but also for any consumer who ends up paying
a premium for a lesser-quality fish. The U.S. Food and Drug Administration identifies this practice as species substitution, a violation of
consumer protection law. The most egregious recent example involved
grouper, a white-fleshed kosher species of fish popular in South Florida
that commands top dollar. In August 2006, the *St. Petersburg Times* discovered that Tampa Bay restaurants purporting to sell grouper were
actually serving different, cheaper fish. DNA testing on fish purchased
at eleven local eateries revealed that six were not grouper, but hake,
tilapia, and Asian catfish. Fresh grouper caught in the Gulf of Mexico
wholesales for $10 a pound or more, while *Pangasius hypophthalmus*, the
most common variety of Vietnamese catfish exported to the United
States, usually fetches $3 to $4 a pound. In May of that year, a federal
jury indicted a Florida wholesaler on charges of importing one million
pounds of frozen Asian catfish for as low as $1.52 a pound, calling it
grouper, and selling it at up to four times the price.[10]

Supervising kosher fish production is quite labor-intensive. With
wild fish, some agencies require a mashgiach to go out with the fishing
boats to watch as the fish is caught. The Orthodox Union does not
require that level of oversight, allowing its supervisors to wait on the
dock for the boats to come in and watch as the fish are unloaded, to
make sure no non-kosher varieties are mixed in. As with fishermen, a
kosher supervisor's schedule is at the whim of the waves. Salmon runs
are notoriously unpredictable, so supervisors have to be ready at a
moment's notice to jump on a plane when the boats go out, to make
sure they are at the dock or processing plant when the fish arrive.

Most of the kosher fish processed in the Far East is tuna. Plants are
scattered throughout Indonesia, Thailand, Vietnam, the South Seas,
and, increasingly, China. The tuna season is much longer and more
predictable than the salmon season, so the mashgiach usually gets a
few days' warning when a big catch is on its way. He arrives at the plant

in the wee hours of the morning to sit and wait until the boats come in. Again, the level of supervision varies among kosher agencies. If a factory processes just one kind of tuna, the Orthodox Union requires only quarterly inspections, relying on a ruling by Rabbi Joseph Soloveitchik, considered the seminal rabbinic figure in Modern Orthodox Judaism. The Star-K follows a much stricter ruling by Rabbi Feinstein, requiring a mashgiach to be present in the factory whenever fish is being processed, watching each individual fish the entire time.

In a Star-K plant, at least two mashgichim are needed for each run. The first picks up each fish as it arrives in the prep room, to check that it is the species it's meant to be. Once he approves a small group of fish, a second mashgiach walks the group into the next room, keeping an eagle eye on every fish as it is skinned, filleted, sealed in packaging, and double-marked with Star-K tape and plastic tabs. The tape and markers are changed with each run for added security. When the fish arrives in the United States, a third mashgiach meets it at the receiving dock and supervises as the seals are broken on the shipping containers.

On a good day, a fish mashgiach can work twenty hours straight, running from room to room until all the fish are processed. It's miserable work—cold, wet, physically exhausting, and not particularly stimulating.

Joel Weinberger, who now runs the kosher dining program at the California Institute of Technology, supervised Star-K fish production in the Far East for eight years. He started at a family-owned plant in Taiwan, then moved to a large industrial factory in Thailand that canned tuna for Bumble Bee and other multinational corporations. The Thai operation had rooms the size of football fields, he says, filled with hundreds of workers gutting, cleaning, and steaming fish around the clock. As the mashgiach, he would have to turn on the boilers that created the steam to avoid *bishul akum*, or cooking by a non-Jew. After steaming, the tuna went into a cooking chamber and was then cooled, skinned, and beheaded before canning. Canned tuna would go to the United States, and whole cooked loins were shipped to Israel for final processing.

The Star-K requirements for kosher fish certification are so strict, and the work is so unappealing, that the agency actually discourages companies seeking it. The agency no longer does Passover fish certification, following an unhappy incident some years back with a major

Canadian tuna company. As Weinberger tells it, Canada imposes a 30 percent duty on imported canned fish, but fish brought into the country for religious rituals is exempt. It was worth it for this company to pay tens of thousands of dollars for Star-K Passover certification of all its canned tuna, just to avoid that import tax.


TWO DAYS AFTER his trip to Jiangsu province, Rabbi Grunberg is back in Shanghai manning the OU booth at Food Ingredients China, the largest food additives and ingredients trade fair in Asia. Held every March, the show draws more than one thousand exhibitors, 20 percent of them overseas companies. Virtually all the domestic companies at the show produce goods for export.

Outside the exhibition center, crowds mob the main entrance, waving their event badges and shouting into cell phones. A river of gray-suited young men and women funnels noisily through the heavily guarded front door and fans out excitedly across the massive hall. The OU, Star-K, Kof-K, and OK all have booths at the show, handing out information and trying to drum up new clients. Representatives of smaller kosher agencies walk the floor, sizing up the competition and schmoozing with customers. No serious contender in the world of kosher supervision would miss this event.

The OU has prime placement, all the way to the left in a busy corner of the main hall. Its booth is festooned with blue and white ribbons, and the name of every OU-certified plant in China is listed on a wall underneath the Mandarin phrase *Jie Sah*, meaning "clean food." That's how the kosher agencies translate the word *kosher* for the local market, explains Howard Chen, a Chinese national who works for the OU in Shanghai. "We don't use the phrase 'Jewish food' because that has religious connotations," he says. Jews are very popular in China, admired for their supposed cleverness and business acumen, but Western religions are officially banned, as is proselytizing. None of the local rabbis will perform conversions or permit non-Jewish Chinese citizens to attend their worship services, for fear of being shut down by the government.

Chen Zhi Qing is the twenty-five-year-old manager for Nanjing Rich, a Chinese start-up that makes ginger and garlic oils. She takes a brochure from the OU booth and begins reading it with intense concentration. "I don't know what kosher is, but I'm negotiating with an Israeli company, and they will only work with me if I have kosher certification," she explains.

A young man who says he represents a company that makes flavorings for export is shopping around among the kosher agencies, looking for the best deal. He is shocked by the fee the OU wants to charge him. "Why forty-five hundred dollars, so much more than the others?" he asks Grunberg, speaking through a translator who tries to soften the man's accusatory tone. "Tell him we're the grandfather in the field," Grunberg urges the translator. "Tell him the OU is as old as I am, one hundred years."

Kosher agencies go to trade shows to find customers, their efforts kept in check by a sort of gentleman's agreement. "We don't go after products certified by our competition. We don't steal companies from each other," insists Phyllis Koegel, who works trade shows for the OU as the agency's director of new business development. "At least *we* don't. But if their certification is from a local vaad, or the product carries a kosher symbol I don't recognize, I'll mention to them that it might be more marketable if they used us. I don't push."

In accordance with the prohibition against *lashon hara*, or gossip, kosher agencies will rarely criticize each other publicly. But they have no compunctions about telling potential customers why their agency is best. There is big money at stake in China: Even if every OU-certified plant paid only the minimum annual fee, it would bring the agency nearly $2 million a year. "Kashrus agencies are not holy rollers," says Rabbi Eidlitz. "This is a business."

The American media only caught on to the story of kosher food in China in early 2008, when reporters were sent into the country to churn out copy in the buildup to the Beijing Olympics. The Orthodox Union hired Welfeld Public Relations to help steer those reporters to China's growing kosher industry, particularly the OU's part in it. The Bloomberg News service carried a story about China's kosher explosion on January 17, 2008, followed a few days later by the Associated Press. Major publications, including the *Los Angeles Times* and *USA Today*, reprinted the articles. Within days the Welfeld agency estimated that four million people had read about the OU in China.[11] By the end of the year, the *New York Times*, NPR, and *The New Yorker* had all sent reporters to cover the same story. Rabbi Grunberg, whom most of the reporters followed, took it in good spirits.

Over at the Star-K booth on the opposite side of the exhibition hall, thirty-nine-year-old Rabbi Amos Benjamin is handing out free kosher candy to passersby. The Star-K has been in China longer than the OU and supervises about the same number of companies, with the same number of mashgichim, but struggles neck and neck in the market with the better-known Orthodox Union. Sixty percent of the Star-K's China plants manufacture food chemicals, with another 20 to 30 percent doing fruit or vegetable products—canned, frozen, freeze-dried, or juiced.

The Baltimore-based agency has one leg up on the competition in Benjamin, who has headed its Beijing office for thirteen years. Benjamin speaks "passable" Mandarin, but adds quickly that his wife speaks it much better.

The Food Ingredients China trade show isn't where the big deals are made, Benjamin says. "It's open to the public, so there are a lot of looky-loos, but the other agencies are all here, so we're here, too." In fact, Benjamin says, the years of greatest growth have passed. Until 2005, the number of Star-K factories doubled every year. But now so many agencies are competing against each other in China that growth has slowed somewhat.

Other countries are eager to take up the slack, actively encouraging the major kosher agencies to work with their businesses to help them penetrate the U.S. food market. In 2009, the Philippine government opened a kosher liaison office in Manila to help domestic companies navigate the certification process. And the Turkish government invited the Star-K to address the Aegean Exporters' Association conference in Izmir, lecturing on how kosher certification could help their global marketing.

As the U.S.-based kosher agencies increase their work abroad, they are causing friction with the rabbis and kosher agencies already working in those countries. When the OU tells a Dutch or French company it should drop its domestic kosher certification if it hopes to sell goods in the United States, that's a direct threat to the livelihood of the local rabbinate. Rabbi Isak Haleva, the chief rabbi of Turkey, told a reporter in 2004 that the number of Turkish companies his office supervised had dropped from 180 to 40 in two years because of strong-arm tactics by the big American agencies. The chief rabbi of Holland noted a similar drop-off, adding it hurts the Dutch Jewish community because the fees charged for kosher supervision are used to pay for local Jewish educa- tion and synagogues.[12] There's no law against tough business competi- tion, in the Talmud or the civil courts. But the actions of the Americans leave a bad taste, the Europeans say.

"There's an attitude among the American kosher agencies of coming to a company and laying down the law," charges Rabbi Akiva Padwa of the London Beth Din Kashrut Division, one of the largest European agencies. "They say, this is what you have to do, and the companies resent it. Time and again I come across companies working with Amer- ican agencies, and I get that feedback."

Rabbi Michoel Brukman is representing the Kof-K at the Shanghai trade show. The Kof-K has worked in China since 1997, and by 2009 was certifying two hundred plants, all of them producing simple ingre- dients and additives. Brukman says the Kof-K won't supervise finished products, or anything containing meat or dairy, in China.

"Honestly? I want to sleep at night," he explains. "I've seen too many things here, and if I say something is kosher, I want to feel it's one hun- dred percent." On one visit to a plant in Shandong, managers showed him fifty-gallon drums of chemical ingredients they said came from Dow, a kosher-certified company. Brukman called Dow and learned the company did not even make that compound. At another plant, officials insisted they did not use MSG in their product. Brukman went through the garbage and found empty boxes of MSG. It's impossible to give the level of kosher supervision in China demanded by complicated food products, he says, and with infrequent inspections, the temptation to cheat is too great.

On his very first visit to China, he asked a food technology expert in Shanghai what motivated the Chinese to stay honest. Judaism has a fear factor, he told the man: Observant Jews are afraid of breaking God's laws. What did China have? The man opened his wallet, took out one hundred yuan, about $15, and told Brukman, "This is our reli- gion, and we'll do whatever it takes to get more of it."

No one is going to stop kosher supervision in China. So long as Americans demand inexpensive food and U.S. companies face in- creased pressure to keep production costs under control, food and food ingredients will continue to pour in from Asia, Africa, and the rest of the Third World. The best kosher agencies can do, they say, is take on clients carefully, make sure they understand the rules of kashrut and the penalties for noncompliance, and provide the most rigorous oversight possible within each country's limitations.

Ultimately, it's about choice. Economics needs to be weighed against the challenges of tainted food, lax health and safety regulations, and the difficulties of sending employees abroad. Rabbi Eidlitz points out that mashgichim are now working in the most remote areas of Asia, Africa, and the South Pacific, following the same dollar as the food manufacturers. "On one hand, it's great bringing in a product at a good price. It pays well to the mashgiach. It pays well for the kosher agency. But the question is, Do I want to do business in that place in that way or not?"

Eidlitz's opinion is clear. "At some point the question is going to have to be asked: Is it worth it? Do we really need fifteen types of imitation shrimp? There is a point where the agencies are going to have to decide, do I or don't I send a mashgiach to such a place?"

# 11.

# A Wedding in New Jersey

## Cholov Yisroel to Sushi, the New Kosher Diet

"COME TO my daughter's wedding Monday."

Rabbi Avraham Stone issues the invitation, then hangs up to take another call. Stone is a busy man: He lectures widely on kosher food issues; is a leading force in the Vaad HaKashrus of MetroWest, New Jersey; and is one of the Orthodox Union's three senior rabbinic field supervisors, overseeing kosher certification for all the agency's accounts east of the Ohio River, from Maine to Florida. So when his daughter gets married, the mashgiach in charge sweats bullets to make sure everything is really, really kosher. He knows he will be under intense scrutiny, and besides, Stone is his boss.

That mashgiach is fifty-year-old Pinchas Triestman, supervisor of the glatt kosher kitchen at the Crystal Plaza in Livingston, New Jersey. By 8:30 a.m. the day of the wedding, he is already at work and bustling around the kitchen with nervous energy. It's a crisp Monday morning in November, and he is gearing up for the final ten-hour push. "This is the first *yoshon* event I've done," he worries.[1] "All the top brass of the OU will be here. We'll have four managers on duty."

More than four hundred guests will start arriving at six o'clock, and Triestman has a lot to do, including kashering an entire second kitchen. The Plaza holds both kosher and non-kosher events, and the kosher kitchen is one floor above the main dining room, so the waitstaff can't get the food downstairs fast enough once the meal begins. For big events they use a second kitchen downstairs for last-minute warming and prepping.

But that comes later. First, he does a walk-through of the Plaza's kitchens and storage areas, consulting his checklist and firming up the day's timetable. Kashering the silverware? Later. Clearing the non-kosher alcohol out of the lobby bar? Later. Locking up the non-kosher and non-glatt food and equipment so they don't get used accidentally? Later. "By the time cocktail hour begins, the staff will not be able to access so much as one of their spoons," he says. "I will lock it all down. If they need something, they have to go through me."

Downstairs by the loading dock, he unlocks the glatt kosher storage room where he keeps utensils and serving pieces he doesn't have room for upstairs. Tonight is a meat meal, so all his dairy equipment is locked away here, along with portable stoves, extra plates, and seventeen additional chafing dishes. "Here's the blowtorch I use for kashering ovens," he says, pointing to an eighteen-inch torch connected to a heavy propane tank. "I'm just using boiling water today, so I don't need it."

The Crystal Plaza has been a popular banquet hall since the Janoff family, longtime kosher caterers in central New Jersey, purchased the historic Victorian-era mansion in 1965. In 1994, the Janoffs added glatt kosher to their repertoire, following a rise in requests for that stricter standard. In 2004, they converted the Plaza's bakery into a permanent glatt kitchen and hired Triestman as the full-time mashgiach. The kitchen maintains the highest level of kosher food preparation, including separate ovens for meat and fish. Only glatt meat is permitted in the room. When not in use, the kitchen is kept locked behind a heavy metal grate that pulls down from the ceiling; only Triestman and another mashgiach have keys. An emergency key is kept in a lockbox for firefighters or police, but they have to call Triestman first. The kitchen is under constant video surveillance, not for thieves, but to catch kosher missteps like a worker heating up his own ham-and-cheese sandwich or using a meat knife on a dairy dish.

Not many kosher supervising agencies will permit a banquet hall to operate both glatt and non-glatt events, because of these logistical difficulties and the potential for slipups. Also, the market for non-glatt kosher events is steadily shrinking, so it's not worthwhile for most caterers or hotels to offer them. Even if the host of a kosher affair doesn't keep glatt, the odds are that some of the guests will, meaning the entire meal has to adhere to that stricter standard.

"People either want glatt kosher or non-kosher, nothing in the middle," says Plaza owner Allan Janoff. Fifteen years ago, just 5 percent of his customers requested glatt; today the percentage has risen to half.

Janoff says he'll continue to provide ordinary kosher meals until demand drops below 20 percent of his business, which might happen soon.

Because the Crystal Plaza has so many kitchens serving different kinds of meals, Triestman's security duties are more onerous than they might be. He must be vigilant that dairy never touches meat, that a frying pan used for non-glatt meat is never used for glatt, that waiters running up and down stairs don't inadvertently carry utensils from one kitchen to the other. He checks every can, bottle, and package for a recognized kosher label. He turns on the pilot lights in the morning and relights them if they go out. To ensure that nothing untoward enters his territory, Triestman color-codes every movable object in the kitchen, from baking trays to cutting boards to dish towels—red for meat or chicken, yellow for fish, and blue for dairy. If anyone steps outside, they have to remove their red aprons and dishrags, and put them on again when they return. If anything non-kosher goes into one of his ovens, that oven cannot be used again until it is re-kashered.

By 9:30, Triestman is back upstairs in his kitchen, checking the bowls of vegetables he has prepared over the past four days. He spent sixteen hours yesterday checking, washing, and chopping, plus half a day last Friday and eight hours Thursday. Altogether, checking and cleaning vegetables for possible bug infestation has taken him two and a half days of work. Those are long days spent on his feet, soaking, rinsing, examining, and soaking again.

The salad alone took him fifteen hours, checking and cleaning thirty-five pounds of spring mix, fourteen pounds of frisée, three pounds of radicchio, twenty pounds of endive, and nine pounds of baby spinach. The process is similar to what Rabbi Friedman does at the Dole plant, but Triestman must check every leaf, not just a representative sample. He places the leafy greens in a sink filled with paracetic acid, a solution used in the food industry as a disinfectant. It dissolves the sticky substance insects use to cling to the leaves, so they float freely and can be seen more easily. Then he rinses the leaves in a second sink and puts them in a big green plastic salad spinner called a hopper. He agitates the hopper, pulls out the colander holding the leaves, and examines the leftover water for insects. If he sees any, the entire process is repeated. Once the water runs clean, he checks the leaves visually against white paper or on a light box, using a jeweler's loupe.

In addition to the green salad, there were parsley, basil, and chives to be examined, cleaned, and chopped for the breading on the chicken breasts; cabbage and carrots for the coleslaw; celery, rosemary, scallions, and more. Triestman and two helpers spent much of Friday cleaning twenty-one cases of baby portobello mushrooms, a tricky vegetable because insects can hide in the moist folds under the cap. The job took six hours, with three men working nonstop.

By ten, Triestman starts blocking off the section of the non-kosher kitchen that he will later kasher. He rolls around six-foot-tall wheeled serving racks, pushing them together to make an impassable wall, and then wraps chains around them and secures the chains tightly with heavy iron locks. Now no one can walk through the non-kosher section or grab any utensil or serving piece from it. Before locking up the final chains, he opens the kitchen's pantry, removes every open box, package, or bottle of food—flour, sugar, salt, oil—and shoves them deep behind the makeshift barrier. The food is kosher, he explains, but because the containers are no longer sealed, he cannot guarantee that no one has used a non-kosher spoon in them or poured used cooking oil back into the bottle.

"I feel like the Ghost of Christmas Past," he booms, his arms filled with three-foot-long iron chains and clanking metal locks. "Or was that Jacob Marley?"

As he pushes the heavy rolling racks into place, Triestman says that tonight's wedding is far from the most difficult event he's worked. Sometimes he does back-to-back events and can be on his feet for twenty-four hours at a stretch. And working as a hotel mashgiach for Passover is the worst of all.

"I did Pesach at the Four Seasons up in Whistler, British Columbia, and I still haven't recovered," he says. "I stood at a sink twenty-two hours straight, cleaning hearts of romaine. It was so infested with flies. The next day I had leg cramps from dehydration. I couldn't get out of bed. I had to take all kinds of pills and stuff." Passover is a job for a younger man, he says. "*Bli neder,* I'm never going to do that again."[2]

If Triestman was nervous running a kosher event for his boss, imagine how Rabbi Hillel Baron felt when the White House called.

In December 2005, the administration decided that bringing in prepackaged kosher meals for the president's annual Chanukah party was no longer sufficient for the caliber of Jewish dignitaries invited. It was time to kasher the kitchen.

"President Bush and the first lady got it in their minds to make it all kosher," says Baron, a rabbi in Columbia, Maryland, who was invited to be the mashgiach in charge of the project. "Mrs. Bush found what she thought was a kosher caterer in Philadelphia. Turns out it was kosher-style, not appropriate for this crowd, but she had already booked them. One of the White House aides called us, all in a panic."

Baron and a colleague located a glatt kosher caterer in New Jersey willing to partner with the Philadelphia outfit. The two teams prepared the food in New Jersey, then trucked it down to D.C. along with thousands of pre-kashered dishes, pots and pans, and serving pieces. Baron and his fellow mashgichim swept through the White House kitchen, kashering the ovens and sinks, covering up everything they weren't going to use, and double- and triple-wrapping all exposed counter surfaces where food or utensils might be placed. Because the kitchen was still contaminated with non-kosher food in the refrigerators and particles of past treyf stuck to the undersides of dishes and serving utensils, the mashgichim spent the entire party on high alert to make sure nothing unapproved made its way out to the dining room.

"A lot of the guests were shocked to see us there," Baron says. "They kept asking, Is this really kosher?" Afterward, when the cooking team was invited to have their pictures taken with the president and first lady, Baron thanked Bush for making the event kosher. "President Bush paused and said, 'You know, it was the right thing to do.'"

At eleven, Triestman heads upstairs to start kashering silverware. The silverware in his kitchen is always kosher, but he will need 2,500 forks, 600 steak knives, 600 butter knives, and 1,000 spoons for tonight's event, so he has to kasher a lot of extra pieces. He fills a four-by-two-foot industrial brazier with water, heats it to boiling, and pours in a little ammonia. Then, his arms and hands protected by heavy black rubber gloves, he plunges trays full of silverware into the bubbling cauldron. The silverware is already clean—this process is meant to purify it spiritually, not wash it physically. In about five minutes, when the water returns to boiling, he shoves his arms back in and hauls out the trays, heaving them into a sink of clear water to rinse. This is hot, heavy work, and he has dozens of trays to go. By the middle of the first round, he is sweating profusely.

Triestman is a big, strong man, with beefy arms, ruddy skin, and a gravelly smoker's voice. This job suits his physique and temperament. He started out bartending and cooking while a student at Syracuse University, and in 1993, newly observant and studying at a yeshiva in Morristown, New Jersey, he took up cooking again. Three years of cooking for Jewish summer camps didn't discourage him, nor did a couple of years as a chef-mashgiach for several local caterers and restaurants. He passed on the chance to be a mashgiach in a Manhattan bagel shop, saying he didn't want to be stuck behind a counter, and took the job at the Crystal Plaza instead.

Triestman does not have to do this heavy manual labor; he could supervise while his staff works, like many of his colleagues do. But that's not his style. "I can't see myself doing that," he says. "A lot of places that do kosher events aren't used to seeing a working rabbi. But I can't ask my workers to do anything I won't do."

A top mashgiach needs to know how things work. The world of kosher food production has become so technologically complex that a background in engineering can be just as helpful as knowing the laws of kashrut. "Everything's changed," says Rabbi Seth Mandel of the OU. "The plants have changed, the equipment has changed. You can't work in kashrut unless you know what equipment a plant is using, so you understand what the problems might be."

Rabbi Moshe Perlmutter, longtime mashgiach and kosher educator for the OU, likes to point out that before he went into kosher supervision, he worked as a plumber. Once, while inspecting a food manufacturing plant, he noticed pipes connecting the dairy side of the operation to the pareve side in three separate places. Someone with only book knowledge, unfamiliar with how piping works, would have missed that, and the food produced would not have been kosher.

Perlmutter is telling that story to a group of two dozen rabbinical students at the Grand Hyatt hotel in Manhattan. The students, all from the Rabbi Isaac Elchanan Theological Seminary at Yeshiva University, are taking an optional three-week course in practical kashrut organized by the OU's kosher outreach department. It's the first time such a class has been offered. These future rabbis spend a lot of time studying the laws of kashrut, but if they take pulpit positions they will be called upon to answer all kinds of practical questions from their congregants. They will sit on rabbinical committees in charge of restaurants and kosher stores; they might even give supervision themselves. This course takes them to factories, slaughterhouses, restaurants, and hotel kitchens, so they will have at least a modicum of familiarity with the field.

"The yeshivas were not set up to produce practicing rabbis; they were set up to teach Torah," says Mandel. "To my mind, this is not only long overdue, it's a tremendous thing. Kashrus is too important to be left to the guy who doesn't know what he's doing."

Perlmutter has several dozen silver-plated serving pieces arranged on a table in front of him. One by one he picks them up, telling the class what it is and what it is used for. This isn't just etiquette; it's essential to their job. If they don't know what a gooseneck is or what kind of food is served in it, they won't know how to kasher it.

The students, young men in their early twenties, are furiously taking notes. Cheese knives, fish platters, soup tureens, three-tiered dessert trays, gravy boats—it's all uncharted territory for them. Perlmutter holds up a silver plate cover, the circular half-dome used to keep dishes hot while they're being served. He runs his finger around the rolled rim along its outer edge. "This can be a problem to kasher," he explains. "Any food that gets under the rim can get stuck. A plate could be full of gravy; it's a big concern."

Perlmutter tells of an affair he attended where the mashgichim were arguing over whether nonpermitted food residue might be trapped under the rims of plate covers they wanted to use. They finally took a saw and hacked one apart, just to see. That, he tells the group, is not the best course of action.

Before kashering such items, the mashgiach has to determine whether something is rust or a stain versus actual food particles. "It's good to feel with your fingers," he advises the class. "If there's nothing there, just discoloration, it's okay. But if it's burnt on, there could be *bliya* [odor left behind by hot food] stuck behind there, so that's a problem. If I were kashering a pan like that, I'd go around the edges with a torch."

Next, he hauls an industrial-size percolator up onto the table. "This is a coffeepot," he tells the group, all of them too young to know anything but drip-coffee machines. "Fifteen years ago we didn't kasher them, because they were just used for coffee. Now we kasher them. There's nothing we use for hot that we don't kasher today."

There are three basic ways to make equipment kosher or change its status between milk, meat, or pareve. If the equipment has been used only with cold food or drink, such as the inside of a freezer, a good cleaning with soap or caustic cleansers is usually sufficient. But if it has come into contact with hot food, that same kind of heat must be used to make it kosher. An oven would be kashered using extreme dry heat, such as a blowtorch heating the metal until it glows, whereas a sink or kitchen counter would require wet heat, that is, boiling water thrown over it. A dishwasher is made kosher by undergoing a thorough scrub-down, and then running it through a complete cycle using extra-hot water, upping the usual heat from 190 to at least 212 degrees Fahrenheit.

Sometimes creative solutions are called for. It's a lot easier to haul out the blowtorch for one-time jobs like koshering a restaurant or home kitchen, but hotels and banquet halls won't let anyone near their expensive ovens with such an instrument. One false blast near a thermostat and the whole oven has to be replaced. For such jobs the usual method is to turn the ovens to the highest heat possible for up to three hours, after scrubbing them out with an oven cleaner. So mashgichim have to know about metals, cleansing agents, boiling points, blowtorches, and electrical wiring as well as the laws of food preparation and storage.

They also have to be able to connect the dots. It's common practice in bars and hotels to "marry" partially used bottles of wine, pouring them into one bottle to save storage space. That may not be bad, unless they're pouring non-kosher wine into a kosher bottle. Make sure wine is opened in front of you, Perlmutter warns the class, and look for streaks on the label that indicate the bottle was once in a tub of ice, taken out long enough to dry, and used again. "If you're not on the ball and know to look for these things, you won't *khap*," he says, using Yiddish slang for "get what's going on."

Working well with people is a further job requirement. Rabbi Mayer Kurcfeld is a kashrut administrator at Star-K headquarters in Baltimore. Part of his job is training new mashgichim, and he tells them that without a good relationship with staff, the most carefully laid plans are useless.

"Imagine yourself in a big kitchen. Things are flying, especially when you have a catered event for five hundred people," he posits. "You can't keep running around after everybody; you can't keep yelling. What I find is, if I create a good rapport with the workers, then they want to help. They want to do it right."

A combination of tact and firmness is needed to convince a hotel manager or chef that seemingly small mistakes or innocent substitutions could violate guests' deeply held religious beliefs as well as ruin the mashgiach's and kosher agency's reputation. It's second nature for a cook preparing a vegetable dish to reach for butter when the margarine runs out, but if that dish is being served at a meat meal, it must be thrown out.

"I tell them, imagine if the food is burnt," Kurcfeld says. "The hotel would never dream of serving it, I promise you. It's the same if they reach for the butter. You can yell until tomorrow; there's nothing I can do for you. Go make more soup. If they put butter in it, as far as I'm concerned the soup is burnt. It is not being served."

Rabbi Eliezer Stolzenberg, another OU kosher instructor, tells the students that dining managers and caterers are just as eager as the mashgiach to satisfy their customers, but don't necessarily have the same interests at heart. "If you're in a hotel that has a kosher and a non-kosher kitchen and a caterer runs out of meat for the smorgasbord, what's he going to do? Send a waiter to the other kitchen to heat up some corned beef and bring it in a back door. If the mashgiach happens to see it, the caterer says, 'Oh, I'm so sorry, rabbi. It'll never happen again.' This goes on all the time." A mashgiach told him of one affair he supervised where the kitchen staff waited until he took a bathroom break, and then sneaked in plastic tubs of non-kosher chicken to make up for a last-minute shortage. "They were all working in collusion, waiting for him to step out."

Having enough mashgichim working an event is important, Perlmutter says. Conversely, too many mashgichim is also a mistake. Perlmutter tells of a kosher caterer who brought twenty-seven mashgichim to a Passover job. "They had guys checking the waitresses entering the hotel, looking inside their pocketbooks to make sure they weren't sneaking things in. That's not the way to treat people."

Having good systems in place, knowing your materials, knowing the kosher laws, getting along with your staff—it's a complicated, multi-faceted job. And it all has to be done under pressure of time, money, and human limitations. A mashgiach also has to know when something cannot be done, when a perfectly kosher cake cannot be served because it was delivered on Shabbat, or when a client's grandmother's china cannot be used at her daughter's bat mitzvah dinner because it cannot be kashered.

"There are four types of kashering, not three," says Perlmutter. "The fourth is to say no."

Back at the Crystal Plaza, it's 12:30 p.m. and Triestman is ready to start kashering his second kitchen. He and his staff have scoured all the stainless-steel sinks and countertops with steel wool, and polished every surface to make sure not the slightest scrap of food remains lodged in any cracks. He has a second brazier full to the brim with rapidly boiling water. Ordering everyone out of the kitchen, he dons the heavy-duty elbow gloves, dunks a metal bucket into the brazier, hauls it out, and begins slinging boiling water all around the room. He throws buckets of water on the counters, the cutting tables, the sinks, on top of ovens, on stove doors. The room fills with steam, and his head disappears behind a cloud of white. This is dangerous work. Plenty of guys get scalded.

Before slinging the water, he has turned all the ovens to 550 degrees to burn out any residue from previous jobs. Now he starts in on the stovetop. He covers it with two layers of aluminum foil, lights the burners, and turns them on full blast for about fifteen minutes, until whatever food particles that remain are reduced to ash. Removing the foil is a delicate operation, as the heat buildup underneath is tremendous. Once that procedure is complete, he takes the oven racks, which he has previously cleaned, wraps them in foil, and sets them on top of the stove to be blasted by fire for two to three hours. By now he is sweating and his face is beet red.

At two, Triestman wolfs down half a sandwich and starts locking up all the refrigerators, ovens, storage areas, and pantries he won't be using for this job. He goes through every part of the building, grabbing a bunch of copper pots he discovers hanging underneath a staircase, shutting away a cupboard filled with spices. Walking through the porch that will be used for the cocktail hour, he notices that plates set out by the hibachi grill station do not have the pattern specific to his glatt kosher kitchen. He calls a waiter to remove them.

The cocktail bar is next. An assistant has removed many of the bottles that do not carry kosher symbols, but Triestman is ruthless. He is not taking any chances with this wedding. Plain vodka does not need kosher certification, but flavored vodkas do. Same thing with rum: White rum is usually fine, but not amber or brown, which contain coloring agents that must be produced under kosher supervision. The Bacardi can stay, but the Captain Morgan has to go. Canadian Club is in, Southern Comfort is out. Bottles of Cointreau, Campari, Grand Marnier, Midori, Tia Maria all get carted away. By the time he's through, the bar is decimated. The only liqueur remaining on the shelves is Frangelico. When the bartender arrives he will have to fill in the empty spaces with kosher bottles so it looks less tragic.

At 2:30, Rabbi Stone shows up and makes his first of several visits to the kitchen. Why aren't all the treyf cabinets locked up yet? Ordinarily Triestman might bristle at the intrusion, but not today. Not only is Stone the father of the bride, he is directly responsible for upholding the kashrut standards of any event at the Plaza.

The rest of the kitchen staff begins arriving, and the tempo increases. Most of Triestman's heavy work is done, but he has to stay alert for the rest of the afternoon and evening, mopping up, solving problems, adding an extra pair of hands on the serving line. One sous chef calls him to unlock the pantry so he can get out more tea bags; the bartender needs dishes for limes; the executive chef needs him to clean and check additional leeks, rosemary, and thyme. At four, he's dragged away to make the tenth man for afternoon prayers; he rushes back to light all the butane stoves under the chafing dishes in the cocktail lobby, a job the non-Jewish staff cannot perform. All the while he keeps one brazier filled with boiling water, for last-minute kashering of extra serving utensils that might be needed. "I'm over this thing like a witch's kettle the whole evening," he mutters.

It's been a long day, and an equally long night is ahead. The last guests will leave around midnight, but he won't get home until much later. He has to make sure the kosher kitchen is clean and safely locked up. In a few days, it all happens again. "If I work fourteen-hour, sixteen-hour days, whatever, that's what goes on here," he says. "Still, I'm not getting any younger."

. . .

IN A SMALL ROOM at the Meadowlands Exposition Center in Secaucus, New Jersey, four sushi chefs have their hands on their knives, waiting for moderator Elan Kornblum to start the clock. "Three, two, one!" Kornblum shouts, and the chefs start frantically slicing into piles of raw fish. Each has five minutes to construct a platter of the tastiest, most attractive, most unusual kosher sushi he can.

It's the first day of Kosherfest 2008, the annual trade show of the kosher food industry, and the first time organizers are running a live, *Iron Chef*–style cooking competition. What did they choose for this first showcasing of cutting-edge kosher cuisine? Not gefilte fish. Not chicken soup. Not even the deli sandwich—that's next year's category.

Sushi. That great traditional Jewish food. "It's amazing how popular sushi has become," says Kornblum, publisher of *Great Kosher Restaurants*, an annual guide to kosher eateries around the world. "At first Jews said, Ohhh, raw fish, I can't eat that. But they've been educated. Now no matter what, even if you have a small space, you'll find a place for a sushi bar."

Kornblum dates the kosher sushi boom back about five years, at least a decade later than it hit the rest of the country. Kosher trends always lag a few years behind, he says. The Orthodox community is leery of change, in food as in anything else. Today California rolls and tuna sashimi are de rigueur at even the most Orthodox bar mitzvahs and wedding receptions. It was front and center at the Stone wedding in New Jersey, along with guacamole and chips, Chinese egg rolls, and spicy chicken crepes—all part of the lavish appetizer spread before the main meal. When Jews adopt a food trend from other cultures, they don't necessarily treat it as it was originally conceived. "Sushi has replaced gefilte fish as an appetizer," points out food critic Arthur Schwartz. "The Japanese don't eat sushi as an appetizer and then have a steak afterward, but Jews do."

Binem Naiman, owner of Glatt-A-LaCarte, a kosher restaurant and catering operation in Brooklyn's heavily hassidic Borough Park neighborhood, stands anxiously behind his head chef during the sushi competition, watching the man build little towers of tuna roll. Naiman is a Gerer hassid, a member of a fervently Orthodox sect that follows the

Polish-born Gerer rebbe. He is on a crusade at his restaurant to bring his fellow hassidim into the modern culinary world.

"We started small, with French cuisine, steaks," he says. He served those steaks medium rare, a novelty in a world where beef is traditionally cooked to death. "A regular Jewish guy, a Brooklyn Orthodox, by him a rib steak is charcoal burned, well done. Delicious!" Naiman explains. "What is this, blood I should eat? They didn't know. That's what I grew up with—a steak that was well done in the oven, chewy, and it tasted good. We're educating the people that you should eat it medium, at least. Slowly, the community is learning what is good food."

Same with kosher wine. "There's the kiddush wine, sweet; I don't want to say names. Today more and more we're selling good wine. People want to know if it's a good cabernet. It used to be only cough syrup in the Jewish world. Four or five years ago we didn't even sell wine at all. We had to push them: 'Try this wine together with this.' Educating the people what a good wine is, how to drink it. The moscato wine, everybody likes. At first they thought it was sour—what is this? After a while you acquire the taste. Now when they come in for a good steak, they want a good glass of wine."

The third hurdle was sushi. Naiman's introduction came two years ago, when his chef took him to a kosher Japanese restaurant in Manhattan and pushed him to try a vegetable roll and some spicy tuna. The vegetable wasn't so hard, but raw fish? "I was very nervous," he admits. But he liked it, and in early 2008 he brought it to Brooklyn.

Naiman urges his customers to start slow. First a cucumber roll, then work up to the Godzilla Roll, made of deep-fried fish, nothing raw or slimy. "I say try it. Just close your eyes and try it."

The Naiman kids are hooked. His two-year-old son is crazy for sushi, he says. His five-year-old daughter taught her aunt the correct way to eat steamed and salted soybeans called edamame. You have to pop them out of the shell first, she instructed, appalled that the older woman had put the entire pod in her mouth.

Now sushi is one of the hottest items in his restaurant. "Everyone's excited—they can have a good steak, and sushi, too," he says. "We've come a long way from herring."

There really is no such thing as Jewish food. But when Americans say "Jewish food," they mean the Ashkenazic dishes of Eastern Europe and the Russian Pale of Settlement, the herring, gefilte fish, and stuffed cabbage brought to America by the two million Jewish immigrants who arrived at the turn of the last century.

Jews have always taken from the cuisines of their surrounding cultures, adapting those dishes to kosher requirements. The Jewish population has been scattered so thoroughly throughout the world that there are very few dishes that can claim to be originally Jewish. Pastrami is Romanian, borsch is Ukrainian, herring is Russian, chopped liver is Alsatian, and rye bread, corned beef, even gefilte fish are German. "If Martians landed in New York today, they would think pizza and sushi were the most Jewish foods, because we always eat the food of the culture that we live in," says Schwartz.

The only dishes that can be considered truly Jewish in origin are those developed for specific rituals, such as matzo for Passover, or those that solve a halachic problem, such as cholent, the Sabbath stew that is put in the oven Friday evening and simmered slowly until Saturday lunch without requiring the cook to adjust the heat, which would violate the Sabbath prohibition on lighting a fire. Cholent is so necessary to the Sabbath table that virtually every Jewish community has developed its own version, based on local tastes.

Jewish cooks are constrained by the laws of kashrut. Taste and presentation must take a backseat to kosher requirements, and that has led to low expectations for kosher food. Schwartz says that's why so many kosher restaurants are mediocre. Even he falls into the trap of saying this or that dish in a restaurant he's reviewing "is good, for kosher," before catching himself. "Why do we permit this?" he complains. "We should have the same standards for a restaurant that we have in our own home."

When the first kosher Chinese restaurants and pizza joints appeared in New York City in the 1950s, they didn't have to be good—it was enough that they were kosher, and that they existed. New Yorker Beth Berg says the craze for kosher Chinese food took off in the 1960s, and she recalls the scene on a typical Saturday night at Shmulka Bernstein's on Essex, one of the city's first kosher Chinese restaurants. "The average wait for a table and the privilege of devouring overstuffed pastrami sandwiches and egg rolls was at least an hour or two," she reports. "While you did not enjoy the wait, you knew it was the price to pay for being seen at that 'hot' location."[3]

The best new kosher restaurants, cookbooks, and food products go farther afield, dipping into the Sephardic traditions of Spain and Italy, the Arab-influenced cuisines of Egypt and Iraq, the subtlety of Persian cooking, and the exotic, heavily spiced dishes of Ethiopia. Manhattan set the bar for the new upscale restaurants. First was Levana, which opened in 1979 as a bakery and later wowed customers with kosher exotica like venison in juniper berry and currant sauce, and short ribs with parsnip mousseline. Le Marais, a French-style steak house in the theater district, introduced kosher diners to steak tartare and rare medallions of beef in béarnaise sauce. In March 2008, Solo upped the ante by hiring Vietnamese-born chef Hung Huynh, third-season winner of the *Top Chef* reality show. The tony East Side eatery with the Mediterranean-Asian cuisine and Zen-inspired interior design offered seared yellowfin tuna with shaved fennel and pea shoots for $23 and pan-roasted veal sweetbreads for $24—and those were just the appetizers.

Ironically, the recent proliferation of upscale kosher restaurants in the business neighborhoods of cities like New York and Los Angeles actually breaks down the social barriers kashrut seeks to enforce, by providing dining venues where Orthodox can eat with non-Orthodox, and with non-Jew. Rabbi Jack Wertheimer, provost of the Conservative movement's Jewish Theological Seminary, remembers the first kosher pizza parlors in New York in the 1960s as places where observant Jewish teenagers like himself could hang out. Today's kosher restaurants attract a much more diverse clientele, including Orthodox businessmen and businesswomen meeting non-Jewish clients over a meal. "I've been in kosher restaurants in Manhattan where only a small fraction of the men are wearing kippahs," he reports.

Kosher cookbooks are flying off the shelves. For more than a century, synagogue women's groups have put together books of their favorite recipes and sold them to raise money. In the past decade or so, glossy kosher and kosher-style cookbooks featuring traditional and innovative Jewish dishes have become hot sellers in the mainstream market. There's no reason why kosher cooking should be stuck in a schmaltz-laden rut, these new books suggest. Kosher diners have increasingly sophisticated palates, and they are closely following mainstream food trends.

In 1979, Joan Nathan published *The Jewish Holiday Kitchen*, a collection of hundreds of traditional Ashkenazic recipes interspersed with snippets of food history and Jewish holiday tips. Twenty-five years later she updated it in *Joan Nathan's Jewish Holiday Cookbook*, catering to new food sensibilities with dishes such as low-cholesterol challah. More than half of the eight hundred recipes in Claudia Roden's 1996 *The Book of Jewish Food* focus on Sephardic cuisine, with recipes such as Yemeni wedding soup and *megadarra*, Egyptian-style brown lentils and rice. In 2008, the best-selling *Hip Kosher: 175 Easy-to-Prepare Recipes for Today's Kosher Cooks* demonstrated that a kosher diet could be rich in fresh fruits and vegetables.

Queen of the kosher cookbook is Susie Fishbein, whose six books in as many years have collectively sold half a million copies. *Passover by Design*, released in February 2008, sold out all twenty thousand copies in one day. Her latest release in November 2008, *Kosher by Design Lightens Up: Fabulous Food for a Healthier Lifestyle*, focuses on low-sugar, low-fat recipes featuring whole grains, fresh produce, and lean cuts of meat.

"Ancient grains are hot," says Jeff Nathan, chef-owner of Abigael's on Broadway. "I'm not just talking quinoa, but millet, faro, oats, tamaranthe, kemet, teff. Organic is still going up. It's more expensive, but everybody's talking about it. Probiotics—it's in yogurt, it's in everything. Consumers don't know what it is, but they hear it's good for you."

Nathan presented a workshop on new culinary trends at Kosherfest 2008. His session was designed to help kosher restaurant owners and food manufacturers outguess the competition, and they have a lot more to work with than they used to. Ten years ago, Nathan had difficulty finding kosher-certified rice wine vinegar, pickled ginger, and nori. But now that the Orthodox crowd wants sushi, the products are available. The same applies to health-conscious foods; the general consumer is buying them, and now kosher consumers demand them as well, he says, so restaurants and grocery stores are clamoring for more healthy kosher-certified products.

In urban markets like New York, locally sourced meat and produce are fashionable. The best kosher restaurants are following suit. At Abigael's the menu lists not only a dish's ingredients but also their points of origin. The duck and arugula salad, for example, features midwestern wild rice and "local harvest" arugula. The duck is not fried, it's "pan-crisped." Terminology sells. "No one wants baked food anymore; they want slow roasted," Nathan says. "The kosher consumer is more educated and wants more interesting things."

Those trends are front and center at Kosherfest, which in November 2008 featured hundreds of new kosher-certified products. Booth after booth touts the health benefits of their new offerings. In one aisle, Yochi Katz is handing out samples of gluten-free chocolate cake from Katz Gluten-Free Bake Shoppe in Monroe, New York. The two-year-old company uses recipes his mother developed for two of his siblings who have celiac disease and can't tolerate gluten. Ashkenazic Jews have a genetic disposition for the disease.

In another aisle, the Fiorella Pasta Company is showing off its new cheese ravioli, which is hormone- and antibiotic-free. Managing partner Michael Seiff says Whole Foods asked Fiorella to make the product to cater to their higher-end kosher customers.

The Pittsburgh, Pennsylvania–based NuGo food company has brought its entire supply of healthy gourmet snacks, claiming it is the nation's first line of gluten-free, soy-free, pareve kosher snack products. The packaging is slick and eye-catching, featuring phrases like "Go Organic" and "Smart Carb." The company's dairy-free chocolate-chip bar has "Vegan" written in big letters across the front. In fact, the only word missing on these snacks is *kosher*. A tiny OU on the label is the only tip-off.

Even the traditional ethnically Jewish food manufacturers are making changes. David Ross, vice president of marketing for The Manischewitz Company, holds up a pop-top can of the company's newest product, an all-natural, low-sodium chicken broth. "We're definitely trying to do more all-natural and organic," he says. "We are seeing a trend away from the traditional products." The company still manufactures more than two million pounds of fish every year, but sales of gefilte fish, pike, and jellied whitefish, along with borsch, schav, and other ethnic favorites, is down. "It's not rapidly declining, but it's an older category," he admits, employing an adjective that makes marketers wince.

A big impetus for this revolution in the quality of kosher food, as with wine, is the baal teshuva, or newly religious Jew. There are no hard statistics, but perhaps one-third of the estimated 350,000 kosher-keeping households in the United States include Jews who know what non-kosher food tastes like from past experience. They've tasted aged cheese and tender steaks, and they are not willing to settle for second-rate food just because it has a hekhsher.

"The baal teshuva has had a major influence," says Lévana Kirschenbaum, who for thirty years owned and operated, with her two brothers-in-law, the Manhattan restaurant that bore her name. She is a case in point. Raised Orthodox, she "fell away" from religion for a while and experienced a wide variety of non-kosher foods before becoming observant again.

"As people became religious, they brought good food with them," she says. "The food had to look real and taste real. They didn't say, 'Let's make ersatz versions of the food we used to eat,' but 'Let's use fresh mushrooms, virgin olive oil, sun-dried tomatoes,' things that were there all along but weren't being used."

"If you grow up eating kosher, you don't really know the difference," says Joy Devor. Winner of the 2008 Simply Manischewitz Cook-Off for her flounder recipe, Devor was asked to fine-tune more than three hundred recipes for her next-door neighbor's kosher cookbook. Devor has always kept kosher, so she had to depend on her neighbor to judge the authenticity of her adaptations. "She's a baal teshuva, so I'd bring the dish over to her and ask, Does this taste like the real thing?"

The kosher organic market has been booming for more than a decade. Increasing numbers of food products carry both kosher and organic certification. In 2008, the Star-K became the first kosher agency to partner with an organic certifier when it announced an alliance with Quality Assurance International, a national organization that certifies foods as organic according to USDA specifications. Star-K began training mashgichim in QAI standards, so the same inspector could satisfy both demands.

When American consumers began paying top dollar for higher-quality luxury items such as cheese, coffee, and chocolate, the kosher industry jumped on board. Alyssa Kaplan runs KosherGourmetMart .com, a website she created in 2004 to sell a wide variety of upscale kosher food products. Along with a surge in demand for kosher-certified Asian cooking ingredients, she is noticing a clamoring for imported chocolates and premium cheeses. When the Vermont-based Cabot Creamery, famous for its cheddar cheeses since 1919, came out with kosher-certified sharp cheddar recently, she put it on her site immediately.

"Jews want fresh mozzarella, they want *nam pla* [Thai fish sauce] and bonito flakes," says the forty-year-old Kaplan, who grew up kosher in Brooklyn and sees how the community's culinary options have expanded. "We don't feel we are second-class citizens anymore."

Even treyf can be kosher. The Talmud teaches that for every non-kosher food there exists a perfectly acceptable kosher equivalent. For centuries Jewish cooks have been inventing kosher versions of treyf dishes, substituting oil for butter in meat recipes and using chicken or beef instead of ham. Food historian John Cooper describes a medieval Italian Jewish dish made of veal and chicken known as *chazarello,* or "little pig," no doubt because the original was made of pork.

Modern food technology has greatly widened the kosher culinary imagination. A century ago, Crisco vegetable shortening allowed observant housewives to serve better-tasting cakes and flakier pies after a meat meal. Nondairy creamer, a mid-twentieth-century invention, appeased kosher diners tired of black coffee. Today imitation crab, lobster, and shrimp made of kosher fish such as pollack and bream, artificially colored and reshaped to look like shellfish, are sold in supermarkets and sushi restaurants. Soy is a kosher bonanza, used in tofu hot dogs, nondairy ice cream, and, in the form of soy milk, whipped into a cream sauce and poured over beef or chicken.

In November 2007, Talia's Steakhouse, a glatt kosher restaurant in New York, caused a sensation when it introduced a kosher pareve cheeseburger—a slab of soy cheese melted onto a kosher beef patty. Many Orthodox leaders decried the dish, citing the Jewish custom of avoiding *maaris ayin,* which is doing something that looks sinful even if it's not. The burger may be technically kosher, but to many it smacks of trying too hard to mimic the Gentiles.

"I don't know, maybe I'm old-school," says Rabbi Traub of San Francisco. "I grew up without cheeseburgers. I lived most of my life without cheeseburgers. I assume, God willing, that I will continue to do that." But restaurant owner Ephraim Nagar told reporters that curious Orthodox customers were ordering the dish in droves, as were formerly secular, now observant Jews who missed the taste of the real thing.[4]

Of all the foods forbidden by Jewish law, pork holds pride of place. Some food historians posit that Chinese restaurants became popular with American Jews because the pork is chopped up and mixed in with the vegetables, so it's not noticeable—a sort of "don't ask, don't tell" approach to dietary law.

Although the Torah does not single out pigs as worse than any of the other non-kosher creatures, they have become so through historical experience. Pork carries cultural baggage for Jews that other treyf does not. From Rome to the Inquisition to Nazi Germany, when anti-Semites wanted to taunt Jews, they forced them to eat pork, not lobster. Perhaps that's because pork was more available in the areas of Europe where most Jews lived, but the fact remains that pig became etched in the Jewish and non-Jewish consciousness as the most un-Jewish of foods.

Brian Dentz, a forty-year-old New York videographer, was raised in a kosher home. As a secular adult he kept kosher until he was thirty. Now he eats seafood, mixes milk and meat, but still won't touch pork. "There's no logic to it," he admits. But something in his gut turns over at the thought of downing pig flesh. "You have to draw the line somewhere. For me, it's pig. And I think the world's gonna be okay with that."

"Pork is the ultimate expression of treyf," says writer Jeffrey Yoskowitz, who spent a year in Israel researching the non-kosher food industry. In Israel, where religious parties are the swing vote in government coalitions and laws about kashrut and Shabbat are imposed on a largely secular public, flouting those laws, he says, "is like sticking it to the Man," an act of political rebellion. In America, where Jewish observance is not mandated by the state, eating or not eating treyf is an individual matter. But you still have to answer to your mother for it.

Pork is to Jews like sex is to Catholics—a guilty pleasure that provokes sheepish grins and whispered giggles. It seems as if every American Jew has his or her secret piggy adventure. Thirty-year-old Rebecca Gruber, project director of the Six Points Fellowship at the Foundation for Jewish Culture, grew up in a kosher home in St. Louis where her parents permitted, or pretended to ignore, pepperoni pizza if it was eaten in the basement. "Like if it was underground, somehow it wasn't treyf," says Gruber, who claims she never indulged, only her friends did. "We were fifteen; that was their rebellion," she says. "My rebellion was becoming a vegetarian."

Laughter is a classic nervous reaction to guilt, as anyone who has been in therapy knows. In Jewish circles, Yoskowitz says, the more treyf something is, the funnier it is. What gets a laugh? A Jew eating a cheeseburger. What gets a bigger laugh? A Jew eating a bacon cheeseburger. For its special food issue in September 2006, the Jewish youth magazine *Heeb* featured a piglet on the cover. Scallops would not have been as funny. "People laughed in America when I told them about my project," Yoskowitz says. "In Israel, they didn't. The religious were angry, or disgusted. The secular Jews wondered why I was wasting my time."

Bacon is almost a separate category. It's such a part of the classic American breakfast that some American Jews who otherwise keep kosher make an exception for bacon, and many newly religious Jews say giving up bacon was their most difficult challenge. The Jewish fetish for bacon is an iconic part of American Jewish comedy from Woody Allen to Baconjew.com, one of several online forums that purport to unite Jews who lust after the forbidden meat.

In the quest to find kosher versions of treyf foods, food manufacturers have tackled bacon with particular vigor. Early soy-based versions fooled no one who had ever tasted the real stuff. Kosher turkey bacon is much more successful, but in deference to maaris ayin is rarely marketed as such. Meal Mart calls its version "turkey fry strips," reminiscent of "beef frye," a kosher bacon substitute invented in the 1930s. Jenna Weissman Joselit credits beef frye with holding "out the very real and tantalizing possibility that the observance of kashruth posed no barrier to participation in the wider world, at least in a culinary sense."[5]

In 2007, thirty-five-year-old Dave Lefkow and Justin Esch, twenty-nine, two Seattle friends, developed Bacon Salt, a kosher-certified seasoning mix designed to make any food taste like bacon. Esch, the non-Jewish member of the team, says he came up with the idea at a Jewish wedding when the conversation at his table suddenly turned to the Other White Meat. "Everyone started laughing and talking about bacon," he recalls. "Some of them said, 'I'm a bad Jew. I love bacon.' They called it the 'gateway' meat. One girl said, 'It's not a meat, it's a condiment.' So I thought, why not?"

The duo started experimenting with faux-bacon flavorings in a garage, funding their project with $5,000 Lefkow won from *America's Funniest Home Videos* for a segment of his three-year-old son hitting him in the face with a baseball. After months of working with chefs and food scientists, they came up with an all-vegetarian product. Finding a rabbi to give kosher certification was next. Lefkow called Rabbi Moshe Londinski of Seattle's Square K Kosher Services and told him what they wanted. "There was a long pause, and he said, 'David, I don't know if you know this, but bacon isn't even close to being kosher,'" Lefkow relates. But, says Esch, the rabbi "took pity on us" and agreed to certify the seasoning mix.

Lefkow got a starkly different reaction when he tried to get halal certification. Two agencies hung up on him—they wouldn't even hear him out.

When J&D's Bacon Salt was launched, the company received seventy thousand hits on its website in one day. Within a year, the guys made a million dollars in sales. "The rabbi and I were laughing about it, but it's a legitimate product for people who keep kosher," says Lefkow.

The company ships Bacon Salt for free to U.S. troops in the Middle East who are starved for bacon in the pork-free countries where they serve. Among the hundreds of thank-you cards and letters they've received is a photo of a U.S. Army rabbi stationed in Kuwait who took a picture of himself eating Bacon Salt with a local Muslim—one point for peace in the Middle East. "There are a lot of people who have a hard time giving up bacon," Lefkow says. "There is a group of people called bacon vegetarians: The only meat they eat is bacon. So in a way, we're helping people keep kosher."

# 12.

# Got Shrimp?

## Liberal Jews Take Another Look at Kashrut

ON JULY 11, 1883, Hebrew Union College, the rabbinical seminary of America's nascent Reform movement, held a gala dinner in Cincinnati to honor its initial graduating class, the first four Reform rabbis ordained in North America.

The nine-course meal, which became known as the Trefa Banquet, was elegant, elaborate, and not at all kosher. It featured seafood—littleneck clams, soft-shell crab, shrimp, and frogs' legs—non-kosher beef, and, in flagrant violation of the prohibition on mixing milk and meat, ice cream for dessert. The menu was written in a sort of franglais—"Salade of Shrimp" and "Grenouiles [sic] a la Creme and Cauliflower"—to underscore its Continental aspirations.

The Jewish press reacted harshly to what they saw as a slap in the face of traditional Judaism. In the *Jewish Messenger*, Henrietta Szold, a twenty-two-year-old reporter and later founder of Hadassah, the Women's Zionist Organization of America, recorded her "indignation" at the lack of "regard paid to our dietary laws." She noted that two rabbis left the room when the first course was served, and several others sat stone-faced for the rest of the evening, refusing to touch the food.

The Trefa Banquet has gone down in Jewish lore as an illustration of Reform's contempt for Jewish law and tradition. In fact, Reform leaders at the time were embarrassed by the incident, insisting the violation of kashrut was unintentional. Rabbi Isaac Mayer Wise, president of the college and the preeminent voice of American Reform Judaism, initially blamed the caterer, telling the *American Israelite* in August 1883, "We do not know why he diversified his menu with multipeds and bivalves."

By that fall, the Reform attitude had hardened. Buoyed by support from within his movement and angered at the continued brouhaha in the Orthodox press, Wise in November told *Die Deborah,* another Jewish publication, that he did not need to justify the dinner because most American Jews did not keep kosher anyway.[1]

There is still no consensus on who authorized the Trefa Banquet, although most scholars blame local lay leaders. It was not the first non-kosher meal sponsored by a Reform institution; in 1841, a Reform school in Hamburg, Germany, held a dinner featuring crab, oysters, and a pig's head.[2] But the Reform movement in America had always been more circumspect. Although increasing numbers of American Jews no longer kept kosher by the middle of the nineteenth century, it was rare for a Jewish communal institution to so openly flout the dietary laws.

The Trefa Banquet changed the rules. It represented, according to one scholar, a flexing of young Reform muscle, "a midpoint between the general compliance with traditional kashrut at public events that characterized American Reform Judaism until the 1870s and a radical break with kashrut that increasingly characterized mainstream Reform beginning in the 1880s."[3]

Reform Judaism emerged in Germany in the early nineteenth century as a reaction against what its Enlightenment-era founders considered the antiquated aspects of traditional Jewish practice and belief. Early Reform leaders viewed the Torah as a moral and spiritual guide rather than the word of God, its commandments no longer binding. They emphasized Judaism's ethical and universalist values; rituals and customs that no longer furthered those ideals, such as prayer shawls, ritual baths, and services conducted in Hebrew, were discarded.

This new approach arrived in America in the 1820s, and in 1873 a handful of congregations that followed its practices formed the Union of American Hebrew Congregations, now called the Union for Reform Judaism. They set down their core beliefs in the 1885 Pittsburgh Platform, the foundational document of American Reform Judaism. Among other things, the platform declared Jewish laws regulating "diet, priestly purity and dress" to be outmoded, their observance "apt rather to obstruct than to further modern spiritual elevation." The kosher diet had no place in modern American society, the document declared; it was socially divisive, alienating Jew from Gentile, and culturally backward, relying on arbitrary norms that had no basis in science.

Today most Jews assume that Reform Judaism rejects kashrut out-right. In fact, the Reform attitude has always been more nuanced, shifting along with developments in American Judaism as a whole. Historian Jonathan Sarna suggests that what is most significant about the Trefa Banquet is not what was served but what was *not* served: pork. Shellfish was acceptable to this urbane crowd. Mixing milk and meat was fine. But no hint of bacon, ham, or lard was permitted. The much-maligned banquet is thus a prime example of the emerging prac-tice of "selective kashrut," a pick-and-choose approach to Jewish die-tary law that led to the kosher-style delis of the late nineteenth and early twentieth centuries.

Selective kashrut has never meant anything goes. It operates accord-ing to well-understood, if unspoken, societal rules, themselves influenced by where one lives and with whom one associates. In nineteenth-century America, especially along the eastern seaboard, the genteel Gentiles ate shellfish. In Boston that meant oysters; in Baltimore it was crab. Liberal Jews looking to climb the social or business ladder in those regions followed suit, often incorporating these treyf sea crea-tures into their own versions of a Jewish diet.

The custom persists among some Reform Jews in those regions. Rabbi Lucy Dinner of Temple Beth Or in Raleigh, North Carolina, grew up in the Reform community of New Orleans, where Gulf shrimp was a staple at festive meals. Her childhood synagogue held an annual seafood dinner as late as 2005. As rabbi of her own congregation now, she encourages greater observance of the dietary laws and eschews treyf—except when she's in New Orleans, where she keeps what she calls "New Orleans kosher."

Pig was always different. One scholar writes that there were three kinds of Jewish diets in nineteenth-century America: ritually obser-vant, not observant, and "pork-free."[4] Shrimp salad and lobster bisque might be waved along with a friendly wink, but roast ham was a real statement.

Oysters were particularly popular in Belle Epoque cuisine, and an "antipork, pro-oyster" culture developed in Reform Jewish circles. Sci-ence was brought in as a weapon, again on a selective basis: Prominent Reform leaders argued that pork was dangerous, being prone to con-tamination, but they ignored the similar health risks presented by tainted shellfish. In 1895, Wise wrote in the *American Israelite* that the oyster's shell "is the same to all intents and purposes as the scales of the clean fish, protecting against certain gases in the water."[5]

The antipathy to pork relaxed in liberal Jewish circles as the twentieth century continued. Not only were second and third generations comfortable with American culinary tastes, many of their more traditional coreligionists pouring in from the Russian Pale were eager to fit in to American culture as quickly as possible. In 1910, the Purim Ball at a synagogue on Long Island served lobster, crab, *and* ham sandwiches, prompting the *Hebrew Standard* to declare, tongue in cheek, that Judaism on Long Island was "quite progressive."[6]

Pork became particularly accepted among Jews in the South. In 1935, the National Council of Jewish Women served baked ham for Shabbat dinner at its conference in New Orleans. A dish labeled "Swiss and Bacon" was offered as an alternative.[7] But few Jews tried to justify pork the way they rationalized seafood; those who ate it either knew they were violating kashrut or didn't think about it at all.

While segments of the Reform leadership began reexamining their attitude toward kashrut as early as the 1930s, that was not true of the Reform grassroots. Kashrut was of so little concern to most Reform Jews that movement surveys through midcentury did not even ask about it. In 1979, the Responsa Committee of the Central Conference of American Rabbis (CCAR), the legal body of the movement's rabbinical association, wrote that kashrut had "ceased to be a matter of primary concern for Reform Jews," citing as proof the lack of questions on the topic the committee had received from the public for decades.

By the 1980s, a new Jewish generation was coming of age at a time of greater spiritual exploration and ethnic identification. Whereas their parents and grandparents actively rejected Orthodox traditions, many younger Reform Jews were willing, even eager, to explore the potential these rituals might have to give meaning to their lives. The idea that ethical and spiritual ideals could be furthered rather than cheapened by observing Jewish ritual gained ground as the century progressed, engendering considerable push-back from older Reform Jews who hewed more closely to the Classical Reform line.

The winter 1998 edition of *Reform Judaism* magazine addressed the issue head-on, with a cover photo of Rabbi Richard Levy, then CCAR president, wearing a yarmulke and kissing the fringes of his prayer shawl. The accompanying article published a draft version of Levy's

"Ten Principles for Reform Judaism," intended as the basis for a new platform of principles to replace the 1885 Pittsburgh Platform and its rejection of Jewish ritual. Levy's proposal encouraged Reform Jews to consider adopting certain observances, including kashrut, as part of striving to make their lives more holy.

Now director of the School of Rabbinic Studies at Hebrew Union College's Los Angeles campus, Levy says he was not advocating a particular mode of religious expression; he just wanted Reform Jews to be open to the spiritual possibilities presented by all aspects of Jewish tradition. "The intention is to see eating as a religious act," he explains. "If you like the notion of locally grown food, to see *that* as a religious act. If you pay attention to food grown by farmworkers who are fairly treated, to see that involves *oshek*, freedom from oppression, and it, too, could be a religious act. These are ways of building a spiritual dimension through buying food, preparing it, eating it, blessing it."

Levy's draft immediately drew fire from Reform leaders who bristled at the specific practices he named, including keeping kosher, going to the mikveh, and wearing tallitot (prayer shawls) and tefillin (phylacteries). None of those rituals was mentioned by name in the final platform adopted in May 1999, which was revised to read: "We are committed to the ongoing study of the whole array of mitzvot and to the fulfillment of those that address us as individuals and as a community." The wording was a far cry from the hostility of 1885 but fell short of a hearty embrace of tradition, however altered or adapted.

A decade later, openness to the spiritual potential of Jewish rituals was growing fast, at the grassroots and leadership levels. Several Reform congregations now have mikvehs, or ritual baths, which they use for a wide range of ceremonies in addition to the traditional purposes.[8] Tallitot are common in Reform services, and some younger members are donning tefillin. And Jewish dietary practice, kosher or not, is a hot topic of discussion.

"There's a more general openness to ritual questions," confirms Rabbi Eric Yoffie, president of the Union for Reform Judaism, which represents North America's more than nine hundred affiliated congregations. "I am seeing tremendous interest among many Reform Jews in Jewish eating—the Jewish concerns that come into play, issues of ethical eating, issues of how we infuse sanctity, holiness, into the act of eating."

Yoffie is the movement's preeminent spokesman, and an advocate for increased incorporation of Jewish rituals into Reform life. He spends much of his time traveling to Reform congregations across the country, and says the people he meets want more substance from their Judaism. "There's a sense that [Reform] Judaism has been a disembodied tradition in the past, and that is no longer desirable," he continues. "Judaism is about sanctifying the physical, the day to day, the ordinary, and we have to do that with all aspects of our physical existence, including eating."

The growth of Jewish adult education has contributed to this interest in mining tradition. Carol Oseran Starin grew up in Seattle in the 1950s and '60s in a non-kosher, actively Reform home. Her mother, whom she says cooked with ham and bacon, contributed a recipe for noodles Romanoff to the 1969 Temple De Hirsch Sinai Sisterhood Cookbook. It called for a can of cream of mushroom soup added to two cups of cooked chicken or crab—par for the course, Starin says, in a city with just one kosher butcher.

Today Starin would never think of serving non-kosher food to her guests. Her "consciousness was elevated," she says, after her children came home from their Jewish day school talking about kashrut. She took adult education classes to keep up with what they were learning, and it rubbed off. "No question, as I've learned more it has changed my awareness and my practice."

When Rabbi Sue Levi Elwell, a worship specialist for the Union for Reform Judaism, served as the rabbi of Leo Baeck Temple in Los Angeles in the late 1980s, she says there was "very little interest" in kashrut. But for the last thirteen years she has led High Holiday services at two Reform congregations in Virginia, and she says Rosh Hashanah meals and the break-the-fast after Yom Kippur are dairy-vegetarian at both places. She chalks that up in part to a conscious desire to respect kosher practice, which she did not see two decades ago in the Reform communities where she served.

Reform Jews generally expect their clergy and institutions to set the bar for religious observance. Recent surveys of Reform rabbis and lay leaders show a steadily growing number observing at least some aspects of kashrut, usually by avoiding pork. Some keep "biblical kashrut," a diet that follows the Torah's instructions but not those of the later rabbis. Rabbi Jeffrey Brown of Temple Solel near San Diego, who does not keep biblical kashrut, points out that the practice is based on the understanding that Jewish tradition and law evolve over time, with the older parts carrying more authoritative weight than the newer.

A survey of delegates to the 2005 Reform biennial, comprising clergy and the movement's most active lay leaders, revealed that at home 62 percent avoid pork and 46 percent refrain from shellfish. Larger numbers eat those forbidden foods in restaurants, in keeping with the practice of "eating out." Interestingly, while 28 percent of these Reform leaders claim to eat vegetarian at home, 38 percent said they order vegetarian in restaurants, which the surveyors interpret as a desire to avoid potentially awkward kosher dilemmas.

A telling example of the changing expectations Reform Jews have for their clergy is the forty-five-year-old Reform rabbi who says he "eats treyf" outside his home but doesn't want his congregation to know about it. Whereas older Reform rabbis are open about their lack of observance, he says rabbis his age and younger "are more concerned" with respecting Jewish tradition, and his congregants expect that from him. "People want their rabbi to be 'Jewish,' to represent Judaism," he says, refusing to be quoted by name.

Younger Reform Jews are markedly more observant than their parents. A 2007 survey of fourteen thousand Reform activists and clergy revealed that 58 percent of those older than forty bring shellfish into their homes, versus 39 percent of the younger crowd.[9] Forty-three percent of the older group eat pork at home, compared with 29 percent of those thirty-nine and younger, and 16 percent of younger Reform Jews stick to kosher-certified meat, versus 9 percent of their elders.

Deborah Cohn, a member of Anshe Emeth Memorial Temple in New Brunswick, New Jersey, says her congregation "is doing more and more to accommodate people who keep kosher." Nondairy creamer is served with meat meals at the synagogue, and catered events have a vegetarian option or are completely vegetarian. "There are always people who object and say, 'We're Reform,'" she notes. "Those are usually the older members. It's the younger members who are leading this return to more tradition."

"The younger generation is more ritually comfortable across a wide range of practices, from kashrut to prayer," agrees Rabbi Daniel Freelander, senior vice president of the Union for Reform Judaism.

Reform youth groups, religious schools, and summer camps have been moving toward greater kosher observance for a generation, pushed in many cases by their younger staff members who have studied or traveled in Israel or were exposed to more traditional practice elsewhere.

Jerry Kaye, director of the Olin-Sang-Ruby Union Institute, a large Reform summer camp in Wisconsin, says that when he arrived in 1970, the camp kitchen did not serve pork or shellfish, but the meat was not kosher, and milk and meat were mixed freely at the same meals. As the decade passed, stirrings of discontent emerged along generational lines. A coterie of older rabbis on staff hewed to the Classical Reform line. They actively opposed kashrut and supported putting cartons of milk on the table for the kids during meat meals. But more of the younger faculty and staff members were keeping kosher.

At first those few were on their own, picking out what they could eat from the kitchen's offerings. Then the camp started providing kosher TV dinners, but those who wanted one had to pay extra and go up to the counter to request it. By the 1980s, more campers from kosher homes began enrolling, and the camp removed butter, milk, and sour cream from the table on Friday nights, a Reform take on the Jewish commandment to honor the Shabbat. (Observant Jews customarily honor the Shabbat by serving the best meal they can afford; some nonobservant Jews honor it symbolically, by serving traditional Ashkenazic foods or avoiding overtly non-kosher practices such as mixing meat and milk.)

In 1984, the Great Taco Debate erupted. At issue was the camp's make-your-own-taco buffet, which offered meat along with cheese and sour cream. Some staffers and campers felt this was wrong in a Jewish camp setting. Others didn't understand why the first group cared.

Meanwhile, changes in the dining hall continued. The kitchen bought separate pots to cook kosher meat for the more observant campers and staff. By the mid-1990s, there was no extra charge for kosher or vegetarian meals. And when the camp built a new kitchen and dining hall in 1998, new rules were established. There is no mashgiach to supervise food preparation, and the kitchen does not keep separate meat and dairy dishes, but meals are either dairy or meat (no mixing) and all meat is kosher certified. "Our practice has evolved," says Kaye, who estimates that about 10 percent of his one thousand campers come from Conservative homes, a number that increases every year.

The Great Taco Debate came to a fitful conclusion. First the sour cream and cheese were removed from the buffet table, but people grumbled at eating dry tacos. Then bean tacos were served instead of beef, but that didn't go over well, either. Finally one of the cooks discovered TVP, textured vegetable protein, which is often used as a meat substitute in vegan cuisine. At camp today the "beef" tacos and sloppy joes are made of TVP, a compromise that takes care of the kosher and the vegetarian problem in one swoop.

As the twentieth century came to a close, increasing numbers of Reform synagogues tightened their dietary policies. An unpublished 2000 survey of Reform synagogues in North America reported 10 percent had a kosher kitchen. Eighty percent do not permit pork or shellfish in their building, and nearly half do not mix milk and meat.

Rabbi Sue Ann Wasserman, former worship director at the Union for Reform Judaism, says the survey results would have been very different ten years earlier. She is not surprised by the large number of Reform congregations that forbid pork and shellfish—many Reform institutions have done that for years. But the ban on mixing meat and dairy "takes observance to another level, one I did not expect to see forty-six percent of our congregations going to."

The trend is continuing. At Temple Emanu-El in Honolulu, pork and shellfish are banned, but meat and dairy dishes are served at the same meal, although not on the same platter. Rabbi Peter Schaktman finds the policy increasingly hard to justify, and is pushing the congregation to adopt stricter practice within the synagogue building. "I think there are many people in the congregation who feel like me," he claims. "Even if their own personal observance is not one of kashrut, they feel the temple should be a place where we do not blatantly violate the kosher laws."

Increased Reform Jewish interest in the spiritual potential of a kosher diet has developed concurrently with interest in the ethical, political, and environmental implications of food decisions in general. "Ethical kashrut," a Reform approach to growing, preparing, and eating food that adapts some Jewish dietary laws to modern sensibilities and ethical values, is becoming more widespread. It is closely related to eco-kosher, a term coined in the 1970s by Rabbi Zalman Schachter-

Shalomi, the founder of Jewish Renewal, as part of his campaign to invigorate liberal Judaism with traditional spirituality. Eco-kosher, or eco-Judaism as it became further developed, focuses on living harmoniously with the earth as a Jewish commandment, and supports such things as organic and sustainable agriculture, recycling, and healthy work environments.

Ethical kashrut fits in well with Reform's emphasis on social justice. One of its earliest expressions came in 1976, at the height of Cesar Chavez's efforts to unionize farmworkers in California, when the CCAR passed a resolution urging "all persons of good will to seek out and purchase UFW Black Eagle label grapes and iceberg lettuce . . . as an incentive to growers who are procrastinating in negotiations." Buying grapes and lettuce picked by underpaid, ill-treated workers was un-Jewish, the resolution suggested.

Broadening this notion to a well-thought-out dietary practice took longer, until the new century brought with it a greater interest in food and food policy in general, fueled by books such as *Fast Food Nation* by Eric Schlosser and Michael Pollan's *The Omnivore's Dilemma*. Whereas the founders of Reform Judaism opposed Orthodox religious authority but did not question its right to define the very kashrut they were rejecting, a new generation of rabbis and activists were saying there are other, equally valid ways to eat like a Jew. The commandment in Genesis to be "stewards of the earth" can be interpreted as support for organic and sustainable agriculture. *Tsar baal hayim*, the commandment to treat domestic animals humanely, can lead people to buy free-range eggs and chickens or become vegetarian, while *oshek*, which forbids cheating others out of what is due them (for example, wages), can influence one's choice of which brands of food to buy or which restaurants to patronize.

The notion of basing dietary decisions on a wide range of Jewish teachings quickly spread beyond Reform and Renewal circles to affiliated as well as unaffiliated Jews. Some have no problem using the *k* word to describe what they're doing. "Organic is my kashrut," declares New York videographer Brian Dentz.

Some Reform rabbis and activists are also willing to employ kosher terminology as they develop new dietary practices that draw from Jewish tradition but are not bound by it. "The Reform community should be comfortable taking ownership of the word *kosher*," says Rabbi Mary Zamore of Temple B'nai Or in Morristown, New Jersey. "Kashrut is a *shlemoot*, a wholeness. When we talk about kashrut we are asking, What is our Jewish relationship to food? If we say blessings before we eat or we don't eat pork, that expresses intentionality. The person who fasts on Yom Kippur or eats matzo on Passover is functioning within the world of kashrut. There are values that lie behind our choices every time we go to the grocery store."

But for most of the Reform movement, the word carries too much baggage.

In 2007, the Union for Reform Judaism's worship department posted a "Kashrut Dietary Policies Guide" on the URJ website. The guide neither advocated nor rejected keeping kosher, but urged Reform congregations to adopt some kind of well-reasoned dietary policy, even if that policy is to permit everything.

Two years after the guide was posted, few Reform Jews, including rabbis, even knew it existed, a telling sign of how divided the movement's attitude toward kashrut continues to be. It has since been removed. And when the Reform movement unveiled its first *public* campaign regarding Jewish dietary practice at its November 2009 biennial in Toronto, the Just Table, Green Table initiative, it did not posit kashrut as one of the options for Reform Jews to consider.

"This is not about kashrut," stated Rabbi Yoffie, who outlined the initiative in his presidential sermon delivered during the conference's Saturday morning worship service. "We do not accept the authority of the kashrut establishment, and its problems are for others to resolve."

But acknowledging America's increased interest in food choices in general, and pointing to Jewish values concerning stewardship of the earth, sustainable agriculture, and treatment of workers, he urged Reform Jews to develop consciously Jewish and ethical food policies for themselves and their congregations—ethical kashrut, broadly conceived.

"We need to think about how the food we eat advances the values we hold as Reform Jews." That, Yoffie said, is how Reform Jews can eat food that is "proper and appropriate," which, he reminded the audience of nearly three thousand, is the literal meaning of the word *kosher*.

Eat less red meat, he advised. Plant synagogue gardens. Join Community Supported Agriculture (CSA) programs, where members pre-buy a season's worth of produce from a local farmer. Pay attention to how meat animals are raised and how food workers are treated. Host Shabbat and holiday meals at synagogues to build community.

"Above all," he said, "let's avoid the temptation to do nothing."

Although Yoffie did not speak about the kosher laws, he did point out that preparing and eating food can and should be a sacred act. Whereas animals "eat instinctively," he said, "Jews eat mindfully and thoughtfully." Above all, he said, Jews "invite God in" when they eat. "We understand—as we did not a century ago—that Jewish eating has a profoundly ethical dimension. We now know that God cares what we eat, and that eating can be an entrance to holiness."

That's as far as he went. Even as the Reform leadership and many younger clergy and activists push for greater observance of traditional mitzvot, they face stiff opposition from those in their own movement who believe this represents a betrayal of core Reform principles. "Kashrut is a visceral issue for many Reform Jews, in the negative sense," Yoffie explained after his talk. "It has been seen by many Reform Jews historically as something we rejected—ritual without ethical content."

Largely for this reason, he was careful not to promote it in the movement's Just Table initiative. "My central objective was putting food issues on our religious agenda, and in our movement, kashrut is not the vehicle to open that discussion," he said. "I intentionally put the focus on the ethical and communal dimension, which is central to who we are as Reform Jews. If I'd talked about kashrut, it would have had the opposite impact."

In 2008, a small group of Reform congregations committed to what they see as Reform Judaism's original vision formed the Society for Classical Reform Judaism. In these synagogues, as in the early days of American Reform, men don't cover their heads or wear prayer shawls; there is little Hebrew used in worship services; and kosher laws are not observed. That's what defined Reform Judaism at the outset, declares Rabbi Howard Berman, executive director of the new society, and there is no reason to change it. He says that adopting traditional practices like kashrut puts the movement on a slippery slope toward recognizing Orthodox authority. Indeed, one of the reasons many Reform rabbis continue to oppose kashrut is that the kosher certification process is controlled by Orthodox Jews, whose movement still does not formally recognize Reform Judaism.

Many Reform Jews who believe as Berman does feel under siege as younger people in their congregations, cheered on by the new crop of traditionally leaning rabbis, demand more Hebrew and more ritual. They don't get it, and they don't like it.

Seventy-year-old Harold Eichenbaum of Colorado Springs grew up in the Reform community of Austin. Like his friends, he was confirmed at sixteen. Reform temples in those days did not observe bar or bat mitzvahs; if you wanted one, he says, you joined the Conservatives. Eichenbaum has been an active Jew his entire life and has never kept kosher. "It's part of being a Reform Jew," he maintains. "Keeping a kosher kitchen was not part of my upbringing."

Today his world is in upheaval. His Reform congregation, Temple Beit Torah, where he has been a member since 1970, is moving further toward kosher observance. It already does not permit pork or shellfish in the building, and now some members are clamoring to make the kitchen vegetarian, possibly even kosher. Eichenbaum is not happy. He comes from a long line of Reform Jews: His grandparents immigrated from Germany and Austria in the 1880s, and they never kept kosher. He mourns what he considers the younger generation's ignorance of that strong ideological heritage.

"There are very few of us Classical Reform Jews anymore. People are listening to talk; they read *Reform Judaism*,[10] which is pushing toward kosher; and they think you have to be kosher to be true Jewish people. I disagree. Kosher was fine five thousand years ago, but in the modern day I don't see any purpose to it."

And what of Hebrew Union College, which ignited the initial firestorm more than a century ago? None of the school's three U.S. campuses has a cafeteria today. The Cincinnati campus used to have one. In the 1980s, it offered kosher and non-kosher food; ten years later, the kosher option was replaced by a vegetarian line. Now the only food on campus comes from vending machines.

But on October 13, 2002, when Rabbi David Ellenson was inaugurated as the college's newest president in Cincinnati, in the same temple where the Trefa Banquet was held in 1883, the meal served was entirely kosher.

. . .

AS THE TWENTIETH CENTURY progressed, the number of American Jews not affiliated with any particular denomination grew steadily. Few of these unaffiliated or secular Jews kept kosher, but they did not reject it with the studied fervency of Classical Reform Judaism. Rather, they simply didn't care; keeping kosher was so far from their reality, they didn't even consider it.

Keeping kosher, which used to be common practice even in nominally "nonreligious" Jewish homes, took on denominational significance, marking the Orthodox or Conservative home. If you did not belong to one of those movements, there was no reason to adhere to such restrictions.

That was the attitude of most Jewish communal organizations through the 1970s. Mirroring the observance level of their members, few Jewish federations, Jewish community centers, or national Jewish organizations kept kosher kitchens or required that their events be kosher. In the 1950s and '60s, few even provided a kosher option. Virtually all the leaders of groups such as the Anti-Defamation League, American Jewish Committee (AJC), B'nai B'rith, and United Jewish Appeal were nonobservant and saw no reason to provide kosher food for those who were. Jewish leaders who in the 1950s and '60s attended conferences of the General Assembly of the Jewish Federations of North America (JFNA), the umbrella organization for North America's nearly two hundred local Jewish federations, recall that there were no kosher meals available for conference participants. They had to pre-order bagged lunches of hard-boiled eggs and fruit or bring their own food.

In the 1970s, in the wake of Israel's Six-Day War and growing Jewish ethnic pride, increasing numbers of Jewish organizations in America shifted their focus from defending Jews to promoting Jewish culture and communal identity. They began to adopt kosher policies for public events, both to attract a wider range of participants and to proclaim the organization's Jewish affiliation. The trajectory taken by the AJC was typical. Steven Bayme, director of the organization's department of contemporary Jewish life, says that when he arrived three decades ago, the AJC building in New York did not have a kosher policy. By the early 1980s, all meals served in the building had to be dairy, and in the late '90s they began using a kosher caterer for meetings and events.

"It's a strong statement of Jewish peoplehood, that you want all Jews to participate in the endeavor," he explains. "And a second reason, which will be more important in years to come, is we are witnessing in Jewish public life a growing ascendancy of Orthodoxy. Any Jewish organization looking to its future will say, How can we attract more Orthodox? One way *not* to attract them is not to have kosher food."

Longtime Jewish educator Paul Flexner of Atlanta, former lead staff person at the Jewish Education Service of North America (JESNA), says that through the 1980s, federation and Jewish community center (JCC) events he attended were not kosher. He would show up at a local Jewish organization on behalf of JESNA, which had a kosher policy, and staffers would scramble to pull together a kosher meal on paper plates, clearly not something they were used to doing. "It was like, 'The guy from JESNA is coming,'" Flexner laughs.

Today all JFNA-sponsored events are supposed to be kosher, but that's hard to enforce, says Eric Levine, senior vice president for development. When major donors who do not keep kosher sponsor fundraisers in their homes and want to use their own caterers and dishes, staffers hesitate to antagonize them. "Most federations will say our policy is to do kosher events, and then try to negotiate for a pareve meal, or at least fish," Levine says. Since the 1980s, he says, there has been "increased openness to accommodating religious sensibilities regarding kashrut" and "far more sensitivity to allow people who keep kosher to do so."

Virtually all federations in larger cities and in the eastern half of the United States now require that public events be kosher. Some require formal supervision; others do not.

In Pittsburgh, Jewish federation events are required not only to be kosher but also to maintain cholov Yisroel standards, in deference to the city's large Lubavitch population. "Some people are frustrated by the increased cost, but we want anyone to feel comfortable coming to our events," says marketing manager Ellen Roteman. "Still, we're doing more and more events in people's homes, and while we tell them we would like them to adhere to these standards, if they're paying for the food and it's in their home, we can't really control it."

Smaller cities, particularly in the West, are less likely to enforce kashrut. Jeffrey Frankel, campaign director for the Jewish federation in Palm Springs, California, blames money and logistics. "We're a small community; we don't have kosher butchers or a kosher grocery store," he explains. Kosher meat would have to be brought in from Los Angeles, a two-hour drive. The federation would do it if Orthodox Jews came to its events, but they don't, so why spend the extra money?

Still, as a Jewish communal organization, the federation wants to affirm its Jewish connection, so Frankel says its events are "kosher-style, no biblically prohibited foods, no mixing of meat and milk." At one recent fund-raiser, he asked the hotel kitchen to leave the Parmesan cheese off the chicken dish. "Little things like that. We want the more liberal Jews to feel comfortable without offending the more observant."

That doesn't make twenty-nine-year-old Jodi Berris of Portland, Oregon, feel comfortable or even wanted. In 2008, Berris received her federation's Young Adult Leadership award, to honor her work promoting Jewish events for the under-thirty crowd. The award was to be presented at a dessert reception at a fancy Portland hotel that Berris knew was non-kosher. Not only was she ill at ease being honored by a Jewish organization that did not provide kosher food, but when her mother called to make reservations for the rest of the family, the federation representative she spoke to exclaimed, "Oh, you're the kosher keepers."

"All I could think of when my Mom told me the story was, it's so disappointing that she was singled out as the Jew who keeps kosher, rather than the Jew who's flying in from Detroit to see her daughter get an award," Berris says. "That's the wrong message to give somebody. To me, kosher should be the standard for a Jewish organization, and if you don't keep kosher, fine, who cares? But you shouldn't be singled out because you *do* observe Jewish tradition."

Switching to kosher-only can take a big chunk out of an organization's budget. Rabbi Josh Plaut is the executive director of a major Israeli charity in New York, in charge of multimillion-dollar fund-raising dinners at New York's Grand Hyatt. Every year, he says, there is a discussion about whether or not the meal should be kosher. It costs $175 per person for a non-kosher meal, versus $225 to $250 a head if the meal is kosher. That's money out of the charity's pocket.

Kosher options in Jewish community centers are even more dependent on finances. Typically run on very tight budgets, each center has to decide how high a priority it is to sponsor a kosher eatery that will more than likely lose money. "There are very few JCCs that run successful food establishments," says Eric Koehler, director of the Jewish Community Center of Northern Virginia, which has never provided food services in its building. "In this economy, it doesn't make sense to have something that loses twenty to thirty thousand dollars a year."

Some JCCs make a distinction between events held inside and outside their building, an institutional take on "eating out." The JCC in Pittsburgh has always been kosher, but Flexner recalls that when he lived there in the 1970s, the center ran an annual Halloween event for teenagers on the Friday night closest to the holiday, taking the youngsters trick-or-treating and then out for a meal at McDonald's.

Many JCCs decide they will not house a non-kosher dining establishment. It's a matter of Jewish identity as well as inclusiveness, they say: A Jewish community center should be accessible to the entire Jewish population. JCCs in older Jewish population centers like Detroit, Cleveland, Baltimore, and Atlanta more often fall into this category. Like the JCC of Northern Virginia, these centers would rather offer no food at all than violate kosher law.

In May 2009, the JCC in Louisville, Kentucky, reluctantly shut Café J, its kosher restaurant, after a $7,000 operating loss the previous calendar year. It was the only kosher restaurant in the entire state. Although an Orthodox synagogue shares the same campus space, average daily sales in the café were just $55, not even enough to pay the staff. A campaign to get one hundred JCC members to prebuy $450 worth of Café J vouchers resulted in only fifty-four pledges. Many of those who contributed didn't keep kosher and never used the vouchers; they just felt it was important for the JCC to offer kosher food.

"They were angry when we closed," reports Robin Stratton, the center's executive director. "Everyone saw it as a priority, but we couldn't go on losing money."

Renting space to an outside vendor is one way JCCs can offer kosher food without taking the financial risk themselves. In May 2006, the nation's first kosher Subway opened inside the Mandel Jewish Community Center of Cleveland. The JCC had offered only kosher food since it opened in 1986, but no purveyor had lasted long. The latest, a kosher café, shut in 2004. Ghazi Faddoul, a Lebanese Christian who is co-owner of the franchise, made several changes to bring in a kosher Subway, such as replacing the cheese with a soy-based substitute and removing all pork and seafood from the menu. There is a full-time mashgiach, and the restaurant is closed on Shabbat and Jewish holidays.

The center's executive director, Michael Hyman, says the experiment has been "wildly successful." Since the success of the Cleveland franchise, nine kosher Subways have opened from Miami to Los Angeles, with two more planned by the end of 2009.

The JCC in Wilkes-Barre, Pennsylvania, came up with an even more creative solution, partnering with the city's YMCA to open a kosher deli in that Christian-sponsored institution. The unique arrangement grew out of joint programming already in place between the two institutions, including a jointly run basketball league, says JCC director Rick Evans. Steve Arnovitz, a chef at the former JCC deli, is co-owner of the YMCA eatery, which opened in July 2009. He said he would have preferred to open in the JCC, but there was no room; the building's new fitness center had expanded into the former dining area.

With fewer than two thousand Jews, and only thirty to forty families that keep kosher, Wilkes-Barre does not seem the most likely location for a kosher deli. And it's struggling; the mashgiach's $40,000 salary eats up 60 percent of the restaurant's gross income. But the local Jewish federation wanted a kosher restaurant in town. "It's part of our strategic plan to attract more Jews," says federation executive director Gil August. "Years ago we tried other things—free synagogue membership for a year, free religious school tuition. None of that worked."

In summer 2008, the federation even hired a headhunter, gave him a list of open jobs in the city, and sent him out to find Jews willing to head for central Pennsylvania—right before the market collapsed. Bad timing, August concedes. "But we want to grow the Jewish community. Instead of moving out, Jews should be moving in."

Many JCCs, particularly in the West, host non-kosher restaurants. They say kashrut is expensive and not a priority in their community. From the time the Jewish Community Center of San Francisco opened its magnificent new 235,000-square-foot building in January 2004, none of the restaurants that have moved through its two dining spaces has been kosher. "Our people don't eat kosher," explained a high-ranking staff member at the time.

Wendy Bear, director of adult programs, was involved in the original process of selecting a restaurant for the new building. She says there was no particular desire to go either way; financial considerations were primary. Bids went out to potential operators, and Bear personally sent letters to kosher restaurants in Los Angeles, to see if any would take up the challenge. "No one wanted to do it," she reports. "We would have liked a kosher restaurant, but it was more important to have something that worked. It wasn't our number one priority."

The café that is currently occupying the space is non-kosher, but in accordance with the JCC's request, it does not serve pork or shellfish and offers a few kosher items on its menu.

That's ridiculous, says Kenny Altman, a longtime Jewish community activist in San Francisco who complained about the JCC's dining options in a June 2008 letter to the *J. Weekly.* "Why is it even a question?" he wants to know. "As a Jewish community center, if you don't have a kosher restaurant, you are excluding part of your community. I don't want to be hypocritical. I eat fish or vegetarian out, but I feel it's very important for a Jewish agency not to exclude anyone."

The tension between inclusion and exclusion is very much on the minds of the young Jews active in the independent minyan movement, a loosely connected network of unaffiliated, lay-led Jewish prayer communities that as of 2009 existed in more than a dozen U.S. cities. The twenty- and thirty-something leaders of these minyans, most of them raised in Conservative day schools and summer camps, are very conversant with kashrut, but also hyperaware of its potential to divide Jews who keep different standards. The "indie minyans" reach out to all young Jews, no matter their observance level, and in order to enable everyone to contribute to the potluck meals that are standard at their get-togethers, some instituted a two-table kashrut system, with separate tables for food adhering to different dietary rules.

Ben Dreyfus, a founder of the Kol Zimrah minyan on Manhattan's Upper West Side, describes the meeting that led to the two-table system for the group's first outdoor potluck in May 2003. "We were still operating in the paradigm that we'd have to have a uniform kashrut standard for the community. But whatever we would have chosen would have been problematic. If we said everything has to come from a kitchen that only uses hekhshered food, there would be lots of people in the community who wouldn't be able to bring anything they made. And if we said, okay, just bring vegetarian food, people who need food with a hekhsher wouldn't be able to eat anything."

At Kol Zimrah potlucks, one table is for vegetarian dishes that have a hekhsher and the second table is for any vegetarian dish. Tables are not labeled kosher and non-kosher, because that would signal disrespect for people who consider all vegetarian food kosher, which most Conservative Jews do. At the same time, the system respects people who demand a recognized kosher label. So anyone can bring food, and anyone can eat food, a dietary policy that encourages the widest possible participation, and a broad definition of what constitutes Jewish food choices.

At Kol Zimrah's first outdoor potluck of summer 2008, nearly two hundred young Jews gathered in Riverside Park to watch the sunset over the Hudson River as they prayed the Friday night service. Lamps illuminate the tables of food without forcing participants to violate Shabbat by turning on their own lights, another part of the minyan's efforts at inclusiveness. It is Brenna Cohen's second time at a Kol Zimrah potluck, but she had been to other indie minyans that use the two-table system, and she likes it. "I appreciate that those who keep strictly kosher can eat, and those who don't can also feel comfortable," she says.

Cohen was brought up in a kosher home and does not bring treyf into her kitchen, but is not as strict as some of her friends. If she'd brought a dish tonight, she would have put it on the table with the non-hekhshered food out of respect for those with stricter standards than her own. "One of the ideas I've come to in the past few years is, I love the idea of keeping the home a sacred space, and one of the ways of doing that is keeping kosher," she says. "Paying attention to your diet, to the food you eat and the way it's prepared, makes it holy, takes it out of the everyday world."

Adam Levine, a graduate student at Columbia University, started keeping kosher as an undergraduate when he became more involved in the indie minyan movement. "It's extraordinary how many young non-Orthodox, liberal Jews are keeping some level of kosher. It's part and parcel of being drawn to these kinds of communities. There's obviously a social aspect to it, some level of peer pressure—my friends are doing it, so I will. But I also think people are experiencing Jewish communities that they like, and they want to buy into the values."

The Moishe House Boston: Kavod Jewish Social Justice House, a subsidized communal house for young Jews involved in social action, also uses a two-table kashrut system at its public meals. Joe Gindi, who lives in the house, says the system encourages young Jews to work out their ideas about Judaism and food within a community that accepts this kind of experimentation. Gindi grew up kosher and is now vegetarian, but the kosher food categories are so deeply ingrained in him that he will always consider fish part of a vegetarian diet (kashrut permits fish to be served with a dairy meal). His friend Ari prefers to eat food with a hekhsher because it connects him to Jewish tradition, but when he is in a country where kosher-certified food is unavailable, he will eat any vegetarian food. Both are making food choices based on their Jewish values, Gindi says, but neither choice falls neatly into the category of kosher or vegetarian.

Ben Healey is the only person currently living in Moishe House Boston who does not keep kosher. In addition to the kitchen's blue-taped drawers for dishes and utensils used with vegetarian food that carries a hekhsher and the white-taped drawers for non-hekhshered vegetarian use, there are Healey's striped plates and special pots for use with his non-kosher meat. If he uses the oven or barbecue grill, he kashers it afterward. The system isn't perfect, he acknowledges; both he and the most observant member of the house are not always comfortable. But it allows them to live together in a community that identifies as Jewish.

"I don't think kashrut is exclusive or an insider's club, but it is certainly a marker of identification that others recognize," he says. "This is a Jewish space, and that is a symbol and validation of it."

Some young Jews view kashrut as intrinsically divisive, no matter how many tables are involved. The kosher laws were designed to separate Jews from non-Jews, a goal they say makes no sense in today's multicultural society, and is even offensive.

That's how Alix Wall feels. A forty-year-old chef and food activist in Oakland, California, Wall is very active in her synagogue, cooks Shabbat meals for her husband and friends, and makes ethically based food decisions. Not only does she not need kashrut to feel Jewish, she describes herself as anti-kashrut. "Sharing a meal is one of the most basic human things you can do," she says. "When people reach out to you and invite you to have a glass of tea or a meal in their home and you refuse because you can't eat on their dishes, it's an insult. That's something about Judaism that I really can't stand, and I don't feel it's served us well in the modern world."

Wall's mother was a "hidden child" during World War II, protected by a Catholic family in Poland that regularly ate bacon and ham. As a consequence she enjoyed pork her entire life and raised Wall the same way. Wall was a vegetarian for twenty years but recently began eating humanely raised and slaughtered meat. It took her longer to try pork than turkey, chicken, beef, and lamb, but she forced herself to eat it out of respect for her mother, who is now deceased, and the family that shielded her from the Nazis. "I feel like I would be betraying my mom if I didn't," she said.

For some formerly observant Jews, intellectual opposition to the social divisiveness of kosher practice conflicts with a gut-level distaste for treyf they can't shake. "Often I feel kashrut is an exercise in neurosis," says Brian Dentz. "Jewish culture can be very insular. We almost don't accept other people's humanity. I don't want to be a part of that. I like people. I like other cultures. I don't want to be isolated. And at the same time it's always a struggle. Once I lose my culture, I have nothing to share; I'm part of this bland, American, homogenized culture.

"Probably," he muses, "that's why I stay in New York."

# 13.

# Kosher Law and Its Discontents

*Who Decides What's Kosher?*

BRIAN YARMEISCH steps into the walk-in freezer at Commack Kosher Deli and Market, the store he owns with his brother, Jeffrey, in Suffolk County, Long Island. Climbing up to a top shelf in the back corner, he pulls down a plastic bag so encrusted with frost it's hard to make out the large, grayish object double-wrapped inside. A red tag reading "Seizure Notice, 4/29/88" warns that the bag is being "retained for further examination."

"That's it, the lamb tongue," he says, holding the rock-hard lump in both hands. "You can't eat the stuff now. But there it is."

This freezer-burned piece of meat, quarantined in the Yarmeisches' store for more than two decades, helped lead to a lawsuit that overturned the nation's oldest kosher law and ended the exclusive right of Orthodox authorities to decide what is and is not legally kosher in New York State.

New York was the first state to enact a kosher law in 1915. Jewish immigrants were pouring into Manhattan's Lower East Side and kosher butchers sprang up on every block, with few regulations to control them. Price gouging was common, particularly before Jewish holidays, when demand was greatest, and treyf was sold as kosher. Jewish leaders in the city, unable to control the situation on their own, demanded a legislative solution. New York State's "kosher bill" was designed primarily to protect the kosher consumer from fraud, but also to ward off violent repercussions like the kosher meat riots that rocked the city in 1902.

"Jews took kosher meat pretty seriously, whether it was the availability, the price, or the accurate representation that it met halachic standards," says Rabbi Yitzchok Adlerstein of Loyola Law School in

Los Angeles. "A community that could be victimized by price gouging, or by fraudulent representation that food was kosher, could explode. It made sense to bring its protection under the umbrella of the law."

New York's kosher law made it a misdemeanor to sell food purporting to be kosher if that product did not meet standards "sanctioned by the orthodox Hebrew religious requirements." It was a consumer protection law, with standards determined by religious authority. In 1924, the U.S. Supreme Court considered a challenge to the law on the grounds that the phrase "orthodox Hebrew requirements" was too vague; the court disagreed, ruling that the term was "well enough defined" to be enforceable. Kosher was what Orthodox rabbis determined it to be, a position accepted by everyone; American Jews either kept or did not keep kosher, but they did not question Orthodox authority to decide what the term meant.

Kosher laws spread to other states, all based on the New York model. Massachusetts and Pennsylvania passed kosher laws in 1929, followed by Wisconsin in 1935, Rhode Island in 1937, and Michigan in 1939. Eventually kosher laws were enacted in nearly two dozen states and localities.[1]

Enforcement was hampered by lack of funding. A mayoral committee set up in New York soon after that state's kosher law went into effect found that few kosher butcher shops were supervised by rabbis, and most of those rabbis were paid by the shops they were supposed to oversee. It was only in 1934 that an independent Kosher Law Enforcement Bureau was created within the state's Department of Agriculture, with a director and inspectors in charge of visiting kosher establishments in the state. A separate kosher law enforcement department was set up for New York City, operating as part of the Consumer Law Enforcement section of the Department of Markets.

Inspectors would show up unannounced and had access to all parts of the premises. They had the power to levy fines, which some proprietors challenged in court. In the early years inspectors found it difficult to prove fraud. Writing in 1970, kosher industry expert Rabbi Seymour Freedman said that typically, an inspector would show up at a restaurant suspected of serving non-kosher meat, order a sandwich, see it was treyf, and leave the food on the counter while he went outside to look for a phone booth to call the office. By the time he returned, the sandwich would have mysteriously disappeared, along with his case. By the late 1960s, Freedman continued, kosher inspectors were taught to seize the evidence and put it in a plastic container.[2]

Courts disliked being asked to rule on what they considered religious matters. In March 1963, the Orthodox Rabbinate of Los Angeles sent a letter to every kosher retail market in the county declaring that poultry slaughtered by four local shochtim was non-kosher. The letter was based on a report by Rabbi Juda Glasner, the city's Kosher Food Law Representative, who claimed the shochtim removed the birds' feathers after soaking the carcasses in hot water, a technique that makes the feathers easier to remove but one that is forbidden by kashrut. The shochtim sued the rabbis, claiming the letter defamed them and damaged their business. In her judgment for the defendant, the trial judge said that her court "is not the forum" for deciding whether or not the birds were still kosher.[3]

In *West Coast Poultry v. Glasner*, a case brought against Glasner the following year, the District Court of Appeals for the Second District declined to rule that Glasner was not an Orthodox rabbi, as plaintiffs had asked the court to do. Again, the court indicated this was not within its purview. In *Korn v. Rabbinical Council of California*, a 1983 case, yet another court held that questions of what is kosher and who may give certification are an ecclesiastical matter.

Despite constitutional challenges in several states, kosher laws held everywhere until 1992. That July, the New Jersey Supreme Court struck down its state's kosher regulations, saying they violated federal and state constitutional prohibitions on the establishment of religion. The ruling came in response to a suit filed by Ran-Dav's County Kosher, a New Jersey retailer that had been cited by state kosher inspectors for violations including failing to de-vein calves' tongues and storing non-kosher chicken breasts in the same freezer as kosher chicken breasts. Instead of paying the fine, as others had done before them, the owners of Ran-Dav's took the matter to court, arguing that they had no intention to defraud and were merely following the instructions of the rabbi who certified their store.

By the time the case got to the state's highest court, it had become about government interference in religion, specifically whether the kosher regulations forced the state to decide religious standards properly left to the private sphere. The court ruled that was so, and swept away the existing regulations, which depended upon Orthodox definitions of what was and was not kosher.[4] A new system was put in place that did not require kosher retailers to adhere to one universal standard. They may follow any kosher standard they choose, so long as they disclose what it is.

Rabbi Yakov Dombroff, head of New Jersey's Kosher Food Enforcement Bureau since 1986, was on the losing side of the Ran-Dav's case and helped develop the state's new "full disclosure" system. Every supermarket, restaurant, butcher, baker, importer, and caterer that sells or serves kosher food in New Jersey must now file a form with his office stating what they sell, how they prepare it, and whether or not they operate under rabbinic supervision. A copy of the form must be posted at the place of business, so consumers can decide for themselves whether the establishment is kosher enough for them.

The disclosure form is careful not to make religious judgments. Purveyors must state whether or not they sell pork or shellfish and if they mix milk and meat, all things forbidden by Jewish law, but they are free to call themselves kosher, so long as they don't try to conceal such facts. "You can put down absolutely anything in the world you want," says Dombroff. "Literally, pork could be kosher. The state has no interest in what you call kosher, as long as you're in compliance with the disclosure. The place can be under your German shepherd's supervision, as long as it's disclosed."

The city of Baltimore was next to change its kosher law, removing all reference to Orthodox standards in 1995. The case involved a hot dog vendor fined for placing non-kosher hot dogs too close to kosher hot dogs on his rotisserie, allowing the juices to mix and rendering the kosher dogs non-kosher. Relying on the reasoning of the New Jersey courts in the Ran-Dav's case, the Maryland court ruled that the ordinance the state inspector acted under "protects the tenets and rituals of Orthodox Judaism," and therefore advances a particular religion. The court "acknowledged differences between the various sects of Judaism in the observance of kashrut" and held, as in New Jersey, that the state should not favor one interpretation over another. In October of that year, the U.S. Court of Appeals for the Fourth Circuit upheld a lower court ruling that declared the Baltimore City Code's kosher ordinance a violation of the establishment clause of the First Amendment. The ordinance was changed.[5]

In 1996, New York's kosher law came under fire from a lawsuit filed by Brian and Jeffrey Yarmeisch, whose shop was then called Commack Self-Service Kosher Meats. The Yarmeisches had received several citations from state kosher inspectors beginning in 1986, when they were fined for improper soaking and salting of a package of veal spareribs. The Yarmeisches declared that they always soaked and salted their meat properly, but they did not formally challenge the citation and paid a $600 fine without acknowledging guilt. In 1987, they were cited again for improper soaking and salting, this time of steaks; again they protested, but paid $300.

In April 1988, a vat of lamb tongues was seized from Commack Kosher on the same charges of improper soaking and salting. This time, when the Yarmeisches insisted that they kashered their meat under rabbinic supervision, the Department of Agriculture wrote back charging "in any case, the tongues had not been properly de-veined in accordance with Orthodox Hebrew requirements."[6]

The state eventually abandoned the case over the Yarmeisches' objections; the brothers' attorney wanted to take it to court, believing it was "a perfect illustration of the state legislating religious law." He noted that in its bill of particulars, the state cited Yoreh Deah, the volume of the Shulchan Aruch that deals with kashrut, as the basis for the alleged violation. How could government authorities decide the proper Jewish method of de-veining a lamb's tongue when the rabbis themselves disagreed?

The final straw for the Yarmeisches came in 1993, when they were hit with an $11,100 fine for not marking packages of turkey thighs to indicate whether they had been soaked and salted, as required by the kosher law. The state eventually dismissed the fine,[7] but three years later the brothers brought suit against the kosher law itself, arguing that it represented excessive government entanglement in religion.

In July 2000, the Federal District Court in Brooklyn agreed with the Yarmeisches' contention, ruling that existing regulations "violate the Establishment Clause and are therefore unconstitutional," because they required state officials to enforce religious laws and favored one religious standard in determining what is kosher.[8] A series of appeals failed, in 2003 the U.S. Supreme Court refused to hear the case, and a new system of kosher enforcement was announced for New York similar to New Jersey's full disclosure system.

The New York State Kosher Law Protection Act of 2004 requires producers, distributors, and retailers of food sold as kosher in the state to submit information about their products, including the identity of the person or organization that certifies them as kosher, to the Department of Agriculture and Markets. The information is published in an online directory accessible by the public. As in New Jersey, New York's law has a very narrow focus. The state no longer decides who is and is not qualified to certify products as kosher, or how meat should be kashered or vegetables washed, but simply provides the relevant information to consumers.

Rabbi Luzer Weiss is director of New York's Kosher Law Enforcement Division, in charge of ten inspectors who enforce the new law in 3,500 establishments that make, sell, or serve kosher food. All his inspectors can do, Weiss says, is make sure that each establishment does what it says it does. "It's basically representation," he explains. "You represent what you have, and we confirm it. Joe Rodriguez makes a cookie, and he says all the ingredients are kosher, and he puts a 'K' on it. He represents it as kosher. That's legal in New York State. We can't tell him which rabbi to use."

Weiss and Dombroff both say that the new law doesn't really change the way their departments work. Even under the old laws, they insist they did not seek to monitor religious behavior, a claim the Yarmeisches dispute. As an example, Dombroff says one of his inspectors fined a Bergen County retailer for selling sturgeon, but Dombroff dismissed the charges after the man pointed out that sturgeon is kosher under Conservative standards, which he followed.

"The fellow argued, look, this is what I sell. I'm not hiding it. I have the right to sell it," Dombroff recalls. "So we said, fine, you can sell it. We just want you to put up a sign that says this establishment is not kosher according to Orthodox law; it meets a Conservative standard." Dombroff would have done the same for anyone else, he says, but no one asked. "The idea that we were forcing things down people's throats was simply not true. And it was frustrating that we were so misportrayed."

Attorney Nathan Lewin argued for the existing kosher laws in both the New Jersey and New York cases, on behalf of organizations representing kosher consumers. He says that those laws did not involve a preference for one Jewish denomination above others, but put forth a universally accepted definition of kosher food in order to help consumers looking for such products. "The word *kosher* has a meaning," he says. "It does not mean, to the greatest number of consumers, kosher by Reform standards. It does not mean kosher by whatever standards the seller wants it to mean. The meaning it has always had, the meaning consumers also believed it to have, is kosher by Orthodox standards. That's the reason the laws were adopted in that way."

Lewin calls the New York decision in *Commack* "a great disaster" for kosher enforcement, adding that the new laws hurt the less knowledgeable kosher consumers, the people who relied on the state laws to tell them whether food was really kosher. "That protection has been eliminated, and the substitute laws are toothless and meaningless," he charges.

Even so, Dombroff argues, it's better than nothing. And people shouldn't rely on the state; they should use their judgment, consult their rabbi, and keep their eyes open. "Anybody who is sincere about keeping kosher cannot rely on the disclosure, because you can't rely only on the state," he says. "It's absurd. Did you ever do more than fifty-five on the highway? Were you stopped every time by a trooper? Of course not. So I'm offering the kosher consumer nothing more than awareness. Caveat emptor still has to be there."

Industry experts expected the New Jersey case to affect kosher laws in other states quickly. But in the course of two decades, just three states and one city got rid of the "Orthodox religious requirements" clauses in their kosher regulations. Minnesota managed to do so legislatively, without a court battle. After hearing from both Orthodox and Conservative rabbis, the state legislature revised its kosher laws in August 2004 so that kosher food must be prepared "as prescribed by a rabbinic authority, with the name and institutional affiliation and denominational affiliation, if any, of the rabbinic authority identified." All references to kosher food having to meet "orthodox Hebrew religious requirements" were eliminated.

In August 2009, a Conservative rabbi in Atlanta became the latest to challenge the constitutionality of his state's kosher laws. In a suit filed by the American Civil Liberties Union on his behalf, Rabbi Shalom Lewis of Congregation Etz Chaim claimed that Georgia's 1980 Kosher Food Labeling Act, which adheres to the Orthodox definitions, denies him the right to fulfill his obligations as a Conservative rabbi. Part of his job, the suit explains, is certifying food as kosher for his congregation, but when he does so he must either follow Orthodox standards, going against his own beliefs, or break the law.

"Since 1980 I have technically been a criminal, something I'm not thrilled about," Lewis says.

As of early 2010, Brian and Jeffrey Yarmeisch are still fighting. They have a case pending in federal court challenging New York's new kosher law, the one they helped bring about. Robert Jay Dinerstein, the brothers' attorney, notes that state kosher inspectors can issue a report against an establishment they claim is selling mislabeled kosher food, or food manufactured or distributed by an agency whose kosher supervisor is not registered with the state. Even if the charges are dropped or found to be false, the damage is done. "The mere issuance of such a report can be devastating to a kosher shopkeeper's business," says Dinerstein. When the Jewish media published stories about the Yarmeisches' $11,100 fine ten years ago, their business dropped off dramatically, even though the fine was later dismissed. So in effect, Dinerstein says, the new law still favors Orthodox certification. "There are those who have opined that the new law compels Conservative and other purveyors of kosher food to deal only in products with Orthodox *hashgocha* [certification], with hekhshers readily recognizable to inspectors, so that they can avoid damning inspection reports."

The Yarmeisches also have two cases pending in the New York State Court of Claims, seeking damages. The brothers say the years of legal struggle have hurt them financially and forced them to move into a space half the size of their previous store. And they're still hanging on to the bedraggled remains of the frozen lamb tongue, quarantined by the state as evidence in a trial that never took place.

The brothers believe they were targeted not because they handled their meat incorrectly, but because their store is under Conservative supervision. Rabbi William Berman, who has certified the store for years, follows stricter standards than those dictated by his own movement. Everything the store sells carries nationally recognized kosher certification, including cheese and wine, which do not require it according to Conservative standards. Still, Berman and the Yarmeisches know that few Orthodox Jews will patronize the place, simply because a Conservative rabbi is in charge. That's fine with them— hardly any of the county's eighty-five thousand Jews are Orthodox anyway. All the local synagogues are Reform or Conservative, Berman points out, except for a small Chabad presence. "We make San Francisco look frum," he says.

Berman says he is not in the kashrut business. He supervises Commack Kosher because he lives in the neighborhood and the brothers asked him to do it. He takes no fee for his work; the brothers give him a discount on his holiday orders. The Yarmeisches are the only kosher butchers in the county; if they went under, Jews would have no local source for fresh kosher meat, and that's what Berman wants to prevent.

"Kashrut is a beautiful aspect of Jewish law that has become obsessive, picayune. Instead of an expression of piety, it becomes a mockery of piety. I don't believe the Jewish people can exist without kashrut. But the competitiveness between groups to see who can be more scrupulous just turns people off."

Still, he is tired of fighting. "To tell the truth, I wish the whole thing would just go away," he says with a sigh. "It's been schlepping on for so many years. Any publicity about kashrut, even if you're one hundred percent right, is always bad."

KEEPING KOSHER is a mitzvah, but giving kosher certification is a business. And that means money, politics, and all the other unpleasant temptations that can distract a Jew from fulfilling God's commandments. Some rabbis and smaller agencies do not charge fees to certify local businesses, seeing it as a service they perform for the Jewish community. But they are the exceptions.

"Kashrus today is power and money," says Rabbi Don Yoel Levy, head of the OK kosher agency. "And unfortunately, it's extremely competitive. Instead of people working together to improve kashrus, everybody tries to get business away from the other one."

Levy believes kosher politics caused the death of his father, Rabbi Berel Levy, who bought the OK in 1968 and headed it for two decades. In 1986, the *Jewish Press* reported that the OK was certifying a French company that was using alcohol derived from non-kosher wine to make its vinegar. The company had changed its manufacturing process without alerting the OK, but the damage was done, and the kosher world was scandalized. Here we are relying on the OK symbol, and the stuff's not kosher, people complained. The scandal was compounded when the *Press* reported alleged death threats against the state inspectors who discovered the error.[9]

Levy recalls the incident with bitterness, saying the French company "tricked us into selling non-kosher alcohol as kosher," and instead of the other major kosher agencies rushing to the OK's side, they "teamed up against my father and really, really persecuted him." When the heads of those agencies held the first meeting of what became the Association of Kashrus Organizations, Levy says his father was not invited, an intentional snub that struck deep. In 1987, a year after the scandal, the elder Levy died.

"He had so much aggravation from it that he passed away," his son charges. "At the time I felt he passed away because of his work in kashrus, and I really didn't want to go into the field." He finally did so, after Rabbi Menachem Mendel Schneerson, the Lubavitcher rebbe, urged him to carry on his father's work.

The vast majority of kosher-certified food products are certified by the four largest kosher agencies. But there are still hundreds of individual rabbis and rabbinic committees, or vaads, giving certification to restaurants, retail shops, schools, nursing homes, summer camps, and even some manufacturers; Pepsi, for example, is one of several large companies under the supervision of individual rabbis. As the Big Four get bigger through consolidation, buying up smaller agencies or taking over accounts formerly handled by individual rabbis, those rabbis lose the fees they used to charge for their services.

The large agencies often present the situation as an enforcement problem, noting that it is hard for consumers to know whether a particular kosher symbol is reliable when there are so many different ones. To the local rabbis, however, it's a matter of money and independence. "If I'm a rabbi in Portland, Maine, and I control the local kashrus industry, that's a major source of my income," explains Jeffrey Gurock of Yeshiva University. "I'm going to cede that to some national organization? That's my money. It doesn't mean the guy who won't join is corrupt; it may just mean he wants to be independent."

In spring 2009, four weeks before Passover, the Vaad Harabonim of Queens in New York removed Streit's matzo from its list of approved Passover foods, essentially banning the nation's second-largest producer of matzo from kosher grocery stores. Days later, the Vaad HaKashrus of the Five Towns and Far Rockaway followed suit. In an

April 28 editorial calling for the ouster of the head of the latter agency, the *Jewish Star* of Long Island noted that the two vaads did not explain their ban. They even declared that the matzo was perfectly kosher and did not need to be returned if it was already purchased. If it was kosher enough to eat, why wasn't it kosher enough to buy? "Some kosher consumers were confused and worried," the editorial stated. "Others, quicker to sense 'politics' at work, were infuriated."

Streit's, a family-owned business founded in 1916, had been certified independently since the 1950s by the very well respected Rabbi Ahron Soloveichik. When he died in 2001, the job passed to his son, Rabbi Moshe Soloveichik, who shared the responsibility for five years with the Kof-K. In 2005, Streit's stopped paying the agency, relying solely on Soloveichik and the five mashgichim under him to supervise their production, and company owners believe the ban by the rabbinic boards of Queens and Long Island was thinly veiled punishment for dropping national certification.

That seems to be implied by what Rabbi Yoel Schonfeld, copresident of the Queens vaad, told the *Jewish Star.* Without a national agency overseeing the company, he said, "we don't know enough about Rav Moshe Soloveichik. He just doesn't swim in the kashrus world . . . we're not saying he's bad; not at all. We just don't know." In other comments, Schonfeld and his colleagues hinted at "other problems" with Streit's kosher supervision, although they declined to specify what those were.

Alan Adler, Streit's director of operations and great-grandson of the company's founder, called the ban "an ambush" but caved under the pressure, telling the *Star* he planned to seek certification from a national agency once again.[10]

Personal politics have been at play in kashrut conflicts for a long time. Professor Allan Nadler, director of Jewish Studies at Drew University in Madison, New Jersey, recalls visiting his ninety-two-year-old father in Montreal. The older man had suffered a series of strokes and was slipping in and out of the past. It was Friday afternoon, and as Nadler stood up to go, telling his dad he had to do last-minute Sabbath shopping, his father looked at him and said, "*Kindelach* [my child], be sure to get the chickens from Rabbi Cohen and not from that *shtunk* Herschorn."

Nadler was halfway down the hall before he realized his father was talking about two prominent Montreal rabbis from the early twentieth century—Hirsh Cohen, chief rabbi of the city's Jewish Community Council for years, and Yehoshua Helevy Herschorn, one of his main rivals. "They had competing slaughterhouses," he recalls. "It was the same in every Jewish community. There was always one guy whose chickens were good and one whose weren't."

Kashrut politics are ugly, with business owners using religion to undercut their competitors. New Jersey mashgiach Aaron Leff oversees a number of kosher restaurants, and recalls the owner of one coming to him to report he'd seen the owner of a competing restaurant shopping in Toys "R" Us ten minutes before Shabbat on a Friday afternoon. A guy like that shouldn't be allowed to run a kosher restaurant, the man complained.

"So I said, what were *you* doing in Toys 'R' Us ten minutes before Shabbos?" Leff relates. Both restaurants have since closed, Leff notes, "probably because of all the lashon hara they spread about each other."

Leff went to business school at Yeshiva University, preparing for a career in accounting or marketing. He switched to rabbinical school midway through. "I didn't have the killer instinct, the make-a-buck-no-matter-what attitude. I wanted a more spiritual life." He laughs. "If I'd known that the world of kashrut is just as cutthroat as the business world, I would have gone into business. At least I would have made more money."

The hassidic world is particularly subject to kosher politicking. Members of one community often only accept the kosher certification of their own rabbi, a preference that can have financial as well as religious bases. "Sometimes community A will not accept the hekhsher of community B for valid reasons, or because they want to be in control of the important manufacturing parameters," Adlerstein explains. "But this can lead to community A figuring out that if they demand their own hekhsher in addition to community B's, a good number of jobs will be available for people in their own community."

The long-standing animosity between the Satmar and Lubavitch sects, which has led to street fights in Brooklyn, extends to kashrut as well, with each group refusing to recognize kosher certification given by the other. Many so-called black-hat Orthodox Jews, as well as rival hassidic sects, will not accept Lubavitch kosher certification or eat meat slaughtered under the Lubavitch label, because of opposition to Chabad Messianism, the belief by some Lubavitchers that their late rebbe, who died in 1994, is the Messiah. In May 2008, Avrom Pollak of the Star-K told radio host Zev Brenner that his agency "most likely would not hire" a Lubavitch shochet who held Messianist beliefs. Adlerstein says he knows Jews who will not drink a certain kosher wine from Europe because the rabbis that supervise the wine's production "are known *Moshichists*," he says, using a Hebrew derivation of *Messianist*.

"Those who spurn the kashrut supervision of Moshichists don't view them, God forbid, as apostates," Adlerstein says, downplaying the fact that some critics do, indeed, make that charge. "They simply don't trust them the way they would trust others. Effective supervision requires both knowledge and the ability to make correct judgment calls. The thinking is, how can you trust people who believe in such foolishness?"

The Big Four kosher agencies generally accept one another's certifications, usually refusing only where their standards differ significantly, as with fish processing.[11] But there is still plenty of politicking involved in the struggle for new clients. The people who work for these agencies are not getting rich from their day jobs, but the agencies are not in the business of losing business. They need the fees they charge companies to stay afloat and pay their mashgichim.

There is, therefore, a built-in financial incentive to increase the number of companies under kosher supervision, an incentive that, critics charge, leads to kosher supervision being given to products that do not need it—products like water. The kosher agencies say they do not seek to certify such products, the so-called Group 1 items like water and salt that are inherently kosher. But in fact, most bottled water sold in this country *is* kosher certified, including such popular labels as Crystal Geyser, Arrowhead, and Fiji.

"We have companies call us up for certification, and I tell them, you don't need it, your product is kosher anyway," says Levy, whose agency gives kosher certification to Perrier. "I don't want them to come back later and say, 'Rabbi, why did you take money from us to certify this?' So we tell them they don't need it, but if they insist, we'll give it to them."

Rabbi Yosef Wikler, publisher of *Kashrus Magazine*, has spent thirty years reporting on kosher fraud, changes in kosher supervision, and other items of concern to the observant consumer. Fervently Orthodox in his beliefs and practice, he says the kosher agencies' enthusiasm for growing their business does not always serve the community well. "When I started, Rabbi Rosenberg was head of OU Kosher," he says. "He refused to give hashgocha to anything that didn't need it, not water or aluminum foil. Now we're not only giving kosher certification to nonfood items, we're saying it's healthier. I'm scared about the repercussions when this all hits the fan."

But, Wikler says, despite his misgivings, "there's still plenty of good in kashrus, plenty of quality."

Some people might laugh at the notion of kosher-certified sponges, spatulas, and plastic wrap, but increasing numbers of very observant Jews do not want any non-kosher products to come in contact with their food. They want reassurance that these kitchen items were produced under rabbinic supervision, and they are willing to pay a premium for it. The OK, for one, states on its website that "dish soap, cleanser, and scouring pads used for dishes and pots must have a hekhsher." There is historical precedent for this scrupulousness. In 1890, Polish immigrant Israel Rokeach brought to New York his recipe for kosher soap made without animal fat. He produced it in two versions, blue for dairy and red for meat, giving rise to the color-coding system used in kosher kitchens today.[12]

The increasing variety of products being brought under kosher supervision is part of what David Kraemer calls the humratization of the industry. If the kosher laws as developed by the early rabbis were intended to separate Jews from non-Jews, Kraemer says the increasing strictness of kashrut standards today work to separate Jews from other Jews, based on their level of observance.

Kraemer traces the phenomenon back to German pietists of the twelfth through fourteenth centuries, who distinguished themselves from the rest of the community by following more stringent dietary practices, such as separating their meat and dairy dishes, which ordinary Jews did not do. Few people in those years had more than one pot or dish anyway, he points out. In the sixteenth century, pious Jewish women in Poland adopted the same dish separation to set themselves apart from their less observant neighbors, to "constantly remind themselves, their families and their neighbors *who* they were and *to what com-*

*munity* they belonged."[13] The theme continues in today's Orthodox kitchens, where stringencies such as using light boxes to check vegetables and maintaining separate ovens and refrigerators for meat and dairy identify a household's particular level of observance.

The 1980s were a watershed in kosher humratization. That's the decade kosher agencies stopped certifying non-glatt meat, notes Menachem Lubinsky. By the turn of the twenty-first century, virtually all the kosher meat in the country came from four major suppliers. Only one of them—Agriprocessors, in Postville, Iowa—offered a non-glatt line, certified by an independent rabbi, and it was not widely available. The hegemony of glatt effectively forced kosher-keeping Jews to buy that more expensive meat even if they did not follow that stricter standard.

The 1980s also marked a growing tendency in Orthodox circles to judge kosher establishments on the basis of their owners' religious behavior. Examining articles from mid-decade in the *Jewish Press*, the premier English-language Orthodox publication, Kraemer finds growing criticism of establishments whose owners are not *shomer mitzvot,* or fully observant. No longer was it sufficient for a kosher store or restaurant to be closed on Shabbat; the owner's private observance level impinged on the kashrut of the food offered for sale.

Kraemer cites numerous examples of this trend, which intensified through the 1990s and the first decade of the twenty-first century. A rabbi in Tokyo who had been supervising kosher food production for years had the hekhsher removed from his products when the OU discovered he was Conservative. An Orthodox rabbi was thrown out of his local kosher council for allowing women to dance with the Torah in his synagogue during Simchat Torah services. An Orthodox rabbi in Syracuse, New York, was declared unfit to give kosher supervision because he was the pulpit rabbi of a Conservative synagogue. In none of these cases, Kraemer points out, was the kosher status of the food in question. In the new kosher reality, Kraemer writes, "the food isn't necessarily *treif,* but the rabbi surely is."[14]

"Kashrut is enormously lucrative," says Jonathan Sarna. "Obviously people want to muscle in. One of the ways you muscle in is arguing, I'm more kosher; *they're* not really good enough. Over time, many hekhsher-giving organizations have been pulled to the right. In the early years the goal was to get more people eating kosher. All right, so you don't close on Shabbos, but your food is still kosher. Or, all right, you're using dairy equipment, but the chance of anything *milchig* [dairy] getting into the product is so small that it will certainly be *batul b'shishim* [negated by the one-in-sixty principle]. Over time, these standards changed. Kashrut standards really are a moving target as new humras come in and become normative."

Nowhere is this growing strictness more evident than in Cedarhurst, New York, one of the heavily Jewish Five Towns of Long Island, which together contain about seven thousand Orthodox families. Resident Geri Gindea drives around the town one afternoon, talking about the old days. Thirty years ago, she says, Cedarhurst was a popular shopping destination for Jewish families from all over the tri-state area. She remembers her mother dragging her in from Brooklyn to buy dresses in one of the many fancy shops that dotted Central and Cedarhurst avenues. The town had a sizable Jewish population, but it spanned the range from secular to modern Orthodox.

"The whole aura of Cedarhurst has changed," Gindea says. "The demographic now is really focused on the Orthodox, the right-wing Orthodox." When she was a child, she remembers many non-kosher restaurants doing business next to kosher establishments. Now almost every place on Central Avenue is kosher. And not just kosher, but glatt kosher, pas Yisroel, cholov Yisroel, as proclaimed on the banners across their storefronts. Saturday used to be the main shopping day in town; now Saturday is completely dead. The Cedarhurst Starbucks, a lone holdout for years, the place where non-Orthodox Jews would congregate on Saturdays, finally closed in 2008.

A glatt kosher Burgers Bar and Subway opened in the last year or two, Gindea says, pointing out the car window as she drives down Central. There is Shlomie's Bakery; the Chateau de Vin wine shop; King David's glatt kosher delicatessen; Wok Tov, a Chinese glatt kosher takeout; and Le Chocolat, a gourmet chocolate maker. Kosher pizzerias, coffee shops, bagel stores, and sushi restaurants crowd five downtown blocks. The spacious Gourmet Glatt kosher supermarket, which has absorbed formerly independent kosher bakeries and appetizing shops, is one of five large kosher supermarkets in the area, all of them thriving.

All these eateries are supervised by the Vaad HaKashrus of the Five Towns and Far Rockaway, a powerful board of rabbis that moved to the right in terms of religious standards a decade ago when it merged with the more fervently Orthodox community of Far Rockaway. Headed by Rabbi Yosef Eisen, the vaad supervises sixty-five to seventy retail food establishments and is funded by certification fees paid by those stores as well as contributions from local synagogues and individuals.

In early September 2000, days after the merger and Eisen's hiring, signs began appearing in the windows of kosher food establishments indicating whether the owners were Sabbath observers. The shops were still proclaimed kosher, but the words "not shomer Shabbos" on their certificates were "like a scarlet letter in the Five Towns," as Marcelle Fischler wrote on October 8, 2000, in the *New York Times*. The certificates also noted whether the bread was pas Yisroel, baked by a Jew.

The Jewish community protested the new regulations in several town meetings, and by the end of September the signs were removed. But they had done their damage. Many of the establishments marked as not Sabbath observant saw their Orthodox clientele wither away. And kashrut standards in the Five Towns grew increasingly strict. Even non-meat restaurants had to hire a full-time mashgiach if they wished to retain their kosher certification, as well as pay monthly fees to the vaad ranging from $250 to $800 or more.

Nancy Amar, owner of Primavera restaurant in Cedarhurst, fell under the vaad's scrutiny. She was told she had to hire a full-time mashgiach to check her vegetables for insects and guard her pilot lights against non-Jews trying to light them. "I'm a modern Orthodox woman; I can do that myself," she complains. "But the vaad said no, they were going to send someone, and they told me I had to pay him fifteen dollars an hour." Finally, she decided to rent out her restaurant, renamed Pescato, rather than deal with the headache of running it. "The community was getting more right-wing anyway," she says.

The increasingly strict standards of kosher supervision in this country reflect a general shift to the right within the observant community as a whole. On one hand, they assure this population that the food they are buying or being served is as kosher as they want it to be. On the other hand, the stricter standards cause some kosher proprietors to give up and go non-kosher, as Ziggy Gruber did when he moved his deli business from New York to Los Angeles and then to Houston.

That's also what happened to Noah's Bagels, the famed West Coast bagel chain. Noah Alper, who founded the first Noah's New York Bagels in 1988 in Berkeley, California, recalls the troubles he had over the years with kosher certification. He worked with Rabbi Yehuda Ferris of the Berkeley Chabad to make sure Lubavitchers, the most observant Jews in the area, would be able to eat in his restaurant. But he also wanted to stay open on Shabbat, for economic reasons. Ferris told him about the shtar mechira system—the contract whereby a non-Jew buys the restaurant every Shabbat—a system that few Orthodox accept today, as evidenced by the de facto Orthodox boycott of Manhattan's Second Avenue Deli.

Even then, when stricter standards had not taken firm hold nationwide, Alper remembers ten rabbis crowded into his tiny Berkeley office, arguing over which one would take the risk of supervising his new eatery. "No one wanted to stick his neck out," he says. Finally, they suggested Rabbi David Rue of the Los Angeles Beit Din, who was lenient enough to certify a place that used a shtar mechira, but respected enough so observant Jews would accept his authority. All the branches of Noah's were kosher, certified by different rabbis in different cities. In Los Angeles, Alper met with two of the largest certifying organizations; each told him their people would not patronize his restaurant if their competitor certified it.

Finally, Alper had enough. In 1996, when his thirty-six branches up and down the West Coast made him the owner of the nation's largest kosher restaurant chain, Alper sold the business. "It got into money and into power, Jewish infighting at its worst," he says. "It was big rabbis with big followings, and parts of it were unbelievably ugly. Besides, the whole kosher world had moved to the right, and what we were originally doing was no longer acceptable." The new owners shortened the name of the business to Noah's Bagels and dropped its kosher certification. The only kosher branches today are two stores in Seattle.

Some kosher establishments that operated under the older, looser standards continued to slip under the radar for decades, but as kosher certifiers tightened up nationwide, one by one those older businesses lost their hekhshers. Closing on Shabbat has been a condition for kosher certification for more than a century, at least on paper. The 1902 Constitution of the Union of Orthodox Rabbis instructed rabbis to warn their congregations against buying bread from kosher bakeries that baked on the Sabbath. Not only would purchasing such bread constitute a sin, the document pointed out; it's likely that someone violating one kosher law will violate other, more substantial ones. In practice, however, many such bakeries thrived.

One was Newman's Bakery in Swampscott, Massachusetts. Owned by the Newman family since 1965, it was the last Jewish-owned bakery in the state to carry the kosher approval of the Rabbinical Council of Massachusetts despite the fact that it was open on Shabbat. In May 2008, the council ordered the bakery to close Friday night and Saturday or it would withdraw that approval.

Sixty-year-old Bernard Newman, who took over the bakery when his father retired, protested the decision vehemently, telling the *Boston Globe* that he planned to stay open with or without the council's consent. He and his father had been operating a kosher bakery for forty-three years and had never shut on Shabbat. Their products were the same, just as kosher as they'd always been, he told the *Globe;* the only thing that had changed was the rabbis' standards.

Rabbi Abraham Halbfinger, director of the Rabbinical Council of Massachusetts, says the bakery had operated under a leniency unique to the Boston area. When he arrived forty years ago from New York, Halbfinger says all the Jewish-owned bakeries in the area were open on Shabbat, something that he found "strange" but had to deal with. "I inherited this situation when I got here," he says. "Each community has to work out its own setup, and this is what they did in Boston." Newman's Bakery, along with the others open on Shabbat, were "grandfathered in," but they were never formally certified as kosher. "To accommodate people in the community, our supervisors periodically checked their ingredients to make sure they were kosher, that's all," he explains. "They were on our list of 'approved' bakeries, whose ingredients we check." That, too, is a uniquely Boston arrangement.

Over the years the others either went out of business, sold to non-Jews, or began to shut on Shabbat. Newman's was the last holdout. Halbfinger says he "feels bad" about forcing the owner into a corner. It needn't have happened, he says, if Newman had agreed to shut just one day a week. The Jewish community in Swampscott is more observant than it used to be, and people were complaining about seeing a kosher bakery open on Shabbat. The council's job is to serve the local Jewish community, he points out, noting that none of the rabbis on the council takes a fee for kosher supervision. "We don't charge the mom-and-pop bakeries a nickel," he says. "The mashgichim, it's all free. We do this as a community service."

Newman's Bakery is still open, but the council no longer approves its ingredients as kosher. Rabbi Baruch HaLevi of Congregation Shirat Hayam, a Conservative synagogue in town, says he and his congregants continue to patronize it, because they know and trust Newman and his kashrut level, even without formal supervision. HaLevi, like many non-Orthodox Jews, blasts the increasing strictness of kosher certification, as well as what he considers its awkward loopholes. The local Stop & Shop supermarket is open on Shabbat yet is certified as kosher by the rabbinical council because it is owned by non-Jews. Newman's Bakery, because it is Jewish owned, must close. Where is the sense in that? HaLevi asks.

"It's not truly about kashrut or ethics anymore; it's about something else—power, money, politics, loopholes," he says. "It's a system that has run amok."

LOS ANGELES kosher authority Rabbi Eliezer Eidlitz estimates that 70 to 75 percent of the one thousand agencies and individuals giving kosher certification today are "legitimate." That means several hundred are not, at least in his view. Some are real frauds. A woman called Rabbi Chaim Fogelman of the OK to ask his opinion of the rabbi supervising her restaurant. The rabbi would show up at her restaurant and taste her food to decide whether it was kosher or not, a completely fraudulent way to determine something's kosher status. And he charged her good money for this.

"In an industry as lucrative and important as kashrut, there is ample room for creeping abuse," agrees Adlerstein. "I remember seeing certificates of kashrut in LA butcher shops given by rabbis who had been dead for years."

Some of the kosher supervisors Eidlitz considers less than legitimate might simply be rabbis whose standards are less strict than his. They might be Orthodox rabbis who accept leniencies no longer acceptable to the Orthodox mainstream, such as Rabbi Rafael Saffra, head of the Tablet-K, who does not require a mashgiach for cheese production, or Rabbi Israel Steinberg, who supervises the Second Avenue Deli. Or they might be Conservative rabbis.

Conservative Judaism emerged in 1850s Germany out of the same Enlightenment circles that gave rise to Reform Judaism, but defined itself in opposition to Reform's rejection of halacha, or Jewish religious law. Conservative Judaism, like Orthodox Judaism, accepts the Torah's commandments as obligatory, including the laws of kashrut. The movement is often viewed as occupying a middle ground between the more observant Orthodox and more liberal Reform movements, but that glosses over the substantive differences among the three major Jewish streams. Conservative Judaism views the Torah and Talmud as divine in origin and halacha as binding, but also affirms that halacha should evolve to meet the changing realities of Jewish life; it seeks to conserve Jewish tradition, while constantly refining that tradition in light of modern scholarship.

While Conservative and Orthodox Judaism accept the same laws of kashrut, the Conservative movement applies some of those laws differently. Conservative authorities in the twentieth century knocked down several "fences around the Torah" their Orthodox colleagues had constructed, believing them to be unnecessary or even a detriment to the fulfillment of the mitzvot they were designed to protect. The Conservative movement does not require American-made cheese to carry a hekhsher, although some Conservative rabbis prefer it. The movement also does not require kosher certification of wine, following a 1985 opinion by Rabbi Elliot Dorff, who wrote that the laws regarding its handling by a non-Jew were no longer relevant. The Conservative movement permits greater leniency in kashering methods, and considers chemical additives derived from non-kosher meat products such as rennet and horse-hoof gelatin to be no longer food, and thus permissible in kosher food production. It continues to accept swordfish and sturgeon as kosher even after the Orthodox stopped eating those fish, following the 1951 ruling by Rabbi Moshe Tendler of Yeshiva University.

Despite these differences, the Conservative movement did not challenge the Orthodox hegemony on kosher supervision and certification for most of the century. Individual Conservative rabbis have been giving certification for years in their own synagogues and to bakeries, butcher shops, and caterers that serve their congregations. But when it came to food manufacturing, they left the field to the Orthodox. It wasn't until the New York and Baltimore cases, and the changes made to Minnesota's kosher law, that rumblings emerged from within the Conservative rabbinate to become more active in kosher affairs.

Rabbi Paul Plotkin of Temple Beth Am in Margate, Florida, is the founding chair of the subcommittee on kashrut of the Committee on Jewish Law and Standards, the legal body of the Conservative movement. He dates the growth spurt in Conservative rabbis giving kosher supervision back to the mid-1990s. Some got into the field because they opposed the increasing strictness of Orthodox standards. But most were just filling a gap. "There were communities around the country where the most traditional rabbi in the area was a Conservative rabbi, and if that rabbi did not give hashgocha to the bakery, the nursing home, the deli, the JCC, they wouldn't have it," he says. "Yet our training was notoriously poor. The attitude has been, let the Orthodox handle it, we need enough knowledge for the home, but we don't need to know about industrial kashrut."

In 1990, Plotkin designed a *rav hamachshir*, or supervising mashgiach, training course for Conservative rabbis. It looks much like the OU's course in practical kashrut offered to Yeshiva University rabbinical students, and it has similar aims: to teach how to supervise large-scale kosher events or food-manufacturing concerns. The course has been offered half a dozen times and has trained hundreds of Conservative rabbis.

Even so, Plotkin says, Conservative kosher supervision has not extended much beyond its own movement's synagogue kitchens. Plotkin says he turns down most requests for commercial supervision. Even though he does not charge for his services, why should a bakery or candy manufacturer go through the effort and expense of kashering their operation if only Conservative Jews will patronize them? "I tell them I would be doing them a disservice, and I give them the number of one of the national agencies," he says.

As of 2009, there were just two regional Conservative kashrut boards: the one in Suffolk County, New York, created in 2007, which oversees Commack Kosher, and one in Philadelphia set up in the 1950s.

"Philadelphia is a unique situation," explains Rabbi Robert Rubin, head kosher supervisor of the Philadelphia organization. "It's always had a strong Conservative community and no centralized Orthodox vaad." The Conservative vaad supervises four bakeries, three vegetarian Chinese restaurants, a handful of miscellaneous food establishments such as dessert makers, and six caterers. There are enough events in the Conservative community to keep those caterers in business, Rubin says, and no need for them to follow kosher rules to which almost none of their clients adhere.

The vaad follows Conservative custom but also tries to avoid awkwardness for more observant diners. It permits non-glatt kosher meat, and wine without a kosher label may be poured if that is the practice of the synagogue sponsoring the event. But wine and cheese used in cooking must be kosher certified, so diners don't have to wonder what's in a particular dish. Fish and meat may be served together; it's up to the diner to choose what to take when platters are circulated. The vaad does not require a mashgiach to light the ovens, in keeping with the Conservative distaste for the laws against bishul akum, and allows non-Jewish waitstaff to pour non-mevushal wine. And fruits and vegetables are welcome. "They obviously have to be washed, but we don't panic over the bug issue," he says.

Rubin is very low-key about his work. He doesn't view Conservative supervision as a political struggle. They do it in Philadelphia because there is a need. If any of their clients choose to go with a national agency, they're welcome to do so, no offense taken.

Plotkin, however, believes Conservative supervision is needed, if for no other reason than to provide non-glatt meat to kosher-keeping Jews who are happy with that standard and don't want to be forced to pay the higher price for glatt. A major step in that direction took place in 2004, when the Conservative movement gave its approval to Hebrew National, the company famous for its "We Answer to a Higher Authority" ad campaign.

Hebrew National is one of the most contentious issues in American commercial kashrut. The company bills itself as the world's largest kosher meat processor, making 720 million hot dogs a year, but virtu-

ally no Orthodox Jews will eat its product. Until 2004 few Conservative Jews did, either. The company was supervised by a longtime in-
house mashgiach, Rabbi Tibor Stern, whose supervision was considered "unreliable" by all the national agencies as well as the Orthodox and Conservative leadership. He lived far from the company's
midwestern plants, they operated basically on their own, and no one
could be sure whether kashrut standards were really being observed.
The list of questions put Stern beyond the pale of the kosher mainstream.

In 2004 Stern died, and the company hired the Triangle K, a supervising agency headed by Rabbi Aryeh Ralbag of the Young Israel of
Avenue K in Brooklyn. Soon afterward, Plotkin and two colleagues
from the Jewish Theological Seminary visited all the company's plants
to see whether the Conservative movement would be able to endorse
them. While hot dogs are the company's biggest seller, and three-
quarters of those who buy those hot dogs are not Jewish, the CEO told
Plotkin that the Conservative market was its target for the rest of its
processed meats. Despite Ralbag's strong credentials, the company had
few illusions of being accepted by Orthodox authorities anytime soon,
since it used non-glatt meat.

Plotkin and his fellow rabbis met Ralbag and flew with him to
inspect the company's two slaughterhouses in Wisconsin and Iowa, and
on to Indianapolis to walk through the main processing plant. Satisfied
that kashrut standards were sufficiently tight, the trio presented their
findings to the Conservative movement's law committee, which approved Hebrew National products as kosher in June.

Instead of solving a situation, the Conservative endorsement may
have muddled things further. Before 2004, Hebrew National simply
was not accepted at kosher events. Now its appearance at an event sig-
nals adherence to a particular denominational standard. No Orthodox
authority accepts the company's meat as kosher, but they are loath to
criticize Ralbag himself; it's enough, they point out, that the meat used
for Hebrew National products is not glatt.

Plotkin wants to make more kosher meat available, but he is concerned that Conservative kosher supervision not become seen as less
authentic or watered-down. "If Conservative certification becomes or
is perceived to be the easy way out, we will have demeaned our movement," he says, adding that Conservative Jews "have a lot to learn" from

the Orthodox agencies and mashgichim who speak the language of holiness when discussing kashrut.

"They talk about hashgocha as being a sacred calling," he says. "Based on what you do, you are adding to the holiness of the Jewish people or you are taking away from the holiness of the Jewish people. You have to lose a little sleep lest, God forbid, you bring someone by your actions to accidentally eat treyf."

# 14.

# Postville

## *The Scandal at Agriprocessors Changes the Kosher Conversation*

THE DRIVE TO POSTVILLE, Iowa, winds past miles of verdant, rolling fields filled with soy, corn, and grazing cattle. This is truly America's heartland: the rich, cultivated soil whose bounty feeds the country's great urban centers.

Coming into the town itself, the landscape flattens out and the colors grow more muted. A sign at the entrance to town proclaims Postville "Hometown to the World," homage to the thousands of foreign workers who poured in over two decades to work at the Agriprocessors kosher slaughterhouse and meatpacking plant, the region's largest employer. They started arriving from the time the plant opened in 1987, first single men from Poland and Ukraine, then families from Mexico, Guatemala, and Israel. They settled down, sent their children to school, and forced cultural and social change on the formerly white, Christian population of some 1,500 residents. A multicultural center opened in 2003, the radio station broadcast shows in Spanish and Yiddish, and the Sabor Latino restaurant served margaritas and tacos down the block from the Jewish Resource Center's library and Torah classes.

The former Agriprocessors plant sits at the north end of town, beyond the railroad tracks. It is a collection of long, low buildings punctuated by a tall water tower with the company name emblazoned on it. Large holding pens surround the main processing plant, way stations for the cattle that passed through the doors every morning on their way to slaughter. At one time Agriprocessors was the powerhouse of the country's kosher meat industry, at its peak producing 60 percent of the kosher beef and 40 percent of the kosher poultry sold nationwide. Its nearly one thousand employees processed up to five hundred head of cattle a day, moving them from flatbed trucks to hanging quarters in less than an hour. Annual sales were estimated at $250 million.

On the morning of May 12, 2008, it all came to a screeching halt. Hundreds of federal agents from Immigration and Customs Enforcement (ICE), a division of the Department of Homeland Security, swooped down on the plant with guns and helicopters, and took 389 undocumented workers, most of them Guatemalan, into custody. It was, to date, the largest single immigration raid in U.S. history. By the end of the year the plant was bankrupt, the nation's kosher meat supply was in jeopardy, and the ethics of kashrut was a hot topic of conversation in the Jewish community and beyond.

The Agriprocessors story began with Aaron Rubashkin, a Russian-born Holocaust survivor who came to this country with his young wife and daughter in 1953. Settling in Brooklyn, he went into business with a kosher butcher he knew from Europe. His partner retired in 1985 and he started looking for a way to make more money than what his small butcher shop was taking in. At that time, most cattle were raised in the Midwest and shipped back East for slaughter. Rubashkin came up with the idea of building a slaughterhouse closer to where the animals lived, to save on shipping costs. Less than half the animal's live weight ends up being butchered and used as kosher meat, so why pay for all that extra poundage? In Postville he found a defunct turkey-processing plant, which had closed nine years earlier. It seemed perfect, and in 1987, he moved in and started his operation.

Rubashkin says that by reviving the town's slaughterhouse industry, he saved it from economic distress. "It was a ghost town. Every block had four or five houses for sale; every store on the main street was for rent," he recalls. "We started to build, we raised our kids, and we worked very, very hard."

The company worked hard, and it worked ruthlessly. Within a decade, Agriprocessors had revolutionized the kosher meat and poultry business. Until the 1980s, fresh kosher meat was sold through butchers. It came in raw, hanging quarters from slaughterhouses that were rented per run by kosher operators, and it was rarely available beyond major cities on either coast. Empire Kosher was just starting to make fresh kosher chickens more available, but the company's reach was limited. Aaron Rubashkin brought modern mass-production methods to the kosher meat industry, for the first time putting the processing side of the business under the same roof as the slaughtering. Agriprocessors became the first kosher business to slaughter, soak, salt, butcher, and package its meat all in one location.

"Large-scale production changed the way factories operate," explains Rabbi Seth Mandel, who oversees the four dozen slaughterhouses in North and South America under OU Kosher supervision. "The local model of a heimishe rabbi giving supervision to a meat place is totally inoperable now. They don't look in the places in a modern plant that need to be looked at. There's a difference between supervising a place that does ten animals a day and [one that does] hundreds of animals a day."

Kosher consumers stopped patronizing local butchers, finding it easier and less expensive to buy kosher meat prepackaged and nicely sealed, already carrying the OU logo. Agriprocessors experimented with different ways of wrapping the meat and using chemical dyes so the meat remained red longer and looked more attractive on the shelf. Kosher industry experts credit the company with expanding the availability of fresh kosher meat, which allowed Orthodox communities to move into towns and cities where they never lived before.

As the company grew bigger, it was able to provide meat more and more cheaply. It took advantage of Iowa's status as a right-to-work state, meaning the company could operate without unions to control wages or benefits. Rubashkin, who considered unions part of the Soviet tyranny he'd left behind, fought hard to keep them out of his plants; in two decades, no union managed to get a foothold in his company.

He opened a second plant in Gordon, Nebraska, and as his empire expanded, it began slaughtering as far away as Colorado and Uruguay. Agriprocessors was a tightly held family business, with nearly every aspect controlled by one of his nine sons and daughters or their spouses.

The company's success snowballed. The Rubashkins made it known they would provide kosher meat or poultry to any retail store that wanted to carry it, and at a relatively inexpensive price. Company trucks were willing to make a stop to unload one or two crates of meat, whereas their competitors would schedule only big orders. In many rural towns and smaller cities, the only glatt kosher meat available came from Agriprocessors. Agreements made with supermarkets not to carry competitors' products helped keep it that way. The ShopRite in Livingston, New Jersey, was one of many supermarkets nationwide that knew if it carried Empire Kosher poultry, Agriprocessors would stop supplying it with kosher beef.

Although Agriprocessors was known as a kosher slaughterhouse, about two-thirds of the meat it produced was non-kosher, sold under the Iowa Best Beef label. No slaughterhouse produces just kosher meat. In a kosher run, all the animals are slaughtered according to kosher methods, but then a mashgiach examines the lungs of every animal, both inside and outside of the body, looking for any adhesions or holes that will disqualify it as glatt kosher. If the adhesion is easily removed, the animal can still be sold as non-glatt kosher, under the imprimatur of an independent rabbi; that meat is separated out immediately and held in a different part of the facility. But most of the rejected animals are sold as non-kosher, along with the back half of all the kosher animals. Up to 85 percent of the meat produced in a kosher plant ends up being sold as non-kosher.

Agriprocessors' biggest growth came in its last few years, after it helped fund a $12 million wastewater treatment plant for Postville that enabled the plant to expand tremendously. From four hundred workers in 2002, it ballooned to nearly one thousand in 2007.

Along the way, the company collected a hefty number of fines for health, safety, and labor violations, including a $600,000 settlement paid to the Environmental Protection Agency in 2006 for wastewater pollution. It was charged repeatedly with violating the U.S. Department of Agriculture's Humane Methods of Slaughter Act. In 2004, People for the Ethical Treatment of Animals sent in undercover investigators to shoot video of cows stumbling around in their own blood after their throats were slit, and workers using meat hooks to make second cuts in the throats of animals that didn't die from the first cut. PETA workers shot a similar video at the company's Nebraska plant in 2007. Both videos produced public outcry, even though kosher agencies pointed out the second cut was permitted by kosher law and federal regulations.

On May 26, 2006, the *Jewish Daily Forward* published an investigative piece by reporter Nathaniel Popper alleging horrendous working conditions at the Postville plant, including health and safety violations, numerous injuries, supervisors demanding bribes for jobs and short-changing workers' paychecks, and a general atmosphere of fear among the largely illegal workforce.

The article prompted the Conservative movement to send a five-man investigative team to the plant that summer to meet with workers and managers. The group, which included three rabbis, heard tales of sexual coercion of female workers, of supervisors who demanded that job applicants buy used cars from them in order to secure employment, of wages as low as $5 an hour, paid in cash. The team made note of inadequate safety procedures and worker training, the use of unsafe chemicals, and lack of access to safety equipment, and made recommendations for improvement. The changes were not made and production continued.

In March 2008, the Iowa Occupational Safety and Health Administration cited Agriprocessors with thirty-nine health and safety violations, totaling $182,000 in fines, more than the total of all fines issued to Iowa meat plants the previous year. Between 2002 and 2006, the company received a dozen notices from the Social Security Administration showing hundreds of discrepancies between employee names and Social Security numbers. Throughout the first half of 2008, management received complaints from the state labor board that underage workers were employed at the Postville facility. In April, state agents conducted a spot audit. They lined up workers they suspected were underage, but let them go when no proof could be found.

When the big ICE raid hit on May 12, it wasn't a complete surprise—locals had seen activity at the cattle exhibition grounds seventy-five miles away in Waterloo as federal agents prepared a detention center and makeshift courtroom to handle the expected arrests. Rumors spread that a big immigration raid was being planned, but no one was sure which of several local plants would be targeted.

Forty-year-old Alicia López was at work on the chicken line the morning of the raid. A Mexican citizen in this country without papers, she made $7.50 an hour and worked a shift that lasted from ten to fourteen hours. "I was on my lunch break and I saw my friends running; I didn't know why," she recalls. "I thought they were rushing to take off their gloves for lunch. Then somebody yelled, 'La migra! Run!' A supervisor told us to run because the INS was here. I ran, trying to find a place to hide. I didn't have papers. They had guns, pointing them at us like we were animals. They pulled our clothes to stop us."

López was lined up with a group of other undocumented workers and marched to the factory lunchroom, where their pictures were taken and taped to plastic bags they were given to hold. They were put on a bus, where they sat for nine hours before being taken to the cattle grounds in Waterloo. Late that night, López was released along with four dozen other women with dependent children, and was sent home to await trial, a GPS monitoring device clasped around her ankle to restrict her movements. For the next several months, she had to stand for two hours a day next to a power outlet to recharge the ankle bracelet, a ritual she called her ultimate humiliation.

The devastation in the town was palpable. The morning after the raid, half the students in the elementary school were gone, either kept at home by terrified parents or already on their way back across the border. Hundreds of people had taken shelter in local churches, mainly St. Bridget's Catholic Church, where priests and nuns stood at the door, on the lookout for immigration officials. The town's population dropped by 20 percent overnight. The raid mainly affected families; it took place during the first shift of the day, the preferred shift for families with young children, since it allowed parents to be home by dinnertime.

Most of the workers lived paycheck to paycheck. Now, with the men in jail and the women marked with electronic ankle bracelets and forbidden to work, they had no money and no food. Food banks were set up in the churches, and sad-eyed Mexican and Guatemalan women, children in tow, began showing up every morning to pick up food and scrounge through piles of old clothes. Families that had been in the town for a decade or more were torn apart, trying to find out at which of a dozen jails in various states their loved ones were being held and when they were expected to be deported.

The hearings were rushed through at top speed. The raid was the culmination of a six-month investigation, and the process went like clockwork. Of the 389 people arrested, 306 were charged with fraud-related felonies related to using false documents to get a job. Eighteen of those arrested were between the ages of thirteen and seventeen.

Within a week, 262 illegal workers pleaded guilty to knowingly using false Social Security cards or legal residence documents to gain employment at Agriprocessors; they were sentenced to five months in prison, followed by deportation. The workers pleaded to these reduced charges to avoid facing what court-appointed lawyers told them were more serious charges of identity theft that carried mandatory two-year sentences, followed by deportation anyway. The workers, most of whom were illiterate, were tried in groups and barely had time to meet with their lawyers. They were processed, tried, sentenced, and moved through in a matter of minutes.

In a widely publicized essay, part of which was printed in the *New York Times*, Professor Erik Camayd-Freixas, who worked for twenty-three years as a Spanish interpreter for the federal courts and was called in to work the Postville case, said the defendants did not understand the criminal charges they faced or the rights they had waived.

"Most of the clients we interviewed did not even know what a Social Security number was or what purpose it served," he charged. The workers had followed their bosses' orders, in many cases signing an X instead of their name to whatever forms had been placed in front of them when they were hired.

In the factory, production ground to a halt. Rabbis and yeshiva students from around the country were pressed into emergency duty to fill empty spots on the assembly line. Within days a skeleton crew was managing to keep the lines up and running, but at nowhere near pre-raid levels.

Nationwide, the weakness of a kosher meat system that depended so heavily on one supplier was being felt. Kosher caterers and butchers were unable to fill customer orders, and wholesale prices of kosher meat shot up to two, sometimes three times their pre-raid levels. At the end of May, Jacqueline Lankry, a kosher caterer in Fort Lauderdale, went from paying $2.99 a pound for chopped beef to $6.99. Some butchers couldn't get kosher meat at any price.

On May 23, Aaron Rubashkin bowed to pressure from Jewish and congressional groups that had called for a company overhaul, and announced he would replace his son Sholom, then forty-eight, as CEO. That same day, the Jewish Labor Committee called for a boycott of Agriprocessors meat and poultry, asserting that the company had displayed "a clear pattern of employer negligence and even lawlessness." Uri L'Tzedek, a social-justice advocacy group started by students at Yeshivat Chovevei Torah, a liberal Orthodox rabbinical school in Manhattan, circulated a petition demanding that the company pay its workers at least minimum wage and treat them according to the standards of the Torah and U.S. law.

Meanwhile, Rabbi Genack at the Orthodox Union, the national agency certifying Agriprocessors, told reporters his policy was to rely on federal and state authorities to monitor working conditions and environmental concerns. "We will let the appropriate agencies make their determinations," he said. "We at the OU do not have the expertise to develop standards in those areas. If the company is found to be criminally liable, we will withdraw our certification."

In June, the company brought in outside agencies to recruit and train new workers to replace the Guatemalans, and began using the federal E-Verify system to check every applicant against immigration and Social Security databases. The company now offered wages starting at $10 an hour, and the town swelled with new crops of foreign workers, few of whom spoke the same language. They came from Ukraine, Belarus, and Russia, from Somalia and Sudan. Two hundred workers arrived from the South Seas island nation of Palau, and a group of students from Kyrgyzstan dropped in to make money during their summer vacation.

Americans were recruited, too. Unemployed African American factory workers were brought in by the busload from Chicago and Detroit; red-cheeked boys from the next town showed up looking for a few bucks. People were recruited from homeless shelters in Amarillo, Texas, promised a job and thirty days' free housing, and shipped off to Postville, where they were dumped with no training or resources.

The new arrivals were crowded into substandard housing and milled about the recruiting office in the hot sun every day, spreading rumors and itching for work. Many left almost as soon as they arrived, finding conditions not what they had been promised. The Palauans, who had spent seventy-two hours on planes and buses getting to Postville, clamored to return home after not being paid for two weeks; some had their electricity cut off when they were unable to pay the bills. Fights broke out in the normally quiet downtown streets, and residents started keeping their children inside. Postville was spiraling into chaos.

As June spilled over into July, anger grew: Why were the only people arrested so far low-level workers? Were the feds just biding their time, building a case against the owners and managers, or would those higher-ups manage to slip through without prosecution? Then, on July 3, two supervisors were arrested, the first management-level arrests in the case. A third supervisor skipped the country before he could be jailed. In August, the state issued thirty-one citations against Agri-processors for violations of workplace safety regulations.

On September 9, the first big charges were handed down. Aaron and Sholom Rubashkin and three executives in the human resources department were charged by the Iowa attorney general with 9,311 violations of child labor law involving thirty-two youths under the age of eighteen. Each violation was punishable by up to thirty days in jail and a fine of up to $625. Avi Lyon, a former director of the Jewish Labor Committee, says the Postville school bus used to stop at the plant to pick up kids after the night shift and take them to school; the driver had a list of names to look for.

In late October, the company was hit with nearly $10 million in new state fines for failing to pay proper wages. On October 30, Sholom Rubashkin was arrested on criminal charges of immigration fraud. One of the charges alleged he gave supervisors $4,500 in cash days before the raid to purchase fraudulent work documents. He was released with an ankle bracelet to monitor his movements, but was re-arrested in mid-November on federal charges of bank fraud.

The banks were closing in as well. On October 30, the First Bank of St. Louis filed a lawsuit to foreclose on the company's assets, alleging it had defaulted on a $35 million loan. Agriprocessors declared bankruptcy November 4 but appealed in U.S. Bankruptcy Court the following week to be allowed to use some of the bank's cash collateral to feed 815,000 chickens and turkeys it had on its property waiting to be slaughtered. Beef slaughter had ceased altogether, but crates of dead and dying birds were piling up outside the plant's closed doors.

Throughout it all, Aaron Rubashkin didn't seem to know what hit him. One afternoon in late July 2008, he sat in his second-floor Brooklyn office, next to the butcher shop he'd owned for more than fifty years, surrounded by piles of papers and framed photos of his family with various hassidic rabbis and political leaders. A short, stout man in his early eighties with a long white beard and heavy Russian accent, he discussed his troubles with a mixture of bewilderment and bluster.

"What they write about us on the Internet, they should be ashamed," he said. Shuffling through the photographs, he held up one of a grandson in an Israeli Army uniform and another of his father-in-law as an elderly man standing next to a group of young yeshiva students in prewar Belarus. "We're a family of working people. We didn't come from the streets, not that there's anything wrong with that. People who do not have opportunity, they can come from the streets. And they are nice people. You cannot say they are not human."

He and his wife's family spent the war years in Samarkand, ending up in a displaced persons camp in Austria in 1946. He married at seventeen, and the couple's eldest daughter was born in the camp before they left for Paris and, from there, for the United States. "I have no degrees but the school of hard knocks," he said proudly. "Fort Knox, without the gold."

Even then, two months after the raid, with his company falling down around his ears, Aaron Rubashkin insisted that once people understood he was just an honest working man trying to make a living, his troubles would melt away. "A person comes to us, we got a procedure," he said. "Workers bring a Social Security card and a driver's license; they get a training how not to cut themselves, how to use the machinery. Takes a day or so. Then you're supposed to know how to do your work. The person who likes it, stays."

Working in a slaughterhouse is a dirty job, he acknowledged. "People who come, the first generation, they got no choice," he said. But he always treated his workers fairly, he insists, and did not grow wealthy at their expense. "We don't have no planes. We don't drive no fancy cars. My kids never slept a week in their own beds. Somebody was always coming; they need a bed to sleep, so the kids go in the living room to sleep on the couch or the carpet. And they are accusing us of abusing people? Of not paying them the money we owe them? We never abused nobody! God forbid. Never."

The charges continued to pile up. In January 2009, a federal grand jury indicted Sholom Rubashkin on twenty-five additional charges of bank fraud and ninety-nine federal charges, including money laundering, making false statements, and failing to pay for livestock in a timely manner. By March 2009, the company was limping along with about two hundred employees and was slaughtering some poultry under an agreement with its bank creditors that allowed it to remain open while it sought a buyer. Ironically, some of those working the line were illegal immigrants arrested in the May 2008 raid, who were ordered to return to Postville after their five-month prison term to testify against Sholom Rubashkin in his upcoming immigration trial, which had been separated out from the other charges.

In July 2009, SHF Industries, a company formed by Canadian plastics manufacturer Hershey Friedman and his son-in-law Daniel Hirsch, purchased Agriprocessors for $8.5 million. According to the purchase agreement, the new owners were not liable for more than $22 million the company owed to unsecured creditors, including local businesses, farmers who supplied animals to the company, and former employees. In August, the new owners renamed the company Agri Star Meat & Poultry, and announced plans to continue operation as a kosher slaughterhouse and meatpacking concern.

Meanwhile, other kosher meat and poultry businesses stepped up production to fill the gap caused by Agriprocessors' demise. Small, independent shechting operations sprang up in towns and neighborhoods with large Orthodox populations, such as Lakewood, New Jersey. The hassidic community of New Square, New York, announced plans to open a kosher poultry slaughterhouse with $1.6 million in aid from New York State. In September 2009, a new kosher chicken-processing plant broke ground in Tulare, California, with plans to process forty thousand chickens a day by the following spring, and Whole Foods began carrying a new line of kosher, antibiotic-free chicken from Kosher Valley, a six-month-old kosher slaughterhouse in Plainville, New York.

And Empire Kosher Poultry, which dominated the kosher poultry business before Agriprocessors came along, girded its loins to move into position once again as the country's largest kosher meat and poultry producer. In late summer, it announced plans to increase chicken production from 225,000 birds per week to 350,000 birds per week, going up to 800,000 birds per week during the Jewish holidays. The company also rolled out new product lines of organic and antibiotic-free chicken and turkey, a new line of poultry to be marketed directly to the hassidic community, and its first line of glatt kosher beef.

On November 12, Sholom Rubashkin was convicted of eighty-six federal charges of bank fraud, making false statements to a bank, wire fraud, mail fraud, money laundering, and aiding and abetting. He was the sixth high-level Agriprocessors manager to be convicted on federal charges. The other five struck plea bargains and testified against him.

The jury found, among other crimes, that he had employees create false sales invoices and forge truckers' signatures to defraud First Bank Business Capital, the plant's St. Louis lender, so he could collect larger advances on a $35 million credit line. Faxing the fake invoices across state lines constituted federal wire fraud; mailing monthly reports based on those invoices was mail fraud.

The jury further found that he concealed the fraud by funneling about $20 million through two Postville organizations: Torah Education of Northeast Iowa and the Kosher Community Grocery Store. He then diverted customer payments intended for First Bank into his plant, used the money for operational and personal expenses, and replaced it with money disguised as customer payments from the grocery store and Torah education program.

On these eighty-six counts, he faced a maximum of more than 1,200 years in prison. Sentencing was set for June 2010.

A week after the guilty verdicts, federal prosecutors dropped the seventy-five immigration charges, saying a second trial would add little to the lengthy prison term the disgraced former CEO already faced.

Once the immigration trial was canceled, the illegal immigrants who had been ordered to remain in Postville after their own five-month jail terms to serve as material witnesses against Rubashkin were released. As of December 2009, they did not know whether or not they would be deported.

IN SEPTEMBER 2009, the first book about Postville appeared since the May 2008 raid. *Postville U.S.A.* was written by Mark Grey and Michele Devlin, professors at the University of Northern Iowa, with the help of Aaron Goldsmith, a Lubavitch businessman and former member of the Postville City Council.

The authors' thesis is that the debacle could have happened in any one of hundreds of midwestern towns, all of which went through the same "experiment in diversity" in the 1980s and '90s when immigrant labor poured in to work in physically onerous, low-paying jobs that Americans no longer wanted. Postville stayed in the news because of the Jewish angle—the public loves stories of religious figures gone bad—but it was really just another story of sordid immigration politics and greedy corporations.

Postville was, the book's introduction points out, "a little town on the losing end of global forces bigger than itself and even its country." The solution, the authors insist, is comprehensive immigration reform and the implementation of laws that require for-profit corporations that use immigrant labor to shoulder more of the costs of feeding, educating, and housing those people and integrating them into American society.

Above all, the authors conclude, Americans need to take responsibility for their desire for cheap food and consumer goods. "The Agri plant produced both kosher and non-kosher products," they write. "All consumers benefit from relatively low food costs—costs that are borne on the backs of poorly paid and often vulnerable populations, from migrant workers in the Central Valley of California to Guatemalans at the Postville meat plant."[1]

The Agriprocessors scandal may not have been a Jewish story according to the authors of *Postville, U.S.A.* But the people of Postville experienced it as a Jewish story. Jeff Abbas, manager of the local radio station and a key figure in efforts to help the unemployed Latino workers after the raid, says that the fragile modus vivendi that developed between the town's Orthodox Jews and longtime Gentile residents over fifteen years evaporated in the wake of the raid. "So many people make this a Jewish thing, and it's not a Jewish thing; it's a Rubashkin thing," he says. "But that's not how people see it."

The American Jewish community certainly saw it as a Jewish story. The raid on the Agriprocessors plant and the publicity surrounding the arrests of its managers and owners triggered a national Jewish conversation about what it means to keep kosher, and what the responsibility of the larger Jewish community is when injustice is perpetrated in its name.

"I find it outrageous that this was done to workers so that I could eat kosher food," says Avi Lyon.

In the first days and weeks after the raid, the Jewish and secular press were filled with articles about the ethics of kashrut, something that had rarely been discussed in such a public forum. Rabbis and kosher experts weighed in on both sides: Yes, Jews should be as concerned about the treatment of the workers who produce their food as they are about the kosher status of the food itself; no, the laws of kashrut and the laws of ethical treatment of workers are both part of Judaism, but not dependent on each other. The conversation became more and more heated.

Battle lines were drawn between the Orthodox, who saw themselves as holding up the banner of kashrut on their own, and the non-Orthodox activists, whom Orthodox leaders believed were using the Agriprocessors scandal to justify antireligious views they already held.

Just days after the raid, the Conservative movement seized the initiative by reviving interest in its Hekhsher Tzedek, or certificate of social justice, a project developed by its commission of inquiry after the 2006 visit to the Postville plant. The Hekhsher Tzedek project was presented to the Jewish public as a way to reward kosher food producers that maintained certain ethical standards. The certificate, which manufacturers could apply for, would proclaim that the company pays fair wages and benefits; provides safe working conditions; avoids undue pollution of the environment; engages in honest business practices; and if its products involve meat, treats animals humanely before and during the slaughtering process.

Many Orthodox Jews reacted angrily to the Hekhsher Tzedek campaign, seeing it as an attack on Orthodoxy, which its organizers insisted it was not. "There's the notion in kashrut that food is not kosher if a sin was committed in its preparation," points out David Kraemer. "That's the basis for kosher agencies not giving certification to bakeries and grocery stores open on Shabbat, a transgression that technically has nothing to do with the kosher status of the food served there. By the same token, if food has been prepared by transgressing other mitzvot, such as thou shalt not oppress thy worker, or thou shalt not be cruel to animals, why shouldn't that food also be out of bounds?"

Hekhsher Tzedek became the focus of the Jewish debate over kosher ethics in the second half of 2008. The project was headed by Rabbi Morris Allen, leader of the Conservative movement's 2006 commission of inquiry and rabbi of Beth Jacob Congregation in Mendota Heights, Minnesota. He became the face of the new initiative, drawing parallels between Jewish ethics and Jewish dietary practice for National Public Radio and the *New York Times* alike.

"It's not enough to be concerned with the ritual dimensions of kashrut, but the ethical dimensions of who we are as a people," he said over and over that summer. "Jewish law is concerned not only about the smoothness of a cow's lung, but also the safety of a worker's hand." Kosher meat had become less expensive in recent years, he pointed out, because the average salary of a worker on the killing floor at Agriprocessors was $6.75 an hour. Workers doing the same job in other Iowa meat plants earned an average of $11.25 an hour. "That's why we could buy kosher meat in tray packs in supermarkets," he says. "We were all complicit. No one asked, how are we doing this?"

The campaign caught on quickly in liberal circles. Soon after its official guidelines were outlined in August 2008, the Reform movement announced its support. "The good name of the Jewish community is at stake here," explained Rabbi Eric Yoffie of the Union for Reform Judaism. "Kashrut is a Jewish issue, and if people who provide kosher food to the Jewish community exploit their workers, it's a Jewish concern, whether the majority of Reform Jews keep kosher or not."

The campaign resonated particularly strongly with Jewish teenagers. Several Conservative summer camps stopped serving Rubashkin products in 2008, and teen participants at a B'nai B'rith Youth Organization convention asked organizers not to serve Agriprocessors meat after they heard a fifteen-year-old Guatemalan boy speak about abuses he suffered while working at the plant.

On July 27, two midwestern Jewish rights groups, the Jewish Council on Urban Affairs of Chicago and Jewish Community Action of St. Paul, brought one thousand people to Postville for a march and rally in support of the detained workers. Two busloads arrived from Camp Ramah, a Conservative youth camp in Wisconsin, unloading fifteen- and sixteen-year-olds fired up to take a stand for social justice.

"We're not just here because we want kosher meat; we're here because we care how people are being treated," said fifteen-year-old camper Jonathan Ribnick. "What Rubashkin and Agriprocessors did to their employees is not acceptable by Jewish values, or by any other American values. It was morally wrong."

In September, the Conservative movement asked its rabbis to discuss ethical kashrut during their High Holiday speeches; several hundred did so. Conservative and Reform congregations held informational sessions, bringing in speakers to discuss the ethical implications of kosher food production. In January 2009, Rabbi Julie Schonfeld, the newly installed executive director of the Rabbinical Assembly, pointed to Hekhsher Tzedek, now renamed Magen Tzedek, or "Shield of Justice," as the most important project on the Conservative movement agenda.

"It is not acceptable to our movement to conceive of kosher food produced under circumstances that are abusive of workers, or that cross other boundaries in terms of corporate transparency, worker safety or the environment," she said. "For our people, these pieces go hand in hand: The ethical values of Judaism and the ritual practices of Judaism refine us as human beings and help us develop the kind of communities we want to live in. The life and well-being of the person who prepares and handles our food is as central to its holiness as the rituals involved in its preparation."

Although mainstream Orthodox groups initially opposed the Hekhsher Tzedek campaign, a handful of liberal Orthodox voices joined the outcry. In May 2008, Uri L'Tzedek circulated a petition calling for an Orthodox boycott of Agriprocessors if the company did not demonstrate full compliance with Torah and federal laws regarding treatment of workers.

The boycott was eventually called off, but the organization continued its advocacy work by developing a Tav HaYosher, or "ethical seal," which it began awarding to kosher restaurants that maintained good working conditions and treated employees fairly. Based on a similar initiative in Israel, the Tav HaYosher project got under way in 2009; by that summer, nearly a dozen kosher restaurants in Manhattan carried the seal.

Shmuly Yanklowitz, Uri L'Tzedek cofounder and a rabbinical student at the seminary, says the Orthodox community needed an appropriate way to engage in Jewish social justice work, and focusing on the production of kosher food made perfect sense. It's Orthodox Jews who buy kosher food most regularly, so their dollars and cents have an immediate impact on the industry; and because kashrut is meant to instill holiness in its practitioners, the entire process of producing and preparing the food should share that same level of sanctity.

An Uri L'Tzedek delegation visited Agriprocessors in summer 2008 and spoke to plant workers as their Conservative colleagues had done two years earlier. They came away with similar reactions, and a commitment to organize an ongoing campaign for social justice in the kosher food industry on the basis of Orthodox Jewish values.

"There are a couple ways I experience kashrut now," Yanklowitz says. "A sense of spiritual awareness, that when I eat something I say a bracha on it. That's a way of elevating it for me. I also have a spiritual awareness of understanding how the food has reached my plate. Everything from the slaughtering process, to the country it originated in, to what part of the text deals with how that was handled. I feel commanded by the individual who produced the food; I hear that person crying out to me. And that is the moral aspect of kashrut."

Other Orthodox initiatives emerged around the Agriprocessors issue. Rabbi Shmuel Herzfeld, spiritual leader of Ohev Shalom—The National Synagogue in Washington, D.C., asked the rabbinic board of Greater Washington to suspend purchase of Rubashkin meat at the stores and caterers it supervised until the situation was resolved. Other Orthodox rabbis urged their congregations to hold off on purchasing the meat, at least temporarily. A group of Orthodox rabbis in Los Angeles organized a project similar to Uri L'Tzedek's Tav HaYosher seal, but they expanded their efforts to include any Jewish-owned business, including synagogues and doctors' offices, all of which, they said, had the same Jewish obligation to treat workers fairly and ethically.

In September 2008, the (Orthodox) Rabbinical Council of America created a task force to produce a guide to Jewish principles and ethical guidelines for business and industry. "We attach importance to having ethical guidelines incorporated as a matter of policy by companies receiving kosher supervision," the council stated in a press release.

"This isn't the first time the Jewish community has been talking about ethics and kashrut, but until recently the conversations were marginal, small, and fairly limited to the Renewal community," says Rabbi Jacob Fine, Hillel rabbi at the University of Washington in Seattle. "We have now reached the tipping point. There is no part of the Jewish community, from Reform to Orthodox, where the conversation about kashrut and ethics is not taking place."

The story of the Agriprocessors kosher slaughterhouse and packing plant ignited a communal conversation about Jewish ethics and Jewish dietary practice that appears to be ongoing. It tapped into a growing consciousness about food and food production in America in general, and it built upon a growing interest among young Jews in expressing their Jewish identity through tangible rituals, including the way they eat.

"The end result will be, I hope, that more kosher food will be bought by more Jews," says Allen, who encourages kashrut observance in his own congregation. "You're not going to get the majority of Jews to go out and buy two sets of dishes. But you can get Jews to say, I can make choices about the food I buy based on my identity as a Jew. Because of this conversation, people who had no connection to Jewish dietary practice suddenly have it affect their lives."

# 15.

# Eating Their Way into Heaven, Part II

## The New Jewish Food Movement

ON A COLD, foggy morning in September 2007, two dozen young Jews gathered in a Connecticut field to witness nine goats be shechted, or slaughtered according to Jewish law.

These young people, most in their early twenties, are spending three months studying the connections between Jewish values and sustainable agriculture as part of the Adamah program, an environmental leadership-training course at the Isabella Freedman Jewish Retreat Center. Adamah is one of a handful of Jewish farming projects that have sprung up this past decade, training a cadre of young Jews to grow and harvest their own food.

At nine a truck pulls up, and thirty-one-year-old Aitan Mizrahi, who raises goats for meat and dairy at the center, gently coaxes nine young male animals from the back of the vehicle into a waiting pen. Goats, like cattle, have gender-driven destinies: The females are kept for milking, while the males, except for those lucky few chosen as breeders, are slaughtered for meat.

Four of these goats have been purchased by food activists Naf Hanau and Ian Hertzmark, and two of them by Andy Kastner, a rabbinical student at Yeshivat Chovevei Torah. The three drove up from New York to prepare the kosher forequarters, about twenty pounds per animal. They will give the hindquarters, traditionally not sold as kosher because of forbidden fats and sinews, to non-Jewish friends. The other three goats will go to the Adamah fellows, who will cook them as an educational exercise. Never mind that few of these students actually eat meat—they're committed to the do-it-yourself ethic the project represents.

"I've been a vegetarian for seven years, but I'm not against people eating meat," says Ashley Greenspoon, twenty-four, of Toronto, as she casts nervous, sidelong glances at the goats happily munching on grass in their holding pen. "It's a part of our reality, and I think it's very important for us to face it. So long as there is going to be meat eating in the world, we need to take responsibility and do it in a respectful way that honors life."

The shochet, thirty-two-year-old Rabbi Shalom Kantor, is standing off to the side, removing his prayer shawl and phylacteries. He has finished his morning devotions and is quietly sharpening his halaf, the knife used for Jewish slaughter. Kantor works as the Hillel rabbi at Binghamton University in upstate New York, and is the country's only Conservative shochet. Although he trained under an Orthodox rabbi in Israel, his Conservative ordination means the animals he slaughters cannot be certified as kosher by any supervising agencies. He does this work freelance, he says, because he wants to help Jews take responsibility for the meat they eat.

"There's a piece of me that thinks a Jew who can't participate at least to some degree in the processing of an animal shouldn't necessarily eat that animal," says Kantor, who grew up hunting and fishing in Sun Valley, Idaho. Buying meat already cut up and neatly wrapped in cellophane can lead people to forget that meat was once an animal whose treatment, in life and death, is carefully outlined by Jewish law. "Maybe God and our tradition call upon us to be more involved in our food. When you have to transform an animal from fur and feathers to a piece of meat on your plate, you tend to have much greater respect for what you're eating."

A rough wooden bench has been placed about thirty feet in front of the waiting group. One student sprinkles hay and straw under the bench to soak up the blood as the animals are killed. When everything is ready, Mizrahi gathers the students in a circle. They stand quietly, holding hands, while he talks about how the goats were birthed, nursed by their mothers, and then raised by him. "These animals are giving us their breath and their meat," he reminds the group. "This is a link in the chain between what our ancestors have done, what we do now, and what our children will do after us."

The circle breaks apart, and Mizrahi and Hanau lead the first black-and-white goat to the bench and flip it on its back. Mizrahi leans forward, pressing into the goat's flank, talking quietly into its ear to keep it calm while Hanau bends its head backward over the end of the bench, stretching the neck gently but firmly. A third young man holds its back legs. Kantor steps in quickly, says the bracha in Hebrew—*Blessed are you, O God, Lord of the Universe, Who has commanded us regarding the mitzvah of ritual slaughter*—and makes a quick back-and-forth cut across the goat's neck. Bright red blood spurts out, drenching Hertzmark's shirt and pants. The animal jerks for about ten seconds, and several of the Adamah fellows gasp and hug their neighbors. A few cry softly.

When the animal stops struggling, Hanau and Hertzmark pick it up and lay it down gently in the hay beside the bench. When it is completely still, they carry it to a nearby lean-to, tie ropes around its hind legs, and hang it from hooks they've driven into the wooden beams along the roof. Kantor trades in his halaf for a kitchen knife to demonstrate evisceration. He makes a small horizontal cut above the goat's urethra, then a vertical slice down the middle of the belly all the way to its throat. He cuts very carefully to avoid puncturing any internal organs. When the vertical slice is completed, he reaches inside the carcass and pulls out the first kidney, encased in a milky white membrane. He pulls the membrane off with a small knife, cuts away the *chelev*, or forbidden fat, and passes the kidney to one of the students, who puts it in a plastic bucket labeled "kosher." Another bucket will hold the non-kosher innards: the four-chambered stomach, the intestines, the spleen. Kantor pulls out the lungs and puts his mouth to the windpipe leading to each one, blowing softly to inflate them and make sure there are no holes. His hands are scarred with dozens of tiny cuts from constantly testing his knife for sharpness.

Kantor became more observant in college, abandoning his original plan of going into game conservation for a career in the rabbinate. That's when he learned that the hunting he'd done as a boy was against Jewish law, as animals can be eaten only if they are slaughtered by a shochet. "That was difficult for me to take in," he says. "Hunting was how I related to my dad and my brothers; it's what we did together as a family." When he started to keep kosher, he decided to learn to shecht, so he could preserve the connection to his meat that he knew from hunting. Finding a teacher was a problem—no Orthodox shochet would train a Conservative rabbinical student. The only teacher he could find was an elderly Yemenite shochet in Israel, whom he studied with for a year while he was in Jerusalem as part of his rabbinical training. "He took me to all kinds of wild and crazy places, parking lots, the top of mountains," Kantor recalls.

In spring 2005, Kantor received his certification as a shochet. Reform and Conservative rabbinical students contact him periodically to ask for mentoring, but so far, none has followed through. It's a frustrating business, as no one in the Orthodox community will eat his meat. "I've come to accept it," he says. "That's the reality."

It takes about six hours to kill, skin, eviscerate, and butcher all nine goats. Kantor teaches the students how to do the skinning, but he, Hanau, and Kastner do the evisceration. Kastner is also a shochet, although he is certified only for poultry, and Hanau is learning the same skill. Kastner has never skinned an animal before, and he is working slowly on a small white goat with one of the female students. She is attacking the job with more enthusiasm than he displays, chattering about how she is learning to tan leather and plans to make a wall hanging from this skin. Kastner labors in silence, smiling quietly when asked how he felt holding down a goat as it was slaughtered.

"I was just focused on the moment, to make sure that all members of the team had the same intentionality," he says. "It felt clean, healthy, and peaceful."

Kastner decided to learn shechting after reading "This Steer's Life," a 2002 *New York Times Magazine* article by Michael Pollan that described the life and economics of cattle raised on industrial feedlots. "I thought, what a great way to combine my love for food and my passion for Jewish learning," says Kastner, who was already considering rabbinical school.

He got his first hands-on experience in Israel, tagging along with Shalom Kantor for some of his shechting lessons. In 2008, in his third year at Yeshivat Chovevei Torah, he organized a summer-long shechita course. There were six students, including Kastner. For more than a month, they studied Jewish texts about shechita, acquired and sharpened their halafim, and practiced making quick, straight slices across index cards.

Finally the teacher said they were ready. He brought in three chickens and asked Kastner to go first. Kastner, who had set this whole thing in motion, didn't know whether he could actually kill a living creature. But he steeled himself and took up one bird, cradling it firmly under his left arm as he reached in and made a deep incision across its throat.

"I felt this animal, this life leaving in my hands, and I broke down in tears, because I was holding this animal as it dies," he recalls. "The weight of the experience really shook me. For the first time, I was responsible for procuring meat and for taking a life out of this world to sustain mine. And the rabbi said, 'You're the type of person who should be a shochet, because you have such a reverence for life.'"

Kastner took the chicken home and kashered it, and he and his wife cooked it for their Shabbat meal with fresh vegetables from their Community Supported Agriculture farm. "We were not so eager to eat this bird," he admits. "For the first time, the veil of anonymity was lifted. I had a relationship with this bird. But the meal felt so whole, a complete experience."

Now a certified Orthodox shochet, Kastner could work in any slaughterhouse. But he says he will never work in the industrial system. He would like to provide enough meat for his own family, teach what he's learned to the wider Jewish community, and perhaps work for a small-scale, grass-fed, pastured kosher meat business. "I believe that food is a means to help us cultivate a consciousness of the moment," he says. "As a rabbi and a shochet, I'd like to bring people closer to what they eat."

Mizrahi stands off to the side for much of the day, watching the others skin and butcher his goats. A former Adamah fellow, Mizrahi has taught in Jewish schools and lived in Israel as a teenager with observant relatives. Like most of his friends in the new Jewish food movement, he is intrigued by traditional Jewish rituals but observes only those he finds personally meaningful. He wears a full beard and payot, or side curls, both of which are mentioned in the Torah, but not a kippah, the head covering dictated by later rabbis.

"I very much identify as a biblical Jew," he says. "The beard is symbolic of my Judaism; it reminds me of who my ancestors were and how they would walk the hills of Judea with their goats and their sheep. They had a deeper relationship to the land, and how that land connected them to the holy spirit of God. I very much feel that my work connects me to HaShem. I know how I want to raise my animals, and I believe that how the animal is raised transfers to its meat and milk. If the animal is nervous or stressed, her milk will taste poorly. But when my goats are out in a pasture and are getting good hay and clean water, you can taste that the milk is a lot fresher, a lot cleaner. And I think that translates to the meat as well, on a spiritual level."

By 4:30, Kantor, Hanau, Hertzmark, and Kastner have brought all the goat meat back to Mizrahi's yard and have begun the tedious work of kashering. Kantor is busy cutting the forbidden fats off the skirt steaks, which are usually not koshered in this country because it takes so long to prepare them. The other young men have plunged the forequarters of the nine goats into buckets of water to soak for half an hour, and are butchering and wrapping up the non-kosher hindquarters to take back to their friends in New York.

As he works, Kantor praises his wife for putting up with his passion for shechting, which sometimes has him rushing into the house on Friday evening in bloodied clothes minutes before Shabbat begins. "She just points at the shower and doesn't say anything," he says. "But I am concerned about not permanently scarring my daughter. She's sixteen months old and carries around a soft, furry blanket with a lamb's head sewn on top. At some point she's going to find out her daddy kills lambs."

When he was learning how to shecht in Israel, he was his teacher's only American student. The other young men in the group were always testing him to see if he was tough enough for the job. One of the requirements of a shochet, according to Jewish tradition, is that he not be prone to fainting. The first day Kantor met his teacher, the man took him to the back of a shop where the store owner had a live lamb, and told Kantor to hold the lamb's head. Without warning, the Yemenite took out a knife and slit the animal's throat to see what Kantor's reaction would be.

"Because of my background in hunting, I didn't flinch," Kantor says. "But with hunting you're far away, not looking into the animal's eyes when you slaughter it. So when I got home, I was a little shaken. My wife said, 'Let's go out for barbecue,' and I said, 'Honey, can we not do this today?' She looked straight at me and said, 'Either you get over this, or you quit shechting.' That was my trial by fire."

By six, all the meat is finished soaking and is now laid out on plastic grates, covered in kosher salt to draw out the blood. While this is going on behind Mizrahi's house, the Adamah fellows are sitting in a circle in front of the house processing their reaction to the day. Many speak about being "grateful" or feeling "humbled" by the experience of watching an animal be killed for their food. Most of them grew up in nonobservant homes; this three-month study program is their first real encounter with Jewish dietary practice. Witnessing shechita gave them, they say, an appreciation for kashrut they could not have gotten from books.

"When the rabbi said the bracha right before killing the animal, that raised it to a higher level, the same way that you say a blessing before you eat to acknowledge that the source of this life is not you but something greater, and you are just a part of this great cycle," says twenty-five-year-old Josh Lucknus of Boston. "I gained a deeper appreciation for kashrut. I appreciate the way it tries to sanctify this process, which is part of the cycle of life and death."

Twenty-year-old Abby Weiss of New Rochelle, New York, is one of the few in the group who has kept kosher her entire life. As a committed Orthodox Jew and a meat eater, she thinks it's important for her to witness a shechting. "It brings a mindfulness to the act of eating meat," she says. To illustrate what she means, Weiss tells a story about the Baal Shem Tov, the eighteenth-century founder of hassidism. The Baal Shem Tov once worked as a shochet in a village. When he moved on, another man took his place. As the new slaughterer was sharpening his knife for the kill, an elderly Jewish woman watching him shook her head in disapproval. "You're not doing it right," she said. Annoyed, the man asked why, and she replied, "Our last shochet, the Baal Shem Tov, used to sharpen the knife with his tears."

Another young woman in the group talked about holding one of the goats as it was being slaughtered. "All of a sudden, I felt this shift as the life went out of it. I thought about the distinction Judaism makes between the blood, the life of the animal, and the flesh, the meat. As the blood was flowing out of this animal, it went limp suddenly. And I thought, of course. The blood is its life. It was as if all the animal's weight, all its liveliness was contained in the blood, and when the blood flowed out of it, it became something else. It was a very powerful experience."

The goat shechting in this Connecticut field is part of the small but fast-growing new Jewish food movement. The movement harks back to eco-kosher initiatives of the 1970s, combining back-to-the-land ideas of sustainable agriculture, organics, and local, seasonal farming with Jewish teachings about mindful consumption. Its leaders and activists look to *baal tashchit*, the commandment to avoid wastefulness, expressed in verses such as Deuteronomy 20:19, which commanded the Israelites not to cut down fruit-bearing trees even if they were needed for military purposes. The Talmud extended the principle to prohibit other wasteful activities, such as killing animals for convenience (Chullin 7b), wasting fuel (Shabbat 67b), and engaging in wantonly destructive activities such as breaking vessels, tearing down a building, or clogging a well (Kiddushin 32a). Eco-kashrut applies these examples to the modern world, teaching that drinking from a non-recyclable Styrofoam cup or eating food packaged in layers of plastic might be considered non-kosher, as they involve wasting the earth's resources.

Similarly, *shmirat haguf*, the Jewish commandment to preserve one's body, might suggest avoiding agricultural pesticides and keeping growth hormones out of animal feed, so those poisons do not end up in one's own body. Baal tashchit and shmirat haguf have always been Jewish values, along with treating workers and domestic animals with justice and kindness; what is new is attaching these values to the laws of kashrut to create a particularly Jewish ethos of food production and consumption.

"We are recognizing the fact that we have a tradition thousands of years old of thinking about what it means to eat in a 'fit and proper' way," says food writer Leah Koenig, who created The Jew and the Carrot, the new Jewish food movement's foremost blog. "We don't want Jews to abandon kashrut; we want them to reframe the question of what it means to keep kosher in the twenty-first century. Is it kosher to eat food sprayed with chemicals? Is it kosher to eat eggs from chickens crammed into tiny cages?"

The eco-kosher movement of the 1970s was heavily vegetarian, but that generation's children are now applying the same values to meat, demanding that the animals they eat be raised and slaughtered humanely. "Mixing milk and meat doesn't mean anything to me," says food activist Alix Wall. "Especially after Agriprocessors, kosher meat no longer means clean meat. I only allow organic, humanely treated, grass-fed meat into my home. That to me is the new kashrut."

It's not that hard to remain committed to sustainable agriculture when talking about fruit and vegetables—all one needs is a farmers market or a backyard garden. But obtaining kosher meat outside the industrialized slaughterhouse system is much more difficult. Few American Jews are willing to raise and kill their own animals.

In the last three or four years, however, a handful of young Jewish food activists have been doing just that. Inspired by similar initiatives in the non-kosher world, they have begun organizing their own kosher meat and poultry businesses using ethically raised, humanely killed animals, preselling the meat by phone and e-mail. It feels right, they say, from the perspective of both food ethics and Jewish values. Like the Adamah fellows in that Connecticut field, none of the young people running these new kosher meat operations has a background as a butcher, farmer, or shochet. They are white-collar professionals living in New York, Berkeley, and the suburbs of D.C., and they are learning the business from the ground up.

In June 2006, Brooklyn resident Simon Feil, a professional actor, organized Kosher Conscience, an organic kosher turkey co-op. "The catalyst was the Rubashkin mess," he says, referring to the first *Forward* article. "I kept kosher, and it was surprising to read that this kosher meat was not humanely produced. If I'm going to eat meat, I have to do everything possible to make sure the process is as humane as possible. Even more so with kosher meat, because of the religious aspect."

Feil put all the pieces together himself, from finding a shochet willing to work with him to locating a farm to sell him turkeys and lining up buyers for the birds. The organic aspect wasn't as important to him as making sure the birds were free-range, transported a minimal distance to the place of slaughter, and killed by a shochet who respected the sanctity of the act. The young Lubavitch shochet he found to help him is a vegetarian but eats poultry on Shabbat (as did Rabbi Abraham Kook, the first Ashkenazic chief rabbi of pre-state Israel), and was very interested in what Feil was trying to do.

For Thanksgiving 2007, Feil slaughtered twenty-four pasture-raised turkeys at a farm in upstate New York and drove them back to Manhattan for pickup at an Orthodox synagogue on the Upper West Side. Feil's turkeys were twice as expensive as kosher turkeys from the supermarket, but that didn't stop New York chef and nutritionist Linda Lantos from buying two. "In the last few years, it's become important to me to find organic food that is also kosher," says Lantos, who has kept kosher since childhood. "My grandfather was a butcher, so I was always comfortable with where meat comes from. But I've been uncomfortable not knowing how the animals were treated, so I've been eating less meat lately."

Feil repeated the project in 2008. That November, he and his shochet labored for twenty-two straight hours after their feather-plucking machine malfunctioned and they had to pluck sixty-five birds by hand. In August 2009, he added grass-fed, free-range beef to his offerings. Feil makes no money from this work; it's a mitzvah, one that he, as an observant Jew, cannot ignore. Once he found out how birds and animals are treated in industrial slaughterhouses, how could he not do everything in his power to make sure the meat he eats fulfills all the laws concerning humane treatment of workers and animals, not just the ritual minutiae of kosher slaughter?

"Rather than asking whether it is required by the halacha of kashrut, what on earth is our excuse *not* to do it?" he asks.

In August 2008, Bronx pediatric neurologist Maya Shetreat-Klein launched Mitzvah Meat, a co-op for grass-fed, humanely raised and slaughtered kosher beef and lamb. Like Feil, she is Orthodox and will bring only kosher meat into her home. But whereas Feil was motivated primarily by the Jewish commandments concerning ethical treatment of animals, Shetreat-Klein was pulled in by the organic, nutritional aspect. In spring 2007, her two-year-old son was suffering from terrible allergies. When she took him off soy milk at his doctor's suggestion, his symptoms disappeared. "That was my first epiphany of how powerful food can be," she says.

She started researching food production, learning about different chemical additives and pesticides, and reading studies of their effects on the human body, especially on brain development in children. She began buying organic milk and produce and started recommending grass-fed meat to her patients, but was unable to buy it for her own family, because no kosher grass-fed meat existed. Grass-fed meat is lower in saturated fat than industrial meat, which comes from animals raised on huge feedlots and fattened mainly on corn, which is hard for them to digest. It is also rich in omega-3 fatty acids, important for heart health, as well as vitamin E and beta-carotene. Every week she would pick up her fresh fruit and vegetable box from her CSA co-op, and watch as her non-Jewish friends picked up their own produce boxes along with their packages of naturally raised, locally sourced chicken or beef. It frustrated her that this meat wasn't available for observant Jews.

So she decided to do it herself. "I thought, how hard could it be?" she laughs. "You find a shochet, find a farmer, slaughter a cow, and boom, it's a snap."

It took her a year to organize her first run. She floated the idea past some of her Orthodox friends in New York, and they were very enthusiastic. Word spread quickly, and soon she was getting e-mails from young observant Jews all over the country, asking if her meat would be made available in their areas. "There was this silent but powerful desire for something like this to exist," she says.

Then she encountered her first hurdle. She planned to hire Shalom Kantor as her shochet, but when she told her Orthodox friends who had agreed to purchase the meat, they balked. "I thought, here's an opportunity for these people to get food in the most grassroots way, the way our ancestors did it, and they said no, they would never eat meat shechted by a Conservative rabbi," she relates. "It really surprised me. Some faceless person is shechting their meat, another faceless person is supervising their meat, and it's all under the name of so-and-so, whom they've never met. I thought, what a strange kind of faith to have, when you could meet this person and really know his intentions, and know that the animals were treated well. Instead, they'd rather eat meat that's raised in what I would think of as a concentration camp for animals, pretty much tortured all the way through slaughter, and supervised by someone who may or may not be spiritually dedicated to this. It's an odd place to put your trust."

Organic farmers were eager to sell her their lambs and cattle. "They were excited that the kosher community was showing an interest in their local, grass-fed, naturally raised animals," she says. Finding a slaughterhouse that would let her in for such a small job was more difficult. She found one through the Yellow Pages, but as she was preparing for the three-hour drive to upstate New York to work out the final details, the owner told her he really didn't like working with Jews. "So obviously that wasn't going to work," she deadpans.

The next challenge was finding a rabbi willing to give her kosher supervision. She called a dozen Orthodox rabbis. None called back.

"Kosher meat is so political," she says. "No one wanted to put their name on this. It's all about reputation. Once your name is blown, your career is over. The kosher meat business will give you gray hair like nothing else." Finally she found a sympathetic rabbi through her daughter's Hebrew day school, who referred her to someone who referred her to someone else, and slowly she made her way to a rabbi who agreed to act as her mashgiach. He was interested in starting a similar independent kosher slaughter project in Central America.

Finding a shochet was easier. With the collapse of Agriprocessors, there were plenty of shochtim looking for work in the summer of '08. She lined up a new slaughterhouse, agreed to buy thirty-one lambs and two cows from organic farmers in the Hudson Valley, and settled on three drop-off points for the presold boxes of kosher meat, in Westchester, the Bronx, and New Jersey. But she also had to find buyers for the non-kosher parts of the animals, as well as for any animals that the mashgiach declared non-kosher after slaughter, an additional financial burden for any kosher meatpacking operation. She divided her business in two—Mitzvah Meat for the kosher product and Mindful Meat for the non-kosher product—and customers signed up.

Finally, in August 2008, Shetreat-Klein did her first successful run. A second run followed that November. By early 2009, she had one hundred customers and was fielding requests from Boston, Denver, Arizona, Oregon, and Canada. Somehow, she continues her medical practice as well, integrating what she's learning about the behavioral and neurological impact of nutrition into her treatment of children.

"Judaism is very much about kindness to animals," she says. "You want birds' eggs, you make sure the mother bird is not there to watch. You may stew a lamb, but not in its mother's milk. The whole concept of Judaism is of being thoughtful and mindful about everything that you do, channeling the spirit of God through your actions. And I just can't see how animals raised for kosher slaughter right now fit that definition."

Feil and Shetreat-Klein run small kosher meat operations, and both have kept their day jobs. The only person so far to try to do this as a full-time business is Devora Kimelman-Block of Silver Spring, Maryland, a former magazine editor and educational technology specialist who formed KOL Foods in 2007. KOL stands for Kosher Organic

Local, and Kimelman-Block provides kosher and non-kosher grass-fed, sustainably farmed lamb and beef and pasture-raised poultry to clients nationwide.

Like Feil and Shetreat-Klein, she went into the field to provide kosher meat she herself could feel good about eating. She was never vegetarian, but she and her husband had not brought meat into their home for sixteen years because the only kosher meat they could find came from industrial slaughterhouses that used practices they rejected, such as injecting cattle with growth hormones. Reading about the labor issues at Agriprocessors further cemented her feelings. "A lot of people are faced with the decision—ethics or kashrut? Personally I don't feel it's ethically a problem to eat meat. But I do have a problem with unethical meat processing."

For her first commercial run in July 2007 she slaughtered three head of cattle. Two went kosher, and she sold the four hundred pounds of meat in three weeks. A second run of six kosher head of cattle sold out in less than a week, bringing in $11,000. By late 2008, KOL Foods was slaughtering once a month to the tune of $20,000, but very little of that was profit. It takes a lot of capital to produce kosher meat, especially on such a small scale.

Bringing the kosher and the organic worlds into sync was a challenge. Kimelman-Block spent a lot of time talking to her kosher butchers and slaughterhouses about why she was using such expensive meat, explaining her commitment to pasture-raised beef and pointing out the deeper red color of the flesh. Then her second beef run showed up on her doorstep, neatly packaged by the butcher in non-recyclable Styrofoam—an environmental travesty. "There it was, twelve hundred pounds of meat wrapped in Styrofoam I'd brought into the world." She sighs. "These are very different worlds with very different mind-sets. It's hard to find people who are on the same page."

Demand for her product is growing faster than she can handle. "I could have sold as much meat as I had," she says of those first runs. "People were knocking down the door. I don't know if people are interested more in the ethics or the health aspects, but making this meat available is a joy. The quality is so high, the richness, the taste, it's like night and day compared to commercial meat."

One morning in September 2008, Kimelman-Block is driving north into Maryland to visit one of her farmers and kosher butchers and one of the two slaughterhouses she works with. With her in the car are Roger Studley, a former policy analyst for the University of California who wants to set up a humane kosher meat slaughtering business in Berkeley, and Ariella Reback and Amalia Haas, who are interested in doing the same thing with poultry in Cleveland. In less than a year, Kimelman-Block has become the go-to person in the field of independent kosher slaughter, and she has agreed to show these people the ropes.

Studley and she are discussing the sciatic nerve of a steer, the castrated male most often slaughtered for meat. In Israel, Studley tells the other two women, kosher butchers cut out that nerve and sell the animal's hindquarters as kosher. But in North America, where there is a large enough market for non-kosher meat, kosher agencies will not certify hindquarters as kosher because of the extra work and expense involved. Kimelman-Block's meat is certified by the Star-K and the OU, as well as two local kosher agencies, and she is trying to convince one of them to give kosher approval to an entire animal, so more of her beef and lamb can go to kosher customers. "I know butchers who can do the *treybering,* but they won't," she says, using the Hebrew word for removing forbidden fats and sinews.

Kimelman-Block also wants to be able to sell non-glatt kosher meat, which is all most of her customers need, but again, the kosher agencies won't certify it, and her butchers won't jeopardize their standing with the agencies by working with it. The kosher agencies didn't establish their regulations to be malicious, she says; the rules just ended up serving the interests of industrial slaughterhouses. If a slaughterhouse is processing large quantities, like the five hundred head of cattle a day Agriprocessors used to slaughter, even if one hundred of those animals turn out to be non-glatt, the company can absorb the loss. But if someone like her is slaughtering just two head of cattle, and one or neither goes kosher, she's out thousands of dollars and has to deal with her angry customers face-to-face.

About 50 percent of the animals she brings to slaughter end up "going glatt," whereas 70 percent would fulfill the standards of ordinary, non-glatt kosher meat. If she could sell that meat, her overall yield would be greater and she could lower her prices. She sells her beef and lamb that go non-kosher to organic restaurants in the D.C. area, but she gets less money for that meat while her expenses remain the same.

"The national kosher agencies really dictate whether or not people can buy local or only industrial meat," she says. "They are handicapping nonindustrial small operations, and that is why kosher consumers can't get anything but feedlot beef. There are very few slaughterhouses that will work with someone small like me. Lots of people want to do this, have a kosher meat CSA or do a few animals a month, but they can't. They could if it weren't kosher."

Some Jews concerned about local sourcing, humane treatment of animals, and organics have stopped buying kosher meat altogether, preferring non-kosher meat that meets their ethical standards. Deborah Goldstein of South Orange, New Jersey, recalls telling her rabbi that if she and her family had to choose between eating kosher and eating ethically, they would choose ethics. Today Goldstein is the coordinator of KOL Foods distribution at her synagogue, one of many young Jews who have returned to eating kosher meat because of these new kosher operations.

Rabbi Mandel of the OU sympathizes with Kimelman-Block and supports the work she is doing. But, he explains, the national kosher agencies are not going to change their policies anytime soon. It's a matter of money and logistics. By certifying only glatt meat, the agencies give themselves a little leeway. If an animal has a lung problem or the shochet makes a mistake, it can be quickly taken off the line. But if the agencies certified all kosher animals, glatt as well as non-glatt, production would have to slow down every time a questionable lung mass was discovered, to give the mashgichim time to examine it and discuss whether or not to accept that animal.

"In a mass-production plant, you don't have that time," he says. "The animals are going by too fast for you to sit down and talk about each one." Individual slaughterhouses can decide whether or not they want to bother paying a rabbi to certify their non-glatt product, but the agencies are not going to do it for them.

By 10:00 a.m., the group reaches Groff's Content Farm in Rocky Ridge, Maryland. Julie Bolton, who bought the farm with her husband in 2001, raises free-range turkeys, chickens, guinea fowl, cattle, and sheep on eighty-five pastured acres of her four-hundred-acre property. She sells eggs and meat at farmers markets and to private clients like Kimelman-Block, who did her first poultry shechting here one cold November afternoon.

"It was raining cats and dogs," Kimelman-Block recalls. She, her daughter, and a few volunteers from her synagogue spent twelve hours processing sixty-five birds. They removed the feathers on half the chickens by hand, which took half an hour per bird, then gave up and skinned the rest. "We shechted for an entire day in the rain. It was a miserable experience." The worst part was when the shochet caught fire. His lab coat brushed past a propane heater the group was using to keep warm. "He was very religious and didn't have a lot of exposure to people like us," Kimelman-Block says. "He said he's not interested in ever doing this again."

Bolton shows the group her poultry processing shed, where she's set up a long stainless-steel table, three metal hanging cones for draining the blood, a double sink, and a drum plucker, a four-foot-tall blue plastic barrel with dozens of four-inch rubber fingers sticking out of the interior walls. The slaughtered birds are put inside, the barrel rotates, and the rubber fingers pull out the feathers. Bolton's neighbor made this machine for her for about $500, from odds and ends. Similar machines are available commercially at twice the price, but they don't work well if the birds haven't been scalded first to loosen their feathers, so it's not a usable system for kosher processing.

Bolton buys her turkey chicks the day after they hatch. She raises the birds in a brooder until they're hardy enough to live outside, and then they wander freely around a large enclosure eating grass supplemented with a custom-mixed diet free of medications and chemicals. Her egg-laying hens live in a mini-trailer that she moves to a different part of the pasture every few days, so the birds will have fresh grass. At night they hop back into the trailer, and she closes the hatch to protect them from predators.

Haas and Reback are particularly interested in this part of the farm, as they want to limit their business to poultry. Because they don't own land, they will have to buy birds from other farmers, and not all farms are set up to take care of the waste left behind after slaughter. Maybe they'll buy a mobile processing unit: a trailer outfitted with all their equipment, including refrigerators, that they could drive from farm to farm. That would avoid the cost and stress of shipping the birds to them. There's still a lot they have to work out.

Haas, a Jewish environmental educator and Orthodox mother of four, decided to try raising and shechting her own poultry a few years earlier. She ordered fourteen ducklings online and they arrived at her doorstep in a box, two days old. "We got a heat lamp, put cardboard fences around them, and fed them all our leftovers," she says. When the birds were big enough to eat, she and her children brought them to a shochet's home, and she held each one as he slaughtered it. They cleaned the ducks right there, plucking and kashering them, with Haas teaching her children each step of the way. All the birds went kosher; they ate the first one that Friday night for Shabbat dinner.

After the turkeys and chickens, Bolton shows off her herd of cattle. In one pasture, fourteen cows and an older bull she uses for breeding are feeding contentedly. A couple of younger bulls are fenced off quite a distance away from the main herd. They were born earlier in the year, and Bolton decided not to castrate them. That increases their testosterone production, so their forequarters grow larger, yielding more kosher meat, which makes Kimelman-Block happier, but it also makes them more aggressive, and Bolton doesn't want them to fight with her breeder bulls for access to the fertile cows.

Bolton also raises sheep. She keeps seventy-five adult ewes for breeding, and this summer has forty male lambs and forty female lambs, most of which she'll slaughter. Many of the young rams are also not castrated, because Muslims buy them for Eid al-Ahda, the festival during which it's traditional to slaughter an intact male animal for the first-night feast. But the rams are prone to impregnating young lambs that crawl under the fence to be with their mothers, which derails her breeding schedule.

"It's all sex, all the time here on the farm," she says.

By noon, the group has arrived at J.W. Treuth & Sons, a small family-owned kosher slaughterhouse in Catonsville, just outside Baltimore. All the animals at Treuth's are slaughtered according to kosher regulations. Treuth's can handle just 100 to 120 head of cattle a day, so the only way they can make a living is by sticking to a lucrative niche like the kosher market. About one-third of the animals they slaughter go kosher, the usual yield for feedlot animals. Since they can use only the front half, that means about one-sixth or less of their product can be sold as kosher. The company has regular clients for its non-kosher meat.

Every part of the animal is used for something at Treuth's. The blood and offal drain through holes in the floor into a ten-thousand-gallon tanker truck parked under the building. The truck takes its load to a rendering plant in Virginia, where it is made into blood meal, and the fat is used for biodiesel fuel and cosmetics. The cheeks are sold as kosher, the lips and ears are frozen until spring and then sold as crab bait, and Latino customers buy the rest of the heads for cooking. The hides are swirled around in a saltwater pool behind the plant for twenty-four hours, dried and pressed under concrete blocks, and shipped to China.

Kimelman-Block has developed a good relationship with the Treuth brothers. She pays their shochet $80 per animal and adds her cattle in when they're doing a regular Star-K run. Today Nathan Thomas, one of the farmers she works with, is bringing some steers and lambs from his property in western Pennsylvania. She's a little nervous because sometimes he brings her too many lambs, which she has a harder time selling. He e-mailed her yesterday, saying he was bringing twenty-five lambs, and she begged him not to. A few weeks earlier, she had five head of cattle and thirty-five lambs go kosher in a single day. She sold all the beef but has sixty-three boxes of lamb in her freezer to get rid of. Still, she likes to work with Thomas because he buys back the hindquarters, as well as any animals that go non-kosher, so she doesn't have to deal with selling the non-kosher meat to her restaurants.

Once Kimelman-Block accompanied a *New York Times* reporter with Thomas as he transported three steers and some lambs from his farm to Baltimore for slaughter. They stopped at a gas station, and while they were filling up, manure began dripping out of the bottom of the truck. "All these people in the gas station were like, oh my God, what do you have in there?" Kimelman-Block recalls. "The manure just kept dribbling out. The owner came out and said, 'You can't leave that here. You better take that with you.'" Kimelman-Block and the startled reporter grabbed a shovel and some garbage bags, and started shoveling up the steaming mess. They had to carry it with them the rest of the trip.

Finally Thomas pulls up with just one animal in his trailer: a twenty-two-month-old, 1,800-pound Black Angus bull. Not a steer, a full-blown bull. Like Bolton, Thomas has started to raise his males intact for Kimelman-Block, so they yield larger forequarters. But this big guy took almost three hours to wrestle into the trailer, and he had two men helping him. He planned to bring three bulls but ran out of time. The bull is kicking and snorting loudly inside the metal trailer, raising a tremendous racket.

Now Kimelman-Block is really nervous. If this bull ends up with the smallest lung adhesion and the mashgiach declares it non-glatt, she'll be $3,000 in the hole. But she puts on a brave face as the trailer is backed up to the holding pen and the bull is gingerly unloaded. He lumbers placidly toward a line of cattle that is making its way through a series of wooden chutes toward the slaughtering pen.

The pen used at Treuth's is based on a 1994 ASPCA design by Temple Grandin, the country's foremost designer of humane livestock handling equipment. The animal enters the pen, rests its neck in a hollow on a metal gate, and then a guillotine-like top plate comes down to enclose the top half of the neck. A metal belly plate rises from the floor to cradle the animal's body weight. The entire procedure takes a matter of seconds and is almost without sound; the animal chews its cud calmly the whole time.

While the cow or steer is being secured, the shochet, a red-haired Israeli in his early thirties, washes his knife, checks it for nicks that might have occurred during the last kill, and says the required blessing. Quickly, with almost balletic grace, he swoops in underneath the animal's neck, reaches upward for a swift back-and-forth slice, then dances back out of the way. There is a split second of silence; then the animal throws back its head, and a bright red stream of blood gushes from its neck. Within eight to ten seconds it collapses, and a chain around one hind foot hoists it into the air and begins moving it along a row of previously slaughtered cattle. Some of the animals jerk for a few more seconds after they are hoisted. The experts say they are insensate at that point, but Kimelman-Block's guests, who are seeing this for the first time, wince.

After the killing pen, the head and feet are cut off, a skinning machine peels off the hide in one piece, and a worker slices open the belly to remove the internal organs for checking. A *bodek*, or kosher inspector, feels the lungs inside the carcass, and a USDA inspector examines the liver, spleen, and heart for disease. Then the bodek looks at the lungs on a light table. If they are entirely smooth, the carcass gets a white Star-K tag and the mashgiach carves the Hebrew date into the animal's ribs, as a sign that he approves its glatt status. If there is a membranous adhesion, the bodek tries to remove it without causing a tear in the lung. If he manages to do the job cleanly, the animal gets a red tag and is sold as non-glatt kosher under the mashgiach's private label. If a hole results, the beef is entirely non-kosher. Finally the carcass is sliced into quarters for hanging in one of three cold-storage areas. The entire process from slaughter to storage takes about forty-five minutes.

Kimelman-Block is anxiously watching her bull make its way toward slaughter. At last it is his turn in the pen. The shochet has to slice back and forth five or six times to cut through the bull's tough neck hide, and the huge animal collapses almost immediately. As its hanging carcass moves through the assembly line, the workers glance over at it from time to time, to make sure everything is going well. When it's time for the bodek to put his hand inside the rib cage to feel the lungs, he, the shochet, and the mashgiach hold their breath. They are fascinated by Kimelman-Block's project and tickled to have a group of visitors so interested in and knowledgeable about their work. They trained hard and get little appreciation from the kosher-keeping public they serve.

The bodek frowns. He's felt a lump on one lung, meaning the bull is definitely not glatt kosher. He puts the lung on his checking table and tries to scrape off a tiny mucous membrane barely half a centimeter in length. He pulls it away from the lung with the edge of his nail, taking more than a minute, hoping to avoid even the tiniest tear. But when he submerges the lung in a bowl of water, bubbles rise to the surface. Not kosher. Kimelman-Block's face is like stone. Thomas is stunned. Everyone on the normally noisy killing floor is silent. They all know how much this meant to her.

Thomas and Kimelman-Block step outside to negotiate the fate of the now non-kosher carcass, which yielded 925 pounds of dressed meat. Who will take the financial hit? Kimelman-Block decides to do it. She will sell the entire bull to one of her restaurants. She won't make as much money as if it were kosher, and she'll have some explaining to do to her customers, many of whom are also her friends, but that's the risk you take in this kind of small-scale, hands-on business.

Pasture-raised, grass-fed kosher beef and lamb and organic, free-range kosher poultry will always be a niche market. It's more risky, and more expensive. But this is the only meat Kimelman-Block and her observant colleagues feel good about eating.

"There will always be people who look for cheap meat," Kimelman-Block says. "But meat used to be a luxury. People did not eat it for breakfast, lunch, and dinner. We've lost sight of that, because meat is so inexpensive in this country. That luxury has come at the cost of our ethics. I have no problem with meat being more expensive and people eating less of it."

ON DECEMBER 25, 2008, nearly six hundred Jewish educators, rabbis, and food activists gathered at the Asilomar Conference Center in Pacific Grove, California, for the third annual Hazon Jewish food conference.

"We're here to talk about how our Jewish tradition influences how we should think about food and the policies around food," Hazon director Nigel Savage tells the opening-night audience. "This conference will help us galvanize the building of a new Jewish food movement.

Savage created Hazon in 2000 to promote Jewish environmental activism. In 2004, the organization moved into food, launching its Tuv Ha'Aretz campaign and sponsoring the first Jewish CSA at Congregation Ansche Chesed in Manhattan. Tuv Ha'Aretz is a pun in Hebrew, meaning "bounty of the earth" and "good for the earth." Seventy-eight people at Ansche Chesed bought a season's worth of shares in an organic farm on Long Island, receiving twenty-six weekly fresh produce boxes in return. By 2009, the program had spread to thirty synagogues and Jewish community centers.

"Not only did we want to put Jewish purchasing power behind local organic farms, which is a moral good, not only did we want people to buy local organic produce at fair prices, but we also wanted to do something about reframing what it means to be Jewish," Savage tells his audience. "Being Jewish means not only going to shul on Shabbat, but going on Wednesday or Thursday to pick up your fresh fruits and vegetables. We are heirs to a three-thousand-year-old tradition of keeping kosher, of asking whether food is fit to be consumed, and surely in the twenty-first century that raises new questions."

Looking out at the room, Savage asks how many have read the entire Torah, all five books. About a third raise their hands. "And how many of you have read *The Omnivore's Dilemma?*" he asks. Virtually every hand goes up. Michael Pollan is a guru to this crowd. (Throughout the weekend, his mantra is constantly repeated: "Eat food. Not too much. Mostly plants.") But many of these young activists have sketchy Jewish backgrounds. To help correct that, Hazon published *Food for Thought,* a workbook of Jewish texts related to food, agriculture, and the environment, to ground the new Jewish food movement more deeply in Torah and the rabbinic tradition.

"Everyone should learn about what traditional kashrut is, because we should all be informed about what our laws are around food," says conference cochair Zelig Golden, thirty-four, a former Adamah fellow and environmental lawyer. "And then like everything in Torah, we should go from that point and ask, What are the intentions behind the laws, and what are our values today? Which laws make sense and which don't make sense?"

Golden does not keep kosher, although his diet is heavily based on what he grows in his organic backyard garden. Like most leaders of the new Jewish food movement, Golden has great respect for Jewish tradition and not much for how the kosher food system actually operates. "The system is totally broken," he says. "It's a joke. They've lost sight of the spiritual nature of our tradition."

The new Jewish farm schools are taking the same approach as Hazon, integrating Jewish text study and discussion into their training in organic and sustainable agriculture. The pioneers, less than a decade old, are the Adamah leadership course in Connecticut and the Teva Learning Center, a Jewish environmental education institute that runs programs for children and young adults at three sites in New York, Connecticut, and Baltimore. Graduates of those programs established the Jewish Farm School in 2005 and Kayam Farm in 2006. In just a few years, more than ten thousand people have taken part in one or more classes run by these farm schools, and close to two hundred young activists a year are trained as Jewish farmers.

The goal of these schools is not to turn all Jews into farmers, but to make farming a normative part of mainstream Jewish life. "Not every Jew needs to go pick carrots," says Simcha Schwartz, the thirty-year-old cofounder of the Jewish Farm School, which runs programs in New York and Philadelphia. "But let's be connected to our food in one way or another and to this rich Jewish farming tradition that can inform our lives whether or not we're farmers."

The Jewish Farm School used a $2,000 grant from Hazon to run a Jewish environmental organic gardening seminar for teachers and camp counselors in 2005. They repeated the seminar in 2006 and added a workshop in urban sustainability. Since then, the small staff has planted an organic garden in a Jewish special needs summer camp in the Poconos, and runs farm immersion programs for Jewish college students during spring and summer breaks.

A big part of the Farm School's curriculum is introducing Jews to their own agricultural traditions. One-sixth of the Talmud deals with agricultural laws, Schwartz points out. The Mishna actually shows diagrams of how to plant different crops together without mixing them, which is forbidden in Jewish law. These texts contain practical farming lessons, as well as moral commandments such as leaving a corner of one's field unharvested for the poor. Agriculture is a huge part of the Jewish tradition, but most Jews today are divorced from the land, and from that part of their heritage. "We're looking in the Torah and Talmud and finding out there are great instructions on how to plant," Schwartz says. "It's a blessing to unearth it, literally and figuratively."

The Kayam Farm, located at the Pearlstone Conference and Retreat Center in Reisterstown, Maryland, grew 3,500 pounds of organic produce in 2007, its first year of operation, and drew three thousand people to its workshops, most of them Jewish school groups and residents of a Jewish senior center. One of the farm's projects is a Jewish Educational Garden, where crops are planted according to the Mishna's diagrams, and a Calendar Garden, divided into twelve sections, where an appropriate crop is planted for each Hebrew month.

"In the next few years, we are going to see Jewish agricultural education popping up all over," predicts Jakir Manela, the farm's twenty-seven-year-old director. "We want to encourage every Jewish institution to have a Jewish community garden. It's not just important to Jews that we eat local, but that we recognize we have a particular tradition related to our food." The student groups that come to the farm "plant according to the Mishna and harvest according to the law of tithing," he says, explaining that the children put a tenth of what they grow into a box for charity.

Manela and Schwartz are part of a core group of three or four dozen young Jewish food activists connected to this network of Jewish farm schools. Most are Adamah alumni. They travel in a pack at the Hazon conference, sitting together at meals and running many of the workshops. Some of them keep kosher and others do not, but they are all deeply invested in mining Jewish tradition for what it teaches about food and the environment. And because they take food choices so seriously, they respect and are intrigued by each other's choices regarding kashrut.

Manela does not keep kosher, even though he spends all day teaching others about Jewish food traditions. He used to keep kosher, and says he's "not proud" that he currently does not, but he's still working out what is meaningful to him within kashrut. "I would say, I don't keep kosher at the moment," he explains. He hopes to start raising goats on the farm, and plans to shecht them according to kosher and halal regulations, to serve an interfaith home school the farm runs three days a week. "Ideally I want to get to a place where I mostly eat food I grow myself, including meat we slaughter on our farm according to the laws of kashrut," he says. "I hope to eat as locally and sustainably as possible, and as kosher as possible."

Twenty-three-year-old Naf Hanau has been certified as a shochet since that day in the Connecticut field and is about to launch Grow and Behold Foods, a company that produces kosher pastured meats. His new wife, the former Anna Stevenson, twenty-seven, has spent the past two years as Adamah's farm manager, in charge of the center's five acres under cultivation, and is about to return to Hazon as the organization's assistant food director. The Hanaus call themselves Jewish farmers and intend to spend their lives bringing forth food from the earth in tandem with Jewish values.

Hanau has always kept kosher, but the practice is new for Stevenson. The home they will create together will be kosher. "To me, eating organic, sustainably raised meat is of the utmost importance now, but having a Jewish home is also important to me, having a home where we both feel comfortable," Stevenson says. Even if she had not met Hanau, her experience in the new Jewish food movement would have led her to explore kashrut on her own. "The reason I'm willing to push myself toward it is the idea that I can't just have whatever I want," she says. "That is a profoundly different way to be in the world than American culture teaches. It fosters self-respect. For that, I'm able to engage in conversations about the specific laws."

Thirty-one-year-old Tali Weinberg was Adamah's farm manager before Stevenson, and then spent a few years working for a seed company on Salt Spring Island, off the coast of British Columbia. She grew up in a non-kosher home and first learned about the historical Jewish connection to agriculture while at Adamah. "Before Adamah I would say I was a farmer who happened to be a Jew, but I've learned so much now about the nature of our people, of our roots in the land of Israel two thousand years ago. All our holidays are agricultural festivals. I've not only become more of a Jewish farmer, I understand more of what it means to be a Jew."

She is now "experimenting" with keeping kosher. Over the past few years she has stopped eating pork or shellfish and no longer mixes meat and milk. She has also started blessing her food before eating, a practice the Adamah fellows follow, even if they don't always use the appropriate Hebrew prayer. Eating this way makes her feel Jewish, she says. "I abstain from certain foods, or certain combinations of foods, as a mark of being Jewish, not because it's 'religious.'"

In summer 2008, Weinberg was outfitting a new home. She bought used dishes, bowls, and utensils at garage sales, and when she brought them home, she felt that she wanted to purify them. She didn't know why, but she started washing every item she bought, not because they were dirty but because she felt the need to bring a new energy to them as they entered her home.

"It was really intuitive," she says. "I was washing out all these vessels with water, and while I was doing it I realized, oh my God, this is exactly the practice of *toyveling*, of kashering dishes, that Jewish tradition speaks about. I thought about how observant Jews say, Listen, you don't have to understand the reasons behind all these laws, just do them and trust that there's some truth to it. While I was toyveling this stuff, those words had resonance. I realized, wow, maybe there really is something to all this."

FRIDAY NIGHT DINNER at the Hazon conference was a Bay Area riff on the traditional Ashkenazic Shabbat meal of roast chicken and vegetables. The menu, designed by Wall, prepared by Asilomar's chefs, and supervised by the kosher vaad of Northern California, featured apple-squash soup, quinoa sunchoke pilaf, red lentil rice loaf with coconut-cilantro sauce, and (a first for this group) herb-roasted kosher local turkey.

Earlier that summer, the Hazon conference planning committee had a long, heated discussion about whether to serve meat at all during the four-day gathering. Many Jewish food activists are vegetarian, and the only sustainably raised kosher meat is produced on the East Coast. Shipping it to California would go against the food movement's emphasis on local sourcing of food.

"I think we can only serve pasture raised, humanely slaughtered, kosher meat, and if there is none of that, we should just not serve meat," argued committee member Brenda Berry. Hanau strongly disagreed. "There is a very strong basis in Jewish tradition for eating meat on Shabbat, and it is an important tradition to engage with," he said. "I do not think the Jewish community is going to stop eating meat anytime soon, so we need to find a way to give them meat that is acceptable to our values."

The committee agreed that the only way they could serve meat that met their standards was if they slaughtered and processed it themselves. At Hazon's 2007 conference, three goats were shechted and cooked into a cholent that participants were invited to taste, but that was done as an educational exercise. This year the goal was to shecht enough poultry for an entire Shabbat meal.

Roger Studley volunteered to take charge of the operation, as a dry run for what he hoped would become a West Coast affiliate of KOL Foods. On a blustery cold December 24 morning, twenty shivering volunteers found themselves ankle-deep in feathers and mud on an organic turkey farm ninety miles north of San Francisco; they prepared for a day of shechting, plucking, and eviscerating.

Farmer Lisa Leonard held a tom turkey under her arm in the freezing rain as Studley explained what was about to happen. "As Jews, we are required to take these steps to make our meat suitable for eating," he said. "We're doing this old-school and hands-on. We're doing it as a community, making meat for the conference we are about to attend. This is a project bringing us closer to the source of the food we are eating, making real the fact that we are taking the lives of animals in order to sustain ourselves."

Andy Kastner flew in from New York to act as the shochet. Seth Mandel of the OU was on hand as the mashgiach, in charge of checking the lungs and intestines of the birds for signs of disease or internal damage. Hanau and Stevenson were among the volunteers, along with Kimelman-Block and Noah Alper of Noah's Bagels fame. The rest were students, rabbis, Jewish educators, and other conference participants interested in a personal, highly physical introduction to their meat.

Kastner stood under a hastily erected tarpaulin, shechting turkeys to the rhythm of the driving rain, while Kimelman-Block showed the group how to pluck out the feathers by grabbing hold of a small bunch with one hand and pulling firmly but not so hard as to tear the skin. Soon a sea of feathers rose inside the corrugated iron shed. The farmers set a pot of water on a propane tank to boil, ostensibly for kashering utensils but really so Kastner could restore feeling to his near-frozen hands by warming them in the steam.

The bravest in the group learned to eviscerate the birds, digging their hands into the dark recesses of the still-warm bodies to remove the internal organs. The turkeys would be soaked for half an hour and salted for an hour, rinsed three times, and then sealed and packed on ice for transport to the conference kitchen.

Elizheva Hurwich, a Bay Area artist and Jewish educator, was volunteering in honor of her great-grandmother, who shechted poultry for the kosher delicatessen she ran with her husband a century ago in Memphis. Hurwich knew there was a strong possibility she would be "totally grossed out and not able to do this," but an hour into the process, she was deeply engaged in her work. She soon moved from plucking feathers to the evisceration table and finally took up the position of head salter, rubbing coarse-ground salt into every body cavity and lining up the finished birds on a grated table to drain.

"I was fascinated," she says afterward. "I loved watching the rabbi as he checked the guts. We talked about what he was looking for; he explained to me about polyps and other things he might find.

"It was hard watching the birds be killed," she reflects. "But there was also something very whole and beautiful about it."

Kimelman-Block spends much of the day lobbying Mandel for OU supervision of non-glatt meat, but he won't budge. Mandel is a big fan of these new alternative kosher meat operations, and loves it that young Jews are taking kashrut and meat seriously enough to do such labor-intensive work. That's why he's come to the past two Hazon conferences. But, he points out, these small-scale operations are not an answer to the problems of industrial meat production.

"Efforts like these to get close to the ground will always be small," he says. "It's valuable as education, but not economical."

Much needs to be fixed in the industrial meat system, he says. When hundreds of cattle or thousands of chickens are rushing past, it's impossible to examine each one for kosher violations as carefully as one can do in a small operation. That means kashrut standards can suffer. And other Jewish values might fall by the wayside as well. Mandel will not eat veal or foie gras. These products may be kosher, but the way the animals are treated before slaughter violates other Jewish values he also considers important. Leading an observant Jewish life means juggling many mitzvot at once, he points out.

The young meat activists in the new Jewish food movement have few illusions about changing the nature of kosher meat production anytime soon. As Mandel pointed out, kosher meat from small-scale operations is expensive and hard to find. The pasture-raised, organically fed meat and poultry produced by Shetreat-Klein, Feil, and Kimelman-Block is even more expensive and less widely available. It would take a huge cultural shift within the nation's kosher community to make it viable, and thus normative.

So long as kosher consumers demand cheap meat, and a lot of it, the big slaughterhouses and packing plants will continue to churn it out as quickly and inexpensively as possible. And it will take more than goat shechting in a Connecticut field or turkey slaughter on a California farm to change that.

# EPILOGUE

In mid-2010, the American kosher market showed no signs of slowing down. Last December, the first OU-certified kosher Tootsie Rolls rolled off the line. In January, glatt kosher food was available for the first time at the Super Bowl. In April, Gatorade became good for the Jews.

The industry's global reach continues apace. Kosher milk is now being produced in China, despite fears mentioned earlier in this book that the level of supervision required for such religiously complex food products would not be possible in China or most of the Third World.

Kosher penetration of the organic market also continues at great speed, with more and more processed food items carrying both kosher and organic labeling. Kosher meat and poultry producers are catering to increased consumer preference for natural, antibiotic-free, and hormone-free animals. In late 2009, Whole Foods began carrying the new Kosher Valley line of antibiotic-free kosher chicken, which are fed an exclusively vegetarian diet. It's not strictly organic, but it is 40 percent less expensive than most kosher organic chicken. It's more expensive, however, than nonorganic kosher poultry. Yet people are buying it.

The question remains: Is there really a need for that much kosher-certified food? Half the food products in the supermarket? Given the world economic slowdown and Americans' increased frugality, will millions of non-Jewish consumers continue to pay a premium for the kosher label? Or will kosher food once again become the province of observant Jews?

One thing is certain: The Agriprocessors scandal and its fallout seem to have permanently altered the kosher world. First, less kosher meat is available. Since Agriprocessors ceased production nearly two years ago, no one else has been able to fill its shoes, or to duplicate its prices. Agri Star Meat & Poultry, the Canadian-owned company that took over the Agriprocessors facility in Postville, has been turning out some kosher poultry but, as of spring 2010, still has not resumed beef production. To fill the void, smaller kosher meat operations continue to pop up here and there. More kosher meat is being imported, largely from South America. And many kosher-observant Jews say they're simply eating less meat than they did before.

On June 22, 2010, former Agriprocessors manager Sholom Rubashkin was sentenced to twenty-seven years in a federal prison on the eighty-six felony fraud charges he was convicted of in November 2009. On June 7, 2010, he was acquitted of sixty-seven misdemeanor counts of child-labor violations in an Iowa state court, but if his conviction on the federal fraud charges is not reversed on appeal, he could spend the rest of his life behind bars.

And what of the hundreds of illegal workers who once worked at Agriprocessors, whose low wages and poor working conditions were at the heart of the scandal that brought the company to its knees? They lost their jobs and homes, saw their families torn apart, spent months in prison, and were finally deported. Thirty-seven who served their five-month prison sentences and were under federal order to remain in Postville as material witnesses against the Rubashkins and other top executives were eventually released from what amounted to house arrest and ordered to return to Guatemala. As a final indignity, they had to pay their own way home.

A further, happier repercussion from the Agriprocessors imbroglio is increased concern about the ethics of kashrut across the American Jewish spectrum. That, too, may be long lasting.

Reform Jews have been asked by their movement leaders to eat less meat, and conversations about workers' rights, the environmental impact of meat production, and the benefits of sustainable agriculture are ongoing in Reform circles.

The new Jewish food movement is growing, in North America and now in Israel, where experiments in sustainable, pesticide-free growing practices are beginning to dot the land. Much of the Israeli activism is driven by the success of the North American movement.

The Conservative Magen Tzedek initiative, which would reward kosher food manufacturers for meeting certain ethical standards, hopes to have its seal in the marketplace by 2011. As of early 2010, thirty-eight kosher restaurants in New York, New Jersey, Pennsylvania, Maryland, and Illinois have earned a Tav HaYosher, or ethical business certificate, from the Orthodox-run Uri L'Tzedek organization. And in January 2010, the Rabbinical Council of America (RCA), the country's main Orthodox rabbinical body, issued "Jewish Principles and Ethical Guidelines for the Kosher Food Industry," the council's answer to the Agriprocessors scandal.

The RCA guidelines have been criticized as not going far enough. They require kosher food manufacturers to comply with secular laws regarding worker treatment, animal welfare, and commitment to public safety, but do not ask those companies to go *beyond* the letter of the law. They do not suggest that kosher food production should answer to a higher ethical authority.

The mashgichim I had the pleasure of following for this book *do* believe their work demands that extra diligence. They believe they are engaged in godly work. But the financial pressure on food manufacturers, supermarkets, slaughterhouses, restaurants, and every other aspect of the kosher food industry carries its own brutal logic, one that can be overcome only by the collective will of America's kosher consumers.

At the December 2009 Hazon Food Conference in Northern California, Maya Shetreat-Klein of Mitzvah Meat said the following:

> In 2009, we saw the fall-out from Agriprocessors and the closing of Sara Lee's kosher meat-processing facility. To meet demand, the Empire plant increased production of factory-farmed chicken by fifty percent. At the same time, we've seen real growth in hormone-free, antibiotic-free, and even organic kosher meats.
>
> Although much of this meat remains factory-farmed and slaughtered, we may be in the midst of a burgeoning Jewish food consciousness that extends beyond kashrut alone.

Her words echoed the hopes of growing numbers of American Jews concerned with where their food comes from and how it fits their Jewish and universal values. Only when the entire kashrut industry "answers to a higher authority" will it be possible to ensure a kosher food supply that is fit and proper, in every sense of the term.

Sue Fishkoff
Oakland, California
April 2010

# NOTES

## 1. IT'S A KOSHER, KOSHER WORLD

1. The company developed the slogan in 1965, but the Uncle Sam television commercial seven years later brought the message to a national audience.

2. *Kosher Foods—U.S.—January 2009*, report by Mintel, a Chicago-based market research firm that regularly analyzes the kosher and sacred foods markets, p. 29; http://oxygen.mintel.com/sinatra/oxygen/display/id=393 508,forsaleonly.

3. Ibid.

4. *MarketTrend: Kosher- and Halal-Certified Foods in the U.S.*, 2009 report by Packaged Facts, a publisher of market research for the food, beverage, and consumer goods industries; http://www.packagedfacts.com/MarketTrend-Kosher -Halal-1282406.

5. Mintel Global New Products Database; http://www.mintel.com/gnpd,for saleonly.

6. Number extrapolated from Mintel data *(Kosher Foods—U.S.—January 2009)* showing that 13 percent of respondents regularly buy kosher food.

7. Ten percent of American Jewry considers itself Orthodox, according to the National Jewish Population Study 2000–2001. They form the core kosher market. While many Conservative and some other Jews also keep kosher, the vast majority of American Jews do not. See http://www.jewishdata bank.org/NJPS2000.asp.

8. 2009 interview with Marcia Mogelonsky (research analyst for Mintel's kosher food reports).

9. Mintel's *Kosher Foods—U.S.—January 2009*.

10. *Kashrus Magazine*, 2009 Kosher Supervision Guide.

11. The 2008 *U.S. Religious Landscape Survey* of the Pew Forum on Religion and Public Life (http://religions.pewforum.org/) reported 72 percent of Jews are absolutely or fairly certain God exists, versus 93 to 98 percent of Christians; 10 percent of Jews do not believe in God, versus 1 percent of Catholics and other Christians; 28 percent of Jews say religion is not important in their lives, versus 9 percent of Catholics and 2 to 17 percent of other Christians; 17 percent of Jews say they never pray outside worship services, versus 1 to 3 percent of Catholics and Christians.

12. Data from 1970 (http://www.jewishdatabank.org/NJPS1971.asp), 1990 (http://www.jewishdatabank.org/NJPS1990.asp), and 2000–2001 National Jewish Population Surveys.

13. Ilan Ramon interview with Gil Mann in *Being Jewish*, Fall 2001, http://www.beingjewish.org/magazine/fall2001/article3.html.

14. This restriction applies only in North America. In Israel, for example, kosher butchers routinely remove the sciatic nerve and forbidden fats from the entire animal, rendering both front and hindquarters kosher.

15. Exodus 13:1–6, 34:18.

16. Exodus 23:10–11; Leviticus 25:1–7.

17. Numbers 15:17–21.

18. Leviticus 23:9–14.

19. Leviticus 11:1–44; Deuteronomy 14:3–21.

20. Exodus 32:30; Leviticus 3:17, 7:22–27, 22:8; Deuteronomy 12:20–25.

21. Exodus 23:19, 34:26; Deuteronomy 14:21.

22. There are two versions of the Talmud, a Palestinian version and the more authoritative Babylonian Talmud, reflecting the two greatest centers of rabbinic thought in the centuries after the destruction of the Second Temple in 70 CE.

23. Some isolated Jewish communities followed only the Torah, not the later rabbinic writings, and practiced "biblical kosher," including eating poultry with dairy. Their numbers were few, but the practice has been revived by some liberal Jews today.

24. Rabbi E. Eidlitz, *Is it Kosher? An Encyclopedia of Kosher Foods, Facts and Fallacies* (New York: Feldheim, 2004), p. 3.

25. Data from a 2006 survey by Cannondale Associates of Evanston, Illinois.

26. Pareve food can contain eggs or honey, which most vegans avoid.

27. *New York Times*, January 12, 2003.

28. Posted on http://www.ou.org., October 25, 2006.

29. The 2000–2001 National Jewish Population Survey reported 21 percent of American Jews keep kosher homes.

30. Interview with Joel Felderman, *USA Today*, November 26, 2006.

31. Philip Graitcer, "Always Coca-Cola, Not Always Kosher," *Tablet*, April 6, 2009, http://www.tabletmag.com.

32. *Heritage*, newsletter of the American Jewish Historical Society, Fall 2008, p. 13; http://www.ajhs.org/about/newsletter/2008/Heritage_2008.pdf.

33. Joshua Hammerman, "The Forbidden Oreo," *New York Times Magazine*, January 11, 1998.

34. Ibid.

## 2. EATING THEIR WAY INTO HEAVEN

1. John Cooper, *Eat and Be Satisfied: A Social History of Jewish Food* (Northvale, N.J.: Jason Aronson, 1993), p. 93.

2. Leviticus 19:2; translation from *Tanakh: The Holy Scriptures* (Philadelphia: Jewish Publication Society, 1985).

3. Hebrew for "the Name." This is a common way for observant Jews to refer to God in casual conversation.

4. Periodic attempts to ban kosher slaughter claim that other modern slaughter techniques are more humane. Some countries have outlawed shechita on this basis, including Iceland, Norway, Sweden, and New Zealand.

5. Blu Greenberg, *How to Run a Traditional Jewish Household* (Northvale, N.J.: Jason Aronson, 1989), p. 97.

6. Maria Diemling, "'As the Jews Like to Eat Garlick': Garlic in Christian-Jewish Polemical Discourse in Early Modern Germany," in *Studies in Jewish Civilization*, volume 15, *Food and Judaism*, edited by Leonard J. Greenspoon, Ronald A. Simkins, and Gerald Shapiro (Omaha: Creighton University Press, 2005), p. 216.

7. Hasia R. Diner, *Hungering for America: Italian, Irish, and Jewish Foodways in the Age of Migration* (Cambridge, Mass.: Harvard University Press, 2001), pp. 211–12.

8. Jenna Weissman Joselit, *The Wonders of America: Reinventing Jewish Culture, 1880–1950* (New York: Henry Holt, 2002), p. 178.

9. Jenna Weissman Joselit, "Food Fight: The Americanization of Kashrut in Twentieth-Century America," in Greenspoon, Simkins, and Shapiro, *Food and Judaism*, pp. 340–41.

10. Diner, *Hungering for America*, p. 212.

11. Jenna Weissman Joselit, *New York's Jewish Jews: The Orthodox Community in the Interwar Years* (Bloomington: Indiana University Press, 1990), pp. 109–10.

12. Joselit, *Wonders of America*, p. 177.

13. The Pew Forum on Religion & Public Life, *U.S. Religious Landscape Survey*, released February 2008; http://religions.pewforum.org.

14. Estimates range from the 2000–2001 National Jewish Population Survey's figure of 5.2 million to 6.4 million in the 2008 *American Jewish Yearbook*, an annual publication of the American Jewish Committee.

15. Literally: "If there's no flour, there's no Torah."

## 3. BIG BROTHER IS WATCHING

1. Joan Nathan, *Jewish Cooking in America* (New York: Alfred A. Knopf, 2006), p. 21.

2. Jenna Weissman Joselit, *New York's Jewish Jews: The Orthodox Community in the Interwar Years* (Bloomington: Indiana University Press, 1990), pp. 112–13.

3. Ibid., p. 113.

4. Harold P. Gastwirt, *Fraud, Corruption, and Holiness: The Controversy over the Supervision of Jewish Dietary Practice in New York City, 1881–1940* (Port Washington, N.Y.: Kennikat Press, 1974), p. 11.

5. Hasia R. Diner, *Hungering for America: Italian, Irish, and Jewish Foodways in the Age of Migration* (Cambridge, Mass.: Harvard University Press, 2001), p. 212.

6. Rabbi Eliezer Eidlitz, *Is It Kosher? An Encyclopedia of Kosher Foods, Facts and Fallacies* (New York: Feldheim, 2009), p. 31.

7. Gastwirt, *Fraud, Corruption, and Holiness*, p. 36.

8. Jeffrey Gurock, *Orthodox Jews in America* (Bloomington: Indiana University Press, 2009), p. 19.

9. Gastwirt, *Fraud, Corruption, and Holiness*, p. 23.

10. Moses Weinberger, *People Walk on Their Heads: Jews and Judaism in New York*, trans. Jonathan Sarna (Teaneck, N.J.: Holmes & Meier, 1982), quoted in Saul Bernstein, *The Orthodox Union Story* (Northvale, N.J.: Jason Aronson, 1997), pp. 23–24.

11. Arthur A. Goren, *New York Jews and the Quest for Community: The Kehilla Experiment 1908–1922* (New York: Columbia University Press, 1970), p. 80.

12. Gastwirt, *Fraud, Corruption, and Holiness*, p. 103.

13. Ibid., p. 36.

14. "Abraham Rice," http://www.jewishencyclopedia.com.

15. Nathan, *Jewish Cooking in America*, p. 18.

16. Gastwirt, *Fraud, Corruption, and Holiness*, p. 44.

17. Ibid., p. 84.

18. Ibid., pp. 74–95.

19. Diner, *Hungering for America*, p. 183.

20. Gastwirt, *Fraud, Corruption, and Holiness*, p. 93.

21. "This Day in History: May 27, 1935," Jewish Women's Archive, http://www.jwa.org.

22. Gastwirt, *Fraud, Corruption, and Holiness*, p. 46.

23. Ibid., p. 47.

24. Ibid., p. 48.

25. *Forward*, November 26, 2004.

26. Gastwirt, *Fraud, Corruption, and Holiness*, p. 9.

27. Ibid., p. 10.

28. Ibid., pp. 129–30.

29. Seymour E. Freedman, *The Book of Kashruth: A Treasury of Kosher Facts and Frauds* (Jacksonville, Fla.: Bloch, 1970), pp. 174–77.

30. Rabbi Morris Casriel Katz, *Deception and Fraud with a Kosher Front: A Study in Trickery and Chicanery in the Manufacturing, Distributing and Retailing of Kosher-Labeled Processed Meat Products* (monograph published by author, 1968), p. 38.

31. Ibid., p. 2.

32. "Nonkosher Food," *New York Times*, September 28, 1983.

33. "Concerns Agree to Quit Kosher Meat Business," *New York Times*, February 27, 1988.

34. *South Florida Sun-Sentinel*, October 23, 2006.

35. *New York Post*, March 23, 2009.

36. *New York Times*, January 25, 2009.

37. *Kosher Today*, August 10, 2009.

38. *Daily Record* (Reisterstown, Md.), September 1, 2008.

## 4. ON FIRE FOR KASHRUS

1. Orthodox and Conservative Jews outside Israel celebrate Sukkot for eight days.
2. *The Jerusalem Bible* (Jerusalem: Koren, 1989).
3. According to the one-in-sixty rule of nullification, if the offending food is less than one-sixtieth the volume of the entire dish, it does not invalidate the dish's kosher status.

## 5. PASTRAMI ON RYE

1. David Sax, *Save the Deli* (New York: Houghton Mifflin Harcourt, 2009), pp. 25–26.
2. Jenna Weissman Joselit, *The Wonders of America: Reinventing Jewish Culture, 1880–1950* (New York: Henry Holt, 2002), p. 203.
3. Leah Koenig, "Goldbergers and Cheeseburgers: Particularism and the Culinary Jew," *Zeek*, Fall 2006, p. 14.
4. Esther Levy, *The First Jewish-American Cookbook* (Mineola, N.Y.: Dover, 2004), facsimile of *Jewish Cookery Book* by Mrs. Esther Levy (Philadelphia: W. S. Turner, 1871), pp. 127, 41, 178–79.
5. John Cooper, *Eat and Be Satisfied: A Social History of Jewish Food* (Northvale, N.J.: Jason Aronson, 1993), p. xv.
6. Hasia R. Diner, *Hungering for America: Italian, Irish, and Jewish Foodways in the Age of Migration* (Cambridge, Mass.: Harvard University Press, 2001), p. 184.
7. Joselit, *Wonders of America*, p. 174.
8. Data from 2006 survey by Professor Steven M. Cohen of Conservative leadership beliefs and practices sponsored by the Jewish Theological Seminary, United Synagogue of Conservative Judaism, and the Rabbinical Assembly.
9. David Kraemer, *Jewish Eating and Identity Through the Ages* (New York: Routledge, 2007).
10. Amy Klein, "Table for None? Revolving Door of Kosher Restaurant Closings," http://www.jewishjournal.com, May 2, 2008.

## 6. BEYOND MANISCHEWITZ

1. *New Voices*, December 2008, p. 25.
2. David Kraemer, *Jewish Eating and Identity Through the Ages* (New York: Routledge, 2007), p. 136.
3. Responsum by Rabbi Elliot Dorff in the Rabbinical Assembly's *Proceedings of the Committee on Jewish Law and Standards 1986–1990*, pp. 213, 215, quoting Rema, Y.D. 124:24 and M.T., *Hilkhot Ma'akhalot Assurot* 11:7, 13:11; Tur, Yoreh Deah 124; S.A., Yoreh Deah 124:6–7, 24, and gloss.
4. Jonathan Sarna, *Forward*, August 5, 2009.
5. Lin Weber, *Under the Vine and the Fig Tree: The Jews of the Napa Valley* (St. Helena, Calif.: Wine Ventures, 2003), pp. 77–78.

## 7. GOOD-BYE, MOISHA'S

1. Peter Slevin, "Big-Box Orthodox: It's Kosher, but . . . ," *Washington Post,* January 4, 2005.
2. Ron Grossman, "Kosher Davids Facing a Goliath," *Chicago Tribune,* November 14, 2004.
3. 1931 Macy's advertisement in the *Hebrew Standard,* from digital archives of the American Jewish Legacy, http://www.ajlegacy.org.
4. July 10, 2008, posting at chaptzem.blogspot.com.
5. Melissa Clark, "Sushi and Kishke Under One Roof," *New York Times,* August 20, 2008.
6. "Area's Lone Kosher Butcher Moving to Queens," *Sacramento Bee,* September 29, 2007.
7. Debrah Rubin, "Any Way You Slice It, It's the End of an Era," *New Jersey Jewish News,* December 16, 2008.
8. Daniel Newman, "An End of an Era—Bexley Kosher to Close," *New Standard,* March 4, 2008, http://www.thenewstandard.com.
9. Amanda Rivkin, "Worldly Avenue: A Glimpse of Chicago," *Forward,* August 13, 2008.
10. Data from a 2005 survey of South Palm Beach County's Jewish community conducted by the Jewish Demography Project of the Sue and Leonard Miller Center for Contemporary Judaic Studies at the University of Miami.

## 8. KILLING IT SOFTLY

1. Mintel's 2007 report looked at all "sacred foods," including kosher, but the January 2009 report returned to an exclusive focus on kosher food.
2. Numbers range from *The CIA World Factbook's* figure of 1.8 million in June 2009 to the Islamic Council of America's estimate of 8 million.
3. *Sacred Foods and Food Traditions—U.S.—January 2008,* a report by Mintel International; http://reports.mintel.com/sinatra/reports/index/&letter=10/display/id=295914&anchor=a295914forsaleonly.
4. Jerry Hirsch, "In Praise of Faith-Based Food," *Los Angeles Times,* March 24, 2006.
5. Howard Blas, "One Man's Meat," *The Jerusalem Report,* December 31, 2001.
6. Seymour E. Freedman, *The Book of Kashruth: A Treasury of Kosher Facts and Frauds* (Jacksonville, Fla.: Bloch, 1970), pp. 53–64.

## 9. PLEASE DON'T EAT THE BROCCOLI

1. The Torah permits certain locusts and grasshoppers to be eaten, as stated in Leviticus 11:20–23: "The only flying insects with four walking legs that you may eat are those which have knees extending above their feet, [using these longer legs] to hop on the ground. Among these you may only eat members of the red locust family, the yellow locust family, the spotted gray locust family and the white locust family." Modern commentators hold, however, that only Jews whose communities have a tradition of eating such

bugs may do so. Jews visiting such communities (Morocco, Yemen) may eat these insects during their visits.

2. David Kraemer, *Jewish Eating and Identity Through the Ages* (New York: Routledge, 2007), pp. 55–56.
3. *New York Times*, June 1, 2004.
4. Kraemer, *Jewish Eating and Identity*, p. 158.

## 10. MADE IN CHINA

1. "Israeli Food Distributor Gets Kosher Milk from Michigan," *StreetInsider.com*, April 2, 2008.
2. Agence France-Presse, "China Adjusts 2008 Record Trade Surplus Upward," January 4, 2009.
3. Data from "Made in China: The People's Republic of Profit," a CNBC television special that originally aired July 30, 2009.
4. Associated Press, "China's Food Safety Woes Now a Global Concern," April 12, 2007.
5. Gordon Fairclough, "Tainting of Milk Is Open Secret in China," *Wall Street Journal*, November 3, 2008.
6. "Timeline: China Milk Scandal," *BBC News*, January 22, 2009, http://news.bbc.co.uk.
7. Chinese plant owners are not the only ones to make this error. When I arrived in New York in 1992 as the *Jerusalem Post's* local correspondent, I recall the Manhattan phone book carrying a listing for "New York Board of Rabbits."
8. Mark Drajem, "China Goes Kosher as Exporters Use Rabbis to Reassure Consumers," *Bloomberg.com*, January 17, 2008.
9. "The Kashrus and Safety of Food from China," *Kashrus Magazine*, October 2007.
10. Terry Tomalin, "State Hunts Bogus Grouper," *St. Petersburg Times*, November 22, 2006.
11. *Behind the Union Symbol*, Spring 2008.
12. Yigal Schleifer, "Kashrut Goes Global," *The Jerusalem Report*, December 13, 2004.

## 11. A WEDDING IN NEW JERSEY

1. *Yoshon*, or "old," refers to grain planted before the previous Passover. Increasing numbers of Orthodox Jews will use only products baked from yoshon flour in observance of the biblical commandment not to eat *chodosh*, or "new" flour, until after the second day of Passover.
2. *Bli neder* literally means "without vowing," a Hebrew phrase observant Jews use when making a promise, indicating that they cannot be held halachically liable if the promised action does not take place.
3. *Great Kosher Restaurants*, Spring 2008.
4. Angela Montefinise, "Jews Have a 'Beef,'" *New York Post*, March 2, 2008.

5. Jenna Weissman Joselit, *The Wonders of America: Reinventing Jewish Culture, 1880–1950* (New York: Henry Holt, 2002), p. 193.

## 12. GOT SHRIMP?

1. John J. Appel, "The Trefa Banquet," *Commentary*, February 1966.
2. Michael A. Meyer, *Response to Modernity: A History of the Reform Movement in Judaism* (Detroit: Wayne State University Press, 1988), p. 114.
3. Lance J. Sussman, "The Myth of the Trefa Banquet: American Culinary Culture and the Radicalization of Food Policy in American Reform Judaism," *American Jewish Archives Journal* 57 (2005): 29.
4. Ibid., p. 37.
5. Ibid., pp. 38–39.
6. Jenna Weissman Joselit, *The Wonders of America: Reinventing Jewish Culture, 1880–1950* (New York: Henry Holt, 2002), p. 175.
7. Sussman, "The Myth of the Trefa Banquet," p. 46.
8. In Orthodox practice, the mikveh is used for conversion, by brides and grooms before marriage, and monthly by married women after their menstrual periods.
9. The unpublished survey was sponsored by the Union for Reform Judaism to see where its most active members stood on questions of belief and ritual observance; results were culled from the first 6,221 responses.
10. The official publication of the Union for Reform Judaism.

## 13. KOSHER LAW AND ITS DISCONTENTS

1. Arkansas, California, Connecticut, Illinois, Kentucky, Louisiana, Maryland, Massachusetts, Minnesota, Missouri, New Jersey, New York, Ohio, Pennsylvania, Rhode Island, Texas, Virginia, the City of Baltimore, and two counties in Florida had and/or still have kosher laws.
2. Seymour E. Freedman, *The Book of Kashruth: A Treasury of Kosher Facts and Frauds* (Jacksonville, Fla: Bloch, 1970), pp. 76–77.
3. *Glickman v. Glasner,* 40 Cal. Rptr. 719 (Dist. Ct. of Appeals, 2d Dist. 1964).
4. *Perretti v. Ran-Dav's County Kosher Inc.,* 289 N.J. 618, 674 A.2d 647 (Superior Ct., Appellate Div. 1996).
5. *Barghout v. Bureau of Kosher Meat & Food Control,* 66 F.3d 1337 (4th Cir. 1995).
6. *Commack Self-Serv. Kosher Meats, Inc. v. Weiss,* 294 F.3d 415 (2d Cir. 2002), 45 ATLA L. Rep. 282 (October 2002).
7. The Yarmeisches protested the penalty on several grounds, including that the turkey packages were marked "OU," and the OU certifies prepackaged meat and poultry only if it is already soaked and salted. No further marking was needed, they argued.
8. *Commack Self-Service Kosher Meats, Inc. v. Rubin,* 106 F. Supp. 2d 445, 459 (E.D.N.Y. 2000).
9. "Kosher Food Inspectors Get Death Threats," *Jewish Press,* February 28, 1986.

10. Mayer Fertig, "The Decision, the Fallout and the Regrets," *Jewish Star,* April 10, 2009.

11. As stated in chapter 8, some agencies require a mashgiach to be present during the entire time fish is processed; other agencies do not require this level of stringency.

12. Lisë Stern, *How to Keep Kosher: A Comprehensive Guide to Understanding Jewish Dietary Laws* (New York: William Morrow, 2004), pp. 84–85.

13. David Kraemer, *Jewish Eating and Identity Through the Ages* (New York: Routledge, 2007), p. 121.

14. Ibid., p. 153.

## 14. POSTVILLE

1. Mark Grey, Michele Devlin, and Aaron Goldsmith, *Postville U.S.A.: Surviving Diversity in Small-Town America* (Boston: GemmaMedia, 2009), p. 135.

# GLOSSARY

**Ashkenazic**: Pertaining to German and East European Jewry, including the Russian Pale of Settlement.

*baal teshuva* (pl. *baalei teshuva*): Literally, "returnee to the faith"; term used to describe a newly observant Jew.

**bar** or **bat mitzvah**: A Jewish child who has reached the age of religious responsibility—generally twelve for a girl, thirteen for a boy; also refers to the ceremony marking this occasion.

*bet din* or *bais din:* Rabbinic court; a body empowered to render religious decisions and to arbitrate nonreligious disputes between Jews.

*bishul akum:* Food cooked by a non-Jew.

*bodek:* Inspector who checks animal carcasses after slaughter to make sure there is no evidence of disease or other imperfections, which would render the meat not kosher.

*bracha:* A blessing.

**Chabad-Lubavitch**: A worldwide hassidic movement headquartered in Crown Heights, Brooklyn, noted for its active outreach to Jews it considers non-observant.

**challah**: Braided bread served at Sabbath and holiday meals.

**Chanukah**: The "festival of lights," an eight-day holiday in Kislev/December commemorating the Maccabees' victory, in Israel in the second century BCE, over the occupying Syrian-Greek army; celebrated by lighting the menorah, a nine-branched candelabra, each night of the holiday.

**cholent**: A meat and/or vegetable stew that is slow-cooked beginning Friday before sundown to avoid the prohibition of cooking on the Sabbath.

*cholov Yisroel:* Literally, "milk of Israel"; milk that is supervised by an observant Jew from the time it leaves the cow until it is bottled.

**daven, davening**: Yiddish for "pray" and "praying," respectively.

*frum:* Yiddish for "religiously observant."

**Gemara**: Multigenerational rabbinic commentary on the Mishna; the Babylonian edition was compiled in the sixth century CE, the smaller Jerusalem edition in the fifth century CE; printed together, the Mishna and Gemara make up the Talmud.

*glatt:* Yiddish for "smooth"; has also come to mean meat from an animal whose lungs, upon postslaughter inspection, reveal no scarring or adhesions, the presence of which would require additional rabbinic consultation to determine if the animal was diseased; the presence of disease in an otherwise kosher animal renders it unfit for consumption.

*halacha* (adj. *halachic*): Jewish law.

*halaf* (pl. *halafim*): Specially sharpened knife used for Jewish ritual slaughter.

halal: Food that is permitted to be eaten under Islamic law.

HaShem: Literally, "the name"; a euphemism Orthodox Jews use to refer to God in ordinary conversation so as to avoid taking God's name in vain.

*hashgocha:* Kosher certification.

hassid (pl. hassidim), hassidic, hassidism: Of or pertaining to a religious movement founded in the eighteenth century by Rabbi Yisroel ben Eliezer, also known as the Baal Shem Tov, which emphasizes serving God through joy and may include mystical practices; also noted for the devotion of its adherents to the rebbe, or spiritual leader, of any of the subgroups that were formed throughout Eastern and Central Europe by followers of the Baal Shem Tov.

*hassidishe shechita:* Ritual slaughter performed by a hassidic Jew.

heimishe: Yiddish for "homey"; among observant Jews, refers to that which recalls or reflects the ethos, practices, or values of the Old World, i.e., Europe.

*hekhsher* (pl. *hekhsherim*): Kosher certification.

Hekhsher Tzedek: Now known as Magen Tzedek (literally, "Shield of Justice"); a certification process indicating kosher food produced according to specific ethical and environmental standards laid out by the Conservative movement; developed in 2008 following the Agriprocessors scandal.

*humra:* A particularly strict interpretation of a Jewish law.

Kabbalah (adj. kabbalistic): Literally, "that which is received," refers to Jewish mystical teachings when capitalized; when lowercase, also refers to a shochet's certificate.

kasha varnishkes: Buckwheat; popular among Eastern European Jews.

*kasher:* To make kosher.

kashrut or kashrus: The entire complex of Jewish dietary law and practice.

*kiddush:* The blessing over wine recited on the Sabbath and on certain holidays.

kippah (also yarmulke): Skullcap worn by observant Jewish men (and women, in the liberal movements).

kishka: Yiddish for "intestine"; also, the sausage made from meat, vegetables, and grain that was originally stuffed into a casing made from a cow's intestines.

Kof-K Kosher Supervision: One of the Big Four kosher certification agencies, based in Teaneck, New Jersey.

*kollel:* A yeshiva, or Talmudic institute, for married men.

kreplach: Dumplings.

**kugel:** A cooked pudding; traditionally made of noodles or potatoes, it can have any vegetable base.

**l'chaim:** Literally, "to life"; the traditional Jewish toast.

*maaris ayin:* Literally, "how it looks to the eye"; the practice of avoiding behavior that might be interpreted as sinful even if it is not.

*mashgiach* (pl. *mashgichim;* fem. *mashgicha;* fem. pl. *mashgichot*): Kosher supervisor.

**matzo:** Unleavened bread consumed primarily during Passover, when the consumption of leavened bread is prohibited.

*mechitza* (pl. *mechitzot*): A wall or other type of divider that separates men and women during synagogue worship and at other ritual occasions.

*mevushal:* Literally, "cooked"; also, kosher wine that has been heated to almost boiling; according to Jewish law, only boiled wine may be handled by non-Jews without it becoming non-kosher.

**mikveh:** Ritual bath; used by women and men for periodic spiritual purification, as part of the conversion process, and for the initial kashering of glass and metal kitchen utensils.

**minyan:** Ten Jewish men age thirteen or older who form the quorum needed for group prayer; non-Orthodox Jews count women as part of a minyan. Also refers to a prayer community, as in the independent minyan movement.

**Mishna:** The second-century CE redaction by Rabbi Yehuda HaNasi of rabbinic discussions of Jewish law and practice that had for centuries been part of an oral transmission process.

*misnagid* (pl. *misnagdim*): Literally, "opponent"; Orthodox Jews who opposed the hassidic movement upon its emergence in the eighteenth century and its growing popularity in the nineteenth century.

**mitzvah** (pl. *mitzvot* or *mitzvos*): Literally, "commandment"; used colloquially to mean a good deed.

**Moshichist:** Messianist; refers to Chabad-Lubavitch hassidim who believe their late rebbe, Menachem Mendel Schneerson, is the Jewish Messiah.

*motzi:* Colloquial term for the blessing over bread (". . . *hamotzi lechem min haaretz*").

*neshama:* Soul.

**OK Kosher Certification:** Second largest of the Big Four kosher certification agencies, based in Crown Heights, Brooklyn.

**Orthodox Union,** or **OU:** Manhattan-based umbrella association of North American Orthodox congregations; it houses the oldest and largest kosher certification agency, OU Kosher.

*pareve:* Yiddish for "neutral"; food that is neither meat nor dairy.

*pas Yisroel:* Literally, "dough of Israel"; grain-based food baked or cooked with the participation of an observant Jew.

**Passover** (in Hebrew, *Pesach*): The eight-day holiday in Nissan/April commemorating the ancient Israelites' Exodus from slavery in Egypt, during which no leavened food products are consumed. Israeli Jews and Reform Jews observe the holiday for seven days.

*plumba:* Seal affixed to kosher chicken to indicate it has been slaughtered and prepared according to Jewish law.

*posek:* Rabbi empowered to render authoritative decisions of Jewish law.

**rugelach:** Crescent-rolled pastry-dough cookies that can be filled with cinnamon, nuts, chocolate, or cheese.

**schmaltz:** Chicken fat.

**seder:** The festive meal celebrated on the first two nights of Passover, during which the Haggadah, the book that recounts the story of the Israelites' Exodus from Egypt, is read and ritual foods are eaten. Israeli and Reform Jews hold only one seder, on the first night.

**Sephardic:** Pertaining to Jews throughout the world who trace their ancestry to the exiled communities of Spain and Portugal.

**Shabbat** or **Shabbos:** The Jewish Sabbath, extending from sundown Friday until sundown Saturday.

*shechita* (v. *shecht*): Ritual slaughter according to Jewish law.

*sheitel:* Yiddish for "wig"; worn by some Orthodox Jewish women to cover their hair for modesty.

**shiva:** Literally, "seven"; also the seven-day mourning period following a Jewish funeral.

**shochet** (pl. **shochtim**): Jewish ritual slaughterer.

**shofar:** Ram's horn blown in the synagogue on Rosh Hashannah to stir congregants to repentance; also blown during the month leading up to Rosh Hashannah and to mark the conclusion of the Yom Kippur service.

*shomer mitzvot:* Literally, "observer of the commandments"; used to refer to a religiously observant Jew.

*shomer Shabbat* or *shomer Shabbos:* Literally, "a person who observes the Sabbath"; used to refer to a religiously observant Jew.

*shtar mechira:* Bill of sale given by the Jewish proprietor of a kosher establishment to a non-Jew to transfer ownership of the establishment to the non-Jew over the Sabbath or a Jewish holiday, when a Jew is forbidden to operate or realize profit from a business; at the conclusion of the Sabbath/holiday, the establishment is sold back to the Jewish owner.

**shtetl:** Yiddish for "small village"; small town in pre–World War II Eastern or Central Europe with a significant Jewish population.

**shul:** Yiddish for "synagogue."

**Shulchan Aruch:** Literally, "ordered table"; the authoritative four-volume compendium of Jewish laws compiled by the sixteenth-century sage Rabbi Joseph Caro.

**Simchat Torah:** Holiday that celebrates both the conclusion and the beginning of the annual cycle of weekly readings from the Torah on the Sabbath; it falls on the day after the concluding day of the Sukkot holiday.

**Star-K Kosher Certification:** One of the Big Four kosher certification agencies, based in Baltimore, Maryland.

**Sukkot** or **Sukkos:** The fall harvest festival that also commemorates the forty years of wandering in the Sinai desert by the former Israelite slaves prior to their arrival in the land of Israel; meals are eaten in a sukkah, a nonpermanent hut meant to re-create the wandering experience.

**tallit** (pl. **tallitot**): Prayer shawl.

**Talmud:** Judaism's central legal text, a multivolume work of rabbinic commentary compiled between the fifth and seventh centuries CE and composed of the Mishna and the Gemara.

**Tanya:** Central text of Chabad-Lubavitch hassidism, written by the first Chabad rebbe, Shneur Zalman of Liadi, in the late eighteenth century.

**tefillin:** Phylacteries; leather boxes containing parchment on which has been handwritten a portion of Deuteronomy that is part of daily prayer; at the beginning of the morning prayer service the boxes are secured to the forehead and upper arm with leather straps.

*teudah:* Certificate that indicates an establishment is under authorized kosher supervision.

**Torah:** The Pentateuch; the five books of Moses, which are considered by observant Jews to be the word of God as revealed to Moses.

*toyvel:* To make glass dishware and metal utensils permissible for use by observant Jews by dipping them in a mikveh.

*treyf:* Non-kosher food; from the Hebrew *toref,* or "to tear," referring to flesh torn from the living body of an animal, which is forbidden by Jewish law.

**tzimmes:** Stew consisting of carrots, sweet potatoes, and sugar.

*tzitzit:* Woolen fringes at the four corners of a prayer shawl or ritual undergarment.

*vaad:* Committee; used in text to refer to a rabbinic body that oversees the kashrut of retail stores, restaurants, and/or food-manufacturing operations.

**yeshiva:** A Jewish religious school; the same term is used for elementary, secondary, and postsecondary schools of higher learning.

*yetzer hara:* Literally, "the evil impulse"; the internal impulse that tempts people to do wrong.

*Yiddishkeit:* Jewish life, or "Jewishness."

# SELECT BIBLIOGRAPHY

Alpern, Laura Manischewitz. *Manischewitz: The Matzo Family; The Making of an American Jewish Icon.* Jersey City, N.J.: KTAV, 2008.

Bernstein, Saul. *The Orthodox Union Story.* Northvale, N.J.: Jason Aronson, 1997.

Blech, Zushe Yosef. *Kosher Food Production.* Ames, Iowa: Wiley-Blackwell, 2009.

Bloom, Stephen G. *Postville: A Clash of Cultures in Heartland America.* Orlando: Harcourt, 2000.

Cooper, John. *Eat and Be Satisfied: A Social History of Jewish Food.* Northvale, N.J.: Jason Aronson, 1993.

Diner, Hasia R. *Hungering for America: Italian, Irish, and Jewish Foodways in the Age of Migration.* Cambridge, Mass.: Harvard University Press, 2001.

———. *The Jews of the United States: 1654 to 2000.* Berkeley and Los Angeles: University of California Press, 2004.

Eidlitz, Rabbi Eliezer. *Is It Kosher? An Encyclopedia of Kosher Foods, Facts and Fallacies.* New York: Feldheim, 2004.

Fishkoff, Sue. *The Rebbe's Army: Inside the World of Chabad-Lubavitch.* New York: Schocken Books, 2003.

Freedman, Samuel G. *Jew vs. Jew: The Struggle for the Soul of American Jewry.* New York: Simon & Schuster, 2000.

Freedman, Seymour E. *The Book of Kashruth: A Treasury of Kosher Facts and Frauds.* Jacksonville, Fla.: Bloch, 1970.

Gastwirt, Harold P. *Fraud, Corruption, and Holiness: The Controversy over the Supervision of Jewish Dietary Practice in New York City, 1881–1940.* Port Washington, N.Y.: Kennikat Press, 1974.

Goldstein, Rabbi Zalman. *Going Kosher in 30 Days.* Monsey, N.Y.: Jewish Learning Group, 2007.

Goren, Arthur A. *New York Jews and the Quest for Community: The Kehilla Experiment 1908–1922.* New York: Columbia University Press, 1970.

Greenberg, Blu. *How to Run a Traditional Jewish Household.* Northvale, N.J.: Jason Aronson, 1989.

Greenspoon, Leonard J., Ronald A. Simkins, and Gerald Shapiro, eds. *A Special Issue of Studies in Jewish Civilization.* Vol. 15, Food and Judaism. Omaha: Creighton University Press, 2005.

Grey, Mark, Michele Devlin, and Aaron Goldsmith. *Postville U.S.A.: Surviving Diversity in Small-Town America*. Boston: GemmaMedia, 2009.

Gurock, Jeffrey. *Orthodox Jews in America*. Bloomington: Indiana University Press, 2009.

Heilman, Samuel. *Defenders of the Faith: Inside Ultra-Orthodox Jewry*. Berkeley: University of California Press, 2000.

Joselit, Jenna Weissman. *New York's Jewish Jews: The Orthodox Community in the Interwar Years*. Bloomington: Indiana University Press, 1990.

————.*The Wonders of America: Reinventing Jewish Culture, 1880–1950*. New York: Henry Holt, 2002.

Judd, Robin. *Contested Rituals: Circumcision, Kosher Butchering, and Jewish Political Life in Germany, 1843–1933*. Ithaca, N.Y.: Cornell University Press, 2007.

Katz, Rabbi Morris Casriel. *Deception and Fraud with a Kosher Front: A Study in Trickery and Chicanery in the Manufacturing, Distributing and Retailing of Kosher-Labeled Processed Meat Products*. Monograph published by author, 1968.

Kraemer, David. *Jewish Eating and Identity Through the Ages*. New York: Routledge, 2007.

Levy, Esther. *The First Jewish-American Cookbook*. Mineola, N.Y.: Dover, 2004.

Lipschutz, Rabbi Yacov. *Kashruth: A Comprehensive Background and Reference Guide to the Principles of Kashruth*. Brooklyn, N.Y.: Mesorah, 1988.

Meyer, Michael A. *Response to Modernity: A History of the Reform Movement in Judaism*. Detroit: Wayne State University Press, 1995.

Nathan, Joan. *Jewish Cooking in America*. New York: Alfred A. Knopf, 2006.

Roden, Claudia. *The Book of Jewish Food: An Odyssey from Samarkand to New York*. New York: Alfred A. Knopf, 2007.

Safran, Eliyahu. *Meditations at Sixty: One Person, Under God, Indivisible; Kashrut, Modesty, Mourning, Prayer and Love*. Jersey City, N.J.: KTAV, 2008.

Sarna, Jonathan. *American Judaism*. New Haven, Conn.: Yale University Press, 2004.

Sax, David. *Save the Deli*. New York: Houghton Mifflin Harcourt, 2009.

Schachter-Shalomi, Zalman, and Joel Siegel. *Jewish with Feeling: A Guide to Meaningful Jewish Practice*. New York: Riverhead Books, 2005.

Schochet, Jacob Immanuel. *The Mystical Dimension*. Vol. 3, *Chassidic Dimensions*. Brooklyn, N.Y.: Kehot Publication Society, 1990.

Stern, Lisë. *How to Keep Kosher: A Comprehensive Guide to Understanding Jewish Dietary Laws*. New York: William Morrow, 2004.

Sussman, Lance J. "The Myth of the Trefa Banquet: American Culinary Culture and the Radicalization of Food Policy in American Reform Judaism." *American Jewish Archives Journal* 57 (2005): 29–52.

Weber, Lin. *Under the Vine and the Fig Tree: The Jews of the Napa Valley*. St. Helena, Calif.: Wine Ventures, 2003.

Welfed, Irving. *Why Kosher? An Anthology of Answers*. Northvale, N.J.: Jason Aronson, 1996.

# INDEX